W9-BOM-092

Secretariat:
The Making of a Champion

Secretariat:
The Making of a
Champion

by
William Nack

DA CAPO PRESS

Cataloging-in-Publication data for this book is available from the
Library of Congress.
Second Da Capo Press edition 2002; first Da Capo Press edition 1988
ISBN 0–306–81133–2

Secretariat: The Making of a Champion was originally published in
1975 with the title *Big Red of Meadow Stable.* Reprinted by arrangement
with the author.

Reprinted courtesy of *Sports Illustrated:* "Pure Heart" by William
Nack, SPORTS ILLUSTRATED, June 4, 1990, Copyright © 1990,
Time Inc. All rights reserved.
Secretariat Racing Record is reprinted with permission from
Champions, published by DRF Press LLC.

Published by Da Capo Press
A Member of the Perseus Books Group
http://www.dacapopress.com

Da Capo Press books are available at special discounts for bulk purchases in the U.S. by corporations, institutions, and other organiza-
tions. For more information, please contact the Special Markets
Department at the Perseus Books Group, 11 Cambridge Center,
Cambridge, MA 02142, or call (800) 255-1514 or (617) 252-5298, or
e-mail j.mccrary@perseusbooks.com.

1 2 3 4 5 6 7 8 9—06 05 04 03 02

To my parents and to Mary

Contents

Preface to
the 2002 Edition

Nearly thirty years after Secretariat made his final bow at Aqueduct that autumn day in 1973, the questions most frequently asked about him are: How great was he? How fast? Is his reputation all a product of myth, museum history, and media hype?

Horsemen have always been loath to compare horses from different eras, and any attempt to do so amounts to nothing more than a parlor game, a diverting but futile exercise. Could Secretariat have beaten Man o' War or Citation? Could either of them have whipped Swaps, Seattle Slew, or Dr. Fager? Could any of them have run down Count Fleet? Or outgutted the determined Seabiscuit at his match-race best? To these and other such entertaining questions, of course, there are no glib and certain answers. All that is really known, over the passage of almost three decades, is that Secretariat's legend remains as vibrant and secure as ever, and he continues to be viewed as the modern standard against which all members of his tribe are judged. If anything, time has only enriched and embellished his name. On ESPN's acclaimed TV series portraying the fifty greatest athletes of the twentieth century, for instance, he was ranked thirty-fifth, the only horse included in the series. In another end-of-the-century series celebrating the decade of the '70s, the U.S. Postal Service put his comely mug on a 33-cent postage stamp. And a three-quarter-size bronze statue of Secretariat, commissioned by Paul Mellon and portraying the horse in full flight, decorates the middle of the walking ring at Belmont Park—a symbolic centerpiece forever representing the best of the sport and breed.

Statues and postage stamps aside, this ineluctable fact remains: nearly one million thoroughbred foals have come of age since Secretariat's year, yet today he still owns the Kentucky Derby record of 1:59 2/5 seconds—last year, in 2001, Monarchos became the only other Derby winner to shade two minutes when he flew home at Churchill Downs in 1:59 4/5—and no horse has come even remotely close to challenging his standard of 2:24 flat in the twelve-furlong Belmont Stakes. It may also be asserted, without a doubt, that no racehorse on the planet has ever hung up faster morning workouts than Secretariat. After winning that record Derby, he prepared for the Preakness by tearing five-eighths around Pimlico in a stunning :57 2/5, then galloped out six furlongs in 1:10 flat, stakes race time on Old Hilltop. Following the Preakness victory, he came to the Belmont after scorching a morning mile in 1:34 4/5, a time that would have won most mile stakes, and then galloped out nine furlongs in a florid 1:48 3/5. What was so remarkable about all of this, when viewed in retrospect, is that these morning flights came in the middle and near the end of a record-setting, five-week Triple Crown whose three races, in and of themselves, were enervating enough. But Secretariat always flourished in the wake of prodigious workouts, to be sure, and how fast he went in the mornings actually predicted his performance in the afternoons. After he worked five-eighths of a mile in :57, galloping out six furlongs in an unbelievable 1:08 4/5, three days prior to the nine-furlong Marlboro Cup, it came as no surprise when he set a new world record in that race of 1:45 2/5. Nor was it unexpected, after working five-eighths in a monstrous :56 4/5, galloping out a swift 1:09 for six furlongs, that he would break the one-and-a-half-mile track record on the turf at Belmont Park. Finally, that lustrous five-furlong work at Woodbine, where the trees swayed as he charged past the pole in a blazing :57 3/5, set him up perfectly to win the Canadian International by six and a half lengths, the last race of his life.

"What a workout line!" exclaimed Andrew Beyer, the racing writer of the *Washington Post*, after studying Secretariat's morning regimen years later. "We may never see this kind of line again."

So how fast did Secretariat really run in the Belmont Stakes, his most memorable performance? In a recent column for the *Daily Racing Form*, of which he is editor and publisher, speed handicapper Steven Crist wrote the most definitive tale to end all tales about the Belmont and Secretariat's ability. Speed handicappers determine the quality of a horse's performance in a race relative to the surface over which he ran it. Looking back on the charts of that Belmont day, after analyzing the six dirt races run at Belmont Park and the running times of the horses who ran them, Crist was utterly blown away by the figure he computed to define Secretariat's performance in the Belmont. The 2:24 final time simply didn't compute on any rational scale. "Unbelievable," he wrote. "Astronomical. I needed confirmation." So Crist enlisted the help of two other noted speed handicappers, Mike Watchmaker and Andrew Beyer, the father of figs, and all three came up, relatively, with the same fig—a Beyer number of 138, by far the largest speed figure any of them had ever given to a horse's performance. "I've never made one that high," Watchmaker told Crist. "Not even close."

"The reason speed handicappers slave over their numbers is because things are often not what they seem to the race watcher's eye," Crist wrote in the *Form*. "A lengthy winner can be running slowly against a horrendous field, and raw times can be as much a product of the racetrack as the horses running over it. In the case of Secretariat, though, appearances were not deceiving. His Belmont figure is as spectacular as he was—simply the best."

For all that Secretariat accomplished, it remains his most enduring signature on the sport.

Chapter 1

It was almost midnight in Virginia, late for the farmlands north of Richmond, when the breathing quickened in the stall, the phone rang in the Gentry home, and two men came out the front door, hastily crossing the lawn to the car.

They swung out the driveway onto the deserted road and took off north. It was one of those hours when time is measured not by clocks but by contractions; the intervals between were getting shorter. In a small wooden barn set off at the edge of a nearby field, beneath a solitary light in an expanse of darkness, a mare was about to give birth. The men were rushing to the barn to help her.

The man behind the wheel was Howard M. Gentry, sixty-two years old, for almost twenty years a manager of the Meadow Stud in Doswell, one of the most successful breeding farms in America. Sitting with him in the front seat was Raymond W. Wood, a railroad conductor, fifty-four years old, Gentry's long-time friend and neighbor, for years his steady companion at straight pool, and himself a modest breeder of thoroughbred horses.

It was the night of March 29, 1970, not the kind of night for anyone to leave the velvet green warmth of a pool table and rush outdoors. The weather had been bleak all day—the sky perpetually overcast, a drizzle falling through the morning and afternoon, and a fog that clung to the farm and the uplands and the bottomlands of Caroline County. A wind, mounting occasional gusts, blew out of the north from Washington. The temperature had been in the high forties during the day, but by evening it had dropped into the thirties, and sometime past eleven o'clock, when the call came, it was almost freezing.

Gentry instantly recognized the voice of Bob Southworth, the nightwatchman at the foaling barn. In a characteristic monotone Southworth told him what he had been waiting to hear. "Mistah Gentry! You better come on down here to the foalin' barn in the field. That mare's gettin' ready to foal."

That mare is what put an edge on the moment for Gentry. He had delivered hundreds of foals in the years he worked around thorough-breds, but *that* mare was not just another broodmare carrying a foal by just another sire. Down in Barn 17A, the two-stall foaling barn near the western border of the farm, an eighteen-year-old broodmare named Somethingroyal, a daughter of the late Princequillo, was going into labor for the fourteenth time in her life. She was carrying a foal by Bold Ruler, the preeminent sire in America, year after year the nation's leading stallion. It was a union of established aristoc-racy.

Somethingroyal was the kind of mare breeders seek to raise dynas-ties. She was the dam of the fleet Sir Gaylord, probably the most gifted racehorse of his generation, the colt favored to win the 1962 Kentucky Derby until he broke down the day before the race. She was the mother of First Family, a multiple stakes winner in the mid-1960s. In 1965 she bore her first Bold Ruler foal, a filly called Syrian Sea, winner of the rich Selima Stakes in 1967. Another Bold Ruler filly, The Bride, was a yearling, and tonight Somethingroyal was having her last Bold Ruler foal: the stallion was dying in Ken-tucky.

So Howard Gentry felt more anxious than usual to get the foal delivered. The foal would be virtually priceless, and Gentry hoped the delivery would be easy. Gentry had stopped to see Something-royal earlier that night, just before he went home for supper at six. She didn't appear to be near labor then, but when he and Southworth made the rounds two hours later, as they often did together during breeding season, her condition had begun to change. Labor seemed imminent. The mare was "waxing heavily," as Gentry called it, with milk congealing at the tips of her nipples like beads of candle wax —the tentative sign that labor is near—perhaps a few hours away, perhaps a day. It was then he decided to stay awake, instead of going to bed at nine, his regular time, and to call Wood and ask him to wait it out over a pool table.

Gentry edged his beige 1969 Chrysler across the highway dividing the farm, past the big house on the hill, past the towering stand of trees around the house, around the gravel driveway crunching underneath, down the gentle slope and past the fences and the pastures and through the gate where the broodmares walk to and from the fields during the day, and finally stopped about a hundred feet from where the lights were burning and where Bob Southworth, standing by the stall, was waiting.

Gentry and Wood cut across the wet grass on the field, walking briskly—hurrying—through the pasture toward the barn. Wood jogged to keep up, stumbling once in the dark, skimming through the pastureland to keep up with Gentry, midwife for Somethingroyal.

Gentry looked in the stall and walked quietly inside. Somethingroyal was breathing quickly now. Her nostrils were flared. She was walking the stall and seemed edgy, nervous. Gentry felt her neck and shoulder. She was warm and sweating lightly.

"She's gettin' ready," Gentry said. A quick routine began. He checked for the iodine, the enema, the cup for the iodine, and the bowl for the water to wash the nipples for the suckling foal. Then he spotted his Unionalls, picked them off the hook, and slipped them on. The three men waited at the door, watching the old mare pace the stall, circling it as if caged, and they spoke idly in unremembered conversations.

At midnight, almost to the stroke, Gentry saw Somethingroyal stop pacing and lie down, collapsing her bulk on the bed of straw. She faced the rear of the stall, lying on her left side. Gentry slipped on his rubber gloves and dropped to his knees beside her. Her water bag broke, spilling fluid from her vagina. Any moment now, the foal.

Just past midnight, the tip of the left foot appeared, and Gentry waited for the other. In a normal birth, the front feet come out together, with the head between the legs, so Gentry watched and waited. When the foot failed to emerge, he decided to wait no longer. He feared the leg might be folded under or twisted, a position that could cause injury to the shoulder under the extreme pressures of birth. So, kneeling closer to the mare, he reached his arm inside the vagina and felt the head, which was in a good position, and then dropped his hand down to the right leg and felt for the hoof. As he suspected, he found it curled under, so he uncurled it gently, bringing the leg out of the vagina. "Won't be long now," he said to Wood.

Somethingroyal pushed, paused panting, and pushed again. Gentry guided but did not pull the legs—not yet. He always waited for the shoulder to emerge before pulling. The legs came out together.

Then the head, with a splash of white down the face, slipped through the opening. A water bubble preceded it, and Gentry slit the bubble open. The neck slipped out, slowly, and finally the shoulders emerged. The mare paused, and Gentry took the front legs and waited for her to rest, always letting her lead: push and relax, push and relax.

Somethingroyal pushed, straining, and Gentry pulled on the legs, hard. It was a good-sized foal. Then he called Wood to his side, telling him to put on a pair of rubber gloves. Returning, Wood kneeled down next to Gentry and took one leg, Gentry the other.

"Take it easy now," Gentry told him. "No hurry—and not too hard—take your time." They pulled together for several moments. As the foal came out, and Gentry saw the size of the shoulders and the size of the bone, he feared the foal might hip lock—his hips were so wide—and have difficulty clearing the opening. When the rib cage cleared, Gentry guided the hips.

Moments later the foal was out and lying on the bed of straw, the mare was panting and sweating, and Gentry was asking Southworth for the cup of iodine. Southworth broke the umbilical by pulling the foal around to the mare's head so she could lick him. Gentry cauterized the wound with iodine and gave the foal four milliliters of the combiotics—an antibiotic combination of streptomycin and penicillin—as a precautionary measure, and Southworth rubbed him down with a towel to dry him and circulate the blood.

Gentry looked at his watch. It was ten minutes after midnight, March 30, 1970, the moment the whole foal emerged. He was a chestnut, with three white feet—the right front and the two behind. The colt lay at his mother's head when Gentry, looking at him, stepped back and shook his head and said to Wood, "There is a whopper."

Chapter 2

The Virginia of Caroline County—acres of porous soil and roughly tree-mantled countryside—is not the Old South of cotton farms and magnolias under moonlight and willowy, straight-backed women drifting among the lawns and gardens of the Tidewater. This is not the Virginia where buses stop at overlooks on any of the approved tours, lying outside the limits of the Tidewater and far to the southeast of the Blue Ridge Mountains and the Shenandoah Valley, with its pungent orchards and its own haunting song.

Caroline County seems closer in spirit to Stephen Crane than Stephen Foster—a starker and less storybook Virginia than the mountains and the valleys, a place where old times are often just as well forgotten. It is tomato and melon country—watermelons and muskmelons—and it has fields for grazing horses and cattle and cultivated stretches for growing corn and soybeans, but it was not always so prosperous or so peaceful there.

The Meadow is part of a neck of land almost midway between Richmond and Washington. For four years, two armies crawled around it feeling for each other's jugular. The fighting began just seventy miles to the north, at Bull Run, and it ended not far to the southwest, at Appomattox Court House. The Morris family, living on The Meadow at the time, hid the family silver in the well. Some of the largest set-piece battles of the war, with their cavalry sweeps and scouting parties, took place nearby. The land, and whatever civilization had been built on it, came out of the war years badly gored.

The war radically altered the course of the lives of the people who somehow survived it and left James Hollis Chenery the sole male support of three families, including the Morrises of The Meadow. The war had left the Morrises and other families nearly destitute, though it did not destroy them. Chenery ended up as a clerk in a dry goods store in Richmond.

The war also picked up Richard Johnson Hancock in the Deep South, marched him into Virginia, and then left him nearly dead outside a city in the Shenandoah Valley. Hancock was born in Alabama, the son of a farmer, but he was raised and ultimately orphaned in Louisiana, where he joined the Bossier Volunteers when the war broke out. Hancock's unit was ordered to Virginia and eventually came under the command of Stonewall Jackson. Hancock was wounded three times in the next two years, the first time superficially at the Second Battle of Manassas on August 30, 1862.

The second wound gave him a limp, but it also remade him into a Virginian and in time led him to found what would become one of the largest and most important thoroughbred breeding establishments in the world. In July of 1863, Hancock was jumping a fence in an assault on Cemetery Ridge during the Battle of Gettysburg when a Union soldier turned on him and fired. The ball struck Hancock in the hip. He was dispatched to a Confederate hospital in Charlottesville. While convalescing, Hancock often attended Sunday services at the Christian Church, and one morning he met Thomasia Overton Harris. She was the daughter of John Harris, a prominent landowner on whose 1450-acre farm, called Ellerslie, about one hundred slaves bred and raised livestock and planted corn and tobacco.

The courtship that developed was interrupted when Hancock, recovered from the hip wound, rejoined the Bossier Volunteers. The fighting in the months that followed carried him to the mountains, to the Shenandoah Valley beyond the mountains, and finally to the city of Winchester in the valley. There, on September 19, 1864, a Union soldier shot him in the stomach as he and other members of the unit retreated south from the city. He was a prisoner of war and badly wounded, though he was not either very long. Hancock, with some help, contrived to escape, slipping away unseen and skirting Sheridan's right flank at Cedar Creek, making his way to the Confederate lines and then on to Ellerslie. There, in November of 1864, he and Miss Harris were married. Richard Hancock had always liked thoroughbreds, and when he returned to the farm after the war, one of the things he wanted to do was raise them at Ellerslie.

James Hollis Chenery had no such visions. He was only sixteen years old when he started work at the dry goods store in Richmond. Sixteen years later, when he was thirty-two years old, Chenery married his second cousin—it was in the family tradition—Ida Burnley Taylor. They had six children, one of whom died young. Ida Chenery, a disciplinarian, pushed and raised and shaped them.

The oldest boy, William, went through journalism school and rose to be the editor of the *Rocky Mountain News* and then an editor at *Collier's* magazine. A daughter, Blanche, attended the University of Chicago, married an advertising man, and settled down in Pelham Manor, New York, where practically the whole family wound up living at one time. The youngest boy, Alan Chenery, went through Richmond Medical School and became a urologist with a practice in Washington, D.C. Charlie, the only one of the children who did not go to college, eventually worked for his brother Chris. And there was Chris.

Christopher Tompkins Chenery became what he set out to become —a man of substance and horses and a part of the landed gentry. He was born in Richmond on September 19, 1886, but his parents soon moved to Ashland, north of Richmond and just south of The Meadow, where he acquired a feeling for the land and place that never left him.

Helen (Penny) Chenery Tweedy, Christopher Chenery's youngest daughter, once wrote in a personal family history that poverty was a central emptiness in their lives:

> The boys went barefoot from March first to October first to save their shoes. They did not have servants other than a cook, but they were too proud to admit it, so Chris would wait until after dark to carry the laundry in a wagon down to a colored washerwoman so the neighbors wouldn't know. The best Christmas present was a tangerine in the toe of their stockings—a rare luxury. But they were a close family, fiercely fond of each other and fearful of insult. . . . Each of the boys grew up craving something—mostly to be relieved of poverty. Bill wanted books, Charlie, the third son, loved cards and girls, but Chris loved horses. A distant cousin, Bernard Doswell, still had a half-mile track at his place adjoining The Meadow, and when they weren't out in Caroline, Chris would walk the seven miles to exercise the few remaining horses. He not only loved them, but they became a symbol to him of all the things he couldn't have. . . . His mother kept his feet on the ground, however, and ruled him and his brothers with a magnificent and ladylike temper. If they got out of line, they spent a week in the yard or cut an extra cord of wood. There was no appealing for

clemency or using boyish charm with her. She stiffened their spines and sent them out into the world with a great sense of family obligation.

The children shared their opportunities for education. Each boy was allowed to attend Randolph-Macon College in Ashland for two years, but was then expected to quit and work three years to allow another of the boys his two years of study. And that is what sent Chris Chenery into the mountainous terrain of West Virginia when still a boy of sixteen.

By then he had already finished two years of college at Randolph-Macon, and he had taken a job as a surveyor with an engineering party laying tracks for the Virginian Railroad, one of America's largest lines of coal carriers. He worked there for three years, and when he left, in 1907, he took with him enough money to return to college, this time to study engineering at Washington and Lee. Scholastically, he behaved like a man possessed, poring over the texts, teaching a course in engineering, and pushing himself to the top of his class. By the time he graduated in 1909, he had acquired a Bachelor of Science degree in engineering, a Phi Beta Kappa key, and a taste for wild adventure that sent him west, beyond the Appalachians to the Pacific. There he joined another engineering party that reconnoitered the uncharted interior of Alaska by pack train, looking for potential railroad routes from Cook inlet to the Yukon. The job involved surveying 600 miles of land in difficult weather. "It took two polar bears to live through one winter," said turfwriter Charles Hatton, a friend of Chenery. The terrain was hazardous, the mosquitoes in the summer malevolent.

In idle moments Chenery read and reread the complete works of William Shakespeare and the Bible from Genesis to Revelation, and in later years he quoted liberally from both, especially when he was with people educated in the arts and letters he had missed.

"When he got back to Oregon," Penny Tweedy wrote, "he was quite a 'hell-raiser' and the minister's daughter he wooed in Portland spurned him. Later he found her again in Chicago, and after two stormy, indecisive years they were married." Her name was Helen Bates, and she descended from a long line of New England homeopaths who moved slowly from the east coast to the west, by way of Rochester, Minnesota. Helen Bates was pretty, resented her richer cousins' hand-me-downs, and found a favorite uncle who sent her to Smith College. She went to Chicago to strike out on her own and improve herself, there married Chenery and left Chicago when America entered World War I:

> Christopher "joined up" right after they were married in 1917. Helen did not relish living with her mother-in-law in Ashland. Mrs. Chenery had remarked, hearing that Chris was engaged to an Oregon girl, "I thought they only had barmaids out there." But these two strong-minded women survived, and Chris survived the war—spent ignominiously teaching cavalrymen to ride at nearby Fort Belvoir.

Chenery left the service in 1918, and in the next decade he switched from engineering to finance and began one of those inexorable American climbs to the presidency of a string of utility companies. In 1927 he quickly became wealthy and began to acquire all the accoutrements of money and position and substance as they had been defined for him and as he had defined them for himself. He moved to Pelham Manor, New York, and founded the Boulder Brook Club —a riding club—in Scarsdale. He played some polo and fox hunted with the Goldens Bridge Hounds. He had an office in Manhattan. And he sent his children to good schools. Chenery was never a haughty man, never a man who flaunted his wealth, and he was enough of a romantic and sentimentalist to want to finally return to The Meadow.

One day, in 1935, he took his daughter Penny and his wife Helen to see a boarding school that Penny would attend in Washington, D.C. She would recall the day many years later, picture it as she and her father and mother drove south toward Richmond from Washington and bumped toward The Meadow, where he had spent summers as a youngster, toward Ashland where he had grown up and learned to know the country to which he was returning now:

> We drove south for several hours that day, on narrow roads that went up and down like a roller coaster over countless hills. The brown winter woods and the sluggish creeks had a sameness that depressed me; they were so unlike the twisting roads and sudden vistas of my familiar New England, but I was excited to be going back to dad's home—not really his, but his cousin's, where he had spent his happiest summers.

Chenery drove further south, toward the "wooded hills dropping down to deep-cut brown rivers, and wide old fields lying in between," across the dirt roads climbing to a bridge, high and rickety, that delivered them from Hanover to Caroline County:

> Here indeed were the broad fields of the farm, but they were sandy and bare of soil. The car climbed a hill with a commanding view of the river flats to find—a gas station, two old pumps and a shed along side the road. About two hundred yards behind it stood an unpainted three-story, gaunt, old, stark wooden house. It stood amid some handsome old trees but the ground around it was bare. A mongrel dog lay under the porch, the chickens pecked around the steps. My memory fills in tattered children and a few pigs, but I wouldn't swear to it.

The car nosed into the drive and the yard. There was a silence, and Penny Tweedy recalled her father looking perplexed, then angry:

> Still standing were a tall story-and-a-half building at one corner of the yard—the office, he fumed. At the other were two smaller shacklike structures, but with definite architectural details, which were the smoke house and the old kitchen. The remnants of a classic revival cupola capped the well house. Below, in a wide loop of the river, there had once been rich fields. Slave labor had built a dike around them to keep the river out, but after the Civil War, it was breached by high water, and the cove, as it was called, was now covered by an immense tangle of brush, trees and brambles. It had been overgrown even when dad was a boy, and he had heard stories of a runaway slave who lived down in there. No one had ventured down in many years.

Chenery stopped the car in the yard and climbed out, looking at the house and the trees and the land around it. He told his wife and daughter to remain in the car, warning them that the house might be louse ridden. Chenery went inside, but he didn't stay long. Moments later he walked back to the car. He said nothing as he slid inside and drove off to the house across the road. Penny wanted to ask him what The Meadow homestead was like inside, what it looked like, but she saw his expression and decided to say nothing at all. He bought The Meadow a year later.

Thus Christopher T. Chenery had repossessed his childhood, reclaiming some old hills and remembrances and a place to raise horses. But if there was some of the Gatsby romantic in him—something of a man trying to recapture his past—his brothers hardly

shared his enthusiasm. They were against his buying back The
Meadow, Penny said:

> They thought Chris was crazy to buy it back—that was all behind
> them—and Virginia would never leave the shackles of its backward
> economy, especially rural Virginia. The Depression was easing, but the
> specter of poverty never left any of them.

But Chenery had made his money by stringing utilities together,
and he was on his way to being a millionaire several times over again.
By 1936, he had already been the president of the Federal Water
Service Corporation for ten years, and that year he also became
chairman and director of Southern Natural Gas Company. Deep in
the Depression, Chris Chenery was making money and incorporat-
ing his holdings and sharing his stock with the family, and with the
gold he set about in earnest to rebuild The Meadow.

He spent thousands of dollars making it a showplace, rebuilding
and enlarging and refurnishing it:

> He built stables for one hundred horses, a mile training track, breed-
> ing sheds, hay barns, and an office—the old one had been beyond
> repair. The poor country boy eventually spent his winters in Palm
> Beach buying at auctions the things that were symbols of wealth in his
> childhood. He first acquired oriental rugs, then turned to nineteenth-
> century paintings, and finally to jade.

He had earned what he was spending and what he owned. He had
a contempt for idle people and for laziness, a disdain for dullness and
the weak witted. Education was not what set men apart. What
distinguished them was the intensity of the drive and the energy and
imagination they possessed and used.

Politically, he was conservative, a staunch anti-Communist—or,
as he would prefer to say, an anti-Bolshevik. Financially, he was bold
but careful, and when he invested in thoroughbreds in the late 1930s
he made small and what appeared to be insignificant acquisitions of
blooded horses. "The price does not always represent what a horse
is worth," Chenery once said. "It is only what some fool thinks he
is worth."

Among his first purchases was a filly named Hildene, a daughter
of the 1926 Kentucky Derby winner, Bubbling Over. He paid only
$600 for her. "Hildene showed speed, but she tired badly eight times

in eight races," he said. So he retired her to the stud, and there she produced a family of some of the finest horses on the American turf.

Sometime during the Depression, when he was getting started in racing, Chenery acquired a set of jockey silks. They were some old silks that had been abandoned, no doubt discarded by some owner who went haywire for a decade and then dropped off into the perpetual twilight that came in October of 1929. The silks were snappy: white and blue blocks on the shirt, and blue and white stripes down the sleeves. And a blue cap.

Chapter 3

In the end it was the land that made them all—the land that raised the horses and made room for the people and supported the empires of chance they built on it.

It was blocked off in white and creosote fences and planted in clover and grass, a deep green shag rug that ran, as if unrolled, across a boundless countryside. The land is where the horses were born, on farms such as Hamburg Place in Kentucky, where still stands a single barn—a historic marker now—in which five Kentucky Derby winners were foaled: Old Rosebud (1914), Sir Barton (1919), Paul Jones (1920), Zev (1923), and Flying Ebony (1925). It is where the horses were raised and weaned, where they romped and grazed and grew to young horses on the racetrack. Some were returned to it as pensioners, many more to serve in studs and nurseries. A chosen few were buried on the land, the best beneath granite headstones chiseled in their names and, at times, in epitaphs rendered in the style of Boot Hill:

> Here lies the fleetest runner the American turf has ever known, and one of the gamest and most generous of horses.

That is the epitaph on the monument of Domino, the "Black Whirlwind," who was buried in 1897 in a grave outside of Lexington. There was no faster horse than Domino in the sprints—he was the Jesse Owens of his species in the Gay Nineties—and when they retired him to stud, he whirled the wind again as a progenitor. Domino died at six, twenty years too soon for a sire of his prepotency, and he left only twenty offspring from his duty as a stud horse, eleven daughters and nine sons. But among the sons was Commando, a horse who would strike his and his sire's names into the pedigree charts of champions for many years. Through Pink Domino, a daughter, his name would surface often in the family trees of numerous racehorses, appearing in the distant collateral reaches of the bloodlines of many modern horses, including the colt Gentry delivered that night at The Meadow.

Domino was a phenomenon, a complete thoroughbred, sui generis. He remains today one of the few American racehorses in history who left the land and became one of the fastest horses of his era, then returned to it and made an even deeper imprint on the breed itself. Most thoroughbreds, in the days of Domino and since him, left the land and failed at the races—if they ever got to the races at all, which many did not—or they raced through careers of declining mediocrity. Many colts were gelded along the way, destroyed for a variety of reasons, sold for use as saddle horses or jumping or hunting horses, or hitched to wagons or rented out, by the hour, at livery stables everywhere.

Scores of stallions, coming off superior racing careers, failed as stud horses, some more ignominiously than others. Sir Barton, winner of the 1919 Triple Crown, failed to transmit much of his speed to his offspring, and he finished out his stud career at a cavalry remount station in Douglas, Wyoming. Grey Lag, one of the most gifted runners in the early 1920s—winner of the 1921 Belmont Stakes and the prestigious Brooklyn Handicap—was virtually sterile when sent to stud. Returned to the races at age nine, he had trouble beating horses that could not have warmed him up in his younger days. He was retired a second time, given away, and a few years later was discovered again, at the age of thirteen, running against cheap $1000 claiming horses in Canada. Harry F. Sinclair, who raced Grey Lag in his prime while leasing oil fields at Teapot Dome, was in no need of more adverse publicity. Quietly, he dispatched an agent to Canada, bought the horse, and retired him to his Rancocas Farm. Grey Lag never raced again, living out his life as a pensioner. The other famous impotent, 1946 Triple Crown winner Assault, did the same, as did many fine geldings, such as Exterminator and Armed.

But most of the horses sent back to the farms, the many fillies and mares and the few colts and horses, were pressed into the service of breeding enterprises, of large stud farms such as Hamburg Place and Himyar, Rancocas and Idle Hour and Calumet Farm. The fortunes of the farms and their owners, in some ways, ran with the fortunes of the horses and the bloodlines they produced. All of them would rise to prominence in their day, wane, reemerge, or die away. There is no great Himyar anymore, no flourishing Idle Hour since Colonel E.R. Bradley died, though the land still raises horses. Sinclair sold the last of the Rancocas horses in 1932, all but Zev and Grey Lag. Hamburg Place, once the showplace of American breeding, is no longer what it once was, though it still exists. And Calumet Farm is no longer the 1927 Yankees it was when Bull Lea filled the farm's stable with so many high-classed runners, three Derby winners and all those nimble-footed tomboys. But what is behind them, behind all the young horses and the new owners and breeders of thorough-breds, is the land.

While Christopher T. Chenery was piecing together the shards of his family homestead, the descendants of Richard J. Hancock emerged as the leading breeders of thoroughbreds in America. It had taken seventy years.

R. J. Hancock founded Ellerslie Stud and within ten years of the war had bought his first stallion, Scathelock, and his first broodmare, War Song. That was the start.

Hancock's rise to prominence as a Virginia breeder actually began after he acquired the stallion Eolus from a Maryland breeder, swap-ping Scathelock in an even trade. The transaction revealed Han-cock's shrewd eye for horses. Eolus sired a number of winners, giving a measure of prestige to the Hancock name among Virginia horse-men. Among the best was Knight of Ellerslie, who not only won the 1884 Preakness Stakes, but also made a name as the sire of Henry of Navarre, the chestnut colt who battled Domino, the "Black Whirl-wind," in one of the most celebrated struggles in the history of the American turf. High-rolling Pittsburgh Phil bet $100,000 on Domino and calmly ate figs out of a bag as he watched the two horses struggle to a dead heat.

Eolus died three years later, in 1897, but by then Ellerslie had become a major thoroughbred nursery in Virginia, selling its year-lings every year at auction, buying and raising its own bloodstock. And by then, too, Richard Hancock's son, Arthur, had graduated from the University of Chicago, a reedy young man, 6 feet 6 inches and 165 pounds, who came home in 1895 to be about his father's business. He became his father's assistant, attending yearling sales and doing his novitiate on the farm. And then, within one three-year period, a series of events occurred in Arthur Hancock's life that enlarged its scope and potential, multiplying the possibilities open to him as a breeder.

In 1907, seeking a man without local ties or friendships, Senator Camden Johnson of Kentucky invited Hancock to judge a class of thoroughbreds at the Blue Grass Fair in Kentucky. Hancock accepted. While he was there, he met Nancy Tucker Clay, one of the many Clays of Bourbon County. Like the Harrises of Virginia, the Clays of Kentucky were landed gentry, owning lots of land, acres of some of the choicest real estate in the Blue Grass country. Nancy Clay and Arthur Hancock were married the following year, in 1908, fusing a family owning one of the finest estates in Virginia with another owning miles of rolling greenery in Kentucky.

In 1909, Arthur Hancock took over the operation of Ellerslie from his aging father.

In 1910, within a span of four days, Nancy Clay Hancock's father and mother died. Nancy Hancock inherited 1300 acres of property in Paris, Kentucky, rich farmland set off Winchester Road. So the events of the year made Hancock the steward of two manors, and they left him an heir to his fortune and name. Earlier in the year, Nancy Hancock had given birth to a son, Arthur Boyd Hancock, Jr., a man whose influence on American bloodstock would one day exceed that of his father's. Arthur Hancock, Sr., did not take long to coordinate the operations at Ellerslie and Claiborne Farm, the name they chose for the land in Paris. The Hancock stud at Ellerslie survived the horse-racing blackout of 1911–1912, when the sport was outlawed in New York during an outburst of moral fervor, but Hancock had to cut back the broodmare band to all but about twelve mares. Over the next twenty-five years, Hancock's long climb to preeminence as a breeder began. He moved his family permanently to the Kentucky farm in 1912, a move suggesting that he knew Kentucky would one day be the home of thoroughbred breeding in America.

A year later he bought the stallion Celt, a son of Commando, for $20,000 in a dispersal sale at Madison Square Garden. Under Celt, the Hancock stud regained the vigor it possessed in the days of Eolus. Hancock's interest in foreign bloodstock heightened when the prices dropped in Europe at the start of World War I. In 1915 he bought the English stallion, Wrack, for $8000 from Archibald Philip Rosbery. It marked Hancock's first major acquisition of a foreign stallion, and it launched a breeding operation at Claiborne Farm, where Wrack was sent to stud. Barns were built near Kennedy Creek. Part of the land was fenced with planking. A grazing paddock was built for Wrack to loll away his idle hours. And the farm itself expanded, growing in size from 1300 to 2100 acres.

The Hancock studs flourished in the 1920s, grew in influence and prestige. In 1921 Celt was America's leading thoroughbred sire in the amount of money won by his offspring, his fifty-two performing sons and daughters winning 124 races and $206,167 in purses. Hancock reached out for more foreign blood. His acquisition of foreign bloodstock reached its zenith in 1926, when he formed a four-man group —composed of Hanover Bank president William Woodward, Marshall Field, Robert Fairbairn, and himself—and bought Sir Gallahad III, a French stallion and a son of Teddy, for $125,000. Sir Gallahad's impact at the stud was felt almost at once.

Bred his first year in America to Marguerite, a daughter of Celt, he sired Belair Stud's Gallant Fox. "The Fox of Belair," as he came to be known, won the Triple Crown in 1930, the second horse to do it. Sir Gallahad III was the leading American sire that year, with just sixteen offspring winning forty-nine races and $422,200, a record in purses that stood until 1942. He led the sire list three more times, his horses winning more than the horses sired by any other stallion.

Through the importation of the potent Teddy blood, through Sir Gallahad III and later his full brother, Bull Dog, American and other imported blood was freshened and invigorated. Sir Gallahad III's influence became unusually pervasive in his role as a "broodmare sire," so pervasive that he led the annual broodmare sire list for twelve years, ten years in a row, from 1943 to 1952. The broodmare sire list is a special category that singles out stallions whose daughters are exceptional producers. For twelve years the daughters of Sir Gallahad III produced racehorses that won more money than the racehorses produced by the daughters of any other sire. No horse in American history, before or since, ever dominated that list so long. He sired La France, dam of the 1939 Kentucky Derby and Belmont Stakes winner, Johnstown; and he sired Gallette, dam of champion handicap mare Gallorette; Fighting Lady, dam of the speedy Armageddon; and Black Wave, dam of the 1947 Kentucky Derby winner, Jet Pilot.

In 1936, Hancock was instrumental in bringing Blenheim II, the 1930 Epsom Derby winner, to America. Blenheim II cost an American syndicate $250,000. Among Blenheim II's first sons to reach the races in America was Whirlaway, winner of the 1941 Triple Crown, the fifth horse to win it.

Hancock's fortunes as a breeder soared. In 1935 horses bred by Hancock won more races—392—and more money—$359,218—than the horses bred by any other breeder. He led the breeder lists for the next two years. Hancock was not racing his homebreds. Following a policy adopted originally by his father in 1886, he sold his yearlings at auction every year. Through the years, he developed a reputation as a breeder knowledgeable about bloodlines, both foreign and domestic, who could recall in minute detail the distant reaches of a pedigree.

By then his son Arthur was a student of breeding too. "I grew up at Claiborne and when I was twelve, my father was paying me fifty cents a day to sweep out after the yearlings," he once said. That was in the summer of 1922, the year before he left the public school system in Paris and went to Saint Mark's Academy in Southborough, Massachusettes, a bastion of righteous Episcopalianism, where he subscribed to the *Daily Racing Form,* the industry's trade newspaper and the horseplayer's bible. He transferred to Woodberry Forest, a Virginia school, and there picked up his nickname, Bull, by which he would one day be known throughout all the major world marketplaces for the blooded horse. His central ambition was to be a thoroughbred breeder.

In the summers of his youth, when his jobs went beyond sweeping out after the yearlings, he worked with the broodmares, the stud horses, the yearlings, the farm veterinarian, alternating jobs summer after summer. He went to Princeton, played baseball and football, and earned letters. He was a six-foot-two raconteur with a reverberating baritone voice.

At Princeton he studied eugenics, French, and genetics. And when he graduated in 1933 he returned to Clairborne, as his father had returned to Ellerslie almost forty years before, to become his father's assistant. He learned, as his father learned, from the grass up—about the care and feeding of the yearlings and the broodmares and the stud horses, starting from the beginning. He learned about the land, too, walking it so often that one day he would know every tree and plank on it.

"I never wanted to be anything but a horseman," Bull once said. "I just never thought of anything else."

Chapter 4

Claiborne Farm was no empire of prepotent young stallions and mares of promise when Bull Hancock returned to it in 1945, the year the air corps released him after his father suffered the first of several heart attacks.

Bull was thirty-five then and much had begun to wane since he became his father's assistant. What he came back to was a farm with a twilight presence to it—old stallions and old mares and an aging, ailing owner who would not let go. Arthur Hancock, Sr., had been the leading breeder again in America, but there had been no infusion of fresh bloodstock. Breeding blooded horses is an enterprise that flourishes most vigorously with recurrent transfusions of young horses and mares of quality, with the culling of the failures and the replacement of the aging stock with younger animals. Stallions and mares—with some notorious exceptions—usually produce their finest offspring before they reach the age of fifteen.

In 1945, Blenheim II was already eighteen years old and beyond his prime, though he later sired several excellent runners. Sir Gallahad III, whose influence as a broodmare sire was growing, was a ripened twenty-five and only four years away from Valhalla. The younger stallions were not successful. In general, the 250 mares living on the farm, most of them owned by Claiborne's clients, who boarded them there, were well bred but not exceptional producers. Hancock was unenthusiastic about the quality of Claiborne's own mares. "We had gone twelve years without replacing stock," he once recalled. "He [Arthur, Sr.] had sold everything. When I took over he had about seventy-five mares and I didn't like any of them, except two. I started rebuilding. I made up my mind that my children wouldn't have to go through what I did." And by 1950, when he was refreshing the bloodstock with mares like Miss Disco, he already had two sons. The oldest was Arthur B. Hancock, III. And the youngest, an infant at the time, was Seth.

The rebirth of the Hancock breeding dynasty actually began to take place six years earlier, launched by an event so inconspicuous that it stirred only the mildest notice of a day. It occurred when the Georgian Prince Dimitri Djordjadze and his wife Audrey, a Cincinnati heiress, decided to retire their little bay colt, Princequillo, and arranged to have him stand at stud in Virginia.

Almost two decades earlier, in 1928, two figures connected with the Belgian turf purchased a weanling—a colt by the stallion Rose Prince out of a mare named Indolence. The cost was 260 guineas. The weanling, shipped to Belgium, was named Prince Rose.

Prince Rose became the greatest racehorse in the Belgium of his day—probably the best that had ever run in that country—and one of its greatest sires. He had the bloodlines: Prince Rose's sire, Rose Prince, was by Prince Palatine, a son of Persimmon, who was himself a son of one of the greatest sires in thoroughbred history, the undefeated St. Simon. As a direct male-line descendant of St. Simon, Prince Rose descended in what is called "tail male" from St. Simon, a potentially valuable genetic trait. The St. Simon male line produced an unusual number of superior horses.

As Prince Rose was establishing himself as Belgium's leading sire, the American representative in France for Metro-Goldwyn-Mayer, Laudy Lawrence, obtained the horse from Belgium on a three-year lease. Lawrence brought the horse to France in 1938 and installed him in his Haras de Cheffreville. In the spring of 1939, he bred Prince Rose to his mare Cosquilla, a daughter of Papyrus, winner of the Epsom Derby. She conceived. The breeding occurred in a turbulent time. War was coming to Europe. The German armies were menacing France. Pregnant, Cosquilla didn't stay there long. She was dispatched across the English Channel, while in foal, to be bred in England the next spring.

In early 1940, as the Battle of Britain was about to begin, Cosquilla gave birth to her bay colt at the Banstead Stud at Newmarket, near Suffolk, about ninety miles outside of London. The air war over England began in July of 1940, and later that summer or fall—after the colt had been weaned—he was sent to Lawrence's farm in Ireland. Then, in 1941, he and a number of yearlings were shipped across the North Atlantic, by then a lair of submarines, to New York. The colt disembarked as a refugee of sorts.

Named Princequillo, he was broken at the Mill River Farm in New York and put in training there. Prior to leaving the country again, Lawrence leased Princequillo to Chicago owner Anthony Pelleteri. One of the clauses of the lease permitted Pelleteri to run Princequillo in claiming races—in which the horse could be bought or "claimed" for a specific price—even though Pelleteri did not own him.

Pelleteri raced Princequillo for the first time under a $1500 claiming tag. No one took him.

He then ran the colt back for a $2500 claiming price, and again there were no takers.

Pelleteri then raced Princequillo for $2500 in his fourth start, winning with him then, and that was the last time Pelleteri had him. Trainer Horatio Luro, acting for the Boone Hall Stables of Princess Djordjadze, claimed him for the price. Luro ran him as a claimer, too. Aside from his pedigree, there was no apparent reason for anyone to believe that Princequillo would develop into the best long-distance runner in America in 1943. But he did, running best beyond a mile and an eighth.

In 1943 the spring classics were dominated by Count Fleet, an extremely fast horse who raced to easy victories in the Kentucky Derby, Preakness, and Belmont stakes and became the sixth horse in history to win the American Triple Crown. He won the Belmont Stakes by twenty-five lengths, the longest margin by which it had ever been won. Princequillo began his three-year-old year modestly. He won an allowance race in New Orleans, not a major racetrack compared with those in New York, then lost two others there, but he quickly became sharp. On June 12, seven days after Count Fleet rushed to his record-breaking clocking in the Belmont Stakes—clipping two-fifths of a second off War Admiral's stakes record of 2:28 ⅗ for the mile and a half—Princequillo ran the best race in his career. He defeated Bolingbroke, the great long distancer, beating him going a mile and five-eighths.

Princequillo then hooked the older Bolingbroke and Shut Out, winner of the 1942 Kentucky Derby, at a mile and a quarter in the Saratoga Handicap. Princequillo won it. The farther they ran, the better he liked it. He would leave the gate and simply roll on. A week after the Saratoga Handicap, he raced Bolingbroke over a mile and three-quarters, thus far the longest race of his career, and he won a head-bobbing stretch duel in record time. He closed out his year with a triumph in one of the longest races in America, the two-mile Jockey Club Gold Cup at Belmont Park.

Princequillo, by acclaim, was the best cup horse—that is, the best long-distance runner—in America, beating the most accomplished routers consistently. He won two more races in 1944, when he was a four-year-old, then pulled up lame at Saratoga. He won $96,550 and twelve of thirty-three races over three years.

Arthur B. Hancock, Sr., liked Princequillo's racing record—his ability to stay a distance of ground—and he liked his pedigree. So Princequillo was installed at Ellerslie in 1945. There were no breeders leaping over one another to get their mares to Princequillo. He may have been the best long-distance runner in America, but he was not a fashionable stallion like Count Fleet or War Admiral. Princequillo was held in such uncertain esteem, in fact, that Hancock was unable to get enough mares to breed to him, the thirty-five or so mares needed to fill his book. But those who did decide to send him mares at Ellerslie made the difference. One was William Woodward. Another was Christopher T. Chenery.

Chapter 5

Princequillo was bred to Chenery's Hildene in the spring of 1946, a year that ushered in a quick succession of landmark years in the fortunes of Hancock and Chenery and in the course of breeding thoroughbreds in America.

In 1946, the Hancocks sold Ellerslie, which had been losing money and declining as a stud farm for years, and consolidated all their thoroughbred holdings at Claiborne. Among the horses dispatched from Charlottesville to Paris was Princequillo. For him it was a long journey's end. And Hildene, one of the last of the hundreds of mares bred at Ellerslie since the days of Richard Hancock's Eolus, was returned to The Meadow in foal. The following year, in the spring of 1947, Hildene gave birth to a bay son of Princequillo. Chenery named him Hill Prince.

The racing fortunes of the Chenery horses were rising. More pivotally, 1947 was also the year that Chenery attended a dispersal sale of the estate of W. A. La Boyteaux at Saratoga and decided to join the bidding when the mare, Imperatrice, winner of the 1941 Test Stakes, was led into the sales ring. It was perhaps the most important decision of Chenery's extraordinary career as a breeder.

Imperatrice was not much to look at, but she liked to hear her feet rattle. She was a big-barreled, short-legged, floppy-eared bay mare with a stirring gust of speed. Sprinting was her trump.

Imperatrice also won the Test and New Rochelle—both sprints— but she had a depth of quality about her that almost carried her home in the 1941 Beldame Stakes, an important middle-distance race at Aqueduct. She finished a close second.

At her side in 1947 was a colt by the stallion Piping Rock, and the gallery at the sale was advised that she was in foal to him again. So Chenery, seeing a once-speedy race mare with a Piping Rock foal beside her and another advertised within, jumped into the bidding and moved it upward, finally upward to $30,000. The gavel slammed down, and they were his. Then down to The Meadow went Imperatrice. Later in the year Dr. William Caslick, a veterinarian, made his regular rounds of the Chenery broodmares to pronounce them either *in* or *not* in foal.

Chenery happened to be at The Meadow that day. Caslick moved from mare to mare, coming finally to the stall of Imperatrice. He walked inside and began the examination, inserting his hand in the mare's rectum and reaching far inside, to where he could feel the outside of the uterine wall through the intestines. He was feeling for the fetus.

Moments passed. Caslick probed carefully for the signs of life. More time passed. Chenery, standing by Howard Gentry, wondered out loud what was taking so long.

"That mare's empty," Caslick finally said.

Chenery plopped down on a bale of straw: "Thirty Thousand dollars, and empty!"

Imperatrice did not stay empty long.

In the autumn of the year, another kind of milestone was reached. Hundreds of men and women drove or walked the twelve miles from Lexington to Faraway Farm, filing through the gates until all of them, some horsemen and some not, gathered near the grave and listened as the mayor of Lexington gave a speech, and the head of the American Horse and Mule Association, Ira Drymon, delivered a eulogy. Bull Hancock was among the breeders there.

The mood was reverential. Man o' War was lying in an oak coffin at the edge of an open grave. The top of the coffin was open. Man o' War had died with an erection, and someone had discreetly placed a black cloth or blanket over it. He had suffered a series of heart attacks within a forty-eight hour period, getting to his feet repeatedly until the last one put him down for good. He was thirty then, extremely old for a horse. The crowd listened as the eulogy ended, watched as the coffin was closed. They had paid the ultimate tribute to a racehorse—giving him a funeral fit for a prince of the blood, celebrating the cherished belief in Kentucky that Man o' War was the greatest horse America had ever produced.

In the winter of 1948, trainer Jimmy Jones saddled Citation for the Ground Hog Course at Hialeah Racetrack in Florida, where many top three-year-olds would begin their campaigning for the Triple Crown. On May 1, he won the Kentucky Derby by three and a half, beating a stablemate, Coaltown. Two weeks later he won the Preakness Stakes at Pimlico by five and a half lengths. On June 12, at Belmont Park on Long Island, he raced to an eight-length victory in the Belmont Stakes. Thus Citation became the eighth Triple Crown winner in American turf history and earned a reputation as one of the greatest runners of all time.

In 1949, the winnings of the Chenery horses soared to $141,005, with Hill Prince winning the World's Playground Stakes at Atlantic City, worth $11,275, and the Cowdin Stakes at Belmont Park under Eddie Arcaro. Hill Prince was voted the leading two-year-old in America. The value of Princequillo's stud services started climbing. At Claiborne Farm meanwhile, Bull Hancock was engineering the masterstroke in modern American breeding, the pièce de résistance.

Toward the end of 1949, sometime in the fall of the year, Dr. Eslie Asbury, a Cincinnati surgeon, received a telephone call from Hancock, his long-time friend and counselor on thoroughbred breeding. The call concerned Nasrullah, the Irish stallion that Hancock wanted to import to America. He had tried twice without success to purchase him. Foaled in 1940 at the Aga Khan's Sheshoon Stud in Ireland, Nasrullah was a son of the unbeaten Nearco, the greatest racehorse of his day in Europe. Nasrullah was a stubborn if gifted animal, a rogue at the barrier, a rogue sometimes in the morning. If the spirit did not move him to gallop on the racetrack, which was often, an umbrella opened behind him usually did; that became one of the techniques used to make him run at Newmarket. He was a champion two-year-old in England, and Hancock believed the horse was unlucky when he finished third in the 1943 Epsom Derby. Bull Hancock liked him.

In fact, Hancock tried to buy him once in 1948 for £100,000 in partnership with Captain Harry F. Guggenheim, the copper baron, and banker Woodward, but the pound was devalued and the deal caved in with it.

And now a year later Hancock had tried again and finally succeeded in getting him. Nasrullah, at last, was coming to America.

"We have the horse," Hancock said to Asbury. "Do you want in?"

Asbury did not hesitate. Nasrullah was not new to him. Years later he recalled that he and Hancock during various conversations had spoken of Nasrullah's prospects as a sire, his racing record, his temperament, and the vigor he might infuse into American strains. Hancock had always wanted a stallion from the Nearco line, a powerful line only tokenly represented in America at the time. Nearco had been the leading sire in England in 1947 and 1948 and was on his way to being the leading sire again in 1949. Asbury recalled that he and Hancock had spoken specifically about the invigorating effect the Nasrullah blood might have on the blood of Sir Gallahad III and Bull Dog, the sons of Teddy. "We had felt Nasrullah was an outcross for all the Teddy blood here," said Asbury. "We had so much Teddy blood here, especially at Claiborne and in my own mares."

Hancock told Asbury that the syndication was almost complete: the stallion had been acquired for $340,000 and the price was $10,000 per share. The syndicate included some of the most prominent names in American turf: Guggenheim and Woodward, H. C. Phipps, and George D. Widener, chairman of the Jockey Club, among others.

The announcement that appeared on page 572 of the December 10, 1949, issue of the *Blood-Horse* began ironically in the passive voice:

> The purchase by a syndicate of American breeders of the nine-year-old stallion Nasrullah was announced this week by Arthur B. Hancock Jr. of Claiborne Stud, Paris. The son of Nearco–Mumtaz Begum by Blenheim II . . . was purchased from Joseph McGrath of the Brownstown Stud, County Kildaire, Eire.

The resurgence of the Hancock dynasty was now at hand.

The following year, in 1950, Hill Prince finished second in the Kentucky Derby, a race Hancock and Chenery always wanted to win. The son of Princequillo romped to a five-length victory in the Preakness Stakes, worth $56,115 to Chenery, and to victories in the Withers Stakes and the Jerome Handicap. As Hill Prince was making a run for Horse of the Year honors on the East Coast, a five-year-old horse named Noor beat Citation fairly four times. For the showdown, Noor came east to meet Hill Prince in the two-mile Jockey Club Gold Cup. Hill Prince rolled to the lead and never lost it, easily winning the race his sire won in 1943. Noor, an Irish-bred horse, finished second. The significance of these events was only gradually dawning.

Hill Prince was named Horse of the Year in 1950.

Prince Simon, another son of Princequillo, was among the best three-year-olds in Europe. He was owned by William Woodward. And Noor was a son of Nasrullah, one of his first sons imported to America.

Nasrullah had arrived in America in July 1950, and he started his first days in stud there—his paddock was near that of Princequillo—in the early part of 1951.

That same year, with one champion son of Princequillo in his barn, Chenery sought another from him. But he didn't return Hildene to him. Instead, in 1951, Chenery sent Imperatrice to Princequillo and on January 9, 1952, she had a filly foal at The Meadow. She was a bay, and Mrs. Helen Bates Chenery—who named most of the horses—called her Somethingroyal.

Chapter 6

Jockey Eddie Arcaro was riding Bold Ruler toward the winner's circle late that afternoon of 1956, moments after the colt had raced to a two-length victory in the Futurity at Belmont Park, when Mrs. Henry Carnegie Phipps stepped forward to meet them. Bold Ruler had just beaten the fastest two-year-old colts in America, running in near-record time, and he was dancing home, his nostrils flaring hotly, his neck bowed and lathered with sweat, moving powerfully toward his seventy-three-year-old owner. Turfwriter Charles Hatton watched her meet him.

"Mrs. Phipps was out at the gap to get him and lead him down that silly victory lane they had there. And she must have weighed all of ninety pounds, and here is this big young stud horse—and she walked right up to him and held out her hand, and he just settled right down and dropped his head so she could get ahold of the chin strap, and Bold Ruler just walked like an old cow along that lane and she wasn't putting any pressure on him to quiet him down or make him be still. It was one of the most amazing sights I've ever seen. It was incredible to me because anyone else reaching for that horse—and he was hot!—you'd have had to snatch him or he'd throw you off your feet or step all over you. But not with her. For her he was just a real chivalrous prince of a colt. He came back to her and stopped all the monkeyshines, ducked down his head and held out his chin, and here was this little old lady with a big young stud horse on the other end and he was just as gentle as he could be."

Even growing old, as her walnut face withdrew inside a frame of white hair, she had a mind as quick as a crack of lightning and always drove to the racetrack in the morning by herself, without a chauffeur, steering her Bentley south from Spring Hill, the marble palace on Long Island.

Mrs. Phipps must have seemed the picture of some innocent eccentric—the way she tipped back her head to see the road above the dash, the way she gripped the wheel with both hands, the way she climbed from the car with the poodles beside her and walked into the barn at Belmont Park. Her horses turned to watch her coming. She carried sugar, and she wore a plain dress, sometimes a stocking with a run in it and sometimes moccasins or gym shoes. The men at work in the stables stepped gingerly around her when she walked up the shed, some nodding deferentially and saying hello, and she returned the salutations but did not speak at length to them, only to Sunny Jim Fitzsimmons, her crippled trainer.

On summer mornings they would sit as if enthroned like ancients from another time. He was the sage, a former trolley car motorman from Sheepshead Bay in Brooklyn who became one of the finest horsemen of all time, the only man to train two winners of the Triple Crown, Gallant Fox and Omaha, and almost three and four in Johnstown and Nashua. She was the patron, fulfilling the aristocratic role, racing horses for the sport of it and never complaining, win or lose. She was the stable bookkeeper and knew how much each horse had won. She would ask how they were doing, how they were eating, and when and how they were working, and when and where they would race again. She was an independent little statue of a woman who went her own way, and she would walk up to the shed and stop to pet and feed her horses, complimenting those who had won, scolding softly those who had just lost: "You dope," she would say, holding a cube of sugar. "I don't know if I should give you one." But she always did.

She was the grande dame of the American turf, and she hardly ever spoke in public. The news accounts in words attributed directly to her are sparse, and one newsman confided that he always left her alone when he saw her sitting in the box seat because he sensed a privacy inviolate.

She was born Gladys Mills on June 19, 1883, in Newport, Rhode Island, a twin daughter of Ruth Livingston and Ogden Mills, her name minted from a marriage between heirs of two of the largest family fortunes in America. The Livingstons were old American wealth and aristocracy, pre-Revolutionary real estate and later steamboats up the Hudson. The Millses were nineteenth-century nouveau riche. Darius Ogden Mills made millions in the California Gold Rush. His son Ogden became a financier, and a sportsman. He went into a racing partnership with Lord Derby of England, and together they operated a strong stable of racehorses on the Continent —so strong that in 1928, the year Mills died, it was the leading stable in France. The Mills-Derby racing venture continued to endure when Gladys Mills's twin sister, the Right Honourable Beatrice, Countess of Granard, replaced her father and helped to carry the stable. By then Gladys Mills was an owner, too.

In 1907, when she was twenty-four years old, Gladys Mills married into one of the wealthiest and most powerful families in America, the steel family of her husband, Henry Carnegie Phipps. He was a son of Henry Phipps, who, with Andrew Carnegie, founded a steelworks so profitable that when J. Pierpont Morgan bought them out in 1901, Phipps's share alone came to $50 million.

Gladys Mills and Henry Carnegie Phipps settled down in New York, in a home with a marble facade at Eighty-seventh Street and Fifth Avenue, and on the Long Island estate off Wheatley Road in Roslyn. Phipps was tall, distinguished, and played polo. Mrs. Phipps was small, with a flinty New England dignity about her, a crack shot. In her later years she climbed into a swivel seat mounted on a swamp truck in Florida, and with a shotgun she would spin around, shooting birds. She bagged her limit in quail at the age of eighty-six.

Mrs. Phipps, in partnership with her brother Ogden L. Mills and his wife, bought horses for the first time in the mid-1920s and raced them under the nom de course of the Wheatley Stable. The stable flourished early, launched to a quick success after the leading American breeder of the 1920s, Harry Payne Whitney, a Long Island neighbor of the Phippses, offered her a choice of ten of his yearlings in 1926, reportedly to satisfy a gambling debt incurred during a high-rolling card game with Henry Carnegie Phipps. Whether out of luck or shrewdness—probably part of both—Mrs. Phipps and trainer Sunny Jim Fitzsimmons chose five yearlings that went on to win stakes for her and more than once whipped Whitney's horses. Incredibly, the other five were multiple winners, too, though not of stakes. The best of the ten were Diabolo, a long-distance runner who won the 1929 Jockey Club Gold Cup at two miles, and the unbeaten but ill-fated two-year-old Dice (who died of colic as a youngster), as well as Nixie, Distraction, and Swizzlestick.

Her passion was for horses purely as runners. "I just like to see them perform as thoroughbreds," she once said, in one of her rare public remarks. Her interest in horses involved her as a breeder soon enough. In 1929, the same year Diabolo won the Jockey Club Gold Cup, she purchased a broodmare, Virginia L., in partnership with Marshall Field, who had just helped finance the importation of Sir Gallahad III. Mrs. Phipps never bought a farm of her own for the breeding and raising of thoroughbreds. But she did meet Arthur B. Hancock, Sr., early in her career as an owner, and when she finally did decide to breed as well as race her horses, she became a client of Hancock at Claiborne Farm. Through the next forty years, most of her homebreds were foaled and raised in Paris, Kentucky. It was she who decided which of her mares would be bred to which stallion; she became a student of the pedigrees of all her horses, and though she took advice, she made her own decisions.

In her first twenty-five years as a breeder, by far the fastest thoroughbred she bred was Seabiscuit, the bay horse who bumped off War Admiral in the famous Pimlico match race on November 1, 1938, though "The Biscuit" did not carry the Wheatley gold and purple silks for her then. He had raced eighteen times as a two-year-old before he won his first start for her, thirty-five times in all that year with only five wins. He was just a sluggish selling plater when Mrs. Phipps, becoming impatient and discouraged with him, sold him for $8000 to Charles S. Howard. It was one of the rare mistakes she made in the business. Seabiscuit retired in 1940 with earnings of $437,430, a world record at the time.

The Wheatley-breds won more than $100,000 for the first time in 1935, winning 106 races and $113,834. Never again did they earn less than $100,000 annually. Among the best horses Mrs. Phipps bred were Seabiscuit, High Voltage, and Misty Morn, a daughter of Princequillo who won $212,575. Yet nothing she ever did compared in import to the purchase she made early in the 1950s, when she prevailed upon Hancock to sell her Miss Disco, upon whom the Phippses founded a dynasty.

Miss Disco came to Gladys Phipps at the end of a curious, sometimes unlikely series of events that began unfolding late in 1933, the year Alfred Gwynne Vanderbilt turned twenty-one. Vanderbilt had just begun to involve himself as an owner and breeder of racehorses, as a man of name, means, and ambition in the thoroughbred industry. He grew up, fatherless, with family fortunes on both sides of his pedigree.

He was the son of Alfred G. Vanderbilt, Sr., a wealthy sportsman who perished with 1152 others when a German U-boat sank the *Lusitania* off the Irish coast, and the former Margaret Emerson, the daughter of Isaac Emerson, a Baltimore chemist of modest means until he invented Bromo-Seltzer. Emerson acquired Sagamore Farm, an 848-acre stretch of rolling landscape in the Worthington Valley, and his daughter went into racing. Young Alfred acquired his mother's passion for the sport, dropping out of Yale at the end of his sophomore year to raise and race the running horse.

In the photos taken of him in the early 1930s, he looks strikingly like the James Stewart of *Destry Rides Again,* and what adds to that impression is the whimsy of his humor. One year, prior to the running of a race in which his horse appeared to have no chance, Vanderbilt gave jockey Ted Atkinson a sandwich, a wristwatch, and a flashlight, advising him, "It may be dark before you get back." He never took himself too seriously, not even as a breeder.

When Vanderbilt turned twenty-one on September 22, 1933, he was given $2 million in government bonds, the first of four such installments his father had left him. His mother gave him Sagamore Farm, which Isaac Emerson had given to her. With that, Vanderbilt had money and land, the means to buy and breed and raise and race horses of his own.

In August of 1933, he hopped into his sporty new LaSalle roadster, fire-engine red, and tooled north toward Saratoga. Beside him in the car was a set of his new racing silks, a modified version of his mother's silks of cerise and white blocks. On the advice of trainer Bud Stotler, he was heading north with a check for $25,000 to buy a big, raw-boned chestnut colt named Discovery. Vanderbilt intended to buy him and race him in the Hopeful Stakes. Discovery had been bred by Walter Salmon's Mereworth Farm, and he was a son of a fast if fiery rogue of a horse named Display. Display was a son of Fair Play, who also sired Man o' War, and there was nothing docile about Big Red. But when bred to Ariadne, Display transmitted nothing of his unruliness to their offspring, Discovery, a colt of estimable poise and calm at the post. He launched his racing career in a blaze of indifference, but by the time of the Hopeful Stakes at Saratoga, he had matured considerably.

The sale was delayed until after the Hopeful Stakes, so Vanderbilt didn't get to run Discovery in the race. After the horse finished a sharp third in the event—behind High Quest—his price jumped from $25,000 to $40,000, the equivalent of $400,000 today. Vanderbilt left Saratoga without the horse, but he had been impressed by Discovery and continued following the colt's career. He bought the horse when he had the first chance.

Discovery won eight of his sixteen starts as a three-year-old including the Brooklyn Handicap against older horses. But even that hardly suggested what was coming when he matured to a four-year-old horse, 16.1 hands high and 1200 pounds, about 200 pounds heavier than the average horse. (A horse is measured from the ground to his withers, the highest part of his back, in a unit of measure called "hands"—a hand is 4 inches, so Discovery at 16.1 hands stood 65 inches from the ground to the withers.)

Though Discovery lost his first five starts as a four-year-old, he came alive when he broke from the barrier in the Brooklyn Handicap in June and carried 123 pounds for a new world's record for a mile and an eighth, 1:48⅕, the second year he won the race. And for the next six weeks, until August 10, Discovery rolled across the east and midwest in a boxcar on what remains among the greatest six-week grinds in racing history. As a horse running mostly in handicaps, Discovery had to carry whatever weights the track handicappers decided to load on him. The aim of handicapping horses with weights (inserting lead slabs in the jockey's saddle) is simply to weigh down the horses—with the superior horses carrying more than their inferiors—so that all finish at the same time, in a dead heat. That is the theory, anyway. Discovery, a sensible horse, never paid any attention to that theory.

After the Brooklyn, he won the Detroit Challenge Cup carrying 126 pounds and then the Stars and Stripes Handicap in Chicago, spotting his rivals' weight and winning by six. He kept winning with high weights everywhere.

Known as the "Iron Horse" and the "Big Train," Discovery retired after the 1936 season with a lifetime record of sixty-three starts—twenty-seven wins, ten seconds, and ten thirds—and with a reputation as one of the greatest weight carriers that ever lived, a touchstone by which other handicappers would be measured. Vanderbilt sent him to Sagamore for stud duty beginning in 1937.

"There is no other horse in the entire range of turf history, American or foreign, that ever attempted to do anything so tremendous or came anywhere near Discovery to doing it so successfully," wrote turf historian John Hervey.

Vanderbilt, for his part, did not confine his activities to racing during his first years as an owner. He was buying mares at auction to build up breeding operations. The most crucial purchase he ever made at a sale occurred at the dispersal sale of W. Robertson Coe in 1935, when a mare named Sweep Out was led into the sales ring. The mare was in foal to Pompey, a fast and game horse who won the Futurity Stakes at Belmont Park in 1925.

Vanderbilt bought her for $2000, and the following year she had a filly foal by Pompey that Vanderbilt named Outdone. In 1943, he bred Outdone to Discovery for the third time. She produced a good-looking filly foal in 1944. In fact, they were a grand bunch of foals at Sagamore that year, but Vanderbilt was not there to tend or race them. He had joined the navy in 1942 and was in command of a PT boat in the Pacific. While there, he instructed his farm manager and trainer to "go to the field and pick out twelve yearlings you like best, before they're broken, and sell the rest." Of the yearlings kept, none went on to any distinction either at the racetrack or in the stud. But of the twelve they sold, six eventually won major stakes races. One was Conniver, a daughter of Discovery, who was voted the leading handicap mare of the year in America in 1948. Another was the bay filly by Discovery from Outdone.

Sidney Shupper, not a major owner, bought the filly for $2000 and named her Miss Disco. Shupper raced her from 1946, when she was a two-year-old, until 1950, when she was six. She was a strikingly handsome, racy-looking mare with a beautiful head—a prominent forehead and the face penciled like that of an Arabian. She carried herself elegantly and liked to get her work done in a hurry. She won ten of fifty-four races and $80,250 for Shupper. Nor did she shy away from tangling with the boys. Miss Disco won the Interboro Handicap as a four-year-old, whipping colts over three-quarters of a mile, a sprint. She also won the New Rochelle Handicap. As a three-year-old, Miss Disco won the Test Stakes at Saratoga, a race in which a number of good fillies have run, if not won, over the years.

Miss Disco had speed, and she would transmit it to her many foals, one by one, especially the seal brown bay colt she foaled in 1954. Shupper did not own her then, not when she served in the stud.

At the close of her racing career, Bull Hancock saw the potential in her as a broodmare, so he bought her from Shupper for himself, privately, for a undisclosed price. Bull had the Vanderbilt-bred mare shipped to Claiborne Farm to join the bands of other mares. That was in 1950, when a rebirth at Claiborne Farm was in the making, and when Gladys Phipps prevailed upon Bull to sell the mare and he gave in, since she was an old client and wanted to own Miss Disco so badly.

Owned by Mrs. Phipps, the bay daughter of Discovery was bred to Nasrullah in 1951, and the following year she foaled a bay colt that Mrs. Phipps called Independence, a horse who would become one of the nation's finest steeplechasers. Miss Disco was returned to Nasrullah in 1953, and in the spring of 1954 the whirlwind came, the horse for which all breeders tap their feet and wait.

The evening of April 6, 1954, at Claiborne Farm was perhaps the most remarkable of any in the long history of the American turf, certainly in the annals of Claiborne.

In the foaling barn set back off the road that winds through the farm, two foals were born that night thirty minutes apart. One was a bay son of Princequillo out of a mare called Knight's Daughter. His name was Round Table, and by the time he retired as a racehorse at the end of 1959, running for Oklahoma oilman Travis Kerr, he had won forty-three of sixty-six races, been named America's Horse of the Year in 1958, become regarded as the greatest grass runner in American history, and won more money than any horse in the history of the sport, $1,749,869.

Down the row of stalls Miss Disco gave birth to her son of Nasrullah who, by the time he retired in 1958, had been voted America's Horse of the Year in 1957, won twenty-three races and $764,204, and earned a reputation as a magnificent cripple—one of the fleetest runners the American turf had ever known, and one of the gamest and most generous of horses. He was Bold Ruler.

Bold Ruler had a hernia as a foal, and he was so common looking that Hancock sequestered him in a distant paddock so that visitors to Claiborne Farm wouldn't see him.

"He was a very skinny foal," Hancock would recall. "We had the devil's own time trying to get him to look good, and I was never really pleased with his condition the whole time I had him. But he had a good disposition in many ways and he never missed an oat."

Bold Ruler suffered a painful accident as a yearling, almost cutting off his tongue in his stall one night, and the experience made him forever sensitive about his mouth. Nor was that all. One morning, while being broken under saddle, he fell and got tangled under a watering trough, almost breaking a leg while struggling to his feet.

Somehow he survived all this, and made it to Hialeah Race Course in the winter of 1956. One of the first things he did was to begin ripping off quarter-mile sprints in 0:22 during morning workouts. Few quarter miles are run that fast in actual races.

So Fitzsimmons had no trouble cranking up his speedball for his first start at Jamaica on April 9. He won it by three and a half lengths. "Easy score," reads the official past performance charts.

With that began the racing career of the fastest of all Nasrullah's sons or daughters, a tall and leggy runner with a seal brown coat, phenomenal powers of acceleration, and a fiercely combative instinct that held him together when the oxygen was running low. Nothing ever seemed ready-made for him, nothing as easy as it might have been. There was always a measure of adversity to overcome, some trouble plaguing him. He raced three years, and at one time or another he was hounded by arthritis, by torn back muscles, and by what was called a "nerve condition" in his shoulder. A minor cardiac condition came and went during his three-year-old year. He developed splints—bony and sometimes painful growths on his legs—and later osselets—an arthritic condition in the ankle joint. He once wrenched an ankle. And throughout the last year he raced, when he won five of seven races and $209,994, he ran with an undetected two-and-a-half-inch bone sliver sticking into a leg tendon like a splinter. Bold Ruler carried 134 pounds in the mile-and-a-quarter Suburban Handicap of July 4, 1958—one of the epic duels of the turf —spotting the talented Clem 25 pounds. Bold Ruler did not take the lead early in the race, but then bounded past Clem after a half mile. Clem stalked him from there as they raced for the far turn. Banking for home, Bold Ruler was two on top. The crowd grew deafening as Clem moved up on Bold Ruler down the lane, charging on the outside and actually getting the lead at one point in the stretch. Most horses, losing such a lead, would have hung or quit. But jockey Eddie Arcaro dug in and Bold Ruler battled back, getting up just in time to win it by a nose.

He was almost rheumatic in the way he walked from his stall in the morning, but he was capable of tremendous speed, of dazzling bursts. In 1957, his three-year-old year, after spending the winter at Hialeah and Gulfstream Park trading blows with Calumet Farm's Gen. Duke—perhaps the fastest horse Calumet ever produced, though he died before he could prove it—Bold Ruler came north to New York for the Wood Memorial on April 20 at Jamaica. The close of the race was an eyepopper, something like the Suburban a year later, with Bold Ruler and Gallant Man in a desperate stretch fight. Bold Ruler actually lost the lead with about 200 yards to go, but he came back at Gallant Man to win it by the snip of a nose.

He might have won the Kentucky Derby May 4, his next start, but Fitzsimmons and Arcaro decided that the colt should be restrained off the pacesetting Federal Hill, a horse with sharp early speed. They feared Federal Hill would drag Bold Ruler through a dizzying early pace and set it up for a stretch-running Gallant Man. Whether as a son of the temperamental Nasrullah or as a youngster whose tongue had almost been severed as a yearling, Bold Ruler clearly resented the tactic, fighting Arcaro's exertions to restrain him. Iron Liege, Calumet's second-string colt substituting for the injured Gen. Duke, won by a whisker over Gallant Man in one of the Derby's most exciting renewals, with Bill Shoemaker standing up prematurely on Gallant Man, misjudging the finish and probably costing him the race.

Arcaro did not restrain Bold Ruler in the Preakness Stakes. He let him roll, and the son of Nasrullah and Miss Disco raced unchallenged through the mile and three-sixteenths, beating Iron Liege by two lengths.

Bold Ruler's stamina—his ability to run a distance beyond a mile and a quarter—would always be suspect. The origins of this suspicion stemmed in large part from his performance in the mile-and-a-half Belmont Stakes of 1957. Gallant Man's fainthearted stablemate, Bold Nero, dragged Bold Ruler through a set of rapid early fractions, softening him up for Gallant Man's finishing kick. Gallant Man blew past Bold Ruler at the turn for home and raced to an eight-length victory in a record-breaking 2:26 $\frac{3}{5}$. Bold Ruler, exhausted at the end, wound up third.

Bold Ruler came back later that year, gaining in stature as he went on. Like his maternal grandsire, Discovery, he began to show his gifts for lugging high weights at high speeds.

He won the Jerome Handicap by six with 130 pounds.

He won the Vosburgh by nine lengths under 130 pounds in the mud, shattering the track record that had been held by Roseben, the sprinting specialist, for fifty years. He raced the seven-eighths of a mile in a sizzling 1:21$\frac{2}{5}$, three-fifths of a second faster than the old mark.

He won the Queens County Handicap under 133 pounds, spotting the second horse 22 pounds.

Under 136 pounds, an enormous burden for a three-year-old, he won the Ben Franklin Handicap by twelve. "Breezing all the way," said the charts of that race.

The ending of the year was almost poetic. In the $75,000-Added Trenton Handicap at a mile and a quarter, Bold Ruler faced his two archrivals for Horse of the Year honors—Gallant Man and Round Table. The gate sprang, and Arcaro let Bold Ruler bounce, sitting as the colt opened up an eight-length lead at the end of the first three-quarters of a mile. He simply coasted for the final half mile, beating Gallant Man by two and a half. Round Table was third.

That made Bold Ruler Horse of the Year.

In 1958, as a four-year-old, even with that splinter in the tendon, he won the Toboggan Handicap under 133 pounds, spotting Clem 16 pounds, and grabbed the lead in the stretch of the Carter Handicap at seven-eighths of a mile, and won that by a length and a half under a crushing 135 pounds. He failed to spot Gallant Man 5 pounds in the Metropolitan Mile on June 14, losing by two lengths. But he won the Stymie Handicap by five lengths under 133 pounds, and that led to the nose-bobbing struggle with Clem in the Suburban, and finally to a last victory, under 134 pounds, in the mile-and-a-quarter Monmouth Handicap. He wrenched an ankle in the Brooklyn, finishing seventh with 136 pounds on his back, and then Fitzsimmons took x-rays at Saratoga, discovering the splint on the back of a cannon bone. And that ended it for Bold Ruler.

All through his campaigns on the racetrack, from his two-year-old year onward, he endeared himself to the frail old widow, Mrs. Phipps. He was always the first horse she went to in the mornings at the barn, the first horse she asked about, the horse she dwelled with the longest, the one she favored most with her time and sugar cubes. Groom Andy DeSernio used to braid a Saint Christopher's medal into Bold Ruler's foretop, the lock of hair between his ears, before each race. Mrs. Phipps was not a Catholic, but for Bold Ruler she overlooked nothing.

She never lost her fondness for Bold Ruler, certainly not in the dozen years since that day they sent him off to Claiborne Farm from Saratoga. Bold Ruler was led to the van waiting at the stable area. The colt hesitated a moment, balking at the sight of the van, but Sunny Jim poked him in the rump with a cane and he walked on dutifully. Inside the van, the lead shank was handed to Claiborne Farm groom Ed (Snow) Fields, and Fitzsimmons said, in parting, "Come on, Andy, we've done our job. It's their horse now." Moments later Bold Ruler was rolling southwest toward the Blue Grass.

He seemed destined for some measure of success from the outset. There was so much in his favor. Bold Ruler would begin with the choicest mares. Hancock, as well as Mrs. Phipps and her son, Ogden, and other clients at Claiborne had assembled bands of champion race and broodmares over the years—the foundations of all great studs —and to Bold Ruler many of them would be sent.

He had the pedigree himself, on both the male and the female sides, representing a popular foreign and domestic mixture of bloodlines in his ancestry: the son of a thoroughly European stallion and a completely American mare. Genetically, he was what is known as a "complete outcross," with no name appearing more than once in the first four generations of his family tree.

Since siring Bold Ruler in 1952, Nasrullah himself had become a champion stallion in America, representing the flourishing Nearco male line, and his dam, Mumtaz Begum, was among the most prized of mares in the Aga Khan's magnificent stud. She herself was a daughter of Blenheim II, the stallion later imported to stand at Claiborne Farm, and Europe's "flying filly" Mumtaz Mahal. By the time Bold Ruler was sent to Claiborne, Nasrullah had already led all American sires in 1955, when his performers won 69 races and $1,433,660, and in 1956, when they won 106 races and $1,462,413. Bold Ruler was only one of several champion runners by Nasrullah: he also sired the 1955 Horse of the Year, William Woodward's Nashua, who retired in 1956 with earnings of $1,288,565, a world record until Round Table broke it three years later. Nasrullah had also sired the 1956 two-year-old filly champion, Charlton Clay's Leallah; the 1957 two-year-old colt champion, Nadir, eventual winner of $434,316; and Captain Harry F. Guggenheim's Bald Eagle, America's champion handicap horse of 1960 and the winner of $676,442.

Miss Disco, among the fastest fillies of her generation, was no doubt a source of some of Bold Ruler's quickness, and as a daughter of one of the greatest weight carriers of all time, she gave bone and bottom to the underside of Bold Ruler's pedigree. He had everything a sire should have.

Bold Ruler also had the brilliant speed of the Nearco tribe—speed is an important characteristic for a stud horse to have—and he had it in greater abundance than any other of Nasrullah's sons and daughters. Moreover, he carried that speed the classic distance of a mile and a quarter, and he did it carrying high weights against horses who were just as serious about their business as he—Clem, Gallant Man, Sharpsburg, and Round Table.

Yet no one, not even a breeder as experienced and astute as Bull Hancock, could have foreseen the extent to which Bold Ruler would dominate the American sire championships. He became a phenomenon at the stud, and some believe the greatest sire in the history of American bloodstock.

For seven successive years Bold Ruler was the leading American stallion. Only Lexington, a stallion from a different era, was America's leading sire more often, for sixteen years between 1861 and 1878. But the two horses are hardly comparable. The "Blind Hero of Woodburn," as Lexington was known, competed with only 215 sires of runners in the last year he was the champion, 1878. In 1969, Bold Ruler was competing with 5829 sires of runners. Only three other stallions—Star Shoot, Bull Lea, and Bold Ruler's own sire, Nasrullah—led the list as many as five times.

His reign as America's premier blooded stallion began in 1963, when his twenty-six performers from only two crops of racing age won fifty-six races and $917,531. And this was only a foreshadowing. His influence and power as a stallion grew steadily.

In 1964—44 performers, 88 wins, and $1,457,156.

In 1965—51 performers, 90 wins, and $1,091,924.

In 1966—51 performers, 107 wins, and $2,306,523, the first time in history a stallion's progeny ever won more than $2 million in a single season.

In 1967—63 performers, 135 wins, and $2,249,272.

In 1968—51 performers, 99 wins, and $1,988,427.

In 1969—59 performers, 90 wins, and $1,357,144.

While his two-year-olds were often precocious and brilliant, and for five years he was America's leading sire of juveniles, Bold Ruler's ability to transmit stamina became suspect. His sons Bold Lad, Successor, and Vitriolic, as well as his daughters Queen of the Stage and Queen Empress, were all champion two-year-olds in their divisions. Yet each failed to return as a champion three-year-old, the year the distances stretch out. No son or daughter of Bold Ruler, in all the seven seasons he dominated the sire standings, had ever won the Kentucky Derby, Preakness, or Belmont stakes.

As he added championship upon championship to his record at

the stud, his value as a stallion climbed to an incalculable level. Gladys Phipps was the founder of a major racing dynasty, one supported largely by dozens of valuable broodmares at Claiborne Farm, and she and her heirs were interested in maintaining and building on it, not selling the fruits of it piecemeal.

Money could be made in many ways, but there was only one Bold Ruler, and he was the stuff to build and serve a racing dynasty. William Woodward, Sr., was fond of saying, "Upon the quality of the matron depends the success of the stud." Bull Hancock later agreed with that, but he would add, "Remember, Mr. Woodward's big success came when he got Sir Gallahad III as a stallion. As long as I have a Nasrullah and a Princequillo, an Ambiorix, Double Jay and Hill Prince, I'll be on top." (Ambiorix, another import from France, and Double Jay were leading stallions in America in the postwar resurgence of Claiborne as a thoroughbred nursery.)

Mrs. Phipps had the greatest stallion in the history of the American turf in this century, and his breeding services were not for sale. Owners of mares would have to enter into an unusual agreement with the Phippses to get a mare bred to Bold Ruler. In general, a breeder would offer the Phippses a prospective broodmare for Bold Ruler. If the mare was acceptable, she would be bred to Bold Ruler for two seasons, or until she had two foals. First choice of the foals was determined by the flip of a coin. Thus, Bold Ruler was the Phippses' lever in acquiring foals out of some of the finest broodmares in the world, broodmares they did not own. And one of the breeders with high-class mares was Ogden Phipps's friend, and a fellow member of the Jockey Club, Christopher T. Chenery.

Chenery had been sending mares regularly to Bold Ruler at Claiborne, where he had Hill Prince standing at the stud, since Bold Ruler stood his initial season there. The first mare Chenery sent him was Imperatrice, and in 1960 the twenty-two-year-old matron had a filly foal that Mrs. Chenery named Speedwell. The Meadow Stable's Speedwell was Bold Ruler's first of many stakes winners. Chenery sent his mare First Flush to Bold Ruler in 1961, and she had a filly foal named Bold Experience, who eventually won $91,477 at the races.

In 1965, Chenery ceased sending mares singly to Bold Ruler. Instead, in a coin-flip arrangement with the Phippses, he began sending two mares to Claiborne every year. The Phipps-Chenery deal, matching the greatest sire in America with some of Chenery's choicest mares, was anything but a smash: the biggest winner, the stakes-winning Virginia Delegate who started fifty-five times and won $67,154, ended up a gelding.

Then events began unfolding in the spring of 1968 that set the stage for the most monumental coin toss in racing history, a curious flip in which the winner lost and the loser won—but neither knew it at the time.

For the breeding season of 1968, Chenery sent the mares Somethingroyal and Hasty Matelda across the Alleghenies to Claiborne Farm. Each was bred to Bold Ruler. Each conceived. Each had a foal the following year.

Hasty Matelda had a colt foal.

On March 19, 1969, Somethingroyal had a filly foal.

Just a month later at Claiborne Farm, Somethingroyal entered her heat cycle, and on April 20 she was separated from her suckling foal and taken to a stall at one end of the black creosote board breeding shed at Claiborne. In the adjoining stall, his head sticking into Somethingroyal's stall over an open half door, was a "teasing" stallion named Charlie, a mongrel of Percheron and saddle horse ancestry. Somethingroyal was already believed to be in heat, but the breeding men wanted to be sure, so they walked her into that stall next to Charlie the teaser. Charlie nipped at Somethingroyal, sniffed at her, nuzzled her. She did not protest, backing up to Charlie, squatting, and exposing herself to him. "She was red hot," said the keeper of the stallions, Lawrence Robinson. But Somethingroyal was not mounted by Charlie, as are some of the virgin mares. A few of the thoroughbred stallions at Claiborne come into the breeding shed screaming and whinnying. Such carryings-on can frighten a maiden mare, especially when the screamer mounts her for the first time. Docile Charlie, among his other jobs at the farm, is trotted out to mount such nervous mares—though he does not have intercourse with them—to get them used to it.

Somethingroyal was taken around the breeding shed, where the road runs past the huge sliding front doors, and walked inside the large 35-by-35-foot room. Robinson signaled Snow Fields, Bold Ruler's groom. Fields went to the main cinder block stallion barn and unfastened the sliding bolt from Bold Ruler's stall, with its fireproof ceiling and stained oak walls and heavy oaken door. Snow slipped a bridle on the horse, inserting a straight, stainless-steel bar bit in his mouth, clipped a lead shank to it, and walked the horse the short distance from the stall to the front of the breeding shed.

Robinson met Fields outside the shed, took the shank and walked Bold Ruler through the door, turning him around in the nearest corner so that he faced Somethingroyal, who was standing in the center of the room with her back to him. One man held Somethingroyal. Her hind legs stood in an indentation on the gravel floor where the hind legs of hundreds of other mares had stood while breeding and bearing the weight of the stallion. Other men—including Dr. Walter Kaufman, holding a pint cup—waited nearby.

Bold Ruler's penis dropped from its flap as he walked into the breeding shed. He was a fifteen-year-old horse who knew what he was about. The mood was sober and businesslike.

Fields immediately dipped a sponge into a bucket of warm, clear water and washed Bold Ruler's penis, which was beginning to stiffen. Some stallions excite themselves into readiness by sniffing at a mare, but Bold Ruler was not one of them. All he needed to do was look. Robinson restrained the horse, who soon began prancing, and waited until he saw the horse was ready, watching for the penis to harden fully. Irving Embry, at the front of Somethingroyal, lifted up her left front foot, a precaution designed to prevent her from kicking Bold Ruler while he mounted her. Another man moved in and lifted the mare's tail. Privacy was neither demanded nor afforded.

Robinson brought the horse forward and raised the shank. Bold Ruler mounted Somethingroyal in an instant. Holding the shank with his left hand, standing on the left side of the horse and mare, Robinson gave Bold Ruler one final assist: with his right hand, he guided the penis in. Bold Ruler was inside Somethingroyal no more than two and a half minutes, and Robinson watched for the single most compelling sign that the horse had covered the mare, watched for the flagging of the horse's tail, the dipping of it during orgasm. Some stud horses dismount during copulation, either to rest or prolong the pleasure of it, but Bold Ruler rarely did. "He was one of the most wonderfullest coverin' horses you have ever seen," Robinson said. "The first time up, every time."

Bold Ruler flagged. And as he dismounted Somethingroyal, Dr. Kaufman came to the horse's side with the pint cup to catch a dripping for examination. Then Fields, with a sponge dipped into a soap and disinfectant solution, washed the horse again. Bold Ruler was then led from the barn, no more than five minutes after he walked into it, and was turned out to romp on the greenery of his nearby private pasture.

Kaufman later checked the dripping, in a routine examination, to make sure the horse had ejaculated. He had.

Two days later, on April 22, Somethingroyal was returned to the breeding shed for a second and final mating with Bold Ruler. The same procedure was repeated. There was no way of telling, Robinson said, when Somethingroyal actually got pregnant that spring. But she did.

That year, The Meadow sent Cicada to Bold Ruler as the second mare in the arrangement with Phipps, but she proved barren.

In the summer of 1969, Penny Tweedy was in Saratoga to meet Phipps and Phipps's trainer, Eddie Neloy, in the offices of the chairman of the board of trustees of the New York Racing Association, James Cox Brady. It was time to flip the coin.

Each knew the consequences of winning the toss.

Under the rules of the flip arrangement, the winner of the flip would automatically get *first* choice of the *first* pair of foals—the two born in 1969—either the Somethingroyal filly or the Hasty Matelda colt. The loser, while getting the second choice of the first pair, automatically would get the *first* choice of the *second* pair of foals. And the winner would get the second choice of the second pair.

But there would be no second foal in the second pair. Somethingroyal was pregnant, but Cicada was barren.

So neither party wanted to win. The winner would get only one of the three foals, the first choice of the first pair. The loser of the flip would get the second choice of the first pair *but* also the only foal to be born in 1970—the foal that Somethingroyal was carrying on that day in August.

The coin sailed in the air. Ogden Phipps returned to his box seat and dourly told his son, Ogden Mills Phipps, "We won the toss." And that was it. The Phippses took the filly foal from Somethingroyal. They called her The Bride; she couldn't run a lick, finishing out of the money in four starts as a two-year-old before she was retired to the Phippses' stud at Claiborne. The Meadow Stable got the Hasty Matelda colt, who was named Rising River because he was foaled when the river below The Meadow was flooding. He always had more problems than future.

The Bride was weaned at Claiborne in the fall of 1969 and taken from her mother at Claiborne. On November 14, Somethingroyal was loaded on a van and returned across the Alleghenies to Doswell. She was almost seven months pregnant. She spent the winter that year at The Meadow, with the other broodmares, her belly growing larger and rounder until came that chilly night of March 29, 1970, when Southworth rang Gentry from the foaling barn in the field.

Chapter 7

The newborn Somethingroyal foal gained his legs just forty-five minutes after birth and began suckling when he was an hour and fifteen minutes old. He was well made, well bred, healthy, and hungry, and that made him as much a potential Kentucky Derby winner as any of the other 24,953 thoroughbreds born in America in 1970.

The mare and the foal were turned loose together the following day in a confined one-acre paddock behind the foaling barn. So that the newborn foal does not injure himself trying to stay at her side, a mare is not given much room to run and roam about. After the foal had gained the strength to stay with her—four days later—the pair was turned out with other mares and their foals in a three-acre pasture near the broodmare barn. The routine of farm life began.

For six weeks the mare and foal were pastured in the daytime, and returned at night to their single Stall 3 in the broodmare barn. The routine changed in mid-May, when groom Lewis Tillman began taking them outdoors in the early afternoon, leaving them out all night, and then returning them in the morning to Stall 3. The foal subsisted on Somethingroyal's milk for the first thirty-five days of his life. Then Tillman began to supplement the youngster's regimen with grain, preparing him for the day of weaning in October. Tillman would tie up the mare in the stall and give the colt small portions of crushed oats and sweet feed. He grew quickly as the summer passed. Christopher Chenery's personal secretary of thirty-three years, Elizabeth Ham, visited the farm and looked at the foals. Miss Ham noted in her log, dated July 28, 1970:

Ch. C Bold Ruler–Somethingroyal
Three white stockings—Well-made colt—Might be a little light under the knees—Stands well on pasterns—Good straight hind leg—Good shoulders and hindquarters—You would have to like him.

Summer cooled into October. The daily rations of the Bold Ruler colt were boosted periodically, up to five and finally to six quarts of grain a day by the time he was separated from Somethingroyal on October 6, 1970. Like other newly weaned colts, the youngster howled and stomped around the stall and field, but that passed in a couple of days. Somethingroyal was far into pregnancy once again by then, this time carrying a foal by the Meadow stallion First Landing. The aging Imperatrice, the colt's maternal granddam, had been bred for the last time in 1964, and since then had been pressed into service as baby-sitter for nervous, young, and uncertain mares, especially for broodmares visiting the farm. They would gather around her in a field, as if around a grandmother, within the apron and circumference of her calm. Chenery had bought her twenty-three years before, when she was nine in 1947, so while her grandson was romping around toward his yearling year, which would begin January 1, 1971, Imperatrice was already pushing thirty-three. She was aging visibly, three dozen ribs and elbows dressed up inside an old fur coat, but her eyes were clear. Everyone hoped she would live to reach the milestone age of thirty-five.

Her chestnut grandson had begun to fill out into a striking if still pony-sized colt by the day of his weaning, and on October 11, Miss Ham was moved to note: "Three white feet—A lovely colt." *Lovely* was twice underlined.

In autumn it was time to name the weanlings, a tiresome process for many owners. Nine of ten names submitted to the stewards of the Jockey Club, which administers the naming of all thoroughbreds, are rejected for various reasons. Under the rules of the Jockey Club, a name cannot be that of a famous horse, such as Swaps; or advertise a trade name, such as Bromo-Seltzer; or be that of an illustrious or infamous person, such as Jesus Christ or Hitler; or duplicate the name of a horse having either raced or served in the stud during the last fifteen years, such as Virginia Delegate or Imperatrice; or have more than eighteen characters, including spaces and punctuation marks (Man o' War, for instance, counts ten characters). Nor are names of living persons allowed unless they give their written consent, as have Shecky Greene, Pete Rose, and Chris Evert. Most names are rejected because they are identical to the names of existing horses.

The Bold Ruler colt was named with a formidable assist from Miss Ham. The Meadow sent in a total of six names, two sets of three names each, for the colt. The first five were rejected.

The first choice of the first set was Scepter, a name Penny Tweedy liked. The second name, suggested by Miss Ham, was Royal Line. The third was Mrs. Tweedy's Something Special. The three were submitted and quickly rejected. So the owners were forced to try again. A second set of names was submitted for the Bold Ruler colt. Mrs. Tweedy suggested Games of Chance and Deo Volente, Latin for "God Willing."

Miss Ham suggested the third name on the second list. She had once been the personal secretary of Norman Hezekiah Davis, a banker and diplomat who served in a number of ambassadorial posts for the United States. Davis was the financial adviser for President Wilson at the Paris Peace Conference, and later an assistant secretary of the treasury and undersecretary of state under Wilson. Later still he was the chief American delegate to the disarmament conference in Geneva, Switzerland, the home of the League of Nations' secretariat.

Secretariat, Miss Ham thought, had a nice ring to it. It was submitted as the third and last name on the second list. The following January, after rejecting the first two names, the stewards advised The Meadow that the colt by Bold Ruler–Somethingroyal, by Princequillo—with the white star and the three white stockings, born on March 30, 1970—had been registered under the name of Secretariat.

Secretariat grew out above the matchstick legs, his ration of grain increasing from six to seven and then to eight quarts as he lengthened, heightened, and widened through his yearling year of 1971. "A lovely colt. Half brother to Sir Gaylord," Miss Ham noted.

After his weaning, Secretariat lived in the end of a row of stalls by the office behind the big house that Chris Chenery rebuilt and renovated. Barn 14 is an attractive set of stalls withdrawn under a roof topped by a spanking bright blue and white cupola.

Secretariat lived in the premier stall, the one traditionally reserved for the most promising colt yearling, Stall 11. Gentry placed him there because of his superior confirmation and pedigree. Somethingroyal may not have been a runner—starting only once and finishing far up the racetrack—but she had given birth to fine running horses —Sir Gaylord, Syrian Sea, First Family. Putting the most promising colt in Stall 11 was not mere symbolic ceremony to Gentry. Facing the Coke machine and nearest the feed bin, the stall is seen and passed more times a day than any other stall in the shed, so its occupant is observed more closely during the routine of the farm.

Secretariat lived there that fall, winter, spring, and most of the summer of 1971. Danny Mines, a yearling man, would daily walk the youngster to and from the field. Secretariat was nosy, alert, ambitious, playful, playing constantly with other yearlings, and in that shifting pecking order of the yearling crowd he was at times a leader, at times not.

Meanwhile, he grew up. On April 20, 1971, Miss Ham noted that Secretariat had suffered a minor injury at the farm: "Nicked left shoulder—Not serious." Things far worse had happened at the farm. The nick on Secretariat's left shoulder, probably from a fence post, healed and disappeared.

As spring and summer warmed up to August—baking the sand and gravel white on roadside shoulders, dappling the wardrobes of the bays, grays, and chestnuts in the fields—there was a sense of transition in the air at The Meadow. Chris Chenery was ill, and no one was certain what would happen to The Meadow if he died or whether anyone near him would continue it—his horses in the racing stable at Belmont Park and the stud in Virginia. No one knew if it would be sold, dissolved.

Meredith Bailes, for one, sensed the uncertainty, and so did his father Bob, the trainer of the yearlings at The Meadow. Meredith was an exercise boy at the yearling training center. He and his father had talked about what would happen if Chris Chenery died, about who would take it over. They knew change might be in the air and were looking to the future.

Penny Tweedy had been taking an interest in The Meadow in the last few years. The Meadow had been suffering through a dry spell and the farm needed something to give it a push while Chenery was ill; it needed a big horse, a gifted horse.

For that reason, there was a sense of jubilation at the farm when the Meadow Stable's homebred Riva Ridge, a son of Chenery's First Landing, ran off with the $25,000 Flash Stakes at Saratoga August 2, winning by two and a half lengths and running three-quarters of a mile in the swift time of 1:09 4/5, only three-fifths of a second off the track record. The Flash had always been a prestigious two-year-old race, and the victory vaulted Riva Ridge into exclusive prominence among the 24,033 thoroughbreds born to his generation.

A blacksmith shod Secretariat on August 3, fitting him out for a set of racing plates on his front feet. They were of aluminum and signaled the start of a new way of life. Later that morning, groom Charlie Ross and several other men headed for the row of stalls at the yearling barn. It was a day of permanent change.

Ross, clipping a shank on Secretariat, led him out of Stall 11, to which he would never return, lined him up in single file with the other yearlings, and marched him in caravan down the road. Yearling trainer Bob Bailes directed traffic while the youngsters, heads up, moved across the pavement, passing the stretch of the racetrack, across the sandy surface to the infield and offices.

Secretariat was taken to Stall 1, in the corner, and there his training began on August 4.

Ross played with the colt's ears, preparing him for a bridle. Secretariat ducked away from Ross; he did not like his ears touched. Ross also tried to lift a foot to clean it, but Secretariat kicked him away. Meredith Bailes watched from the doorway and heard Ross cussing softly.

Secretariat's spookiness, not uncommon in the young, meant more work for Ross, more trouble teaching, more time. He put a rub rag to the colt, trying to clean him off, and Secretariat dipped away again. So Ross worked with Secretariat the next few days, picking up his feet again and again, toying gently with the sensitive ears, rubbing and patting him and talking, getting him accustomed to the presence of a human in the stall.

On August 9, they fitted a bit into his mouth for the first time, pulling the bridle over his ears. Meredith Bailes put on the saddle. At the odd sensation of the saddle and girth, Secretariat humped his back, arching it. Inside the 220-yard indoor ring, where all the Meadow yearlings are schooled and broken under saddle, the three stopped—Bailes, Ross, and Secretariat.

Bailes put his arms over the colt, patting him. Ross took the bridle with one hand and reached down, giving Bailes a boost.

Up Bailes went, not straddling the colt, only lying across his back, lengthwise, his stomach lying on the saddle. Bailes said nothing, watching what he was doing, his full weight resting on the back. The bridle was reinless. Ross led Secretariat several steps down the ring with Meredith lying across him. Ross stopped the colt. Bailes slid off, jumped back on. Ross walked Secretariat forward again, a few steps at a time around the oval. Bailes was up and off, up and off, Ross walking and stopping, walking and stopping. For three days they went through that routine, accustoming the colt to a saddle and bridle and a body on his back, a bit in his mouth. Secretariat behaved sensibly, Bailes recalled, with poise and equanimity. The lesson changed on August 12.

Bailes again saddled the colt, and he stood for a moment beside him in the indoor ring. Secretariat no longer humped at the feel of the saddle, and he had never tried to "break Western," as they call it on the farm—to buck, kick, or break loose. But August 12 was another day, the one on which Bailes would climb aboard and ride him for the first time, straddling the colt with both legs. Bailes knew the ceiling of the ring was about twelve feet high, perhaps a foot or so more. His head had almost grazed it while riding yearlings that bucked him. Bailes donned his blue fiberglass helmet, steadied himself at the side of Secretariat, talking to him. "Take it easy, old boy. Whoa. Easy now. Whoa."

When a horseman like Bailes communicates with a horse, it is not through language, of course, but through stringing together tone and sounds with a melody, a rhythm of oral unguents, lotions, and balms to soothe and reassure. Secretariat was strapping for his age, and Bailes felt him as a source of great energy, of unusual strength.

On his back, Bailes spoke and Secretariat peered back at him, but he didn't buck, just watched Bailes as Ross took him around the ring. He never turned a hair in menace. Nor did he on August 17, the first day Ross turned Secretariat loose with Bailes on him. The prospect had concerned Bailes. What worried him was that Sir Gaylord had been tough to break as a yearling in training, and he wondered whether Secretariat, his half brother, might be the same—it sometimes ran in a family. But Secretariat behaved with unusual aplomb for a yearling. Bailes walked, stopped, started again, rubbed Secretariat's sides with his legs, and eased back on the reins. Three days later he clucked to the colt—a kissing sound—and Secretariat moved off in a jog, a slow trot. The tempo of the schooling continued to pick up, but always one move at a time.

Bailes urged Secretariat into a canter, then a slow gallop, for the first time on August 24, and during the next eight days the colt walked, jogged, and cantered in the indoor ring. He learned how to canter easily both ways with facility.

That was the key: Bailes cantered the colt clockwise and counterclockwise in the one-furlong shed, teaching Secretariat to use the left and right leads, or strides, a crucial part of any yearling's training. It is important because a horse—when he canters, gallops, or runs

—leads each stride with one front leg, just as a swimmer doing a sidestroke leads each stroke with one arm. A horse will tire leading too long with one foreleg. In races, horses that appear to be tiring will often come on again by simply changing leads. On a racecourse, running counterclockwise in America, horses learn to lead with their left foreleg going around a turn—that is, while turning left—and to switch to the right lead on the straights.

Dr. Olive Britt, a Virginia veterinarian, gave the colt a physical examination for a $200,000 life insurance policy on August 26. He passed. Five days later, the final stage of his indoor training ended, and he was moved outdoors for the rest of his schooling.

That began on September 1, when Ross walked him from the stall and Bailes hopped aboard. Bailes walked him in company with two other yearlings to the training track, a one-mile cushion of soft sand that wraps like a cinch around the training complex. The track runs past a series of interlocking wooden fences and paddocks, past old hurdles that Chris Chenery built for jumping horses years ago. Secretariat walked, jogged at the sound of clucking, and broke into an easy canter that first day, his ears playing, his eyes looking around, a youngster as nosy as he was when he was just a weanling. On a grassy plot called the "filly field," Bailes walked and jogged him through figure eights, teaching him to respond to reins, to guidance at a touch, to pressure on the lines. Week by week the training increased in speed and duration; on September 3, the colt walked a quarter mile, jogged three-quarters, and cantered a half, and after several days Bob Bailes noted in the training log: "Secretariat very good size, well-made colt, good manners."

Training was interrupted routinely. There was a break when the colt was wormed, and he galloped a complete mile, once around the track, for the first time on September 13. It was a slow mile, one of five in the course of as many days. Then again the training stopped when he was inoculated against VEE, Venezuelan equine encephalomyelitis. The colt was lolling about in a lush playpen at The Meadow to prevent aftereffects from the medicine when Bailes and Gentry heard the news from Belmont Park: homebred Riva Ridge, with Ron Turcotte up, raced to a handy victory in the $75,000-Added Futurity Stakes September 18. The youngster hounded the pace from the break, dashed to the lead at the turn for home, and won by a length and a half. The victory was worth $87,636 to the Meadow Stable, and it made Riva Ridge the leading two-year-old in America.

Two days later, the chief delegates from the stable victory party arrived at The Meadow, their faces beaming in the afterglow of the Futurity. There was Penny Chenery Tweedy, who had been making strong, decisive gestures in taking over the running of the Meadow Stable; Elizabeth Ham, who began with Christopher Chenery in 1937 when she answered his want-ad for a secretary; and the new trainer for the Meadow Stable, a volatile little French Canadian named Lucien Laurin.

Racing had not yielded its riches easily to Laurin's touch in the early years, leaving him a mediocre riding career under sheds from West Virginia through New England and Canada. It was a difficult circuit: low purses, sore and crippled horses banished from Long Island, small tracks, and living day to day. He began there.

Laurin was born about fifty miles north of Montreal, in Saint Paul, Quebec. He left school early to work at Delormier Park, a half-mile oval in Montreal, where he first exercised horses and finally, in 1929, became a jockey. He was only moderately successful, reaching a professional zenith of sorts when he rode Sir Michael to victory in the King's Plate in Canada in 1935. His career as a rider bottomed out one summer morning in 1938 when he walked into the jockeys' room at Narragansett Park, took off his jacket and hung it behind him, and sat down to play a game of cards. A while later he was summoned to the stewards' office.

Laurin went downstairs to see the stewards—officials who wield enormous power on racetracks as watchdogs. They have the power to disqualify horses in a race, thus altering the order of finish, and they mete out suspensions, usually with the crisp denouement: "By Order of the Stewards."

The steward put a battery device on the table in front of him. Jockeys have been caught using such illegal gadgets to shock their horses into sudden bursts of speed. "What are you doing with this in your jacket?"

"What am I doing with what in my jacket?" Lucien asked.

It was hopeless. Laurin would later insist that he was framed, that the battery had been planted in his jacket. The final ignominy came when two policemen escorted him from the racetrack. "I was playing cards and some son of a bitch put it in my pocket. That's the truth," he said. He was ruled off the racetrack.

So he went to work at Sagamore Farm, galloping and exercising horses for Vanderbilt. Vanderbilt liked his way with horses and his way of riding. Convinced that the jockey was innocent of any wrongdoing in the Narragansett affair, Vanderbilt moved to get the suspension lifted. In 1941 it *was* lifted, though Vanderbilt maintains he does not know whether his influence had anything to do with clearing Laurin.

Laurin rode only briefly on his return, turning instead to training horses. He wound his way up to the rear staircase of that artful profession, up through the leaky-roof circuit with the cheap horses, up along the eastern coast from Charlestown to New Hampshire and to the day a New York owner, J. U. Gratton, sent him some horses that he trained successfully. "I couldn't do anything but win races for him." So Gratton brought Laurin to New York, and introduced him to businessman Reginald Webster. That made all the difference. For Webster, Laurin had the finest horse he ever trained, his only champion, Quill. She was a daughter of Princequillo and was the American two-year-old filly champion of 1958, a winner of $382,041. She made his name as a trainer.

Lucien Laurin had come a long way in racing, building up steadily if unspectacularly his reputation as a shrewd conditioner of the thoroughbred horse. He finally found his way to Aqueduct, Belmont Park and Saratoga, and ended up making a substantial living on that most competitive of racing circuits in America, working for Reginald Webster and then for America's master breeder and horseman, Bull Hancock. In 1952, in partnership with two other men, Laurin invested in the purchase of a farm in Holly Hill, South Carolina, where for years he ran a training center. He bought his partners out and prospered. He bought a home in Malverne, Long Island; and a home in Florida.

Now he was sixty years old, with silver hair and an elfin grin and traces of French Canada in his voice. He was a man given to uniform pleasantness—courteous, charming, and jovial. He worried visibly, openly, muttering to himself and wiping his face with a hand as if fatigued, thumb and fingers sliding down the bridge of his nose. He sighed a lot.

At sixty, on the brink of retirement, he was at Chris Chenery's farm in northern Virginia with a potential two-year-old champion in his barn at Belmont Park, the winner of the Flash Stakes and Futurity.

One thing Lucien Laurin had never had was the big horse, the champion two-year-old colt who had a shot at the Kentucky Derby, the ability to win the Triple Crown. Laurin had won the 1966 Belmont Stakes with Amberoid, but Amberoid was a nice horse, not a champion. The Derby, as it had for Hancock, Chenery, Vanderbilt, and Mrs. Phipps, had always fallen out of Lucien's reach. Nor had he ever won the Preakness, or many other major races. Now, at the twilight of his training career, he had Riva Ridge and was standing at the moment outside the yearlings' stalls, looking at next year's Meadow two-year-olds, when Meredith Bailes led Secretariat toward the gathering—Lucien, Penny Tweedy, Miss Ham, Howard Gentry, and Bob Bailes. In the notes she took that day, dated September 20, Penny Tweedy wrote under Secretariat's name: "Big (turns out left front—LL), good bone, a bit swaybacked—very nice—lovely smooth gait." (LL meant Lucien Laurin.) But if his left fore turned out slightly and he was a trifle swaybacked to the eye—he quickly grew out of that—Secretariat raised Laurin's eyebrows when Bailes brought him forward, stopping him.

Lucien Laurin did not know it then, but he was moving gradually toward a time in his life that would strain his capacity for understanding, wrench his beliefs in what he had learned about long odds and about a sport shot through and through with chance. After more than forty years on the racetrack, he was about to go to the races.

Through September and October of that year, as Secretariat galloped around the Meadow training track—he went as far as a mile and an eighth with other yearlings galloping beside him, getting used to company—Riva Ridge was doing what no horse had ever done for Lucien Laurin.

On October 9, the day that Secretariat galloped three-quarters of a mile at the farm, Riva Ridge bounced to the lead in the one-mile Champagne Stakes at Belmont Park, opened a four-length lead in midstretch, and won off by seven. First money was $117,090. Riva Ridge was an exceptionally fast horse, even if he did not look it. He had a small head, long legs, and a narrow chest—but Turcotte recalled him as almost deerlike in the way he moved, as if skipping effortlessly. All the two-year-olds were at his mercy now.

At Laurel Race Course in Maryland on October 30, the day Secretariat galloped a mile and an eighth, Riva Ridge lay off the pace going a mile and a sixteenth—the farthest he had ever run—moved to the front as he wished, and ran away to win by eleven. He earned $90,733. His dominance of the two-year-olds was undisputed. Two weeks later—a day after Secretariat breezed his first quarter mile at The Meadow—he went head and head with Ask Not and Last Jewel in about 0:26—Riva Ridge beat seven others in the Garden State Stakes in New Jersey, winning by two and a half lengths and earning $176,334.

At last Lucien had his big chance for the Triple Crown. Riva Ridge won seven of nine races, $503,263 in purses, and following his last start of the year in the Garden State Stakes, was named America's champion two-year-old in a combined staff poll of members of the National Turfwriters Association, the Thoroughbred Racing Associations, and staff members of the *Daily Racing Form.*

Eight days after Riva Ridge won the finale, Laurin returned to The Meadow and again saw Secretariat. Laurin said he wanted the colt sent to him in Florida sometime in January, along with other horses. That was on November 21, 1971—the day Secretariat was taken from training and turned out to pasture. Bailes had hopes for Secretariat—he liked his smooth and easy way of moving and his size and strength—even though he gave no signs of speed in excess or precocity. "He was a big lazy dude, a kind of sleepy colt," Bailes would recall.

Life wound down for Secretariat at the farm during the cold months. He spent part of that winter in a two-acre paddock that rimmed the training track.

Secretariat was being readied for the race track on January 10. Wing Hamilton, an equine dentist, dressed up Secretariat's teeth, knocking off the sharp edges and filing them down. For two days, January 18 and 19, he was loaded onto a van and driven around the farm to prepare him for the jolts of the journey south on January 20.

Bob and Meredith Bailes, Garfield Tillman, and Charlie Ross arose early that morning, and arrived at the training track at 6:15. They took the colt's temperature as a precaution, rubbed his legs with a liniment to cool them, and dressed them in protective cotton bandages. He was led briefly around the walking ring outside his stall, the last chance for exercise before the long ride. Then the blue and white van rolled into the training center. The loading began when two fillies, Ask Not and All or None, were led to the front of the van. Meredith Bailes took Secretariat onto the rear, hooking a hay rack beside him in his narrow but ample stall.

Then at seven-twenty, with the doors fastened and the engine fired up and roaring, the colorful van and its cargo slipped off to Route 30 which divides The Meadow, and within minutes it was plunging south toward the Carolinas.

Chapter 8

By the morning of January 20, 1972, Secretariat had lived almost twenty-two months at The Meadow, but there was more than that behind him as the van rolled south past Richmond and more around him than the James River rushing toward Hampton Roads.

Behind him were the land, lineage, and ancestry stretching back through generations of blooded horses, rows of stone and creosote fencing, ships plunging the Atlantic, trains whistling through the Alleghenies, horsecars and vans rolling down the Catskills, straw beds, Gettysburg, the Aga Khan, gavels slamming, years of grass and snow on fields melting in a pool of a hundred Aprils draining into Stoner Creek, the '58 Suburban Handicap, and the passing of an old order.

Toward the end of August 1958, Alfred Gwynne Vanderbilt headed for Sagamore Farm to see Discovery for the last time. Through the "Iron Horse" Vanderbilt became an enormously influential breeder. Miss Disco was not the only daughter of Discovery to bear an American Horse of the Year at the stud. Another daughter of Discovery, Geisha, foaled Native Dancer, Horse of the Year in 1954, winner of twenty-one of twenty-two starts. Discovery, twenty-seven years old that year, was debilitated in his old age when Vanderbilt came to see him, and on the morning of August 28, 1958, he was destroyed at Sagamore and buried in the farm's horse cemetery on a small rise of ground near the training track.

A year later, on May 26, 1959, groom Snow Fields, Lawrence Robinson, and Bull Hancock were standing in the breeding shed at Claiborne Farm. Nasrullah was in his third year as the nation's leading sire, the year his runners would earn $1,434,543 on American racetracks. Bold Ruler, his fastest son, was standing his first year at stud at Claiborne, a five-year-old who was just getting started. Nasrullah was only nineteen, and he was expected to stand at stud several more years. Princequillo was grazing in a paddock nearby.

Snow Fields cocked his ear and listened out the door of the shed.

"You hear that?" said Snow.

"Hear what?" said Bull.

"Nasrullah's nickerin', Mr. Arthur. Somethin's wrong."

"Hell, he's nickered before. He nickers all the time!"

Robinson and Snow looked at each other, saying nothing for a moment, and finally Snow told Hancock that Nasrullah never nickered in the paddock.

"The only time you hear him nickering is when he comes to the breeding shed," Snow said.

Snow and Larry Robinson walked quickly past the stallion barn and the row of hedges and to the lush acreage belonging to Nasrullah. He was still whinnying but he was sweating profusely too, obviously in distress. Someone rushed off to call Dr. Floyd Sager. Sager arrived just in time to see Nasrullah walk away from the fence and topple over. Sager rushed to him—the most valuable stallion in America—but he was dead. Sager, seeing the autopsy report, could hardly believe it.

Nasrullah died after the left ventricle of his heart, one of the chambers through which blood passes in and out, burst like a tire with a blowout, torn to shreds. The heart kept pumping, but blood was pouring from it and filling the thoracic cavity. He died by suffocation.

As Nasrullah lay dead in the field, Bold Ruler went wild, screaming and running up and down the wooden fence that ran between his paddock and Nasrullah's. Fields was startled: "It was his daddy lyin' there. It's the only day I ever saw Bold Ruler fret. He was hollerin' and pawin' and runnin' up and down that fence—Nasrullah, you see, never nickered, but he nickered that day."

Bull Hancock's decision to bring Nasrullah to America was perhaps the most momentous ever made in the history of American bloodstock, for the rugged bay stallion altered the breed in this country, infusing the domestic strains with the Nearco fire. The

Nasrullahs were fast and they could stay the classic distances, like Bold Ruler and Nashua and Bald Eagle. He represented a milestone in financial investment in racing blooded horses, the beginning of big profits from what were only the most modest investments. An original $10,000 investment in a share of Nasrullah ultimately became worth about $700,000.

Now Nasrullah was dead at Claiborne in the paddock near the stallion barn. He was buried in a grave behind the farm office across from Kennedy Creek, along a gravel walkway that runs behind it shaded by a hedge ten feet high. He was the fifth horse buried there. The other headstones next to his, each a foot and a half high, were carved with the names of Claiborne stallions who had died before him:

> Sir Gallahad III (1920–1949)
> Johnstown (1936–1950)
> Gallant Fox (1927–1953)
> Blenheim II (1927–1958)

And then:

> Nasrullah (1940–1959)

In 1964, the year Northern Dancer won the Derby and the Preakness but faded in the one-and-one-half-mile Belmont Stakes, the little bay Princequillo had a heart attack.

Princequillo was conceived in France, born in England, raised in Ireland, shipped to America as a yearling, and raced in claiming races as a juvenile. He won at the longest of American distances—the farther the better—and even then he stood for only $250 at Ellerslie, and Bull could not get enough mares to breed to him. Chenery's Hill Prince helped change all that. Princequillo was the leading American sire in 1957, the year his offspring won $1,698,427 —a world record until Bold Ruler broke it in 1966—and in 1958, they won $1,394,540. But his impact would be felt most forcefully as a broodmare sire—as the father of mares such as Somethingroyal. He first led the broodmare sire list in 1966, when his 191 daughters produced horses that won $2,007,184. Princequillo was the country's leading broodmare sire for seven years, at last count, and he finally cracked the 1957 record of Mahmoud—whose daughters produced offspring winning $2,593,782—when his daughters' offspring earned more than $2,700,000.

Princequillo declined after his heart attack, but he had the poise and sense to take it easy, never galloping or exerting himself in the paddock. There was nothing anyone could do for him but feed him and hope that death would come easy. He was relieved of stud duties that year.

The son of Prince Rose–Cosquilla died on July 18, at about nine o'clock at night, falling behind the hedge where the graves were lined up, and he was buried there with the others next to Nasrullah. His was the sixth headstone, and it, too, was carved in stone:

Princequillo (1940–1964)

Snow Fields said he first began to sense something wrong with Bold Ruler in 1970. It was the smell of decay, and thinking it might be a dead rodent in Bold Ruler's stall, he looked around for it, but found nothing.

A foulness hung about the horse, filled the stall, and eventually pervaded the barn, making Snow wince at the thought of it years later. Snow bathed the stall with a disinfectant more than once, dousing it more heavily each time, the corners and the sides, but to no avail. It was an odor that Snow Fields would never forget. It was the smell of death.

Dr. Walter Kaufman, the Claiborne Farm veterinarian, had given the horse antibiotics, and his distress cleared up, but then came back on him again.

There had been bleeding, just a trickle in the beginning, then a heavier flow. Bold Ruler had undergone tracheotomy to ease his breathing. A lighted tube had been inserted in his throat, but that exploration revealed only swollen and inflamed tissue, not the cause of it. Bold Ruler was losing weight steadily when it was decided, in early August, to van him to Lexington for exploratory surgery under general anesthesia.

It was a malignancy, deep in the nasal passage and hanging just below the brain. And when Dr. Irene Roeckel told Kaufman that it was not benign—Kaufman had been waiting, like a father, at the medical school for the biopsy report—he called Bull Hancock at Saratoga. Bull told the Phippses.

Gladys Phipps, nearing eighty-seven, ordered her horse destroyed if there were any signs of pain. Those close to the stable said she had a source at the farm, an unknown source, with whom she spoke regularly for reports on the condition of her cripple. They weren't

60

going to fool her, not at this late hour. In an effort to relieve and finally save the horse, she and her son Ogden agreed to send him to Auburn University to undergo a series of unusual and expensive cobalt treatments. Between the time x-rays were first taken and the time Bold Ruler arrived at Auburn, the tumor had grown to the size of a tennis ball and blocked nearly the whole of his nasal passage.

Eight times in eight weeks they bombarded him with cobalt, precision bombings since the tumor lay so near the brain, and each time he was knocked unconscious under general anesthesia. Robinson stayed with him, sleeping in a trailer at the university.

Bold Ruler's condition improved substantially. He ate well, recovering quickly from the anesthesia, and comported himself with calm throughout his two-month stay at Auburn. By the end of the treatments, the mass had diminished in size, and the horse's weight had increased by fifty pounds. Vanned back to Claiborne Farm in October with Robinson, Bold Ruler showed new life and new vigor, his spirits lifting. While there was hope he would continue to stand at stud, there was no definitive prognosis, only guarded opinions and speculation.

Gladys Phipps lived just long enough to learn that Bold Ruler had been returned to Claiborne and that growth of the mass had been retarded. A week after he returned to the farm, she died at the age of eighty-seven on her Long Island estate.

By the late spring of 1971, a full book of thirty-seven mares had been bred to Bold Ruler. The stallion had been behaving well since the cobalt treatments. Then his illness recurred sometime in June. Though he continued eating well, Bold Ruler started losing weight. X-rays taken in May had been clear, but now in June there was trouble again.

Eight months after Mrs. Phipps died, Miss Disco was destroyed "due to the infirmities of old age," according to the farm files. The dam of Bold Ruler was twenty-seven.

Bold Ruler continued declining through June, his general health and vigor deteriorating. An entry in the farm veterinarian log, made June 25, noted: "The horse has lost considerable weight, and appears uneasy and unhappy. Considerable foul-smelling discharge from the nostrils. Horse not moving well. Appears stiff and sore."

A piece of tissue, cut from the horse's neck, was sent for a biopsy to the University of Kentucky. The report, dated July 8, read in part like an order for execution: "This tumor is the same as the first biopsy specimen but appears more anaplastic and malignant."

Nothing more could be done. Bold Ruler grew pathetically ill. One side of his face became paralyzed. By then he had reigned seven years in succession as America's leading sire, his performers having already earned $13,067,364. He was only seventeen years old, and he should have had several more years at stud.

Finally an orange van was rolled up to the office and parked along that gentle incline of a ramp where horses load and unload at Claiborne. Bold Ruler would be destroyed there and taken to Lexington for autopsy. The spot was near the office, the horse cemetery, and the breeding shed, beneath a large grove of trees.

Bull Hancock left almost immediately, as he always did when a horse was about to be put down, getting in his car and driving out along Kennedy Creek and out the stone gate. "Don't even tell me about it," Bull told Robinson, before leaving. "I don't want to know anything. Just put him down and say no more to me."

On July 12, 1971 (three weeks after Secretariat walked in caravan toward the training center from the yearling barn), Snow clipped a lead chain on Bold Ruler and, with Lawrence Robinson alongside, walked the horse from his stall. Leading him toward the van, they walked along the path past the breeding shed—and Bold Ruler raised his head and nickered.

"That rascal thinks he's goin' to the breeding shed," Robinson told Snow.

They walked him to a gate leading to a grassy patch of land behind the shed and toward the gravel surface of the unloading area. They took Bold Ruler inside the van. There, Dr. Kaufman, with a hypodermic needle containing a heavy dose of a potent barbiturate, went into the van with the horse. Dr. Kaufman injected the drug into Bold Ruler's jugular, emptying the syringe, and then jumped hurriedly from the side of the van. For the next several seconds they all stood there—Kaufman, Snow, Robinson, and the van driver—and waited. Forty-five seconds later there was a tremendous crash, rocking the van, and then silence.

He was buried behind the office with Princequillo and Nasrullah and all the others. The stone read:

Bold Ruler (1954–1971)

There were tributes, like that from thoroughbred breeding writer Leon Rasmussen, who wrote an obituary that opened: "The king is dead. . . ."

Chapter 9

The van door opened in Florida on that January day of 1972, and Secretariat first stepped foot on the racetrack at Hialeah Park.

Like Bold Ruler, Secretariat emerged into a new kind of world, insular, superstitious, and perpetually on the make, a world forever in bivouac—whole armies of grooms and hot walkers, exercise boys and trainers and jockeys' agents, feed men peddling alfalfa and medicine men with horse aspirins weighing sixty grains, clockers and jockeys—ready on a moment to move on to other tracks, north to Maryland, New York, New Jersey, California, or Chicago.

Flies on all the windowsills, rows of stalls in rows of barns, hooves clicking on cement, metal gates clanging, springs whining, liniments and alcohol for rubbing, a pint of whiskey holstered like a wallet in the pocket, tips hot at six o'clock in the morning, lukewarm at three, cold at dinner over ham hocks or enchiladas.

As a young two-year-old—plump as he was off the farm—Secretariat had begun to grow into an aesthetic marvel of anatomical slopes and bulges, curves and planes that were stressed and set off by the color of his coat, a reddish gold that ran almost to copper. His shoulders were deep, his bone of good length, and there was no lightness of bone under the knee, as Miss Ham once suggested there might be. He had a sloping rump, the imprimatur of the Nearco tribe, and the slightly dished face of an Arabian. The quality of his head and face set him apart at once from many other Bold Rulers, including Bold Ruler himself. His sire was coarse about the head, with the jug-headedness common to trotters, and transmitted this trait to not a few of his offspring.

Secretariat didn't inherit Bold Ruler's lengthiness; he was shorter of back, more barrel chested and muscular in his physical development. But he had what Bull Hancock regarded as a mark of quality in all the Bold Rulers that could run. "You can pick the Bold Rulers out on their conformation," Bull once said. "I see the same musculature as Nasrullah. They all had an extra layer of muscle beside their tail running down to their hocks. It is a good sign when you see it in a Bold Ruler. It means strength and speed."

All he had was physique in the beginning, the look of an athlete. Lucien Laurin was wary of appearances. In his years spent on the racetrack, he had seen too many equine glamor boys come and go. To Laurin, Secretariat was just another untried thoroughbred.

To jockey Ron Turcotte, he was a potential mount, no more than that. The day after Secretariat arrived from the farm, Turcotte was at the barn at Hialeah, where he worked mornings exercising horses for Laurin. He walked up the shed to see Riva Ridge and glancing down the barn, two stalls away from his Kentucky Derby favorite, he saw the white star, the ears pricked forward, and the neck a mass of red. Secretariat was glancing back at him.

Turcotte went to the stall, took a closer look, and called up the shed to Henny Hoeffner, the assistant trainer. It was the first time Turcotte ever saw Secretariat, whom he described as "a pretty boy."

Penny Tweedy, when she first saw him said, simply, "Wow!"

But the game is a horse race, not a horse show, and the axiom among horsemen is: "Pretty is as pretty does." Secretariat, in the opening weeks, did not do much.

He didn't awe the clockers with the bursts of speed that Bold Ruler loosed at Hialeah as a youngster. There were no quarter-mile workouts in 0:22, no leveling off into a flat run, all business, from the quarter pole at the top of the stretch to the wire. He was still the overgrown kid.

Ron Turcotte was with Lucien Laurin one morning at Hialeah when four two-year-olds were led from the barn and began circling them, grooms holding the bridles.

Turcotte jumped aboard Secretariat that morning for the first time, guiding him out to the racetrack with the others in Indian file, reaching the dirt track and turning right, counterclockwise. Laurin told them to let the youngsters gallop easily, side by side, in a schooling exercise designed to accustom them to having other horses running next to them. The drill was the same as Secretariat had done two months earlier, under Bailes, at the farm. The four colts took off at a slow gallop around the mile-and-an-eighth oval, galloping abreast. The riders stood high in the saddles, going easily, Secretariat almost lackadaisically. The red horse plopped along in casual indifference, his head down, a big, awkward, and clumsy colt, Turcotte thought. Galloping past the palm trees and the infield lake, jockey Miles Neff, riding Twice Bold, reached his stick over and slapped Turcotte on the rump. Turcotte yelled. There was laughter on the backstretch. With Charlie Davis riding inside him on All or None, Turcotte leaned over and jammed Davis in the butt with his stick. Davis almost went over All or None, screaming. This was not all intended for fun. Exercise boys often do this to get young horses accustomed to quick movement, to shouts, to noise, to horse racing.

The colt next to Secretariat drifted out and banged against him and the red horse countered with a grunt.

He didn't alter course, drifting back and taking up the same path he had before the bumping. "He was just a big likeable fellow," Turcotte said. "His attitude was 'Stay out of my way.' " But they didn't. The colt beside him came out again, sideswiping him a second time.

Turcotte remembered the same drill a year before on Riva Ridge. The rangy bay was timid, shy, and leery of all contact. If Riva Ridge had been sideswiped like that when he was a young two-year-old, he would have leaped the fence to get away. Not this one.

Ron Turcotte liked him instantly because he was "a big clown," likable and unruffled among crowds, a handsome colt who relaxed while on the racetrack, who behaved himself, going as kindly as if out in the morning for a playful romp in the Florida sun.

Secretariat became the most popular of the baby two-year-olds to gallop, and one after another the exercise boys and jockeys who worked for Laurin climbed on him. There was Cecil Paul, a thirty-year-old jockey from Trinidad, who jumped aboard one morning and remembered hearing Lucien tell him, "He's a nice colt, Mr. Paul, and he's just a baby. You take care of him."

Mr. Paul galloped Secretariat frequently on those balmy mornings. On his back went Miles Neff, too, the jockey who was about to retire after thirteen years of knocking about on racetracks, and off went he and the colt into an easy gallop.

Neff especially liked the way he moved, feeling something a rider feels after straddling many horses over many years. Part of it had to do with size and strength, but some of it was just a feeling, a sense. "This is your best two-year-old, Mr. Laurin," Neff said one morning, as he slid off Secretariat.

As the days chased one another like colts in a pasture, Secretariat's bearing, his ease and kindliness, increased his popularity among the exercise boys until they were actually competing for his stirrups. Gold Bag, a youngster owned by Lucien Laurin, was quicker on his feet but he was headstrong—rank and speed crazy—often trying to run away with riders in the morning. Twice Bold pulled so hard on the reins that riders used to dismount rubbing the soreness in their arms. All or None, the filly, would buck, jump, kick, spin, and wheel; no one wanted to ride her. "Everyone wanted to gallop Secretariat," Turcotte said. "All you had to do was sit there." As the days passed, Cecil Paul felt the youngster getting stronger, more rhythmic in his strides, and felt him begin to take hold of the bit.

That was pivotal. Turcotte also felt the colt lean against the bit, fall into it, grab it in his mouth, and run against it in a communion transmitted from mouth to hands through the lines stretched taut between them.

"You want to make him think he's doing something, so you sit against him, take a hold of him, and make him think he's doing everything on his own. You have to build his ego. You have to give him confidence," Turcotte said.

Not even confidence came easily for the red horse. In late February Laurin boosted Turcotte on Secretariat for a quarter-mile workout, not an easy gallop but a speed drill, in company with Gold Bag, Twice Bold, and a colt named Young Hitter. It was time to teach them how to run, how to level out and reach for ground, something all horses have to learn.

"No race riding, boys!" Lucien called out to the four as they walked their horses to the racetrack that morning, through Sunny Fitzsimmons Lane and out the quarter-mile bend under the spanking brightness of the morning. The four riders reached the racetrack and moved into a gallop around the turn. They headed for the three-eighths pole at the top of the stretch, then pulled to a stop, lining up abreast and walking several yards. Then they clucked to their horses and went into a jog, picking up speed slowly.

Nearing the quarter pole, the four riders chirped again and the horses started leveling and reaching out, bodies lower to the ground. Twice Bold, Gold Bag, and Young Hitter accelerated rapidly, gathering speed from a gallop to a run as they raced past the quarter pole at the top of the straight.

Turcotte picked up Secretariat's reins and chirped to him, trying to give the colt a feel for the game, not yelling, but urging quietly. He sensed bewilderment in the colt, so he gathered Secretariat together and gave him time to steady himself and get his legs under him, synchronized and meshing. The three others blew away from him. Far up the racetrack, as Secretariat battled along by himself down the stretch, Turcotte saw the three more precocious horses far down the lane as Secretariat started to find himself and gather momentum.

They all dusted Secretariat easily that morning, beating him by about fifteen lengths and racing the quarter mile in 0:23. Secretariat finished in about 0:26.

Periodically, as Secretariat worked out in Florida, Penny Tweedy would ask Laurin about the red horse, and he hardly reflected buoyant hope.

"He hasn't shown me much," Lucien would say. Or, "He's not ready. I have to get the fat off him first." Or, "I have to teach him to run. He's big, awkward, and doesn't know what to do with himself."

Secretariat was beaten more than once in workouts that winter at Hialeah. Gold Bag beat him again. So did Twice Bold and All or None, the filly. So did a colt named Angle Light, a two-year-old bay owned by Edwin Whittaker, a Toronto electronics executive. He wasn't beaten by fifteen lengths again, but the crowd of young horses did beat him by five lengths another time.

Riva Ridge remained the luminary of the Meadow barn. The champion worked sharply for the seven-furlong Hibiscus Stakes March 22, and when he won it briskly coming off the pace, Laurin honed him for the Everglades Stakes—the same race won by Citation twenty-four years earlier—on April 1. That was the day Turcotte sensed a change in Secretariat during a workout. The track was muddy that morning when Laurin put Turcotte on the red horse, Neff on Angle Light, and Charlie Davis on All or None. The filly had thrown Turcotte earlier, so Laurin put Davis, a strong and experienced exercise boy, on her.

He told them he wanted them to work an easy three-eighths of a mile.

It was about eight o'clock. It had been raining heavily earlier in the day, but it had lightened to a drizzle by the time the set of horses headed down the backstretch to the three-eighths pole, midway through the turn for home. About seventy yards from the pole, in unison, the riders took hold of the reins and eased their horses toward the rail, keeping them about five feet out. Turcotte could feel Secretariat fall against the bit, heavy-headedly, and he could see a horse on each side of him. He eased down in the saddle. The tempo picked up as the horses raced past the three-eighths pole and banked into the stretch. Suddenly the horse on the inside of Secretariat drifted out, glancing off his side.

Turcotte steadied Secretariat. Recovering from the bump, the red horse started slowing down, easing himself back. Turcotte reached forward with his whip and waved it in front of the colt's right eye and he picked it up again, slipping back into the breach. He stayed there through the run down the lane, striding hard against the bit to the wire, finishing head and head with the others in 0:36, breathing easily, a sharp move for young two-year-olds in the mud at Hialeah. They had run at a perfect "twelve-clip." It was a fast workout. Secretariat was learning how to run.

Running times vary considerably from track to track, from condition to condition, and according to the sex and age of the horses, so what is fast is relative. But most horsemen agree that horses are stretching out on a fast track when they run a furlong—a distance of 220 yards or one-eighth of a mile—in 0:12. When horses string a few 0:12 furlongs back to back, they are moving at what horsemen call a "twelve-clip."

A twelve-clip is the rate of speed horses must average or maintain to win major stakes races at American middle and classic distances, distances from a mile to a mile and a quarter.

Most horses, even young two-year-olds like Secretariat, Angle Light, and All or None, should be able to run at a twelve-clip for a few furlongs—at least four.

That means they would be running one-eighth of a mile in 0:12, one-quarter in 0:24, three-eighths in 0:36, a half mile in 0:48.

At that rate of speed, a horse would run six furlongs, or three-quarters of a mile, in 1:12, which would win races on some tracks. If a horse strung two more furlongs together at a twelve-clip, he would be running a mile in 1:36, a time that equals or betters the clocking for six of the dozen runnings of the $50,000-Added Jerome Handicap at Belmont Park between 1961 and 1972. The degree of difficulty in sustaining a twelve-clip beyond a mile, unlike sustaining it from four furlongs in 0:48 to five furlongs in one minute, increases in quantum jumps. The degree of difficulty increases vastly beyond a mile.

For another furlong in 0:12 would send a horse a mile and an eighth, or nine furlongs, in 1:48, a clocking that would have won every running of the $100,000 Wood Memorial since it was run at that distance in 1952. And another 0:12-second furlong would send a horse a mile and a quarter in 2:00 flat, which was the Kentucky Derby record set by Northern Dancer in 1964; and a mile and three-eighths in 2:12, two and one-fifth seconds faster than Man o' War's American record; and a mile and a half in 2:24.

That workout was the first time Turcotte could sense that the big clown had any ability at all, any speed. He fell against the bit and ran with two fast youngsters, handling the mud well, handling it better than Riva Ridge did that afternoon in the Everglades Stakes.

Hemmed in on the rail with no place to go, bumping the rail in the stretch, and never getting near the lead, Riva Ridge finished fourth in the race, the first time he had been beaten since the summer of '71. Laurin said he was grateful to get the horse back in one piece. Turcotte was sharply criticized for his ride in the race, and Penny and Lucien talked about firing him and finding another rider. But the big races were coming up, so they decided to keep him on the colt.

It would not be the last time that Turcotte nearly lost a Meadow Stable mount.

It was nearing the time of the spring classics, and Riva Ridge was shipped north to Lexington, Kentucky, for the Blue Grass Stakes on April 27, his final prep race for the May 6 Kentucky Derby. Secretariat and several stablemates were vanned north to Long Island and to Barn 5 at Belmont Park, an indoor shed with a row of stalls that abutted the fence of the clubhouse parking lot. Barn 5 lay just 200 yards from the main track, the biggest oval in America—at one and one half miles in circumference—and there the humdrum of routine began.

In their first workout in New York that year, Angle Light and Gold Bag beat Secretariat badly on a sloppy racetrack, running a half mile in 0:49. Secretariat ran in 0:50 ⅕ with urging, not a sharp move. A fifth of a second is equal to a length, so Gold Bag and Angle Light beat him by six.

In mid-April, on a gray wet morning when the track was a mire, apprentice jockey Paul Feliciano, who worked under contract for Lucien, hopped aboard Secretariat for a routine gallop on the training track about a quarter mile away.

Feliciano had his feet out of the stirrups, dangling them at Secretariat's side, when Laurin spotted him and raised his voice in warning.

"Put your feet in the irons!" he yelled. "Be careful with that horse! Don't take no chances. He plays and he'll drop you, I swear to God."

Feliciano's feet rose into the stirrups, which he was wearing too short, and someone dimly recalled Laurin's calling to Feliciano, "Drop your irons." What Laurin wanted Feliciano to do was lengthen his stirrups for surer balance.

The horses moved toward the training track, and Laurin turned to Dave Hoeffner, Henny's son, and said, "Hey, you want to take a ride to the training track with me?" They slipped into Lucien's station wagon.

Laurin, muttering and still peeved at Feliciano, told Hoeffner in the car, "I bet that horse throws this kid. He's frisky and I bet he throws him. The kid's not listening to what I'm saying."

Secretariat, and the other horses in the set, strode through the stable area to the gap leading to the training track. They walked onto the muddy surface and began, one by one, to take off at a slow gallop. Feliciano, his reins loose, guided Secretariat near the outside rail and stood up in the saddle as the colt cantered through the long stretch toward the clocker's shed, passed the shed, and began heading into the first bend. He heard a horse working to his left, on the rail, his hooves slapping and splashing at the mud as he drilled past on the rails.

"I heard the noise. It was a split-second thing. He stopped, propped and wheeled, and turned left and I knew what was going to happen. I think he knew I was going off, too, already slipping, because he turned around from under me. I landed on my face."

Secretariat, riderless, his head and tail up and his reins flapping across his neck, took off clockwise around the racetrack, the wrong way, racing back toward the gap. Laurin saw him and, in an instant, was speeding out of the training track infield.

The car zipped through the tunnel and reentered the fence at the stable area. Laurin and Hoeffner saw Secretariat standing calmly at the gap by the training track, as if he were waiting for a taxi.

Dave Hoeffner climbed out from the car, walking with stealth toward Secretariat, who stood looking at him curiously. He reached out and grabbed the reins. Laurin immediately took off back to the barn, leaving Dave to walk Secretariat home alone. The colt walked like a prince for a quarter mile.

Paul Feliciano unscrewed his face from the mud at the seven-eighths pole and started walking around the oval toward the stable area.

He did not want to return to Barn 5, where Lucien Laurin was waiting for him. Paul Feliciano, twenty, born and raised on Union Street in the Park Slope section of Brooklyn, feared Laurin. Earlier, the headstrong Gold Bag had run off with him, as he had done with other riders, and Laurin had ranted at him. Paul had not forgotten the incident, so he had no illusions about what Lucien would say to him.

It was a ten-minute walk to the stable. By then Secretariat was standing in his stall, with blankets stacked up on his back. His back muscles were tied up so badly he couldn't move. Secretariat wouldn't leave the barn for almost two weeks.

"That son of a bitch ain't worth a quarter!" Laurin howled. Paul arrived shortly after.

He would remember only bits and pieces of what was said. "You better listen to me right now, young man! You better pay attention when you're on those horses! Wake up!" Then Feliciano saw the unmistakable sign of the Laurinian anger, the tipoff that he was in dead earnest. Lucien tilted his hat to one side as he walked away, setting it askew. Turning, Laurin said, "I want to see you in my office."

In the screened-in porch, just at the top of the staircase by the office, Feliciano stood and listened for five minutes as Laurin reproached and scolded him. He told him at last, "You come by in the morning and pick up your contract and your check."

"What could I do?" Paul said. "He stopped when that other horse came by and I lost my balance."

It was no use.

Laurin had told him the same thing after Gold Bag had run away with him earlier, and the next day had acted as if nothing had happened. But this time, Feliciano thought, Laurin had raised such hell, seemed so angry, that he had to be dead serious. Feliciano took that home with him to his apartment in Elmont, despondent and confused. He believed Laurin had given him a good chance to ride all but the best horses. Laurin was known for helping young people start in the game. He certainly had been generous about giving Feliciano good mounts, live mounts, not bums. Now that was finished, and with it any good chance to make it as a jockey. Feliciano wondered where he would go.

The following morning, he walked under the shed of Barn 5, coming early to pick up his contract and look for another job. Lucien, arriving about seven, came into the shed telling Henny Hoeffner what exercise boy to ride on what horse. He looked at Paul, who was waiting for his contract, and said, "Put Paul on *that* horse to gallop."

And that was the last Feliciano heard of it.

Chapter 10

Jimmy Gaffney drove past the Meadow Stable office in April, waving to Henny Hoeffner from his Oldsmobile, saying hello and jumping from the car and moving quickly, as always, a reedy stick of a man with a hawkish set of eyes, a fine sculpted jaw, and a love for horses.

He was thirty-seven years old. He had just returned to work as a mutuel clerk selling five-dollar place and show tickets in the grandstand section at Aqueduct. The clerks had been on strike for three weeks, but that was over, and once again Gaffney was working his artistry behind the window.

Gaffney was also an exercise boy, riding and working horses in the mornings. He had worked for Lucien briefly in 1963, and they had liked each other. They had gone fishing on Lucien's boat, and when Gaffney left him several months later, they had parted on friendly terms. Now, seven years later, Gaffney saw Henny as he drove past the Meadow Stable. He stopped to chat, and in the course of the conversation, Henny asked him if he was working. When he said no, Henny offered him a job as an exercise boy and Gaffney took it.

Gaffney joined the Meadow Stable at a time of heightened expectations and morale raised by Riva Ridge, who on April 27, went to the front not long after the start of the Blue Grass Stakes, shook off one challenge deep in the stretch, and ran off to win by four. That was only the prelude.

Nine days later, in front of 130,564 people at Churchill Downs and millions more on nationwide television, Riva Ridge galloped to the front in the run past the stands the first time, running easily under Turcotte, repulsed three challenges by the gritty little Hold Your

Peace, and won the ninety-eighth running of the Kentucky Derby by more than three.

Turcotte, wearing the blue and white silks of the Meadow Stable, had just won his first Kentucky Derby, and he fairly glided on the colt toward the grassy winner's circle. There was Lucien Laurin beaming, a man on the brink of retirement who woke up suddenly one morning with Riva Ridge in his barn.

There was Penny Tweedy, wearing a white and blue polka-dot dress and a choker of pearls, pivoting through the crowd like a princess newly crowned, her gestures contained but emphatic, her voice husky and assured on television, her manner courteous yet exuberant. She was too good to be true, and the press promptly collapsed at her feet.

On to the Preakness Stakes at Pimlico they went.

To this ecstatic aftermath came Gaffney, and one of the first things Henny Hoeffner told him to do was get on Secretariat. There were less than two months to Secretariat's first race, and the red horse was just recovering from the tied-up muscles he suffered the day he backed out from under Feliciano. Groom Mordecai Williams would put a saddle and a bridle on the colt and boost Gaffney aboard, sending both on a walk around the inside of the shed.

Secretariat, with Gaffney on him, walked to the training track that morning, taking the same route Feliciano had taken him the last time. The red horse stopped at the gap and stood there for several seconds, looking to the left and right, raising his head, as horses do when they are looking off into a distance. Gaffney did not hurry him, but let him stand there and watch the morning activity. It was a habit the colt acquired early in life—he liked to stop and see what he was getting into before he got into it—and he did that every time anyone ever took him to the racetrack.

Near the clocker's shed a quarter mile away, Secretariat began doing his number: he dipped his shoulder and pulled, but Gaffney, riding with long stirrups, rode with him. The colt had been confined for a few weeks, and he was feeling his unburned oats. He galloped off strongly, pulling hard on the bit, but every day Gaffney gave him more rein, exerting less pressure, and after several days the colt relaxed. As he had done at Hialeah he started plopping along easily, moving easily and relaxed.

Secretariat soon stopped dipping his right shoulder. Gaffney, putting a special bit in the colt's mouth with a prong on its left side, worked for days on the problem. Pressing both hands on his mount's neck, Gaffney kept pressure on the right line, and every time the colt started to dip to the left Gaffney pressed down on the colt's neck and exerted pressure on the rein.

Gaffney had been riding horses for almost two decades—he had ridden big and small horses, some fast and slow horses, stiff and supple horses—but in Secretariat he sensed the finest running machine he had ever straddled.

That the red horse had never run a race did not temper Gaffney's public enthusiasm, an enthusiasm rooted in the way he looked and moved to Gaffney. "He was strictly a powerhouse—his movement, stride, and for a horse who is not supposed to know much at his age, he sure knew a lot. He would change strides just right coming in and out of a turn, and he seemed to me so intelligent for a young horse. Nothing bothered him. I had been on a lot of two-year-olds in my life, but this one really struck me."

Gaffney's mornings at the racetrack revolved around Secretariat. He rode the red horse steadily, building him up in his own mind, telling stablehands of the youngster's extraordinary future, boasting about him to grooms and hot walkers and even to his wife, Mary. He began calling the horse "Big Red."

Gaffney told his mother about the colt, too, and she replied by knitting and sending him a pommel pad—which is inserted as protection under the front of the saddle—with Secretariat's name knitted in blue lettering across a white background. As if to flaunt his confidence and to reaffirm his instincts, translating them into something tangible, Gaffney purchased two blue saddlecloths, protective pads that prevent the saddle from abrading the colt. He took the saddlecloths—for which he paid four dollars each—to a woman in Queens who did needlework. Gaffney paid her twenty-four dollars to stitch "Secretariat" into the section that hangs, visibly, below the rear of the saddle. He took one of Lucien's exercise saddles home—it was the saddle he always used when he rode the colt—and for several hours, with his leather-working kit, Gaffney hammered "Secretariat" into it, giving the letters a cursive flourish.

The red horse returned to serious work on the racetrack Thursday, May 18, when he went three-eighths of a mile in 0:37; yet no one but a few clockers—Meadow Stable hands and avid horseplayers—paid any attention. Lucien, for one, had his mind on things of greater moment: the Preakness Stakes, the second race in the Triple Crown series, was consuming all his energy. Penny Tweedy was confident of the outcome, feeling certain Riva Ridge would win it. This only made her disappointment at what happened all the more bitter.

The ninety-seventh running of the Preakness Stakes was a 1:55 ³/₅ horror show, a mudslinger during the running and after it. Riva Ridge broke in a tangle, crowded Festive Mood on the first turn and down the backstretch, and began dueling his archrival Key to the Mint for second position. On the lead, his ears playing and pricking at the sight of the swipes and hot walkers draped over the backstretch fence, was William Farish III's Bee Bee Bee. He was galloping along with consummate nonchalance, and neither Riva Ridge nor Key to the Mint ever got close enough to bite him, much less beat him, while veteran jockey Eldon Nelson sat chilly on him in a superbly judged piece of race riding.

Bee Bee Bee won it. Stretch-running No Le Hace was second, Key to the Mint a neck in front of Riva Ridge for third. The next day Lucien accused Turcotte of losing the race by not letting Riva Ridge move to the leader at the far turn. He said Turcotte was so busy watching jockey Braulio Baeza on Key to the Mint that he let Bee Bee Bee steal away with the race unchallenged. Elliott Burch, trainer of Key to the Mint, made no accusations against Baeza. Turcotte said only that Riva Ridge could not handle the muddy track.

Laurin was furious with Turcotte, howling to turfwriter Joe Hirsch early Sunday morning. Laurin and Penny Tweedy talked about taking Turcotte off the horse again. "It was the second race he blew for us," Penny Tweedy said. But again, rather than switch at a critical juncture, they decided to keep Turcotte for the Belmont Stakes June 9. Several days after the Preakness, Lucien had cooled off, and his opinion of Turcotte's ride had mellowed considerably.

Hope for the Triple Crown was gone, just when it had seemed within their grasp.

If not for the Preakness Stakes, the bay might have won all three. For on June 10, Riva Ridge cruised to the front of the mile-and-a-half Belmont Stakes, opening the bidding with a half mile in 0:48 and six furlongs in 1:12, a perfect twelve-clip, and he almost strung two more twelves together heading for the far turn. Riva Ridge reached the mile in 1:36 ³/₅ when Smiling Jack, racing with Riva all the way, began to stagger. Key to the Mint, probably overtrained for the race, spit out the bit turning for home, and Riva Ridge slowed down but galloped to win by seven in 2:28, the third fastest time of the race since it was first run at that distance in 1926, the year Man o' War's son, Crusader, won it.

Thus Riva Ridge reclaimed whatever prestige he had lost in the Preakness, establishing himself as the leading three-year-old in America and seemingly destined for Horse-of-the-Year honors. Then it happened.

The big mistake—one that would hound Penny Tweedy and Lucien Laurin—was deciding to take Riva Ridge to California for the mile-and-a-quarter Hollywood Derby, a race that appeared a soft touch for "The Ridge." It was not. He carried high weight of 129 pounds, and he was desperate to win it.

He was like Olympic quarter miler Lee Evans running against a good high school sprint relay team. Finalista made two runs at Riva Ridge, Royal Champion took one close look early before calling it an afternoon, and finally Bicker ran at him in the final yards. Riva Ridge just lasted to win. The race exhausted him, leaving him dead on his feet, and many believe he never was the same horse again all year. They had no way of knowing it then, of course, but Riva Ridge would race six more times before the end of the year, losing his final start by thirty-eight lengths, and wouldn't win another race.

Through May and June, with Gaffney galloping him and others working him, Secretariat grew in strength and ability, gained in fitness, and appeared to begin learning in earnest how to run. Other two-year-olds were appearing, too, such as Cornelius Vanderbilt Whitney's chestnut colt Pvt. Smiles. On June 1 another unraced youngster headed down the path past Barn 5, walking from the stable of Bull Hancock. He was a son of Pretense, the one-time Claiborne stallion, out of the mare Sequoia, who like Somethingroyal was a daughter of Princequillo.

His name was Sham, and that morning he worked an easy half mile in 0:51 ⁴/₅. Sham was growing quickly, and he would fill out one day into a rangy, good-looking dark bay colt, but on June 1 he, too, was still an ungainly youngster who hadn't yet caught on to the game. Sham would learn soon enough.

On Thursday morning, June 6, three days before Riva Ridge's Belmont Stakes, Secretariat wore blinkers for the first time—blue and white blocks, with leather cups partially shielding his eyes to keep his mind on the business up front—and went a half mile in 0:47 ³/₅. That was the fastest half-mile work in his life, but not fast enough to stay with Voler, a two-year-old filly who whipped him by four lengths in a rapid 0:46 ⁴/₅, one of the fastest moves of the day. Voler could shake a leg in the morning, and that day Secretariat pinned his ears at her precocity as she pulled away from him.

His work picked up through the last part of June. Again with blinkers, he worked from the starting gate and dashed five-eighths of a mile in 1:00 ⅕ on June 15, with Feliciano up. It was among the fastest moves that day at five furlongs.

Secretariat was within three weeks of his first race.

On June 24, on a sloppy track, the official clockers for *Daily Racing Form,* the horseplayers' scripture, noted a Secretariat workout in boldface letters on the workout sheets, meaning that his clocking of 1:12 ⅘ for six furlongs was the fastest workout at the distance that morning. The clockers, in their eyrie near the roof of the clubhouse, watched Secretariat closely, and in the paper underneath the boldface type they wrote: "Secretariat is on edge."

The clockers themselves had come a long way since the red horse first appeared in Florida, where they were spelling his name "Secretarial." Not only had they learned how to spell him, they had learned to like him.

Walking the colt back from the six-furlong workout that morning, Paul Feliciano saw Lucien waiting for him by the gap in the fence. The trainer was wearing his cheshire-cat grin, turning up the corners of his mouth.

"Do you know how fast you went, young man?"

"No, sir," said Paul. Lucien told him.

Penny Tweedy was still living in Colorado when Lucien called her long distance one morning. He asked her if she could be at Aqueduct one day next week, telling her that he wanted her to see Secretariat run his first race.

They finally decided to enter the colt on July 4, when Penny could be there. It was an $8000 maiden (nonwinner) race for colts and geldings at five and a half furlongs, with the start on the backstretch and facing the far turn.

The red horse was no secret, not since his sharp six-furlong workout ten days before. He had since worked another three-eighths in 0:35 flat. Sweep, the nom de plume for *Daily Racing Form* handicapper Jules Schanzer, advised his readers on July 4:

> Secretariat, a half-brother to Sir Gaylord, appears greatly advanced in his training. The newcomer by Bold Ruler stepped 6 furlongs in 1:12 ⅘ over a sloppy Belmont course June 24 and such outstanding speed entitles him to top billing.

Members of the Meadow Stable bet with both hands, some more than others, most of it on the red horse's nose. They thought he couldn't lose. Gaffney, selling tickets at the grandstand window, would not bet on Secretariat because he didn't think Paul Feliciano liked the colt or had enough confidence in him.

Lucien was sitting in a box seat with Penny Tweedy while the horses walked past the grandstand in the single-file post parade, turned and broke into warm-up gallops past the finish line, around the first turn. In the front row of the box seats by the finish line sat sixty-year-old Alfred Gwynne Vanderbilt, recently appointed chairman of the board of trustees of the New York Racing Association, the organization that runs Aqueduct, Belmont Park, and Saratoga.

It was nearing two o'clock. There was a wind blowing south against the horses walking to the starting gate up the backstretch, south toward Kennedy International Airport across the highway, toward Jamaica Bay. Bettors, some already moving to the rail on the homestretch, were busy making Secretariat the tepid $3.10 to $1.00 favorite.

Big Burn, jockey Braulio Baeza up, stepped into Post Position 1. An assistant starter took hold of Secretariat, who was wearing his blue and white checked blinkers, and led him into Post 2. The door slammed shut behind him. Feliciano patted the colt's neck and waited. Strike The Line stood in gate 3 next to Secretariat, while Jacinto Vasquez sat on Quebec in Post 4. Binoculars rose to eyes.

Dave Johnson, the track announcer, looked through his binoculars toward the starting gate, clicked on the lever of the loudspeaker system, and drove his voice through the clubhouse and grandstand.

"It is now post time," said Johnson.

It came all at once—the break, the sounds, and the collision—three seconds stitched into a triangle of time.

The gates crashed open, the bell screamed, and the horses vaulted upward and came down in a bound, Secretariat breaking sharply through one-two-three strides when Quebec sliced across Strike The Line and Vasquez hollered, but there was nothing anyone could do.

Quebec slammed dully into Secretariat, almost perpendicularly, plowing into his right shoulder. Like a fullback struck on his blind side, Secretariat staggered and fell left, crashing into Big Burn, and for several frames it appeared as if the red horse had two tacklers hanging on him. Quebec and Big Burn were leaning on him and trying to bring him down. Secretariat's legs were chopping savagely and Feliciano heard him groaning as he was struck and worked to regain his legs. It was a wonder he didn't go down.

He raced down the backside in eleventh place, next to Strike The Line, and Feliciano started scrubbing with his arms. Secretariat was digging, trying to pick up speed as they headed for the turn 300 yards ahead. He was not getting with it as fast as the others. Count Successor raced to the front, Knightly Dawn lapped on him in second, Calumet Farm's Herbull third, and Master Achiever nearby in fourth.

The horses strung out charging for the turn when Secretariat started drifting aimlessly, his path a wavering line, his neck thrust out and pumping. Moving to the bend, he seemed confused as he drifted momentarily to the right, bumping a roan called Rove. Feliciano took back on the left rein, leaving the right line flapping, and the red horse leaned left to make the bend. There was nothing else Feliciano could do, nothing since the collision. Paul looked around and began seeing everything go wrong.

There was no place to run, and the rail was clogged up in front. Horses were pounding on his right, and they left no room for him to swing Secretariat out and get him rolling in the clear. A wall of four horses was shifting around in front of him. He had two horses beaten, racing for the three-eighths pole midway at the turn for home, and he had nowhere to go. The colt started to run up a hole opening in front of him, but that squeezed shut, too. He was working to get with it, as if looking for the holes himself.

Secretariat was a Cadillac in a traffic jam of Chevrolets and Datsuns, trapped hopelessly in the shifting, dimly unfolding mess around him. Lucien Laurin, looking through his binoculars, was astounded. Watching the break from the side, he missed seeing the crunch at the start. He was astounded because the red horse had always broken well in his morning trials, not slow like this and floundering rudderlessly. As the field made the bend, passing the five-sixteenths pole near the top of the stretch, Count Successor was still on the lead, Knightly Dawn beside him, Master Achiever now third, and Herbull on the outside fourth. The pace was not slow. The leader was carrying his field through a half mile in 0:46 ⅕, brisk for two-year-olds, with Secretariat about ten lengths behind in 0:48. As the field straightened into the lane, racing past the grandstand bettors howling at them, it appeared for a moment as if Feliciano was going to swing the colt to the outside. Almost running up on horses' heels, Feliciano had to slow the colt entering the lane, to check him.

Nearing the three-sixteenth pole, Secretariat suddenly veered on a sharp diagonal to the left, lunging for space as it opened on the rail, and took off. He was looking for spots, looking and moving for running room. Daylight in front of him, horses on the outside off the rail, scrubbing on the red horse furiously, Feliciano drove Secretariat down the lane. Secretariat gained, passing a tiring Knightly Dawn and then Jacques Who. He was gathering momentum, picking up speed, cutting into Master Achiever's lead, from eight lengths nearing the furlong marker in midstretch to seven and then to six as Master Achiever raced for the wire.

The frontrunners were battling it out, and passing the eighth pole the red horse appeared. He cut the lead to five lengths, then to four and a half, then finally to four lengths passing the sixteenth pole. He was in the hunt, and Feliciano was asking him for more steam, reaching back and strapping him once right-handed.

A small hole opened between Master Achiever and the rail near the wire. Feliciano drove the colt toward it. Secretariat was now running faster than all the others, closing the lane and cutting the lead to three lengths, then two lengths as the wire loomed, then one and a half lengths. Suddenly the hole on the rail closed as Master Achiever came over, and as the wire swept overhead Feliciano had to stand up and take Secretariat back again—"He gave me three runs that day! Three!"—to prevent him from running up Master Achiever's heels. He closed about eight lengths on the leaders in a powerful run through the stretch, finished fourth, and earned $480, beaten only a length and a quarter by Herbull. As he crossed the finish line, the first thought that came to Paul Feliciano was, "God damn, I'm going to catch hell."

Up in the press box, trackman Jack Wilson had already seen Secretariat's run and sat down to write a brief summary of the race for the official chart, which read in part: "Secretariat, impeded after the start, lacked room between horses racing into the turn, ducked to the inside after getting through in the stretch and finished full of run."

Down in the box seats, Penny Tweedy smiled as the colt raced across the line—she too was unaware of the collision—and told Lucien, "That's pretty good for a first start."

Lucien jumped from his chair in the box seat, kicked it, and growled, "He should have *never* been beaten!" His reaction startled Penny Tweedy. Lucien had told her only that he thought she ought to be there for the colt's first start—not that the colt was going to win, only that his workouts were impressive and he appeared to be learning fast. Lucien's reaction made her realize for the first time how much he thought of Secretariat.

Feliciano pulled the colt to a halt at the bend, turned him around, clucked to him, and galloped slowly back to the unsaddling area by the paddock scale, where the jockeys weigh in after a race. As he galloped back, he happened to look over his left shoulder, toward the paddock, and as he pulled up he saw precisely what he expected— Lucien standing in the paddock waiting for him.

Jumping off Secretariat, Feliciano began preparing himself. All he could do, he thought, was tell the truth.

Feliciano weighed in at the scales, and turning around he handed the saddle and pads to a valet and walked over to Lucien. The trainer waved a finger in Feliciano's face. "God damn!" he said. "You sure as hell messed that one up."

What was worse for the young apprentice was that he was scheduled to ride another horse for Lucien in a later race—Sovereign in the seventh. But between races, Lucien and Penny had seen the films, and as Paul came to the paddock for the seventh, Lucien was smiling. Quietly, Lucien apologized for yelling at him, and Feliciano recalled Laurin telling him he hadn't seen the films then and didn't realize the battering he'd taken at the start.

Yet, even with that, it surprised Paul when he picked up an overnight list of entries nine days later and glanced at it as he left the jockeys' room. Under the entries for the fourth race on July 15, a three-quarter-mile sprint for colts and geldings, he read: "Secretariat . . . Feliciano, P."

Chapter 11

Secretariat walked away from his first race staring, his eyes still wide open to the startling snap of the gate and to the collision—and no doubt to the suddenly quickening beat of his life.

Lucien did not hesitate to fuel his intensity, to keep him on his toes through July. Six days after his first start, Secretariat worked to three-eighths of a mile in 0:35 ³/₅ at Belmont Park. Four days later Lucien sent him out to zip three-eighths again, this time breezing in 0:36 on a sloppy track, the day before his second race on July 15.

Jules Schanzer didn't abandon Secretariat July 15, writing in the *Daily Racing Form:*

> Secretariat turned in a remarkable performance after being badly sloughed at the start of his rough recent preview. The half-brother to Sir Gaylord turned on full steam after settling into his best stride and was devouring ground rapidly through the stretch run. Today's added distance is a plus factor that can help him leave the maiden ranks.

Nor did the bettors abandon Secretariat at Aqueduct, sending him off as the $1.30-to-$1.00 favorite over Master Achiever.

Paul Feliciano emerged from the tunnel by the jockeys' room and walked to Lucien in the paddock. They huddled briefly. "Don't do like you did last time. Just stay out of trouble and let him run. He shouldn't get beat."

Lucien then gave Feliciano a leg up on the colt, and to the sound of Sam Koza's Aida trumpet signaling the field of eleven horses to the post, Feliciano was already thinking about what he would do. He was more nervous than usual that afternoon because he himself believed—as Lucien and thousands of bettors no doubt believed—that he should not have lost his first start, that he should not be beaten this time, and that he was sitting on a horse who needed only room to run. He thought about the opening jump from the gate, hoping the colt would break well and in the clear, not in a tangle of horses again, and he thought he would try to keep him on the outside where he would have room to move.

What made Lucien the angriest, thought Feliciano, was a jockey getting a horse in trouble and getting him beat when he should not have been beaten. That was inexcusable. So he was rehearsing what he would do to keep Secretariat in the clear, free to move when he wanted to. He decided he wouldn't rush the horse, even if he broke slowly, but rather would let him settle into stride and move out when he put it together.

Into stall 1 moved Fleet 'n Royal, the colt who had finished third, a nose in front of Secretariat, on July 4. The youngsters loaded each in turn. An assistant starter took a hold of Secretariat's rein on the left side and led him into Stall 8, to the outside of Jacques Who and to the inside of the post of Bet On It, a gelding with a quick turn of foot. The instant before the red horse stepped into the starting gate, Feliciano pulled a pair of plastic goggles over his eyes. Secretariat gave no signs of nervousness at the post, no feeling that he would bust hell-bent for the turn. Secretariat stood relaxed inside the gate, Feliciano recalled, looking casually ahead.

Starter George Cassidy, standing atop a platform about ten yards in front of the gate, watched for the moment when the heads stopped turning. Then Cassidy pressed the button, the gates popped open, and the eleven liberated horses started bounding.

Secretariat broke alertly, as he did July 4, his head emerging from the gate with the others in the first jump, but with that first single stride he was already running last, already a half length behind Jacques Who at the break. Ten feet from the gate, with the others barreling for the lead and beginning to string out, he was still nearly trailing the field. This start, among others, would later give rise to the false notion that the battering he took in his first race made him timid in all his starts, made him afraid to leave the slip with his field, causing him to take himself back.

But he didn't take himself back that afternoon. He was pumping and driving with his front and back legs, trying to move his bulk apace with the field. He was reaching for whatever ground he could grab beneath himself, but he wasn't getting there as fast as the others.

Up in the box seats, Laurin's mouth dropped open as the colt fell back to last, astounded that it was all happening a second time.

Feliciano sensed the colt was having no easy time finding his stride, so he sat tight on him as they started to race for the bend, not reaching back and strapping him, not hollering at him. Instead, Feliciano sat pumping with his arms, in rhythm with the stride. Through that first quarter mile, Feliciano wondered whether Secretariat ever would find his stride. All he could do for the moment was keep the colt to the outside, clear of traffic, and wait for him to find himself. He began to worry in earnest as the field pounded through the first 220 yards, leaving him with only five furlongs to go and still no running horse beneath him. He was asking Secretariat to run, but without the whip, pumping on him as they raced to the bend.

Bet On It was sprinting toward the half-mile pole a length in front, zipping along at an eleven-second clip through the first eighth, with Master Achiever right behind and Impromptu third. They were rolling as Secretariat finally came alive.

As the field raced down the backside for the turn, Paul suddenly began to feel it happening beneath him, a coming together of stride and movement, a leveling out and smoothing of motion that retired exercise boy Jimmy (The Squirrel) Weininger once recalled, in tones of reverence: "It's the oddest thing. It's like you're a pilot and you're out there warming up the engine and then it shifts into that one gear that sends your ass down the runway. A horse drops down and he's in first gear and then he's in fourth gear and it's sort of like flying, taking off."

Feliciano recalled seeing horses on his left, remembered the sense of Secretariat running easily and the feeling of the colt generating power beneath him. The red horse grabbed the bit between his teeth, and Paul felt the momentum forward. He sat still and felt the surge.

Secretariat was on the outside then and moving past Monetary Crisis and Scantling and finally Fleet 'n Royal, moving into sixth as Bet On It finished the first quarter mile in 0:22 ⅕, a fast clip, with Secretariat almost seven lengths behind in 0:23 ⅗. Irish Flavor was on the inside, running with Secretariat for a few jumps as Bet On It drove around the bend and headed for the three-furlong pole. By the time the field had raced midway of the turn for home, Secretariat had bounded past Irish Flavor and was moving six horses wide toward home. He was losing ground on the outside but gaining in a rush on the leaders. He was a running horse with nothing in front of him now but running room, moving on his left lead as he swung around the horses.

Nearing the stretch, Secretariat passed Impromptu, and entering the straight he had Jacques Who measured, charging past him at the three-sixteenths pole, Feliciano still sitting and pumping as Secretariat raced past Master Achiever and moved to Bet On It nearing the eighth pole. He was a half length behind, then head and head, then in front.

The crowd was shouting. Feliciano reached back and hit Secretariat once as he was getting to the front. The colt led Bet On It a half length with 220 yards to run, increased his lead to two lengths and then three lengths passing the sixteenth pole, finally to four lengths and to five lengths and to six as he raced under the wire.

Paul stood up in the stirrups and felt the sweet elation flowing as he galloped toward the clubhouse turn, easing back on his reins and bringing the red horse to a stop at the turn.

Secretariat had raced the fastest six furlongs in his life, 1:10 ³/₅, coming off a speedy half mile of 0:45 ²/₅. He won $4800, but that was only a promise of more to come. He was a son of Bold Ruler from a Princequillo mare, and he had won his second race by six. It was enough to make the palms of a jockey agent's hands itch.

Like exceptional broodmares on the breeding farm, the promising two-year-olds on a racetrack are the gold men covet. To a jockey, whether an apprentice like Paul Feliciano, or a journeyman like Ron Turcotte, a talented two-year-old means a potentially talented three-year-old and four-year-old, a money winner for several years running. To have a two-year-old is to have a future.

Secretariat ran as if he had a future.

Lucien Laurin liked what he saw that day—the way Secretariat lost all that ground and won by himself—but most trainers of Laurin's experience have emotional brakes that draw them up short before allowing them to make the mistake of liking a two-year-old too much too early. He remained skeptical because the colt had only beaten a bunch of nonwinners and horses who might never make it. Lucien had seen so many horses break their maidens and never make the lead again. It was an old story on the racetrack.

Up in the press box, Baltimore turfwriter Clem Florio jumped to his feet as Secretariat crossed the line, turned to colleague Mike Quinn, and said loudly, enthusiastically, "That's my Derby horse for next year!" Everyone heard him in the press box, even rival handicapper Mannie Kalish of New York, who advised Florio that there was a long way to go to the 1973 Kentucky Derby and that he might do well to temper his enthusiasm. Florio, a prominent Maryland handicapper, had seen Secretariat's first start, had seen the crunch at the outset, had seen how the red horse had been impeded and was running wild at the end. So when he saw him tour the high ground on July 15, making it so difficult on himself, and watched him accelerate down the lane and pick up horses relentlessly from the turn to the wire, he wasted no time making his revelation known.

At his home in Valley Stream, Long Island, Ron Turcotte was dopey from the painkiller he had been taking for almost ten days. On July 6, Turcotte had nearly been killed on the homestretch at Aqueduct.

That day, trainer Walter Kelley had put Turcotte on Overproof, telling him the horse needed to be pushed and hustled along if he were going to get the money.

As the field paraded to the post, nearing the starting gate on the racetrack, Turcotte began working on the colt, waking him up and telling the pony boy, "Either he'll do it today or he'll die." He was only kidding.

Turcotte laid into Overproof as the field left the gate, racing head and head for the lead right from the start. He was making Overproof bounce. Turcotte made the lead, turning into the homestretch, and was battling for it when the horse began acting oddly at the three-sixteenths pole. "All of a sudden he started wandering. I hit him left-handed. Then I hit him right-handed. And then I went to switching the stick when I realized he was getting hard under me. His neck muscles were tightening right up. That's when I realized something was really wrong. I couldn't hit him again. Then all of a sudden he jumped up, just like he was dead, and he fell over to the right." Turcotte struck the ground near the sixteenth pole, thrown there with such tremendous force that his rib cage bent inward, causing contusions of his heart muscle, lungs, and back. He lay there and couldn't move. The horse lay dead nearby, dead at the three-sixteenths pole and running on instinct or adrenalin or whatever it is that horses run on when they die of heart attacks during races.

Turcotte was rushed to Physicians Hospital in Queens. He was out of action for twenty days, until July 26.

He couldn't ride Secretariat in his first start, July 4, because he was committed to ride Summer Guest in the Monmouth Oaks at Monmouth Park, a major filly race. He won the Oaks on Summer Guest for Paul Mellon's Rokeby Stable. On July 1, the morning of the day Riva Ridge won the Hollywood Derby, Lucien had mentioned casually to Turcotte—as they drove through the parking lot at Hollywood Park—that he would have liked to see him ride the red horse in his first race. Turcotte thought no more about it. To him, Secretariat was a likable colt of no particular distinction at the time—handsome, well bred but untested.

Turcotte was in bed, at home in Queens, when the colt won his second start under Feliciano.

As Turcotte lay sedated with painkillers that day, his wife Gaetane left their home near Merrick Boulevard in Queens and drove off to a medical supply store in Laurelton, Queens. During the drive she turned on the radio. The first voice that came on was that of the off-track betting announcer who gave the results of the Aqueduct races by recreating them in a studio, calling them as if he were there.

As Gae pulled up to the medical supply house, the race came on. She stopped the car and listened. She had forbidden Ron to listen to any racing while he recovered, but she thought he might like to know who won the fourth that day at Aqueduct.

Gaetane thought she recognized the name of Secretariat as the race was called, but she wasn't sure. She thought it was the horse Ron had spoken about some weeks before, the colt he had told her had all the trouble in his first race, the pretty boy.

A week later, finally able to climb out of bed, Turcotte got restless at home and one morning drove to see Laurin at Barn 5. His back was still sore, and he was taking Butazolidin—an aspirinlike painkiller—when he sat down with Laurin in the office near the barn. They talked awhile of Riva Ridge and of the other horses in the barn and finally of Secretariat. Lucien asked Ron if he would be able to ride opening day at Saratoga.

Turcotte told Laurin that despite the pain he would start working horses in the morning before Saratoga opened. Lucien said he thought the red horse had some class, might be a stakes horse, even off that one victory, and so it was important for Turcotte to ride the colt as soon as possible. Secretariat's next start would be on opening day, July 31, at Saratoga, an allowance race with fast horses in it.

"If I put somebody else on him, I might have to ride him back in the stakes. You feel all right?"

"Yeh," Turcotte said. "I'm all right now."

Secretariat's first victory set other things into motion, too, one of them in the back of Penny Tweedy's mind.

Sitting in the clubhouse section that day in mid-July, watching Secretariat widen his lead through the final 200 yards down the lane, she began to sense within herself a feeling of resentment toward this red horse.

"I resented him because I was so high on Riva and I thought, 'This isn't fair; this lousy dude is so good-looking and if he can run, too, it isn't fair.' This was my immediate reaction after the first victory. I was very pleased, but I had this lingering resentment. Riva represented the golden boy, yes—and also the ugly duckling and the underdog because he is so oddly put together aesthetically. His legs are too long. He's terribly narrow chested and ewe necked. You know how a sheep's neck curves? And the head is a little small for the rest of the body and then the floppy ears. It just doesn't all hang together. It works but it doesn't look good—I thought it would be great if Secretariat turned out to be a winner, but in my heart I didn't want him to jeopardize Riva's eminence. But that was my own problem; I got over it."

Chapter 12

Can the girl from Colorado find success and happiness among the ruthless and powerful men of New York racing? Well, most of them are old friends of my father and have been pretty helpful, and my faith in trying to play this game is based on having a stacked deck to play with. I'm banking on the Meadow mares having such superior qualities that they can overcome my inexperience, for I have undertaken to continue the operation of my father's racing stable and breeding farm. I am optimistic that another good stakes winner will come out of the horses we have just sent to the track. I can't believe the chain of winners is going to stop. Time alone will tell.

> Penny Tweedy, addressing the Fortnightly Club of Denver,
> March 1971.

Penny Chenery Tweedy was at home in Denver when the phone rang for her on an autumn day in 1967. Answering it, she heard the imperative voice of her father's long-time attorney, John Fager, who was calling from New York.

It was October 27, and the call marked the beginning of a time of transition and flux for her, a period of breaking away from her life as a housewife in Colorado and creating a place for herself in the eastern racing world. If there was not a touch of alarm in John Fager's voice, there was a sense of urgency in what he told her that day.

Christopher T. Chenery had just turned eighty-one years old a month before, and his health was failing. There had been no sudden decline, but he was beginning to suffer moments when his thinking lacked clarity, moments of limited lucidity and impaired judgment; a mind as precise as a surveyor's compass had been dulled by age. The lapses in clarity were threatening to affect the way he handled his corporate affairs and his management of the Meadow Stable and breeding farm. It was just such a matter involving the horses, in fact, that prompted John Fager to call Penny Tweedy. If anyone could help in dealing with C. T. Chenery, she could.

Chris Chenery had decided to sell four of his most prized broodmares for $40,000 each, an unwise decision. A breeder might sell or syndicate his stallions, might sell his colts and cull his cripples, but whatever else he might do, he should keep his well-bred broodmares, especially the stakes-winning mares that he bred, raised, and raced himself. The success of the stud depends upon the quality of the mares. Without Hildene and Imperatrice, Chenery would not have had such good fortune in the game. They were the foundation mares, the genetic underpinnings of the Meadow horses. And, though not deeply involved in racing at the time, Penny Tweedy understood the value of such mares to breeding.

The four mares were Speedwell, Bold Ruler's first stakes winner, who was out of Imperatrice; Imperial Hill, a stakes-winning daughter of Chenery's champion Hill Prince out of Imperatrice; Hula Girl, a daughter of Vanderbilt's Native Dancer out of Imperial Hill herself; and finally Hasty Matelda, a stakes-winning daughter of the 1954 Preakness winner, Hasty Road, and the dam of the fleet Gay Matelda.

Understanding the source of the problem to be her father's illness, but thinking she might persuade him not to go through with the deal, she flew to New York at once from Denver, meeting with him in the family home in Pelham Manor. When they spoke of the sale, he was adamant about it, she judiciously circumspect.

But there was no dissuading him. In fact, when she pointed out that The Meadow was in no need of cash, he told her she was looking at the wrong books.

When she failed to convince him to cancel the sale, there was an emergency meeting of the board of the Meadow Stud—Fager, Elizabeth Ham, Chenery's wife, Helen, and Penny. The four board members spoke at length about the sale, talking over the possibility of disavowing the agreement, something they could have done if they chose, since the Meadow Stud was a corporation and all such agreements of sale are subject to ratification by the board. They considered refusing to ratify it, but they considered the consequences, too.

Penny Tweedy recalled: "We decided that the alternative of disavowing the agreement which dad made would involve too much humiliation of the man who had developed all these things we were trying to protect, so we went along with it and sold the three mares (we were able to extract one on a technicality) for $40,000 each. The foal Speedwell was carrying at the time sold as a yearling for $40,000. A foal from Imperial Hill sold this winter [1971] for $66,000. I still get angry about this sale, but my father could still get angry then, too, and I dared not thwart him, even if he didn't know what he was doing."

The mare they were able to extract on a technicality was Hasty Matelda.

Helen Chenery died just three weeks later, and the loss of his wife wore further at Christopher Chenery, altering his attitude. Penny explained: "Dad seemed to give up trying. He was very docile when, at the next board meeting, a carefully prepared script saw me elected vice-president and John [her husband], Elizabeth, and me constituted as the executive committee. This gave us the tools to carry on the Meadow Stud operation. But did we have the skill? John was a tax lawyer and Elizabeth, who had followed orders for thirty years, answered every question with, 'We'll do it the same way Mr. Chenery did.' I had doubts, but no experience and no confidence in my judgment, so I watched and studied, talked to everyone I could, read everything published about racing, and bided my time."

The sale is what first propelled Penny Tweedy into racing and breeding horses at The Meadow. It taught her that the stable and the farm needed active management and guidance, that without leadership the breeding operation—and eventually, the racing stable so dependent on it—would slip quickly into twilight. By 1967, Chris Chenery was no longer paying attention to the horses he once had. Like Arthur B. Hancock, Sr., twenty years earlier, he had been failing for several years to cull unproductive mares, a deadly kind of neglect in a breeding establishment, as Bull Hancock learned when he took over Claiborne Farm. Chenery was breeding them to stallions who were not siring winners. Now in his absence Penny became his surrogate, taking his place out of loyalty to him and to what he built in Virginia and out of fear, too, of what would happen to it if The Meadow were left to drift. "The sale made me realize that the horses just couldn't sit there and run themselves, that into the void created by the departure of this very strong man a lot of people would move."

She was christened Helen Bates Chenery, after her mother, but she was her father's daughter.

She was supposed to be a boy, and almost from the start she swung into the orbit of her father's fields of interest—first toward horses, which she learned to ride at age five, to the prep school of his choice, to war work, and to business school at Columbia University, where she studied corporate finance, and finally back to his horses again.

She was born in 1922, the youngest of Chenery's three children, and grew up idolizing her father. She had an older sister, Margaret, and a brother, Hollis, who never had Chris Chenery's interests in horses or business. Hollis was a scholar, brilliant, conceptual, moving comfortably from being a tenured professor at Harvard University to the position of chief economic adviser to Robert S. McNamara at the World Bank. McNamara was the only man Hollis ever met, he once conceded, who was more brilliant than himself.

When she and her father and mother drove south to see The Meadow in 1935, Penny had been attending elementary school at Pelham Manor, where the family lived on Park Lane, and was about to enroll in the Madiera School of Greenway, Virginia. Her father chose the school. "Madiera was a very horsey school outside Washington. It had riding clubs, and I took my own horse with me. I rode to hounds in the Fairfax Hunt."

She had already been absorbing her father's values, adopting his loves as her own, often traveling with him. "I rode from the time I was five and every weekend was spent at a horse show or watching my father play polo. My father really loved horses. I think a parent often communicates his loves to a child."

Out of Madiera, Penny enrolled in Smith College, her mother's alma mater, and studied American history in Northampton, Massachusetts. She made her debut with thirty other girls in Westchester County, New York, a swank suburb north of Manhattan. She graduated from Smith in 1943, about the time of year Count Fleet won the Triple Crown and her father was just beginning to renovate The Meadow.

After Smith, from 1943 to 1944, she was an assistant for the chief of electrical procurement at Gibbs and Cox in New York, a firm that designed landing craft for the Normandy invasion. The invasion put her out of work. Home in Pelham Manor, Penny plopped down at the breakfast table in a robe, on the verge of doing absolutely nothing; her father peered across the table at her and growled, "If the Bolsheviks take over this country and examine your war record, they'll shoot you!"

She joined the Red Cross, going overseas to work in a Red Cross clubmobile. She was a doughnut girl.

She was home again by 1946, in Pelham Manor and not about to do anything in particular. Chris Chenery said to her one day, "Well, if you don't want to get married, why don't you get a job?" She mentioned that she did have a Bachelor of Arts degree from Smith, but he scoffed at that. "As far as the labor market is concerned, you are unskilled," Chris Chenery told her.

So he made his daughter an offer. He told her to apply for jobs, to look for the highest paying job she could find, promising her that he would match the highest offer made to her and give her that amount in allowance to attend the Columbia school of business. She was one of only twenty women out of eight hundred men in the business school that year. She also met John Bayard Tweedy, a graduate of Princeton, who was attending Columbia law school at the time. Instead of marching out of Morningside Heights to Wall Street downtown, she followed the instructions detailed in a telegram John Tweedy sent her after going to Denver to set up a law practice: "Have job. Have apartment. Plan wedding."

They were married in May 1949, and for the next eighteen years she was a star-spangled All-American housewife from the snows of Colorado, successful, her children's mother and her father's daughter, a doorbell ringer for Ike (her husband was a committeeman), and a dead ringer for the perfect woman in a Cheer commercial. Her voice was rich and warmly modulated, her hair light, her features sharp and photogenic, her skin healthy, and her eyes as clear a blue as the dome above the ski slopes at the resort she and John helped to build in Vail, above the three-mile slope called Riva Ridge.

Penny camped with her husband in Montana, where he loved to fish ("His father took him fishing, as mine took me riding") and she cooked, though not well because she never liked it, and wore aprons, and did the dishes. She was diaper changer for Sally and Christopher and Kate and John. She rode to hounds on Crescent City, a son of Hildene, one of that mare's few offspring who couldn't run. "He was a chestnut, and all her chestnuts were bad."

Penny was a fund raiser for the American Red Cross, the Mile-

High United Fund, the Republican Party, the Symphony Fund Drive, the American Cancer Society, and the March of Dimes; a member of the Junior League of Denver; a member of the Children's Theater Committee; and for seven years a discussion leader for the League of Women Voters.

After eighteen years of settled family living as a housewife in Denver ("I really enjoyed it, I worked very hard at it"), she woke up one morning in Denver and took the telephone call from John Fager.

C. T. Chenery was admitted to New Rochelle Hospital in late February 1968 with an acute kidney condition. He would never leave the hospital, suffering a series of small strokes, a gradual hardening of the arteries, and a long decline toward death. They had been awkward times for those seeking to protect him. Miss Ham, whose loyalty to Chenery was unquestioned, monitored his telephone calls to prevent him from embarrassing himself in business, Penny recalled, and at one point Chris Chenery refused at a board meeting to give Howard Gentry a raise. "Dad was devoted to Howard, but he felt Howard had enough. Howard was there and it was very embarrassing. Dad was a generous man. That's when we realized we had to operate the farm for dad's benefit, behind his back."

Behind his back in the late 1960s was a farm of 2798 acres, over thirty broodmares and six stallions and upwards of fifty yearlings, two-year-olds, and older horses on the racetracks. Since that extraordinary year in 1950—when Hill Prince was Horse of the Year and the stable won $391,835—the Meadow horses had carried the stable and helped support the farm. Between 1951 and 1960, Meadow Stable horses won 231 races, many of them major stakes, and $2,627,734. The stable was a money-making enterprise, not just a hobby, and Chenery enjoyed it more than anything, more than stringing his utilities together and making millions in water companies and natural gas, because he loved horses.

He purchased his foundation mares at sales, just as he did his other fine broodmare, Iberia, the dam of Riva Ridge and the stakes-winning Hydrologist. Chenery's sense of creative accomplishment attained its peak in the brilliant career of Cicada, winner of twenty-three races and $783,664—a world's record for a female racehorse when she was retired in 1963. She was a daughter of Bryan G., a stakes winner whom Chenery bred and raced himself, and she was out of Satsuma, a daughter herself of Hildene—another Chenery homebred. So Cicada's sire and dam were bred by The Meadow, and Cicada became Chenery's greatest source of pride. He adored her.

Hildene, bred to Captain Harry Guggenheim's stallion, Turn-to, had a colt foal named First Landing. He was the second highest earner of any horse to race for the Meadow Stable during its first thirty years, winning $779,577. First Landing was America's champion two-year-old in 1958, winner of the Hopeful Stakes and the Garden State Stakes. Bred to Iberia in 1967, he sired Riva Ridge.

Through most of the 1960s, under Chenery's direction, the stable and the stud made more money than it had the previous decade. There was never a year in which the Meadow Stable made less than $150,000. Between 1961 and 1968, when Chenery entered the hospital, the horses grossed $2,756,259, winning 144 races, and in 1967 alone—the year Chenery told his daughter that The Meadow needed cash—the stable had the third best year of its existence, winning 21 races and $508,646. Between 1940 and 1967, Meadow Stable horses earned a total of $5,914,912.

"After eighteen years of housewifery, I felt out of touch and unsure. I was at the age when many of my friends had gone back to college for teaching degrees, taken public relations jobs, or opened gift shops."

Counting on her father's mares, on the experience of farm managers like Gentry and Bailes, Penny didn't feel she was plunging into racing unassisted. Nor did she feel the sudden rush of pressure to learn, as she might have felt had her father died. She had time to feel her way around while she adjusted to a world away from the ski slopes of Vail and the machinations of Colorado politics. She had always been interested in her father's racing stable, though she had never participated in the operation of it. "My father never needed help. He wanted an audience."

Still in Denver, she began reading and studying the variety of racing publications—the *Blood-Horse,* the *Thoroughbred Record,* the *Daily Racing Form,* and books about racing. She conferred frequently with Bull Hancock, asking him what she regarded later as "dumb questions." They were the questions of a novice: it was amateur night at The Meadow.

Yet one of the decisions she made that year, however new she was to active involvement in the sport, had major historical repercussions. Despite its evident failure, Penny decided to continue with the Phippses the two-year flip arrangement to which her father had already agreed, so she sent Somethingroyal to Bold Ruler twice, in 1968 and 1969. Not bad for an amateur.

Thus Penny Tweedy was beginning to involve herself in what became a central passion and ambition in her life. She was her father's daughter, moving to save The Meadow—the land and the mares and the stallions and the yearlings and the paddocks and the barns and the manor house—and the racing stable and the Chenery name in racing.

She became the nominal leader of the Meadow Stud, assuming control by default more than anything else. Neither her brother, the scholarly Hollis, nor her sister, Margaret Carmichael, shared her enthusiasm for racing. She sensed that their attitude was, "If Penny wants to do it, let her do it. Dad isn't going to live much longer, and when he's gone we're going to sell it all anyway."

At family meetings during her father's illness and the stable's drift —when the future of it was uncertain and she was still running a household in Denver—Penny sensed this unspoken understanding that with the passing of her father would come the passing of the farm. And she was determined not to let that happen.

The stable started losing money in the late 1960s—something it had rarely done—a total of $85,000 in 1969. That was the year in which she sensed the strongest pressure, among family members, to begin considering the sale of the farm, the breeding stock, and the racing stable. It was also the year when Casey Hayes, Chenery's private trainer for more than twenty-five years, resigned. It was a major turn of events. Seeking counsel to find a new trainer, Penny turned to Bull Hancock for advice, and he suggested Roger Laurin, thirty-three, the son of Bull's own trainer, Lucien Laurin. Roger, a public trainer who conditioned horses for various clients, accepted the job with the proviso that for two years he would make all the decisions on training the horses and rise or fall with them. She agreed.

Of the twenty horses in training at the Meadow Stable when he took over, Roger sent fourteen back to the farm, saying they were unfit to race. He sliced stable expenses sharply from $250,000 to about $120,000 a year. While the stable had lost almost $100,000 the year before he took it over, it began showing a profit during his first year of running it. And Penny was asserting herself more forcefully.

The many nonproducing broodmares at The Meadow were sharply culled. In that enterprise she sought and received counsel of

Bull Hancock. All mares, from then on, would have three years to produce. Culling the failures became a rule. There would be no unproductive boarders living and dining for years at The Meadow. They would be sold privately or at auction. Instead of breeding the mares to the farm stallions who were not producing winners, Penny and Howard Gentry sought to breed the broodmares to young or proved stallions. They soon had mares booked to proved studs such as Round Table and Northern Dancer, and to the young and promising Dr. Fager and his archrival on the racetrack, Damascus.

Penny Tweedy took over the running of The Meadow as a businesswoman, with a tough attitude, seeking to reestablish it on a sound financial basis. Behind the Cheer smile and the procelain sparkle of her teeth, behind the radiance and the friendliness and the warmth—behind all the charm, gentility, and good Episcopalianism —was a mind with a thermostat idling at sixty degrees. "I got tough fighting with my brother and sister as a child. My father wanted his children to be tough and self-reliant and to defend their points of view." By upbringing and education Penny Tweedy was a scion of the corporate class, and she fit snugly and without fear into racing's ruling structure. Racing's establishment had changed markedly since the early Vanderbilt days when the ruling guard had names like Whitney, Woodward, and Belmont. The old names were still on the Jockey Club roll, but the power had shifted to financiers and industrial moguls like John Galbreath, John Hanes, George M. Humphrey (President Eisenhower's former secretary of the treasury), Captain Guggenheim, and C. T. Chenery.

Penny Tweedy's fear was not of her father's friends, some of whom encouraged her to keep the silks in racing. Her concern was the sentiment, as expressed by brother Hollis at the Meadow Stud board meeting in August 1969, that they might consider selling the farm, the breeding stock, and racing stable and invest it all in the stock market. Penny objected, quietly, to the idea. "I don't think we have the right to sell dad's horses while he is alive," she said, "because I don't think he would want that."

There was no argument, no raised voices, but the sentiment for sale was there. Her hope to keep the farm and stable was based in part on the belief, a kind of cosmic belief, that good horses and good times come in cycles to breeding and racing operations. The Meadow Stable, she believed, was ready to go into orbit again, into a winning cycle. She recalled that, after Hill Prince retired in 1951, there was a seven-year hiatus until the emergence of First Landing in 1958.

There was another, though shorter, wait for champion Cicada five years later, but since Cicada The Meadow had not produced a champion.

She believed that a good horse, a big money winner, would shift the sentiment against selling the farm and stable and turn it in favor of keeping them. There was money to be made in racing—more than ever in the history of the sport—and she knew that one top horse could show that dramatically and quell the belief that there were more possibilities on Wall Street than shed row. She believed that a star would bring Hollis and her sister into the sport, exposing them to racing and the drama of it, the excitement and the glamor, and involve them as participants.

What The Meadow needed was the big horse, and in March of 1971, Penny Tweedy addressed the Fortnightly Club and told the thirty largely Smith and Vassar women that she was banking on the Meadow mares, "optimistic that another good stakes winner will come out of the horses we have just sent to the track." They had just sent Iberia's son Riva Ridge to the track as a two-year-old, with Secretariat a young yearling near training. Roger Laurin trained Riva Ridge briefly, not long enough for his own mortal good.

An opportunity arose for Roger Laurin that few men would pass without reaching for it, and Roger reached. At the age of thirty-five he was offered the chance of training the Phipps family's string of horses—the most prestigious stable of runners in the country, by reputation the most powerful band of horses in America. Trainer Eddie Neloy, the man who had joked with Penny Tweedy during that monumental coin flip of 1969, had died of a heart attack on the morning of May 26, 1971, just six weeks before Bold Ruler died, two months before Secretariat went into training, and only fourteen days before Riva Ridge would make his first lifetime start.

Ogden Phipps was suddenly without a trainer for all his blue-bloods in Elmont, Long Island, in the stable area at Belmont Park not far from Lucien's barn.

Bull approached Roger, and Roger accepted. There was hardly a way a young man could refuse. It was managing the New York Yankees in the 1950s, the Green Bay Packers of the early 1960s, the Miami Dolphins of today—he would train the finest blooded horses in America and he would be backed up, on Claiborne Farm, by scores of the finest broodmares on earth, by stallions such as Phipps's Buckpasser, and by a variety of others such as Round Table, Damascus, Bold Lad, and Dr. Fager. It was the stable for which trainer

Neloy had set a record in 1966 by winning forty-one stakes races and purses worth $2,456,250, a money-winning record that exceeded Jimmy Jones's 1947 record by more than $1 million.

"Who do you think I should try?" Penny asked Roger, seeking a replacement for him.

"How about my dad?" he asked.

"No," she said.

Penny Tweedy had already seen Lucien that past winter at Hialeah, and she feared he might be patronizing toward her—the old-timer talking down to the young upstart kid. Roger's stable, including the Meadow horses, had been near Lucien's barn in Florida, and she remembered that Lucien was there infrequently, that he was letting his son run his stable much of the time, and that he acted as if he were about to retire altogether, which in fact he was. He was not her idea of a trainer for the Meadow horses. She wanted a second-generation trainer, for one thing, as she was a second-generation owner, someone like Roger himself.

She sat in Colorado a couple of days, with Roger's brief notice running out, and no time to fly to New York to interview trainers for the job, refusing to call Bull for help since Bull, on behalf of the Phippses, had just lured her trainer away. She decided instead to call Roger back. "Maybe if your dad could help us out until we get going," she said to Roger. "I know you have to leave. I would appreciate it. But if you could explain to him that I'm hiring him on an interim basis, and that if he doesn't want to stay he doesn't have to, and if I don't want to keep him I don't have to."

The arrangements were made first through Roger, acting as intermediary. Then the details of the agreement with Lucien were reached during a meeting on a rainy afternoon at the racetrack. The Meadow Stable box seat was so near the front of the section that the rain was falling into it, so Penny and Miss Ham and Lucien fumbled around for a few moments in search of a dry place to talk.

The meeting did not take long. They agreed that Lucien would be paid his usual daily rate per horse, twenty-five dollars at the time, and that he would get 10 percent of the winnings and 10 percent of all the sales he negotiated, but no salary since he was a public trainer with other clients. It was essentially the same agreement they had with Roger.

Shortly thereafter, Lucien saw the first hints of promise. Less than two weeks after taking over the stable, on June 9, he watched Riva Ridge bumped and badly beaten under Chuck Baltazar. On June 23, wheeling the horse back again, Lucien saw him run off and win by almost six lengths under Baltazar. In an allowance race he won again, whipping his field by four, and by then Lucien knew he had a horse in his barn. And so, at one point, Lucien changed his mind about retiring.

The bay was beaten in a stakes race at Aqueduct July 21, after Baltazar was forced to steady him in heavy traffic. The jockey was then suspended for a riding infraction at Aqueduct, and Lucien decided to put his fellow French Canadian, Ron Turcotte, on the colt. Ron had been working horses for Lucien in the morning. He was on Riva Ridge when he raced to his first stakes victory in the Flash on opening day at Saratoga. Turcotte knew he was connected to a live wire, telling Lucien that Riva moved with freakish ease, and Penny Tweedy began to believe she had the colt she had been waiting for, the winner who would save the farm. The day Riva Ridge won the Futurity and started his $500,000 climb to the championship was the turning point, the day she believed the pendulum was swinging upward once again.

Thus Riva Ridge became the golden boy, the ugly duckling, and the underdog, so homely, his ears twirling floppily above a gentle if not striking mien, but he moved like a deer. Iberia was her father's mare, First Landing her father's stallion, and it was as if Penny were living a storybook tale about the prince who was a horse and would save her dying father's farm if only he could get there fast enough.

Riva, as she came to call him, was her pet, her favorite, the one to whom she went first in the mornings at the barns. His homeliness only enhanced his appeal. Hollis Chenery and Mrs. Carmichael, swept up with the others in the excitement generated by the bay, flew to Louisville for the Kentucky Derby, joining the family in the ecstatic aftermath of the winner's circle at Churchill Downs. They were at Belmont Park to watch him romp by seven, rejoining the family there in the winner's circle. Riva Ridge pulled the entire family into racing, and in the days of a bearish market, made hundreds of thousands of dollars quickly. There was no more talk of selling the horses and the farm.

At the start of it all—the Thursday after Riva's victory in the Flash Stakes—Lucien and his wife Juliette took Penny Tweedy to dinner at Chez Pierre in Saratoga. That was the point at which she began genuinely to like and understand Lucien. "I realized then that this was a tremendous individual. He might not be receptive to my ideas but he knew a great deal more than I did." She would not forget that night. They had a grand time over a French dinner, drinking wine and singing and talking of Riva Ridge. And just that morning, Charlie Ross had started toying with Secretariat's ears down at The Meadow, getting the red horse ready for the bridle.

Chapter 13

In the beginning Penny resented Secretariat—resented his outrageous good looks and his physique, his first victory by six, and his promise as a two-year-old, fearing for the eminence of Riva, her golden boy.

This ambivalent feeling was essentially a contradiction of her wish to make and keep The Meadow solvent and profitable. She easily overcame it. The superstition about opening day at Saratoga was more entrenched, and she followed it north from her rented house on Long Island. A year before, Riva Ridge was running in the Flash Stakes on opening day, and she flew all night to see him run in it. She missed her connection at La Guardia, the airlines lost her bags, she was miserable, tired, and almost missed the race. She sensed then that The Meadow was coming back and that it was important for her to be there. And she didn't want to miss Secretariat's race on opening day, July 31.

"I said to myself, 'Maybe lightning is going to strike twice. You better be there.'"

Sometime in late June and July of 1972, Secretariat woke up as a racehorse, ceased being the overgrown pumpkin of a colt, and began to like the business of racing: to get with it when the gates opened, pumping the legs and the neck and tracking the leaders for a while and then—once the legs began to mesh and the rhythm took over—picking up speed, grabbing the bit, and racing hell-bent past them for the wire. Some horses loaf; others refuse to run at all; others spit out the bit and back off when they are in a fight. Others fear close contact, shying away when bumped, hemmed in, or impeded. Not Secretariat.

He began to come alive, and after his first win he started training faster, running faster and harder against the bit. Then he was off to Saratoga, traveling north by van up along the Hudson River to the historic old spa, the mile-and-an-eighth sandbox where the rich play in August, where the beams are still made of wood and the awnings at the racetrack are peppermint striped and the people eat corn on the cob and chicken in a basket.

On July 29, two days before his third start, Lucien sent Secretariat three-eighths in 0:35 under hand-urging, a sharp move at Saratoga, whose surface is not as fast as Belmont Park's. It primed the pump for Monday. Lucien had the red horse entered in the fourth race, a six-furlong sprint for two-year-olds who had never won two races. The purse was $9000, with $5400 to the winner, and he was in with six others. The feature that day was the Test Stakes, the prestigious filly race that Imperatrice and Miss Disco had won in the 1940s. About the time Penny Tweedy and Lucien Laurin headed toward the paddock and Turcotte donned the Meadow silks, one elderly turf-writer who had seen the grandmothers but never the grandson was awaiting quietly the colt's arrival for the fourth.

> The cognoscenti give Mrs. Helen Tweedy's Secretariat the nod for potentiality. He has electrifying acceleration, duende, charisma, and starfire raised to the steenth power. He also is pretty good.
>
> Charles Hatton in the July 19 *Daily Racing Form.*

Wearing tinted glasses and a summer suit, smoking mentholated cigarettes in a holder, his gray hair drawn back, his voice carried along on the soft southerlies of an old Louisville accent, Charles Hatton sat on a bench near the paddock and watched for Secretariat.

Hatton had been coming to the races for more than fifty years, working around them almost as long. His tutor was the former black slave and the rider of Ten Broeck, Billy Walker. Walker had retired as a jockey and was timing horses in Kentucky when Hatton came under his tutorial care. Billy Walker taught him the intricacies of a horse's conformation—the proper angulation of the skeletal parts, the muscular investiture, the set of the eyes and the jowls and the length of the cannon bone relative to the length of the forearm. Horses were anatomical puzzles, all of a piece but in pieces.

Hatton had no way of knowing it then as he sat on the bench, but there was a young racehorse turning the corner of the racetrack— perhaps 150 yards away—who would fulfill some ideal that he had been turning over in his head since Billy Walker put it there more than fifty years ago.

Secretariat walked down the pathway toward the paddock, toward the towering canopy of trees above the saddling area, toward Hatton, who saw the colt and came to his feet. The red horse filled Hatton's eyes of an instant, not striding into his field of vision but swimming into it, pulling Hatton from the bench to a standstill before him.

Hatton had seen thousands of horses in his life, thousands of two-year-olds, and suddenly on this July afternoon of 1972 he found the 106-carat diamond: "It was like seeing a bunch of gravel and there was the Kohinoor lying in there. It was so unexpected. I thought, 'Jesus Christ, I never saw a horse that looked like that before.'"

Hatton followed the youngster to the saddling area. "First thing I know, I look around and there was a circle of people standing there like Man o' War was being saddled," Hatton recalled.

Hatton was in momentary awe. "You carry an ideal around in your head, and boy, I thought, 'This is it.' I never saw perfection before. I absolutely could not fault him in any way. And neither could the rest of them and that was the amazing thing about it. The body and the head and the eye and the general attitude. It was just incredible. I couldn't believe my eyes, frankly. I just couldn't because I've made a kind of thing of looking at horses since before the First World War, when I was a kid, but I never saw a horse like that."

All was of a piece, in proportion, Hatton thought. Secretariat had depth of barrel, with well-sprung ribs for heart and lung room, and he was not too wide in the front fork, nor too close together, and he came packaged with tremendous hindquarters. Hatton noted the underpinnings, stunned at the straightness of the hindleg, an unusual and valuable trait—straightness, not as seen from the front or back, but rather straightness when viewed from the side, from the gaskin through the hock to the cannon bone behind. It was as straight a hindleg as Hatton had ever seen and would serve as a source of great propulsive power as it reached far under the body and propelled it forward.

The value of a straight hindleg in a thoroughbred is roughly analogous to the value of the left arm held straight in a golf swing. A straight left arm gives maximum arc to the backswing and downswing and more propulsion to the clubface, greater sweep and power with minimum effort. "This construction comes to a sort of scooting action behind," Hatton later wrote. "He gets his hind parts far under himself in action, and the drive of the hindlegs is tremendous, as he follows through like a golfer."

His eyes moving up, Hatton looked at the head. The nostrils were large, with great flaring room for breathing large quantities of air rapidly—Man o' War had enormous nostrils, too—and the wide spread between the jowls suggested that it housed an ample windpipe. The cannon bone was not too long—the longer it is, the more susceptible it is to stress and injury, as is the tendon—and the forearm above it was of good length. Hatton noticed the sloping rump, the Nearco mark, but rejected it as unimportant. That sloping rump used to be the emblem of sprinters, but the staying Nearcos had remodeled that conception. Secretariat's shoulders were powerful, and he stood slightly over at the knees—that is, seen from the side, his knees were neither concave, an anatomical disaster in a horse, nor perfectly straight, but rather slightly convex. In this particular he was fine to Hatton, slightly over to reduce the concussion of the hooves on the racetrack.

"It was the thrill of a lifetime."

Hatton and the circle of onlookers parted, stepping back as groom Mordecai Williams led Secretariat to the paddock. Turcotte joined them there, conferring briefly with Lucien on the race and the way to ride the colt. This was not a herd of nonwinners of the type he spread-eagled at Aqueduct two weeks earlier. Two of the colts, Russ Miron and Joe Iz, had shown speed, and Turcotte knew he'd have to catch them if the red horse fell back and ran as he had under Feliciano.

"Don't rush this colt," Lucien reminded him. "Let him feel his way and just come on with him. He has a particular way of running. You can't rush him."

The crowd had made Secretariat the odds-on favorite at $0.40 to $1.00, and Turcotte sat ready on him in the starting gate, clutching a handful of his coppery mane for balance when George Cassidy sprang the latch and sent them on.

Secretariat brushed the side of the gate when the doors sprang open, drifting left and brushing Fat Frank as they left the slip, and Turcotte could feel him trying to get with it. He could feel him chopping and struggling to put his mass in motion. So Turcotte sat chilly on him. Secretariat had broken alertly, but was dropping back as the field made off for the turn. Russ Miron rushed to the lead and through an opening quarter in 0:23 ⅕, with Joe Iz a head behind and on the outside of him. Turcotte eased Secretariat to the outside, giving him time to find his stride and room to move when he found it. As Russ Miron raced past the half-mile pole, Secretariat was last, trailing him by four with his own quarter in 0:24. The horses made the bend, and Turcotte had Secretariat five horses wide, giving him the worst of it but no traffic to deal with. The colt started rolling around the turn, picking up speed past the three-eighths pole and moving past Fat Frank, Court Ruling, Blackthorn, and Tropic Action in a matter of jumps, zipping along that second quarter mile in 0:22 ⅗, and moving up on Russ Miron and Joe Iz to the head of the lane. By then he was just a half a length from the lead and on the outside.

With Secretariat moving to them, Joe Iz caved in first, dropping back, and passing the three-sixteenths pole Ron reached back and hit the red colt once, right-handed. Secretariat drifted left. Turcotte switched his stick and straightened him out by rapping him once left-handed. Secretariat had Russ Miron in trouble at the eighth pole. Carlos Marquez worked on him vigorously, but Turcotte eased away from him in the final 220 yards, hand-riding to a length-and-a-half victory in 1:10 ⅘ for the six furlongs, his final quarter in 0:24 ⅕.

Now the colt began to exact more than just casual interest from horsemen. "Mrs. Tweedy," said Virginia breeder Taylor Hardin, turning to her after the race. "I'd like to apply for breeding rights to that horse. I was the first person to ask for breeding rights to Native Dancer and I was right."

Turcotte liked his race that day, too, though he would not do handsprings back to the jockeys' quarters over it. He had given the youngster the worst of the running, taking him to the high ground at the turn and giving away lengths to two fast colts. And the red horse caught them with a rush when his rider chirped to him. Secretariat ran willingly, responded to the whip, and didn't loaf when he made the lead. The early signs were good. Turcotte also recalled his heavy-headed way of running—stylistically, he was the opposite of the airy-going Riva Ridge—the way he pounded the ground as he reached out for more of it. He had beaten maidens, he had beaten nonwinners of two races, and now he would have to run against the best—the best stakes horses on the grounds, and that meant running against the undefeated Linda's Chief. Secretariat and Linda's Chief were both being aimed for the $25,000-Added Sanford Stakes August 16, another six-furlong sprint.

The tempo of Secretariat's life was accelerating, and Lucien found him thriving on it. For The Meadow, the timing was superb. Riva Ridge was beginning to fall from the heights he'd attained following the exhausting journey to Hollywood Park. On August 5, at Monmouth Park in New Jersey, he was beaten in the $100,000 Monmouth Invitational, tiring after tracking the pace to the stretch. He finished fourth, beaten by six. It was the start of a long diminution in value and prestige.

The following evening, back in Saratoga once again, Penny found herself sitting in the Wishing Well restaurant and looking across a plate of steak, corn, and potatoes at Bull Hancock. Sixty-two years old that year, Bull was the head of the most successful and prestigious breeding empire in America—Claiborne Farm—and was known as the godfather of his industry.

By 1972, his son Seth was working under him, learning the breeding business as Bull had learned it himself, from the yearlings to the broodmares to the stallions. Claiborne had become an enormous spread of acreage, growing over the years from 2100 to almost 6000 acres. Bull had added the 1050-acre Marchmont Farm, which he purchased in the estate sale of his late brother-in-law, Charlton Clay, building five new barns on it and planting trees and adding broodmares. Bull leased the 1800-acre Xalapa Farm, with its stone barn and brass-lined stalls with iron hinges, with its broodmare barn chiseled in stone and its stallion barn. Nasrullah had been his masterstroke, in retrospect, but only the beginning of his ascension as the leader in his industry. From 1955 through 1969, with the broodmare bands growing to 350 mares, America's leading sire stood annually at Claiborne—Nasrullah, Princequillo, Ambiorix, and Bold Ruler. On that August evening in 1972, there were 26 stallions standing at Claiborne, 16 of them champion racehorses either in America or abroad, and among the most famous horses in the recent history of the turf—Buckpasser, Nijinsky II, Hoist The Flag, Damascus, and Round Table.

It was a pleasant evening in a quiet town on the eve of a sudden change at Claiborne Farm and another resurge in the Meadow Stable. Bull would not be staying at Saratoga through August. He would spend a few more days at the spa, searching out yearlings for clients, playing golf, and doing some business in the booking of stallions for the coming spring. He would not be in Saratoga for the Sanford Stakes. Instead, he would fly to Scotland to shoot grouse, and he would watch the races in Ireland and fly to France to see a Claiborne horse run there.

Bull was not feeling well that evening at dinner. In fact, he complained to Penny and her friends dining with them that he felt very badly, and for the first time Penny could remember, he had only one drink of bourbon before dinner, declining a second but telling the others not to mind him, to have another. Of course, Bull had seen Secretariat run and he spoke enthusiastically about the red horse during dinner. He didn't live to see him run again.

Chapter 14

On the eve of the Sanford Stakes at Saratoga, Braulio Baeza knew about Secretariat but didn't know what to think of him. The jockey, one of the world's finest, had seen Secretariat lose his first start ("I knew he would have won that day if he hadn't gotten bothered, knew it for sure") and he saw the youngster win his second start. "But you see that too often. Horses get in trouble their first start and then they come back and win and then they don't turn out to be anything." Baeza had been impressed with Secretariat's second victory, but he was confident because he was riding a youngster—the undefeated Linda's Chief—who had already proved himself a superior runner, and consistently so, in far more compelling company than Secretariat had run against. The only colt he feared was Secretariat.

Lucien, meanwhile, did not stop cranking up his red horse through the morning hours at Saratoga. On August 11, just five days before the Sanford, Secretariat drilled five-eighths of a mile in 0:59, the fastest workout in his life. He came back dancing, and he was saddled and standing ready in the paddock for the Sanford Stakes when Lucien and Ron conferred in generalities. Lucien had never given Ron elaborate instructions for a race.

Lucien boosted him aboard. Nearby, trainer Al Scotti gave Baeza a leg up.

This was the fifty-ninth running of the $27,750 Sanford, with $16,650 to the winner, the only race Man o' War ever lost, to Upset in 1919. The crowd was not anticipating any such outlandish surprises that afternoon, making Linda's Chief the heavy favorite at $0.60 to $1.00, Secretariat the second choice at 3–2. Secretariat walked into the four hole on the backstretch, Linda's Chief beside him in the three slip. Then they were in the gate—Linda's Chief, the undefeated, standing next to Secretariat, the unknown factor.

In a moment of fury near the head of the stretch, in the space of a dozen bounds passing the three-sixteenths pole, Secretariat made his name. He broke sharply, but he was outrun in the first jumps out of the gate. It took him a little longer to get in gear. He was running last as the field assembled loosely at the far turn. Trevose led by a half length as they went the quarter in 0:22 ⅗, honest enough bidding, with stablemate Northstar Dancer joining him on the outside. Linda's Chief was bounding along in third, a length and a half in front of Sailor Go Home. Secretariat was trailing inside of Sailor Go Home, as the horses in front of him made the bend. It was a bad place to be.

Secretariat surprised Turcotte, taking longer to get rolling than the first time Ron had ridden him, and he had to steady the colt and let him drop off the leaders. This time he was falling back on his own. The pace was faster, and it seemed to Turcotte that Secretariat was having more trouble getting his things in order. "I was giving him time to find his stride," he said. Sailor Go Home drifted outside the red horse at the turn, leaving him on the rail and hemmed in to it. Up ahead, Turcotte saw the entry in front, but he couldn't swing outside; Sailor Go Home was in that lane. Nor could he drop to the rail; Trevose was holding that down.

Trevose made the straight still leading by a half, in 0:46 ⅕ at the pole, and Secretariat was right behind him a length away. Linda's Chief moved on the outside, running to the leaders. Secretariat was blocked behind the front two. Turcotte waited. Baeza drove up on the outside with Linda's Chief, taking the lead nearing midstretch, and everything happened at once.

Turcotte saw jockey Angel Cordero, riding Northstar Dancer outside Trevose, glance quickly over his right shoulder at Linda's Chief. Ron felt Secretariat grabbing hold of the bit, running powerfully against it, and he waited. Waited for Cordero to drift away from Trevose, waited for the crack to open up between the two, feeling his horse reaching for it and seeming to wait with him as they neared the eighth pole. And that was when Cordero drifted out, and then Ron turned his colt loose and chirped to him.

Secretariat exploded, driving through whatever room there was, skimming both Trevose and Northstar Dancer and driving forward like a wedge, splitting the hole and shouldering Northstar Dancer aside. His head rose as he went through, gaining speed as Turcotte pumped and sent him to the front. He led by a half length at the eighth pole, then accelerated past Linda's Chief and Baeza, who hardly knew what to make of it.

Secretariat raced the six furlongs in a sharp 1:10 flat, and in that time he remade himself into the leading two-year-old in America, not only beating the best, but doing it with a dramatic flourish, as a seasoned five-year-old horse might do it. He threw his weight around in tight quarters. He bulled about the racetrack. He won by three.

Penny Tweedy, prodding Lucien, said to him, "Well, there's *one* horse that came from off the farm that's not afraid of going between other horses." Lucien had not spoken well of Riva Ridge's training at The Meadow, telling her that the farm training was incomplete and had made the bay timid of other horses.

Alfred Vanderbilt walked over to the Meadow Stable box, leaned over and said, "I wasn't worried about your horse, I was worried about those other poor horses." Trainer P. G. Johnson, shaking his head, mused aloud, "I've seen a lot of races and it makes you think. Now, Linda's Chief is a horse of quality, and Secretariat just took him apart, undressed him, beat him all to hell."

Up in the press box, Art Kennedy had not seen anything like it, and days later he was still speaking incredulously that a two-year-old with only three lifetime starts would even conceive of doing anything so bold as splitting two horses as he did.

Charles Hatton left the clubhouse turn a man in search of a metaphor. He rummaged around in print for the next few weeks before finally settling on one he liked. On August 18, in his daily column, Hatton had his first chance to comment on the Sanford, and he wrote:

> In the race, the Tweedy colt proved himself a positive thinker. He required just 1:10, swiftest time of the meeting, to spot unbeaten Linda's Chief and the others two lengths' running start, then simply pulverized them a last quarter in :23 ⁴/₅. Coming to the quarter pole, he lowered his head and hunched his shoulders, like "Orange Juice" Simpson plunging the line and scattering a bunch of rookies from the second team.

A week later, Hatton wrote:

In action he can be terrifying. He swoops down on his field like a monster in a horror movie, and in the Sanford he left shambles of them reeling around the racetrack.

While Charlie Hatton emerged as Secretariat's most loyal and ardent cheerleader in print, Lucien Laurin seemed to be having trouble believing what was taking place. Only a year ago, he abandoned the idea of retirement, and Riva Ridge had yet to win the Futurity. Since then there had been Riva Ridge's victory at the Kentucky Derby, the race Lucien always wanted to win, the galling disappointment of the Preakness, and the victory in the Belmont. He had just missed winning the Triple Crown, but in doing so he had reached his professional summit. Now, in August at Saratoga, Lucien saddled a horse who ran as if he had classic dimensions to him, a colt combative to a degree rarely seen in thoroughbreds and almost never in two-year-olds.

Nothing at a racetrack seems to stir imaginations more than the sudden rise of a two-year-old. The Kentucky Derby is no sooner over one year than the search begins for the winner of the next—the Triple Crown candidate and the champion three-year-old. The older horses grind each other down, beating each other week after week, and the fillies and the sprinters dash; the grass horses drive for the American turf championship, and the three-year-olds head into summer with the Derby behind them. But nothing matches seeing and discovering a baby with a future.

Secretariat's workouts, like those of Riva Ridge, were events. Despite the streak of apathy Turcotte sensed in him, Secretariat thrived on work, and he devoured his hay and oats and sweet feed and mash after even strenuous workouts, never backing off his feed cup, never missing an oat. He bloomed to a spectacular sheen in the Saratoga sun, gleaming on Tuesday morning, August 22, when Ron climbed aboard him for his only serious workout between the Sanford and Hopeful stakes.

Secretariat was feeling sharp, jumping around as Mordecai Williams led him out. Eddie Sweat then walked out Riva Ridge. Riva Ridge was scheduled to gallop that morning, Secretariat to work a fast half mile. Lucien and Penny posted themselves along the wooden fence on the backstretch and watched for Secretariat. Lucien had his stopwatch in his right hand as Riva Ridge galloped slowly past. Heads followed him, turning in silence.

Around the bend, coming to the backstretch, Turcotte galloped

Secretariat slowly. The colt's neck was bowed slightly, and he was following about a half mile behind Riva Ridge. The symbolism was not lost on Lucien, and Secretariat, nearing the half-mile pole, galloped past. As Secretariat reached for the wire in the distance, Laurin snapped the watch and grinned. He caught Secretariat in 0:46 ⅖ for the half, just a fifth of a second slower than Trevose went the first half in the Sanford.

As usual, following a day of a workout, Secretariat walked inside the shed on Wednesday, but on Thursday Williams saddled the colt for a slow gallop around the racetrack. Jimmy Gaffney, as usual, climbed on the colt. It was just past eight o'clock, and it was an idyllic day, one of those Saratoga mornings when bacon smoke filled the air around the stable kitchen and mash for the oats was cooking in the giant tubs, sending the aroma of oatmeal through the barns and wafting toward the backstretch.

Out the gap to the main track, turning right, the colt moved off at a canter, around the turn for home, past the empty grandstand and clubhouse, past the crowds eating ham and eggs and French toast, around the clubhouse turn, and toward the backstretch. Secretariat was galloping easily. Gaffney neared the pole and started easing him to a walk.

Secretariat was dancing as they neared the gap in the fence leading to the barn, frisky and alert to things around him. That half-mile workout had screwed him up tight, and the colt was simply full of himself.

A van driver, climbing into the cab parked by the backstretch fence, slammed the door behind him. Secretariat stopped, stiffening and bowing his neck. He looked at the van and snorted. Motors made Secretariat especially spooky, Gaffney had noticed at Belmont Park. The colt would duck sharply from tractors chugging along pulling furrows on the racetrack.

"Please don't start the truck!" Gaffney shouted.

But the window was closed, and the van driver couldn't hear him. As the diesel fired up, Secretariat ducked out from under him and Gaffney dropped six feet to the very seat of his pants on the racetrack, the bridle still in his left hand. Secretariat took off through the gap toward the barn. Gaffney held on. Secretariat picked up speed bolting through the stable area, and Gaffney remembered the wet dew on the grass as the horse drew him across it like a sled. Secretariat gained speed. Trees rushed by. Finally Gaffney let the colt loose.

Secretariat kept running, disappearing behind a barn, running toward the Meadow Stable, reins flapping.

Gaffney jumped up and headed after him, reaching the stable minutes later. Lucien was ashen. Secretariat was still loose and running around. It took ten minutes to catch him at another stable.

"Jimmy, you just took ten years off my life," Lucien said.

"You? He took fifteen off mine. He's quick."

Chapter 15

Late in the afternoon on the day of the Hopeful Stakes, Lucien Laurin stepped beneath a giant elm in the Saratoga paddock and waited for Secretariat. He was smoking a cigarette and was wrapped in a splash of colors—a red plaid sports coat, white shirt and pants, white shoes, and a white and purple tie. Lucien smoked only when he felt the pressure of the game closing around him, as he did now, with half an hour to post for the Hopeful Stakes.

Traditionally, Saratoga is where the finest racing stables in America have first tried their untested two-year-olds. The $75,000-Added Hopeful, the last stakes race run at Saratoga, is the meeting's crowning touch, an important event that has been won by many horses who went on to greater fame—Man o' War, Whirlaway, Battlefield, Native Dancer, Nashua, Hail to Reason, and Buckpasser. Several horses who finished second in the Hopeful later made major contributions to the American stud—including Fair Play, the sire of Man o' War, the great Bull Lea, and Tom Fool, sire of Buckpasser—as have colts who finished third, such as Discovery, Turn-to, and Sir Gaylord.

Everyone congregated under the tree—the fans, the horsemen, the owners, and the simply curious—waiting to see the colt everyone was talking about. Penny was there, and so were Ogden Phipps and his son, Ogden Mills Phipps, a friendly bear of a man with a pug nose and freckles and a love of speed: power boats and running horses. Ogden Mills Phipps had come to see the full brother to The Bride, the filly his family picked when they won the toss but lost the horse —a good-looking filly with no speed.

More than a hundred people crowded in a circle around the tree when Secretariat was led across the walking ring and through the crowd. His coat was dappling in the sun—a sign of radiant health —and as he strode to the walking ring around the tree there were cameras clicking and choruses of "ooohhhs" and "ahhhhhhs," as at the unveiling of a statue.

Turcotte thought the race was a cinch for Secretariat. Conditions in the race favored the colt. Linda's Chief was not in the field, and Secretariat was coming off a sharp race and a fast work. The distance was 110 yards farther than the Sanford, and Turcotte felt the extra yards would simply give the colt that much more time to catch the leaders. For Turcotte the Hopeful became more than an ordinary race. It had an emotional sweep and cadence to it, becoming a 1:16 ⅕ dash in which his feelings swept from near panic to desperation to a sense of awe.

Secretariat broke from the gate with the field, emerging with the others as the gate popped open, but immediately Turcotte felt him floundering as he tried to pick up speed.

"He was trying to run, trying to get with it and get in his best stride, but he just couldn't."

He fell back to last as Sunny South scooted to the lead, with Brandford Court a neck behind in second on the outside, Step Nicely tucked away in third, Trevose nearby with River of Fire and Flight to Glory tracking them. They strung out racing for the turn, and the red horse bounded along in last.

Turcotte never rushed him a step. He thought the colt was doing his best but having problems getting all the parts to mesh. He was still an overgrown kid. Turcotte sat tight and clucked to him, trying to give him encouragement. As they charged the turn, running on top of it past the five-eighths pole, Turcotte sensed the colt was still having problems and he started thinking that he had to move soon. He was riding a prohibitive favorite, and already the turn was looming up ahead.

"I wasn't panicky, but I was thinking, 'My God, pick it up! Will ya?'"

Then, as the nine horses raced through the opening quarter mile, Sunny South dragging them through it in 0:22 ⅘, Turcotte suddenly felt the colt pulling himself together, taking hold of the bit.

So he coaxed Secretariat, chirping to him, cajoled him, tapping his shoulder with the stick, and asked him for more speed, pumping him and urging him on. They went to the half-mile pole. The crowd stirred as Sunny South raced in front on the turn and track announcer Dave Johnson called out loudly over the speakers: "Secretariat is the trailer as they pass the half-mile pole!"

Then the move began. It was a powerful move, dramatic and compelling to see, devastating in the scope of its execution. In an instant the crowd was on its feet. Driving past the half-mile pole—two, three, perhaps four bounds past it—Secretariat suddenly leveled out under Turcotte, who sensed a lowering of the mass, as if the colt had found the gear, and took off as no two-year-old had ever done under Turcotte before. The jockey steered him to the outside and sat quietly feeling the surge.

Secretariat moved to the field with a rush, accelerating outside as they made the bend, without urging from Turcotte, bounding along as if independent of whatever momentum the race possessed, independent of its pace and tempo, independent of the shifting, slow-motion struggles unfolding within it, the small battles for position and advantage. But Secretariat was not responding to any force the race was generating, but rather moving as though he'd evolved his own kinetic field beyond it, and Turcotte would later recall sitting quietly and feeling awed.

From the clubhouse, where Vanderbilt and Laurin fastened their binoculars on him, Secretariat emerged for the first time as a spectacle in the sport, overpowering in his manner of performance. He ran to his horses in bunches and singly, first to Torsion and then to Flight to Glory and then to River of Fire as he headed around the bend for the three-eighths pole, the blue and white blocks disappearing as he swept past them on the outside, reappearing again in the gaps between them, disappearing again behind Trevose and Step Nicely. Measuring Stop the Music and Brandford Court, he raced into view again, but quickly disappeared behind them. He was sprinting his quarter mile in less than 0:22, as he charged to the throat of Sunny South, who was racing on the lead.

It was executed that quickly, startling veteran horsemen by the brilliance of it and leaving Lucien Laurin watching in disbelief.

The red horse raced from last to first over about 290 yards of ground not passing a single horse until he'd raced well past the half-mile pole. He was already moving to the lead nearing the five-sixteenths pole. It was a spectacular sweep.

He turned for home two lengths in front, and the rest was simply a mop-up. He widened on Flight to Glory through the lane, winning by five and missing Bold Lad's track mark by three-fifths of a second.

As Secretariat's audacity in the Sanford first drew serious attention to him, his run in the Hopeful made him the most exciting racehorse in New York. He had come to Saratoga the winner only of a maiden race at Aqueduct. He promptly won three races in twenty-seven days and returned to Long Island the leading two-year-old in America, the heir apparent to Riva Ridge. The Sanford and the Hopeful turned everything around. No one was saying now that the Meadow Stable could not do it a second year in succession.

Among the believers was Penny Tweedy, convinced by witnessing the Hopeful Stakes that the Meadow Stable owned its second two-year-old champion in succession. "I was perfectly sure that, barring accident, this horse was going on and we were going to have another year like we had last year."

It was then she began to hope that her father—oblivious to life around him in the hospital, unaware of the existence of Secretariat—would live to the end of the year. "All along I had been praying that he would die because his life had become meaningless. There was nothing left of the man I knew except a shell, a 90-pound shell, and once he could no longer speak there was less and less left." Chris Chenery had been in New Rochelle Hospital for four and a half years, and during that time he had deteriorated from a 210-pound man to a childlike invalid, bedridden and helpless.

Then suddenly, with the rise of Secretariat, Chenery's life acquired a new meaning. If he had died in September, the heavy inheritance tax imposed on the estate would have forced the heirs to syndicate Secretariat immediately. Penny believed there would have been irresistible pressure on her to syndicate the horse, since he was a son of the prepotent Bold Ruler, whose sons were already proving exceptional sires. The selling of Secretariat would have been premature in September, the timing of it wrong.

Penny did not feel she could have asked a syndicate for the right to race the horse to the end of 1972 and then through 1973, the first year syndicate members would expect to breed mares to the horse. So she foresaw Secretariat breeding on the farm, not competing at the track, if her father died that autumn. Moreover, off the Sanford and the Hopeful Stakes, she thought the red horse was going to win the same string of rich two-year-old races Riva Ridge had won in 1971—the Futurity, the Champagne Stakes, the Laurel Futurity, and the Garden State Stakes. This would give him the champion two-year-old honors of 1972, giving him a multimillion dollar value as a potential sire on the bloodstock market. He could not have commanded such a price after the Hopeful Stakes.

She had not learned painlessly the lessons of selling horses at their maximum financial potential. Earlier in the autumn, at the Keeneland yearling sales, she had been offered $1,250,000 for Upper Case, the pretty-boy son of Round Table–Bold Experience. While Riva Ridge was working toward the Kentucky Derby, Upper Case actually developed into one of America's leading three-year-olds. He won the $100,000 Florida Derby at Gulfstream Park in Florida, then came back and won the prestigious $100,000 Wood Memorial at Aqueduct. Penny turned down the offer and she soon regretted it. Upper Case tailed off on the racetrack; he seemed to lose interest in his work. When he started losing, his value plummeted. "We finally sold him for $750,000, and very gratefully," Penny said. "I have been playing two games: one is to get the horses to win and the other is to recognize their peak and sell them at their peak." The trick is to figure out when horses are performing at optimal potential on the racetrack and, if the wish is to sell, to sell then. Secretariat was not yet for sale.

"So I was really just praying in my heart that dad would last through December. Then we could syndicate Secretariat with the right to race him through 1973; I just didn't think the chances of being allowed to race him a full year would be any good if dad died in the fall. They would have sent him to the breeding shed that spring. I wanted him to get to his three-year-old year so I could say, 'He hasn't broken down—he's at the peak of his powers, his full potential—and we shouldn't retire him now.' I wanted maximum potential financially from Secretariat because it would enable us to keep the farm and not have to sell the broodmares when dad died."

Chris Chenery lived through the fall of 1972, and through the rich series of two-year-old races—from the $144,200 Futurity through the $298,665 Garden State Stakes—the red horse built upon his record in the Sanford and the Hopeful, embellishing it as the distances grew longer. As a son of Bold Ruler, of course, his stamina would always be suspect, and so would his soundness. In fact later, whenever Secretariat first walked or jogged of mornings on the racetrack, he had a kind of crabbed, stiff way of moving that made horsemen wince when they saw him, reminding them of his rheumatic sire, who walked like an elderly man until he limbered up at the barn. Rumors of unsoundness would follow the red horse for months, none of them substantiated. The colt gave no indication of soreness in the way he raced that autumn through the last four races.

Groom Mordecai Williams was leaning against the reins and almost walking on his heels, holding fast to Secretariat—as they rose from the underground tunnel at Belmont Park between the stables and the paddock, and together went to the Futurity.

If trainer Johnny Campo and the others had a chance to beat Secretariat that fall, as it would turn out in the end, the chance was in the Futurity. Lucien had Turcotte work the colt seven-eighths in 1:24 following the Hopeful Stakes, then came back later for a five-furlong blowout in company with Gold Bag, jockey Jorge Velasquez aboard. As the two men took the youngsters to the racetrack, Lucien told them to let the colts ramble.

"Let him run as fast as he can without abusing him," Lucien told Turcotte. "Don't kill him."

Velasquez had a long lead as he broke Gold Bag past the five-eighths pole, and Turcotte let the red horse run to catch him. Turning into the stretch, having cut the lead to five lengths behind Gold Bag, Turcotte lashed Secretariat twice right-handed, and the colt plunged down the straight. He caught Gold Bag at the sixteenth pole and opened six by the time they hit the wire, running the five-eighths in 0:58, the fastest workout of the day at that distance. It was a sensational move.

"Ronnie, you worked too fast," Lucien scolded. "He's only a baby and I think you asked too much of him."

On Saturday it almost made the difference. A crowd of 34,248 people made the colt the odds-on favorite at $0.20 to $1.00, and he ran to pattern at the start. Swift Courier went to the lead down the backside, Secretariat dropping back to sixth. He was not running well. The racetrack was clodding under horses' hooves, and as he trailed them down the backstretch, hard clods flew up and struck him in the face, causing him to climb with his front legs, rather than reach out with them. So Turcotte swung him to the outside, and Secretariat leveled out, racing the opening quarter in 0:23 ⁴/₅, six lengths behind Swift Courier in 0:22 ³/₅. Around the far turn, picking up speed and staying outside, Secretariat moved closer to the pace, passing Gallant Knave as they banked for home. He was rushing the second quarter in 0:22 ³/₅, and as Swift Courier turned for home, the colt was looping the field and losing ground. Sweeping into the stretch, Secretariat passed Stop the Music and Crimson Falcon. Then he raced to Whatabreeze and Swift Courier, and coming to the eighth pole, in midstretch, he drove past them and drew out by two.

Laffit Pincay, Jr., on Stop the Music, had set out after him, and in the closing seconds he gained some ground. Seeing Pincay, Turcotte went to the whip.

Secretariat won it by one and three-quarters lengths, Stop the Music finishing second.

Penny met the red horse at the top of Victory Lane, just as Mrs. Phipps had met Bold Ruler after his Futurity victory sixteen years before.

The crowd, pressed against the iron fencing, clapped and whistled over flower boxes as Secretariat walked down the path toward the winner's circle. He moved docilely along it, unruffled by the gathering commotion of the moment, by the people waving and clustering around him. Turning his head, he dabbed his nose on Penny's blue and brown print dress, leaving a speck of mud on it. Penny wiped it off.

"He had to lose so much ground on the turn!" she said to Turcotte.

Across the jockeys' room, Turcotte sat on the bench in front of his locker, betraying none of his concern about the race, answering questions in a cool, curt way. It had not gone as well as he had expected. Secretariat had tired at the end of the race, and that plainly worried Turcotte, raising questions in his mind whether the colt would go a mile, whether he might be a stretch-running sprinter: when horses win with bursts of late speed, passing horses around the turn and through the stretch, they create the sometimes mistaken impression that the longer the distances, the better they will perform. That is not necessarily so. There are stretch-running sprinters who would not have the stamina to run farther than six furlongs.

Turcotte had to hustle him in midstretch, hit him left-handed. But the colt had not won off, as he had in the Hopeful. Stop the Music was gaining on him. "I felt like he might hang going a mile and a half," Ron said. "The race left me in doubt about his going a mile."

Tired or not, Secretariat had won his fifth straight race, running just two-fifths behind the track record of 1:16 flat, and had earned the largest purse in his life, $82,320. Up in the trustees' room after the race, Penny called her father's room at New Rochelle Hospital. She spoke briefly to Chenery's nurse.

"We won!" Penny said, hearing the nurse's voice.

"Yes. We know." She said she believed Chenery understood.

Penny said, "This is a birthday present for dad and I hope he understands. Tell him happy birthday."

Chenery was eighty-six that day.

For others close to Secretariat, though, this was not a day for toasts and celebrations.

The doctors believed at first that Bull had pleurisy. He became ill on the hunting trip to Scotland, after leaving Saratoga, and they flew him home to Vanderbilt Medical Center in Nashville. On August 28 —opening day at Belmont Park—he underwent surgery. They found cancer. He died seventeen days later, on September 14.

Graveside services for Bull were held at four-thirty on Saturday afternoon, at about the same time Lucien was saddling Secretariat in New York for the Futurity—and among the family of mourners in Paris Cemetery were Bull's Sons, Arthur III, an independent breeder with a farm down the road from Claiborne, and twenty-three-year-old Seth, who would now assume the business of running the empire of Claiborne Farm, as Bull had assumed it from his father, and his father had assumed it before him.

Chapter 16

By late afternoon of October 14, the one hundred-first running of the Champagne Stakes at Belmont Park, bettors gathered in search of the horse that could beat Secretariat going a flat mile. Life in the nearby suburbs may be as predictable as the appearance of the yellow school bus at eight o'clock in the morning, but nothing is odds-on in Long Island City.

The pattern had been set. Lucien gave Ron no instructions in the paddock as Secretariat and eleven other horses circled the walking ring. The tactic of giving Secretariat time to pull himself together had been working flawlessly, and neither man wanted to tinker with it. For the first time in his life, Secretariat would be running as an entry with Ed Whittaker's Angle Light, also trained by Lucien, who won his first start by three-quarters of a length, his second by six. He finished fourth in the Cowdin Stakes, tiring, but now he was back again. Lucien's opinion had changed since Saratoga: he no longer regarded Angle Light as Secretariat's equal, and throughout that fall, Penny would remember, Lucien assured her that Angle Light had "cheap speed"—could not sustain his speed under pressure—while also warning her not to underestimate the horse. Since he trained both, according to the rules, they would have to run as a single betting interest. Together, they went off as 2–3 favorites.

Breaking from the four hole, staying with the field in the first jump, Secretariat thrashed about as usual and immediately dropped to last. He had just one horse beaten as Angle Light swept Chuck Baltazar through an opening quarter mile in 0:22 ⅘, then through a blazing half mile in 0:45 ⅕. Angle Light was leading by two as he passed the half-mile pole at the turn, and Secretariat was running ninth behind Stop the Music under John (Gentleman John) Rotz. Secretariat raced along in 0:47, then just settled into the drumbeat of his stride. Ron kept him outside the horses once again, about fifteen feet off the rail, and he dashed past Zaca Spirit in several bounds. The colt was running his third quarter in 0:23 ⅗, even losing ground, and it was sweeping him into the hunt midway at the turn. Angle Light chucked it on the bend, looking for a hole in the fence before the straight, and Puntilla made the lead with Linda's Chief lapped on him in second. They ran as a team, as did Secretariat and Stop the Music turning for home. When Secretariat moved to Stop the Music on the turn, Rotz sent the little bay with him, not letting the red horse loose. Turcotte later said that Stop the Music drifted out on him, bumping him twice.

They moved to the lane as a team, head and head on the outside, turning for home with a quarter mile to go. The drive was on. Together, Secretariat on the outside and Stop the Music on his left, they moved to Linda's Chief and Puntilla down the straight. Coming to the three-sixteenths pole, with about 350 yards to run, they were four abreast. It was an eyepopper.

Suddenly, Turcotte raised his right hand and lashed Secretariat once. A second later the red horse, who had been running on his right lead, switched to his left lead. He dropped to the left toward Stop the Music, bumping him and sending him into Linda's Chief. Turcotte loosened his left line and snatched him sharply with his right, pulling him off the bay, who seemed to suck back at the buffeting, as if intimidated by it. Once Turcotte had Secretariat straight, he went to riding him again, and the colt pulled away as Turcotte rode him strongly to the wire. He won it in a drive by two, lengthening his lead through the final yards and running the mile in 1:35 flat, just two-fifths of a second slower than the stakes' record set by Vitriolic, one of the Bold Rulers who failed to light up the sky as a three-year-old. Stop the Music, recovering from the contact, came on again and finished second. Moments after the horses crossed the line, the roar went up. On the tote board in the infield, the inquiry sign was flashing. The stewards called it, suspecting a foul, and quickly went down the elevator to their offices, ready to talk to jockeys and to see the film.

Turcotte went to see the stewards and explain his side of the race.

Still in his blue and white silks, he stood before the stewards in their carpeted office complex and told them that Stop the Music started the contact sports on the turn for home.

"Stop the Music bumped me twice around the turn," he told them. He further said that the colt switched leads near the three-sixteenths pole and came in on the Greentree Stable colt. "I might have bothered him some, but I grabbed my horse real quick. I hurt my horse more than his."

"We'll look at it," said one steward.

The films do not show what, if any, interference the little bay might have caused on the turn. They do show that Secretariat swung into Stop the Music near the three-sixteenths pole, bumping and forcing him into Linda's Chief, and that Turcotte hauled him off immediately.

The second roar from the crowd of 31,494 persons was louder than the first. Secretariat's number, 1A, and Stop the Music's number, 5, had been blinking off and on to show the order of their finish was under inquiry. If the lights stop blinking and the numbers stay lit, it means the order of finish remains as it was in the race; if the lights of the two numbers go dark, it means that the stewards have changed the official finish of the race. The lights went out. Turcotte sat stunned in the jockeys' room wearing precisely the look of a man who had just lost 10 percent of an $87,900 purse, slowly shaking his head and staring in silence at the new order of finish, then the replay of the race on television. About twenty riders gathered in a circle around the set, looking and watching while Secretariat settled down at the turn and began his move.

The stewards placed Secretariat second, moving Stop the Music into first, and left behind not only hundreds of groaning favorite players—Secretariat would have paid $3.40 to win for a $2.00 bet—but the general belief that the best horse lost by Order of the Stewards. "I was surprised that the stewards were so strict with us for what seemed like a minor impediment," Penny said. "Our horse had so clearly won."

Nathaniel J. Hyland, the steward appointed by the Jockey Club, said simply that the stewards, when deliberating over an inquiry, do not speculate whether a horse might have won if a foul had not occurred. That Secretariat would have won (which was the consensus) was beside the point. The point was that Secretariat had committed an infraction, bumping a horse and bothering him, and evidence of that and that alone justified bringing his number down.

Despite the official order of finish, despite his sudden loss of $8700, Ron Turcotte was buoyed by the colt's performance and enormously encouraged by it. "He ran his best race to date," he said that afternoon while dressing to go home. "You never know until you try a mile, but after what I saw today—yes, he'll go on in longer distances." He knew he was not riding a stretch-running sprinter. The red horse, coming off his six furlongs in 1:10 ⅗, zipped the last quarter mile in 0:24 ⅖.

Through autumn, while Secretariat rose to dominate the nation's two-year-olds and each race added more extravagantly to his superiority, Riva Ridge went on sliding toward Laurel, Maryland, last stop before The Meadow and a winter's rest. On September 20, seven weeks after finishing fourth in the Monmouth Handicap, Riva Ridge hooked a buzz saw in the 1971 Kentucky Derby winner, Canonero II, in the Stymie Handicap at Belmont Park. Riva Ridge set a sizzling pace through most of the mile and an eighth, frying himself to a golden brown by the eighth pole, and Canonero ran off to win by five and tie the world's record of 1:46 ⅕ for the distance. Riva Ridge, carrying thirteen pounds more than Canonero, finished second. Ten days later, he finished fourth in the mile-and-a-half Woodward Stakes, more than six lengths behind his archrival Key to the Mint.

Just six months ago he had been the reigning champion of his generation in Florida, the best three-year-old in America, the luminary of shed row. After the Kentucky Derby, the Belmont Stakes, and the Hollywood Derby, he was everyone's three-year-old of the year, the leading contender for Horse of the Year. By September 20, he was just Riva Ridge—fourth, second, and fourth in his last three starts. He was a tired pug whose managers had found too many fights for him, and they did not let up. Lucien entered him in the Jockey Club Gold Cup at two miles. That was for October 28, the day of the rich Laurel Futurity at Laurel Race Course in Maryland, the first time Secretariat would run a mile and one-sixteenth.

Riva Ridge's groom, Eddie Sweat, took Secretariat to Laurel within a week of the race. Sweat had been working for Lucien since the early 1950s, and he was Lucien's most trusted groom, the one to whom he gave the most responsibility. Sweat not only mucked out stalls and groomed and fed his horses, he also drove Lucien's red van, chauffeuring horses cross country—he delivered Secretariat to Laurel that fall. Charlie Davis, who regularly galloped Riva Ridge, also went with Secretariat to Laurel, replacing Gaffney, who couldn't afford to leave his job as a mutuel clerk to exercise the colt. The move to Laurel divided the Meadow Team, as Penny came to call it. Lucien went to Maryland for the Futurity. Turcotte, given his choice, opted to ride Secretariat instead of Riva Ridge, applying his rule to stay with a two-year-old rather than an older horse. Henny Hoeffner stayed behind, to train the stable of horses in Lucien's absence and to saddle Riva Ridge. Penny chose to stay in New York, too, and watch the old golden boy try to get the two miles of the cup.

Penny's life had become a swirl of activity ever since Riva Ridge won the Flash, and the centrifugal force of it was pulling her away from home and drawing her closer to the farm and horses, to her new career in racing. She had wanted a career in the sport, and first Riva Ridge and now Secretariat were demanding her time, thought, and presence. Her involvement in the racing stable had been gradual, not precipitate, so it only slowly altered her relationship with her husband. In late May 1971, she actually considered putting her career with the horses before the wishes of her husband when Roger Laurin had decided to quit and she wanted to be in New York to look for a new trainer. But that would have meant being away from home in Denver for their anniversary. She stopped short of asking him. "It would have precipitated a terrible fight, so I didn't," she recalled. "There is a subtle thing, a point at which I started saying I have to go to New York because of this or that and I can't be with the family for such and such an occasion. Wives work around the demands of their husbands and children. I stopped doing that. I started saying, 'What I have to do is important, too, and I will do it even if it means missing something.'"

When Riva Ridge was racing to the two-year-old championship in the fall of 1971, Penny said, she sat down with her husband one day and asked him whether he could tolerate her moving to New York for six months. The Chenery house in Pelham was empty—with her mother dead and her father hospitalized—so she would have a place to live. "I wanted to follow Riva's career and try to organize the stable so there would be an orderly transition into the estate, and Jack sort of gave an equivocal answer: 'Well, that might work, but what are John and I going to do out there?'" John is their youngest child, then ten.

Jack Tweedy found a job in New York, partly to accommodate her involvement in racing, and she joined him in Pelham in April 1972, just before Riva Ridge won the Kentucky Derby. They moved to a rented home in Cold Spring Harbor later that year, then into the house in Laurel Hollow on September 1, 1972, the week after Secretariat won the Hopeful.

With the rise of Secretariat, naturally the intensity of Penny's involvement quickened. After years of raising four children and responding to the demands of that way of life, she was now asserting her independence, putting herself and her career first. "Once I stopped putting Jack first in terms of plans, I stopped putting him first emotionally," she said. "And that has really been the cut-off point. The more involved I got with racing, the less room there was for him in my life." The day of the Gold Cup conflicted with Parents Day at Saint Paul's, where young John was going to prep school. "Jack went up alone and he was quite resentful that I wouldn't go with him, and I said, 'There will be other Parents Days but there won't be other Gold Cups.'"

So Penny remained in New York, reading Lucien's instructions on riding the horse to jockey Jorge Velasquez in the paddock. She smiled and read them softly to Jorge, the small white paper in her hand, and he listened like a graduate student in theology. The strategy didn't work. Nothing would have worked by then. Riva Ridge stayed close to the pace and then tired, drifting back to nowhere, to third place, eighteen lengths behind Autobiography, three lengths behind archrival Key to the Mint, who would be named the three-year-old champion. So the fall of the bay and the rise of the red horse continued. Forty minutes earlier that afternoon at Laurel, Maryland, Secretariat ran the race of his young life.

He came to the Futurity light on his feet, up on his toes, just where Lucien put him when he sent him five-eighths in 1:00 flat in a workout at Laurel, a racetrack not as fast as Belmont Park. Five other colts, including Stop the Music and Angle Light, went to the post with him, and for the first time in his life he ran in the mud, over a sloppy surface. But nothing seemed to bother him, to discourage him or make any impression on him.

Secretariat went his own way again, just as he had in his other starts, trying to pick up speed out of the gate and falling back to last as the field made the first turn. Ron, sensing that the racing strip was less tiring on the outside, parked himself there and waited. Rocket Pocket, a horse with a quick turn of early foot, dashed to the lead and led past the opening quarter by three, running it in 0:22 ⅘. He was not dragging it. Secretariat passed the pole in 0:25 ⅖, thirteen lengths to the rear. The leader kept up the pressure through the half, racing it in 0:45 ⅘, while Secretariat was just getting with it through a half in 0:47 ⅘, his second quarter mile in 0:22 ⅖, three full seconds faster than his first. He was beginning to roll. Turcotte could feel him pick it up and relax down the backstretch.

Leaving the backstretch and heading into the far turn, Ron let out a notch, chirping to the colt, and he closed ground quickly. His neck outstretched, still pounding heavy-headedly, his legs smashing at the slop, Secretariat banked around the turn for the leaders. Rocket Pocket was tiring through his third quarter in 0:25 ⅗, and Secretariat was just three lengths behind him. They were turning into the stretch. Rocket Pocket quit suddenly. Stop the Music lay third coming to the lane. And Turcotte still had not let his red horse loose. He was a length astern of Stop the Music, who was closing toward the lead. Then Ron chirped to him, let out a notch of line, and felt the colt reach out, blowing past Rotz and Stop the Music with a tremendous rush. He opened one, then two lengths, then three through the lane, five as they reached the eighth pole. Turcotte had stopped clucking by then and was taking the colt in hand as the youngster stretched his lead to six lengths nearing the sixteenth pole, to seven passing it, and then to eight as he raced for the wire. It was his easiest victory so far, and Turcotte would believe later it was his finest performance as a two-year-old. The colt lagged far behind early, but Ron sensed he could have made the lead when he wanted to make it, no rush—untouched by the whip, winning easily in hand, Secretariat raced the mile and a sixteenth in 1:42 ⅘, just a fifth off the Laurel track record, and won $83,395.

Riva Ridge ran progressively worse. He was shipped to Laurel for the $150,000 Washington, D.C., International Stakes on November 11, over Laurel's soft turf course, so-called, at one and one-half miles. He went to the lead under Velasquez and promptly bobbled in a hole going into the backstretch, almost falling. But that only hastened what already appeared inevitable that afternoon. He finished sixth, some thirty-eight lengths behind Droll Role. Riva Ridge was returned to The Meadow not long after the Washington fiasco, earning a long rest but no titles that year, and kept from the races for six months.

Secretariat, in spite of the growth of a small splint on one foreleg —probably the effect of hard pounding on hard racetracks—was shipped off to Garden State for the $298,665 Garden State Stakes at a mile and a sixteenth. Splints, which can be painful, are small, round, bony growths that occur between the splint and cannon bones. They are not unusual in young horses, and Secretariat's was extremely small, giving no one any special concern. The red horse appeared to have the race at his mercy, with $179,199 going to the winner, and the treatment could certainly wait for that, for when the colt began his long winter rest.

Not all went smoothly at Garden State Park. Lucien, at his best when forced to improvise, was at his best again. He put Ron's brother, Rudy, on Secretariat for a three-quarter-mile workout. Lucien wanted the colt to run the last part of it, to finish out in about 1:15. He was nowhere close. Fearing Secretariat might work too fast, Rudy broke him off cautiously, taking a strong hold of him. All was kindly in the morning, Secretariat took himself back, almost to a gallop, and finished out the work about four seconds too slow and not nearly sharp enough.

Lucien arranged for Ron to be in Garden State to work the red horse seven-eighths of a mile just four days later. Thus Lucien improvised. Lucien had his champion walk two days, gallop two more, and on the Wednesday before the Saturday, he wound him up tighter and Secretariat woke up ticking on Saturday.

Angle Light joined Secretariat in a race for the third time that year, and the customers sent them off at 1–10 against four others. Both were ready. Angle Light had worked sharply for the race, actually beating Secretariat in their final half-mile drill, just as he had been doing, off and on, since the winter past. Rudy Turcotte was on him in the Garden State, and when the gates sprang open he let the youngster breathe on the pacesetting Piamem from the outset.

The two ran head and head through a casual first quarter at 0:24 ⅕, relaxing around the first turn. Ron Turcotte, meanwhile, was taking a hold of Secretariat through a galloping first-quarter in 0:26 ⅕, trotting-horse time, when it dawned on him that he might have blown the race already. He thought he had taken Secretariat too far back behind too slow a pace, and began to hope he could gain on speed horses, like Angle Light, whose edges had not been dulled by a quick opener. Secretariat was ten lengths behind at the end of that trotting-horse quarter, but Ron was chirping and feeling him pick up speed through the second 440 yards. He dashed through it in 0:23, a move that left him eight lengths behind Angle Light, who was also accelerating his pace. Angle Light pressured Piamem as the two went the half in 0:47 ⅖. The pace was realistic now. Holding the tempo, sustaining his speed, Secretariat moved past Step Nicely and Knightly Dawn down the backside.

Going into and around the turn, Secretariat never eased off, shaving the lead to seven lengths, then to six, five, four, and finally to three as he raced through the third quarter in 0:23 ⅗. Running past a tiring Piamem, Secretariat was in pursuit of Angle Light. He closed ground on the Whittaker colt, passing Impecunious near the turn for home and setting out for him. Angle Light was leading by three at the turn. Ron, moving on the outside, cut into that lead quickly as they ran down the lane. He ranged alongside the bay.

Ronnie was on the outside, brother Rudy on the rail.

"All right, brother, I've got the other end here," yelled Rudy. "I've got second."

Ronnie went on with his horse.

Secretariat was in front by a length and a half with 220 yards to run, leaving Angle Light to slug it out for second with Step Nicely. The red horse won it finally by three and a half. Angle Light held on to second, worth $59,733 to Whittaker, in what was the sharpest race of his two-year-old year. So Penny worried about Angle Light, respected and feared him in the fall, while Lucien told her not to worry but not to underestimate. Angle Light, after all, was cheap speed.

Thus for Secretariat it ended in a romp in Cherry Hill, New Jersey, of all places, nine months after Gold Bag beat him by fifteen at Hialeah, four months after he broke his maiden, two months after he divided horses in the Sanford Stakes and looped them in the Hopeful.

He won seven of nine races for the record, and began it all nearly on his knees at Aqueduct, no way to get involved in a 1210-yard sprint in a twelve-horse stampede. He crossed the finish line first in eight of the nine, losing one officially, by Order of the Stewards, and no doubt he would have won it if he hadn't intimidated Stop the Music. He won $456,404, winning from six furlongs to a mile and a sixteenth. He relished the mud at Laurel, the fast tracks at Belmont Park, Aqueduct, Saratoga, and Garden State. It was a tour de force, and he emerged from it the strong winter book favorite to win the mile-and-a-quarter Kentucky Derby May 5, even though, by all odds, he wasn't bred to run so far so soon. No son of Bold Ruler ever had, even with Princequillo holding up the bottom side.

Secretariat was voted America's 1972 Horse of the Year in the combined poll of members of the National Turfwriters Association, staff members of the *Daily Racing Form,* and a board of selection from the Thoroughbred Racing Associations. Since the divisional champions and horses of the year were first chosen in 1936, Vanderbilt's Native Dancer and Bull Hancock's Moccasin were the only two-year-olds ever voted Horse of the Year, both in the TRA polls. The honor usually goes to an older horse, as the Heisman Trophy goes to a running back.

For the Meadow Stable it had been a million-dollar year, the first in its history, despite Riva Ridge's coming down with the droops. Upper Case, before he tailed off and Penny sold him for $750,000, won $234,270. Riva Ridge won $395,632. And a third Meadow three-year-old, Quill Gordon, won $50,226. The four horses won a total of $1,136,532.

Lucien Laurin received his 10 percent not only of purses but of the sales, and for the second straight year he would go to Florida with the two-year-old champion in his barn, the Derby favorite.

Penny spent December in Vail, and it was a cheerful Christmas. "Everything was looking up." She gave Jack a hand-knitted sweater, he gave her a piece of jewelry, gold and sapphire. Her father had lived through the year, as she had wished he would, and the colt had grown enormously in value, as she thought he would. And now she could race him his three-year-old year. Events were still breaking for The Meadow.

Ron Turcotte returned home to New Brunswick, Canada, December 6, to watch his father butchering moose and venision in a store in Grand Falls, to Christmas lunch at his parents' home in town, to Christmas dinner with his wife and three children at her parents' home six miles outside town, in the parish of Drummond, then out to the wilds on his jet black snowmobile, visiting hunters' camps deep in the woods and talking to the old French trappers.

Secretariat was shipped to Florida November 27, treated for the splint at Hialeah on December 9. Dr. Mark Gerard, Lucien's veterinarian, fired the bony growth—inserting hot points into it—purposely causing acute inflammation to quicken the healing process. The colt would walk for two weeks, then jog five or ten minutes from December 24 through 26, and start galloping on the racetrack again December 27 under Jimmy Gaffney, whose wife Mary had been asking him to quit. They had both been disturbed by the size of the yearly bonus Lucien had given him, $500 for galloping a horse that won almost $500,000, and she sensed inside that nothing good could come of Jimmy's staying there. But he refused to quit. "I'm going to go all the way with him," he told her. "I'm going to retire on the winner."

The march of things went on, leaving footnotes to a larger past behind.

Imperatrice died on October 25, the Thursday before Secretariat's Laurel Futurity. She was buried near Hildene and Hill Prince.

In November, as a result of Bull's death, there was a dispersal sale of his racehorses at Belmont Park. There, New York construction and real estate magnate Sigmund Sommer, of Great Neck, Long Island, brought Bull's promising if lightly raced two-year-old colt, Sham—a son of Pretense from Princequillo's daughter Sequoia—for $200,000. Sham was still a maiden at the time.

After finishing third to Angle Light August 28, beaten seven and three-quarters lengths, Sham finished second in his next start September 13, the day before Bull died in Tennessee. Ten days later, the rangy bay raced a flat mile at Belmont Park, and he just got nipped, coming to the eighth pole a length in front and missing by a head for all of it. That was his last race before the dispersal. After it, Sham came under the artful watch of trainer Frank (Pancho) Martin, Sigmund and Viola Sommer's private trainer. Martin was impetuous, emotional, moody, brilliant, speaking with a pound of gravel in his voice, his English cracked up in the magnificent grinder of his Cuban accent.

On December 9 at Aqueduct, for Sham's fourth start, Pancho sent him a flat mile against maidens, and he won by six. On New Year's Day, at Santa Anita Park in California, he won by fifteen.

Chapter 17

On the evening of January 3, 1973, Jack Tweedy was working late at home in Laurel Hollow counseling a neighbor who was having legal problems, when Penny and their son, John, drove up.

It was almost ten-thirty. They had driven from Vail to Denver earlier in the day, then flown to New York and then driven along the North Shore toward Oyster Bay. Penny was tired as she walked into the kitchen. Jack met her there to tell her that her father had died.

She showed no visible emotion and even some relief. Yet months later Penny would remember her feelings of resentment at the presence of that neighbor seeking legal counsel in her house—at that hour and that time in her life.

She unpacked the car, brought in the luggage, and called Elizabeth Ham.

The two women made plans that evening to go to The Meadow —Chris would be buried in Virginia, next to his mother and father —and decided to meet in New Rochelle in the morning to pick out the casket, a simple mahogany one without brass.

In the hollow of the chapel of Saint James the Less Episcopal Church in Ashland, Virginia, the Reverend H. Carlton Fox conducted services before the mourners—horsemen like Seth Hancock and William Haggin Perry, Howard Gentry and Meredith Bailes, whose own father Bob had just died.

The service lasted almost half an hour, and at the close the church doors swung wide open to the snowstorm blowing fitfully outside. The procession edged its way the three blocks to Woodland Cemetery. Lucien was there, and so was Chris Chenery's former trainer,

Casey Hayes. They walked bareheaded through the storm and Penny thought that, because they'd flown up from Florida, they must have forgotten to bring their hats.

The friends and family collected in the big house on the hill, with fires crackling in the two fireplaces in the living room, with pink-colored walls and hunting lithographs and a Gainsborough called *The Watering Place,* a Duncan Phyfe dining table, Chippendale chairs. In the dining room, above a carved mantel and a fireplace, hung a full-length portrait of Helen Bates Chenery. She was dressed in blue and wearing a string of pearls, her hands resting gently on her lap. She was a handsome woman, and she was looking toward the front door. In the living room hung a large portrait of Chris Chenery, done in 1946. He wore riding breeches, held a whip, and sported a vest and tie. Down the staircase was the trophy room, its cabinet filled with rows of golden cups and vases etched with scrolls, of silver trays and shining plates and bowls, a room embracing a hundred winner's circle scenes, of blue and white silks billowing on the turn, of bedlam and champagne. Chris Chenery had built this room, a testament to his youthful dreams, and his mares had furnished it.

Stomping their feet inside, the guests entered a festive, cheerful reception following the services, with drinks and a lavish buffet of sliced turkey, Virginia ham and beaten biscuits, cheese and salad.

Throughout the day, Penny didn't dwell on thoughts about the future of the horses and the farm. But by five o'clock in the afternoon, most of the guests had left the manor house at The Meadow. Now there would be time to deal with questions raised by Chenery's death and the disposition of his estate. There would be time to have meetings with consultants and accountants, meetings with family members and beneficiaries, meetings with representatives of the estate. And there would be time to make the big decisions on the sale of the bloodstock.

Penny knew that the estate of C. T. Chenery would have to sell some of the horses to pay inheritance taxes amounting to several million dollars. The question was, which horses? She knew that Riva Ridge's value had declined through his last five races—each race was a desperate, lurching attempt to regain for him his lost prestige—and she knew that he was nowhere near his peak, that he was capable of running as well as he'd already run. It was no time to sell him. There were the mares on the farm, too, the mares that build such places as this, and the crops of yearlings and two-year-olds and the upcoming foals of 1973. There were eighty Meadow horses in all, and some of them would have to be sold to save the farm as well as the others on it, eighty of them including Secretariat. He remained the single most valuable asset.

Soon after the funeral, the search for options began. Family counsel John Fager contacted the house of Fasig-Tipton in New York, the thoroughbred auctioneers, consultants, appraisers, and bloodstock agents, and retained their services for the estate.

Humphey Finney and his son John of Fasig-Tipton agreed to work for the Chenery estate as marketing consultants and appraisers of the bloodstock, and they got immediately down to the business of it. Before the end of the month, in fact, a meeting in Los Angeles had been arranged between the firm and members of the estate. The time and place were convenient for all parties.

So, on Saturday morning, January 27, in Fasig-Tipton's suite of rooms on the seventeenth floor of the Century Plaza Hotel, the Finneys sat down with John Fager and Penny and Elizabeth Ham to talk about the value of the horses, courses of action open to them, and questions bearing on the future of the Meadow Stud and Stable. In a cordial but businesslike atmosphere, the central problem surfaced, and Finney posed it based on his assumption that the death duties would have to be paid in the 70 percent tax bracket. "The problem was how to use the horses to liquidate the inheritance tax problem, and basically I told them that what they had to do was sell $10 million worth of bloodstock to protect $3 million."

He remembered feeling relieved that Penny and Elizabeth were opposed to complete dispersal. In recent years there had been the dispersal sales of George D. Widener, William S. Du Pont, and Fletcher Jones, and in each of them a number of prized mares were bought by foreign breeders, including the Japanese, who had become especially bullish on the world bloodstock market. With complete dispersal rejected, the point of the meeting centered on alternative ways of raising cash for taxes.

The conversation dwelled on the sale of the two half brothers to Secretariat and Riva Ridge. They had just turned two years old on January 1, the official birthday of all thoroughbreds. One was Capital Asset, the colt Somethingroyal was carrying when Secretariat was weaned, and the other was Capito, a son of Riva Ridge's dam, Iberia. Capital Asset was by First Landing, Capito a son of Sir Gaylord. They also talked about the value of other individuals—the broodmare Barranca, a daughter of Sir Gaylord and Iberia; the filly Long

Stemmed Rose, by Bold Ruler's son Jacinto out of First Flush; and Madrid, the bay horse who was born the same year as Secretariat. The Meadow eventually did sell them—Barranca for $100,000 and Long Stemmed Rose for $74,000, Madrid for much less.

They talked further about selling the yearling colts while keeping the yearling fillies for breeding stock, and in fact they nominated the colts for the Saratoga yearling sales scheduled for August by Fasig-Tipton. And, too, they discussed the possibility of selling the unborn foals of 1973 in the weanling sales that fall. For a time, the meeting pivoted on the idea of selling most of the stock in a sale while holding especially valuable broodmares back.

"How much do you get hurt by holding back certain individuals?" Penny asked John Finney.

She wanted to consider selling most of the Meadow bloodstock while, at the same time, keeping seven of the Meadow's most prized and valuable mares, including Conversation Piece, Bold Matron, Bold Experience, Syrian Sea, and Gay Matelda, all beautifully bred mares. Finney advised her that potential buyers would look askance at the mares chosen for sale, wondering why *they* were not retained with the seven others, wondering what was wrong with *them.*

They also talked of Secretariat and Riva Ridge. The two were the most responsible for inflating the worth of the estate and hence the taxes on it, so they were the most eligible for the block. Finney laid out the financial profiles of each, first outlining Riva Ridge's decline in value, to his present worth, then his potential future. Everyone listened as Finney set forth his findings:

"Riva Ridge is now worth about $2.5 million. After the Belmont Stakes he was worth about $4 million. Because he was a champion two-year-old and because he won the Derby and the Belmont Stakes —even if he never wins another race as a four-year-old, even if he falls flat on his face this year—he'll never be worth less than $2 million. So you are looking at a downside potential of a half million dollars. Now, if he comes back and shows good form as a four-year-old, which we have every reason to believe he'll do, he could go back to $4 million, maybe $4.5 million. So he has a downside potential of a half million and an upside potential of $2 million."

Since his potential for growth in value was so much greater than his potential for decline—he had already reached ground water after losing five races—and since there was no reason to suggest he would not come back after a rest, Finney recommended that they keep Riva Ridge until he had the chance to make his comeback at the races.

Elizabeth Ham and John Fager sat taking notes through the discussions.

"Right now," Finney told them, "Secretariat has a value of between $5 million and $7 million. He is the Horse of the Year, he's expected to win the Triple Crown, and if he wins the Triple Crown his value will go up to perhaps $8 million. Now, if he doesn't train —and many Bold Rulers have failed to train for their three-year-old season—if he fails to train, if he falls on his face, his value will drop from between $5 million and $7 million to $3 million very quickly."

"How quickly?" he was asked.

"Like that," he said, snapping his fingers. "So he has a $3 million downside potential, maybe a $4 million downside potential, from $5 million or $7 million to $3 million. And he's got a possible $2 million upside potential if he does *only* what he is supposed to do, which is to win the Triple Crown. So you're gambling with a $3 million differential, which you have in the pocket right now, if he does turn out to be a top three-year-old; and this against $2 million if he carries on and performs as expected."

That posed a central question. Penny Tweedy didn't believe Secretariat would win the Triple Crown, didn't think he'd perform as expected, believed he had too much to overcome in terms of pedigree and style of running. She knew how so many Bold Rulers had failed to train at the age of three and, of all the Bold Rulers of promise, not a single one had trained to win the Kentucky Derby, Preakness, or Belmont stakes. So why should there now be an exception to this rule, a Bold Ruler who would win all three at that? So she feared he might trip and fall on his pedigree, so to speak, that he might suffer from the rheumatism running in his male line. But more than all these things, more than the pedigree and the streak of rheumatism in the line, Penny feared he might break down—fracture a sesamoid bone, a little pivot bone in the ankle, or chip a knee. This fear traced to the style of running that he had: he ran hard and pounded the ground hard.

Secretariat was nothing like the airy, floating Riva Ridge, who skipped across the ground. Secretariat struck it like a hammer, running with his thick neck stuck out and battering along heavy-headedly. She could not envision him running a mile and a half in the Belmont Stakes, not the way he ran.

John Finney recommended that they syndicate Secretariat. At one point, Penny sought to explore the idea of standing Secretariat at stud in Virginia and of actually putting the syndicate together by herself. She wanted to consider sending him to stud at The Meadow because, she believed, his presence there would ensure the continuance of the farm. The Meadow needed a young stallion. Sir Gaylord, who was sent to the stud at Claiborne Farm, had been leased to stand in Europe. First Landing, then seventeen years old, was beyond his prime.

"You'll lose some of your top investors," John cautioned her, adding that it could be done but that the horse's career would have to be supervised by a management committee, a panel of experienced breeders.

"In fact," he said, "you are taking a chance on the horse's career down the road if he isn't an unqualified success. Kentucky breeders will desert him more quickly if he isn't an instant success. They wouldn't do that if he were standing in Kentucky."

There were financial advantages in her handling the syndication, perhaps the chief of which was that the Chenery estate would not have to give away four free stud services a year to the farm syndicating the colt—the usual fee. In effect, The Meadow would get the shares. But that raised problems, too. Penny thought that standing Secretariat at The Meadow might put too much of a strain on the farm workers. They would be forced to handle a parade of extremely high quality mares, higher in quality than ever visited the court of First Landing, Tillman, or Bryan G. She was concerned that this might put too much pressure on Howard Gentry, who was having trouble with his eyesight.

The meeting between Fasig-Tipton and the estate of C. T. Chenery lasted perhaps two hours, and it was convened on a morning when Secretariat galloped casually at Hialeah and just three days after he worked a brisk half mile in 0:47 $^2/_5$, galloping out an extra eighth in 0:13 $^1/_5$. Three days after the meeting the colt worked a half mile in 0:49, and on February 3, he went an easy five-eighths in 1:01 $^3/_5$. The clockers noted in the *Daily Racing Form* the next day: "Secretariat was only breezing." Lucien turned the screws then. With Ron on top, the colt raced through five furlongs in 0:58 $^3/_5$, ripping off the first three-eighths in 0:34 $^2/_5$, the next eighth in 0:12 for a half mile in 0:46 $^2/_5$, and the last eighth in 0:12 $^1/_5$. It was one of the fastest moves of the day.

On these winter mornings at Hialeah, Turcotte began to notice something different about Secretariat, something barely detectable at first but which grew increasingly apparent to him as time went on.

What was so encouraging was that Secretariat was passing

through a critical stage of transition that winter, a stage many fine two-year-olds never do survive intact. For some reason—glandular or psychological—horses enormously talented at the age of two often fizzle out at three. The 1969 two-year-old champion, Silent Screen, was the most recently conspicuous. He was an extraordinary juvenile, a flop as a three-year-old. Not only did Secretariat appear to be making the passage and emerging his old self at three, to Turcotte he appeared to be improving, growing more rhythmic in his stride, and holding himself higher. On and off the racetrack, the business of Secretariat was compelling attention.

Three days after he sizzled the five-eighths at Hialeah, most of the Chenery family met in Arizona at the home of Margaret Carmichael, gathering to make decisions on dividing up the estate among the heirs. Penny, for instance, chose to center her share of the inheritance in the thoroughbred holdings, while brother Hollis put most of his in the Chenery Corporation, a family holding corporation. In Mrs. Carmichael's home outside of Tucson, with a broad view of the desert and the foothills west of town, the Chenery family also talked about the horses and what to do with them to pay the taxes.

They agreed that there would be no general dispersal of the bloodstock. First Riva Ridge, now Secretariat, had demonstrated the speed at which money could be made in racing. Nor would they sell the yearlings now, nor the weanlings of 1973, nor the two half brothers to Secretariat and Riva Ridge. Nor Riva Ridge, whose value had so plummeted.

All that was decided was to syndicate the biggest asset, Secretariat, and to play it by ear the rest of the way—to see if Riva Ridge's value came back and to see if the two colts trained well. They agreed to try for between $175,000 and $200,000 a share for Secretariat.

The Meadow had already established strong historical ties to Claiborne Farm, beginning when Chenery met Arthur Hancock, Sr., in the 1930s, and continuing when Chris became one of the few breeders to send a mare to Princequillo at Ellerslie. Later he sent Hill Prince to stud at Claiborne, later still Sir Gaylord, and he bred his mares regularly to Claiborne stallions. Penny believed that Seth Hancock, though young and inexperienced, had the momentum of a flourishing breeding empire behind him and the counsel of experienced men whose lives had been interwoven with the life of the farm. Some of the managers had been with Claiborne for years, moving to Kentucky with them from Virginia, resettling their lives for the farm. So it was understood that Seth would be asked first to sell their horse for them and stand the colt there once he did.

Meanwhile, as a practical measure, no chances would be taken with the horse until the syndicate was formed. If he lost his first start, indicating he might be a flop as a three-year-old, his value would plunge immediately. So, it was decided in Arizona, the red horse would not run until Seth syndicated him. Lucien had brought the colt to Hialeah under banners that he would point him for the Florida races, including the $100,000 Flamingo Stakes on March 3, but all racing could wait until the big money was in the bank.

The Tucson meetings broke up on February 11, and the move to syndicate the red horse started quickly after that. Having decided to seek out Claiborne for the syndication, the estate sought the counsel of Gayle Mohney, an attorney from Lexington and one of the most experienced lawyers in the business of syndication. Claiborne Farm had not been asked formally to syndicate the horse, and Penny didn't want to say anything until the terms had been worked out. After discussions with Mohney, a contract was drawn up in rough draft. In its final form, it was a sixteen-page document.

The Meadow had the leverage now to ask for the right to race the colt through 1973, under its care and management and for its benefit. Secretariat had been the Horse of the Year, was expected to make a run at the spring three-year-old classics, and was an exceptional prospect. He was in training, galloping and running toward the Kentucky Derby already, and was still working well, despite rumors of his unsoundness.

So it was agreed that Secretariat would race under the silks of the Meadow Stable through his three-year-old year and that he would be shipped to the breeding farm no later than November 15, 1973.

He would be syndicated for breeding purposes in thirty-two shares at $190,000 a share—Penny argued for $200,000—a world-record total of $6,080,000, or $680,000 more than the highest previous syndication price of $5,400,000 paid recently for Nijinsky II, who was then standing at stud at Claiborne. One share would entitle its owner to send one mare a year to Secretariat.

The farm syndicating him would receive four free stud services a year to Secretariat, three the first year, while trainer Lucien Laurin would receive one free nomination. A free service, unlike a share, cannot be sold like property or be bequeathed in a will. It is a privilege that comes up once a year.

Some farms syndicate horses in thirty-six shares, but it was agreed that thirty-two shares imposed less strain on a young stallion and would induce breeders to buy. If Secretariat were syndicated in thirty-six shares, it would mean the colt would have to breed to forty mares his first year—thirty-six shareholders, three free services to the farm, and one to Lucien. "That's too many," Penny said. "You can't guarantee a *young* horse will cover forty mares." By selling thirty-two shares, with five free services, the colt's normal book would include thirty-seven mares, thirty-six his first year.

There was also a teaser in deciding to sell thirty-two shares. While his normal schedule committed him to breeding to thirty-seven mares, Secretariat could be expected to handle more than that as he got older, perhaps a half dozen or more. If the colt's health or state of fertility allowed it, according to the judgment of the syndicate manager, he might be bred to more than forty mares. The additional three nominations would go to the syndicate members, who would draw for them by lot. Since they were asking such a large amount of money, it sweetened the deal to be able to say syndicate members would be able to draw for a free nomination.

The state of the colt's fertility would be determined in tests conducted by a panel of three veterinarians shortly after the colt went to the farm, and whether he passed would depend on their findings. The fertility test would involve microscopic examination of his semen and observation of the colt during test breeding. As finally written, it was agreed that Secretariat would stand at the farm until "the certification of the veterinarians is made and, if he shall die prior thereto, or if a majority of the panel of veterinarians shall certify that the stallion has failed the fertility test, then in either of such events this agreement shall forthwith terminate; any amounts paid to Seller by Buyer on account of the purchase price shall be promptly returned, without interest, and no party shall have any further liability to any other party hereunder."

Such were the essentials. The rough of the draft was finished, late in the afternoon of that February day, and Penny suggested dinner with Mohney and Seth Hancock. Over dinner, Seth Hancock agreed to take on the job of syndicating Secretariat, to try to sell twenty-eight of thirty-two shares—four were retained by the estate—at $190,000 a share.

He inquired about their plans for Secretariat, since the Meadow Stable would continue to race him through 1973, and Penny at one point recalled some sentiment for not racing him at all.

"Well, ma'am, you might want to retire him right away," said Seth. "After all, he's already been Horse of the Year and Bold Rulers haven't wanted to go classic distances."

"I refuse to consider breeding him at three," she replied. "The way he runs, I wouldn't be surprised if he becomes unsound before the end of the year. But I want the opportunity for him to race."

Seth asked Penny what her plans were if the colt were to lose. "If he loses once, I'll wonder why," said Penny. "If he loses twice, I'll consider retiring him."

Seth asked her what she had in mind for the colt in terms of his three-year-old campaign.

"The Triple Crown . . . the Bay Shore . . . the Gotham . . . the Wood . . . the Travers . . . the Woodward . . . and the Gold Cup . . ."

So they would gamble. They had already decided to go to the Kentucky Derby by way of New York instead of by way of Florida —the traditional springboard for the spring classics. Years ago, largely through the influence of Calumet Farm trainer Ben A. Jones and his son, Jimmy, Florida became the starting point for horses aiming to run in the Kentucky Derby. Riva Ridge went to Kentucky through Florida, and now Lucien was planning to bypass racing there and begin his run for the Derby in New York, historically the kiss of death for Derby contenders. No winner of the Bay Shore Stakes or Gotham Stakes had ever won the Derby, and the last winner of the Wood Memorial to win the Derby was Assault, in 1946. "I decided to gamble," Lucien said.

So Lucien would buck the historical odds and send his red horse north to Long Island, to that perilous strait for Derby horses known as Aqueduct.

"It sounds fine to me," Seth told Penny.

Chapter 18

Daddy imported Nasrullah and syndicated him.

Seth Hancock

At home in his modest ranch on the farm, Seth Hancock was waiting through the final hours of Wednesday, February 21. Ellen Hancock was in Florida at the time, and Seth was waiting home alone for word that would turn him loose on the world's bloodstock market. He was set to attempt the syndication of Secretariat, to begin the search for at least twenty-eight people game to spend almost $200,000 for the right to breed one mare a year to Secretariat for the rest of his life at stud.

Following dinner at the Coach House on Tuesday night, Penny had gone to spend Wednesday canvassing members of the family and telling them the terms agreed upon in Lexington and seeking approval from them. Seth was sitting by the telephone in the house, reading the *Daily Racing Form,* and waiting for Penny to call. He was wondering if anything might have gone wrong.

It was eight o'clock, then it was nine-thirty.

Though unaware of it, Seth was not the only man waiting for Penny to call him. There was John Finney, the thoroughbred consultant and appraiser for the estate of C. T. Chenery. Finney was now working for European interests seeking to engineer the most spectacular coup in the history of international bloodstock—the purchase and ultimate importation to Ireland of Secretariat.

The week before the Lexington meetings Irish bloodstock agent Jonathan Irwin called Finney from his office at the British Bloodstock Agency Ltd. in Ireland. Irwin was seeking Fasig-Tipton's help to negotiate with Penny Tweedy for the red horse.

"I have someone here who would be interested in paying over $5 million," he told Finney, adding that he had the backing of Captain Tim Rogers, one of the leading breeders in Europe and the owner of a large, successful stud farm twelve miles west of Dublin, in County Kildare.

John said, "We just appraised the horse for between $5 million and $7 million. I know they could syndicate him in the neighborhood of $6 million."

There was a pause in Dublin. "That's a considerable sum," Jonathan Irwin said.

"Yes it is, but I know if we were given the opportunity to syndicate the horse, we could do it for that. If you want to come into the market, you better be ready to do six."

"I think we could do six and a half. Let me call Tim and get back to you."

That was the limit for Rogers and his associates. "The price I could bear ranged between $6 million and $6.5 million," Rogers would say.

And that put them solidly in the market—perhaps, they thought, at the top of the market. Irwin called Finney back again, and asked him to represent the Irish in America, to bid for the red horse on their behalf. If successful, Fasig-Tipton would receive a fee of $100,000. John Finney, though feeling some ambivalence, accepted the assignment: he was lured by the fee but repelled by the thought of Secretariat leaving the United States. Thus he became an agent for the Irish.

The Irish told Finney to offer Penny Tweedy $6.5 million, $420,000 more than the figure agreed upon several days later in Mohney's office and over dinner. The $100,000 fee would be deducted from the offer. Under the proposal, Secretariat would race in America for the Meadow Stable, and the stable would receive all the colt's earnings as a racehorse. In addition, Secretariat would be permitted to race through 1974, his four-year-old season. The Irish told Finney to stipulate, however, that they would retain the right to retire the horse at any time if they thought he was embarrassing himself or no longer enhancing his value at the stud. And, finally, he would stand at the stud in Ireland.

Irwin having laid out the terms of the proposal, Finney then set forth his plan to win acceptance of them. Finney at once told Irwin that he didn't want the Irish offer used to pressure American competitors into raising their bids. He advised Irwin that he thought the only chance the Irish had to acquire the colt—if they had any chance at all—was to top the high bid at the final moment, to overwhelm it suddenly when it seemed the last bid had been made. Finney believed that $6.5 million would put the Irish either on the pace or in front of all other offers; it was Finney himself, after all, who had appraised the Meadow bloodstock and had put a value of between $5 million and $7 million on the colt. To be avoided was a confrontation between American and Irish interests, open competition that would simply drive up the bidding. Finney knew the Americans would have an edge because the horse would stand in America, a critical consideration for the Meadow Stud as a breeder.

The idea was to wait for the Americans to make an acceptable offer, watch for the syndication to move forward, and then, just as it was about to begin, to knock off its hat with a sharp counterpunch. Success was as dependent on timing as on money. The Irish agreed. There would be no international price war over Secretariat.

Secretariat in Ireland is what Rogers and Irwin had been thinking ever since they first sat down together to talk of buying and ultimately importing the colt. It was a heady, exhilarating thought for the two men. And it began one day when Irwin called Rogers at the farm outside Dublin, asking him if he would come to the city immediately.

The phone call alerted Rogers to the possibilities open to him. He had already seen Secretariat and was familiar with his record. The past October, considering the purchase of Upper Case as a potential stallion in Ireland, Rogers flew from England to New York to see him at the Meadow Stable in Belmont Park. Rogers didn't buy Upper Case, but while he was there Penny also showed him Secretariat.

Rogers didn't then consider ever owning more than a share in Secretariat. But when Chris Chenery died, Rogers knew that the estate would have to find a large chunk of money for inheritance taxes. Still, it simply never occurred to him that Secretariat might be purchased by the Irish.

"Then Jon Irwin rang me," said Rogers. "And Jon said, 'There's a chance we will be able to get Secretariat to come to Ireland.'"

Rogers, suddenly alive now to the chances opening for him, drove to Dublin, to Irwin's home, and for the next two hours the two men talked over the project in Irwin's sitting room. At the time, Rogers regarded their chances as "problematical," but he also knew there was reason for hope. The American dollar, as devalued, was not what it had been in the years after the war. And the Irish had a tax advantage that Americans didn't have. Seeking to stimulate the growth of racing in Ireland, the Irish government didn't tax profits earned in breeding thoroughbreds—that is, if an Irishman bought a share in Secretariat for $200,000 and sold it later for $500,000, the $300,000 profit would be tax free. Americans, having no such exemption, would have to pay a capital gains tax on such profits.

But what excited Rogers most was the opportunity for Ireland to regain something of what it lost in position and eminence in the breeding of thoroughbreds. Rogers saw far more than simply the purchase of a single racehorse. He saw a historic sweep, a chance to reclaim a part of what had been lost to Americans who, like supermarket shoppers, picked the shelves clean—since Bull Hancock caused such a furor among Irish breeders when he reached over their heads and took Nasrullah from them. The Irish suffered damnably as Nasrullah grew in stature and emerged an Irish giant on American shores. And now, less than twenty-five years later, here was a chance to acquire Nasrullah's finest grandson and bring him home.

For years, ever since Bull imported Nasrullah, Americans had imported one European thoroughbred star after another. Now the Europeans, like the Japanese and Australians, were spending as much or more money than the Americans at yearling and dispersal sales. Rogers saw signs of this at the sale dispersing Bull's horses the year before, watching as an Englishman, a Frenchman, and an Irishman—the latter represented by Jonathan Irwin—became the last bidders for a Round Table colt that sold for $250,000.

When Irwin called Finney in Florida, asking him to negotiate to buy the horse for them, Finney agreed. He waited to spring the offer at what he thought would be an opportune time. Finney knew something was imminent, and he waited over the weekend, through Monday and then through Tuesday, the day Penny missed the plane and Seth picked her up in Cincinnati and they all had dinner at the Coach House. Finney didn't know they had agreed to $6,080,000. But he did find out they had met, and he did know he had recommended between $5 million and $7 million. He guessed that their figure was probably somewhere near the middle. On Wednesday he called Penny. It was time for the counterpunch.

John told her of the Irish offer. She listened to him, saying finally, "Hold on a minute. Let me get a pencil and paper. It sounds very interesting." Penny jotted down the details. "My brother is in the Bahamas and he won't be back until Sunday or Monday," she told John. "I'll have to consult with him."

Through Finney, the Irish had made their offer for Secretariat. Rogers and Irwin waited. And Finney waited, too, though not for the Irish alone: he was moving now to protect his domestic flank in the event the Irish deal blew up in his face.

After speaking to Penny for the Irish, Finney then contacted a prominent horseman in Florida whose name would certainly appear on Seth's list of potential syndicate members. So Finney asked his source to advise him if and when he was offered a share and what the terms of the contract were. If he didn't get the whole of Secretariat for his European clients, Finney wanted to get part of him for his American clients.

So Seth and Finney waited together, their deals unknown to each other, while Penny canvassed the members of the family.

At about nine-thirty on Wednesday evening, unknown to Finney, she called Seth as he waited in the house and read the *Racing Form* and wondered what had happened to her.

"All right," she told Seth. "We're ready to start."

"Yes, ma'am."

On Friday morning, he decided, he would embark on the job before him, on his first major job as the president of Claiborne Farm, Inc.

Seth was born on July 22, 1949, about five months before his father arranged the purchase of Nasrullah from the Irishmen. He had just turned twenty-three when Bull died. In fact he was still doing his novitiate when he was forced into the void created by his father's death, but Bull didn't leave the farm in Seth's hands alone. His will created a three-man advisory committee—composed of breeders Ogden Phipps, Charles Kenney, and William Haggin Perry—to oversee the running of the place until Bull's youngest child, then twenty, reached the age of thirty-five. Seth became the president, but his powers of decision making were limited.

Seth didn't have the depth of training and experience on the farm that Bull had when he took over from Arthur Hancock, Sr., in 1948. By then Bull was already nearing forty, and he had had years to learn the business of breeding horses from his father. Seth acquired most of his experience during summers at the farm, spending time with the yearlings and the broodmares between years spent at Woodberry Forest Prep School in Virginia, where Bull had studied, then later at the University of the South in Tennessee and the University of Kentucky. He graduated in agriculture in 1971, knowledgeable about the quality of hay and cattle.

His passion was not for hay and cattle, however, but for horses, the racehorses and the farm. Through all his years in college, he was a voracious reader of racing publications, with a steady diet of the *Daily Racing Form,* the *Thoroughbred Record,* and the *Blood-Horse.* He wanted to work at Claiborne Farm, to learn the business as his father had learned it. After the army, he came to work for his father, permanently, in February of 1972. They had Seth's training program all worked out.

First he would work six months with the broodmares. Then he would work six months with the yearlings. Then he would spend a year riding the giant spread with William Taylor, the farm manager, learning all ends of running the empire. Then Seth would move into the office.

He had just finished working six months with the broodmares when Bull died, and the set-piece training program fell apart. He never got to the yearlings, and he never spent the year trailing after Bill Taylor. Suddenly he had real work to do.

He dove straight into the center of the place—Bull's old office— slipping a picture of his dad beneath the glass on the top of his broad desk and spending hours working over it. "He'd leave early in the morning and he'd be gone all day," said Ellen. "Then he'd come back home for maybe half an hour or an hour for dinner, and then he'd go back to the office and come home again about nine-thirty, and then he'd sit in his office here and read until eleven or eleven-thirty. That's late down here. Most men are in bed by nine. He'd be up at six-fifteen. We were married only six months when all this happened and it was a big switch in our life. But I knew how much he wanted to do it and I wanted him to do it."

Most of the clients were his elders, and he knew he had something to prove about himself. He was intensely serious, and he was least patient and angriest with those who would exploit him because of his age—his most vulnerable point. Seth was not the sort to be shoved around. He liked and respected his father enormously, but he refused in the end to knuckle under to Bull on the matter of his college education.

He wanted to work with horses after high school, and not go to

150

college, but his father insisted that he get a degree, and that he get it at a school away from Kentucky. Seth went along with that for two years, attending Sewanee, then decided to transfer to the University of Kentucky, closer to the farm. Bull objected.

"If you do, you pay your own way," Bull finally told him.

"I thought, 'If he's going to be bull-headed, I can be, too,' " said Seth. "So I decided to pay my own way."

Seth got up early on Friday to begin the selling of a racehorse for more than one had ever been sold before. He walked past the horse cemetery to the office and settled into the green chair behind the desk. He faced the fireplace and the list.

The office was utilitarian—a beige rug, wood panels hung with pictures of horses that Claiborne raised, bred, or owned. To the front, there were oils of Nasrullah and Round Table, and on the mantel above the fireplace was a football, dedicated to Bull the day he was buried, that was used in play in the Villanova-Kentucky football game.

Behind the desk and chair stood a wall of books—volumes of the *American Stud Book, Thoroughbred Broodmare Record,* and *American Produce Record.* To his left, within reach, was the telephone—pale green with three plastic buttons, his instrument of syndication.

The list was his key to it. On it were the names of many prominent owners and breeders, billionaires, millionaires, and six-figure businessmen. There were the names of large and small breeders raising horses for the marketplace, private breeders who raced the horses they bred, old society breeders and newly established breeders and some dependent on the business itself. There were names of well-connected thoroughbred agents—buyers of bloodstock for a wealthy clientele—and names unknown to Seth, friends of Penny's whom she asked him to call. The list was no tight clique of friends of Claiborne, no fraternity of the inbred elite. What they all had in common, if they had anything in common at all, were mares, money, and a serious interest in breeding and raising thoroughbreds. Socially, financially, racially, and nationally, the list was a mixed bag.

Among the names was the Greentree Stable of John Hay Whitney and his sister, Mrs. Joan Payson; the Rokeby Stable of Paul Mellon, the sportsman and patron of the arts; and the Tartan Stable of billionaire William McKnight, who built the colossus of 3-M. From the southwest were Will Farish III, the owner of Bee Bee Bee; Howard Brighton Keck, the oil executive; and Nelson Bunker Hunt, the brother of Lamar and the son of H. L. Hunt, the oil billionaire.

Also on the list was the Calumet Farm of Admiral and Mrs. Gene Markey; the Mereworth Farm of Walter Salmon, Jr., the Darby Dan Farm of John W. Galbreath; and the Fountainebleau Farm of Zenya Yoshida, the prominent Japanese breeder. In Canada there were Jean-Louis Levesque, the insurance millionaire, and sportsman Edward Plunkett Taylor, the father of Canadian racing and a major thoroughbred breeder in two countries. Also on the list were F. Eugene Dixon, who was living on a yacht at the time; the French horseman Alec Head, who once trained for the Aga Khan; the bass-voiced Warner Jones, a breeder and one of Bull's closest friends since boyhood in Kentucky; E. V. Benjamin, Jr.; the Nuckols Brothers; and Dr. William Lockridge, who carries a clipboard at yearling sales and looks like a high school football coach. Seth would also call Bob Kleberg, whose King Ranch is larger than the state of Rhode Island; Dan Lasater, who began working for sixty cents an hour at McDonald's when he was seventeen and retired with $30 million at twenty-nine; Mrs. Richard C. Du Pont, whose husband was a pioneer in glider aviation; Doug and Mary Carver; Mr. and Mrs. Paul Hexter; Milton (Laddie) Dance; Dr. Eslie Asbury, the Cincinnati surgeon; Alfred Gwynne Vanderbilt; and Captain Tim Rogers, who was waiting to hear from Finney. And finally polo-playing Michael G. Phipps, the president of the family's Bessemer Properties and a cousin of Ogden Phipps, and Ogden Phipps himself.

Ogden Phipps would have owned Secretariat if he'd won that coin toss two and a half years ago, and now young Hancock was asking him to buy one-thirty-second of the colt for $190,000, just $10,000 less than he spent on the debut of his daughter Cynthia.

Hancock had just called Phipps seeking permission to syndicate the horse. As a member of the three-man advisory committee set up to oversee the operation of the farm, Phipps would have to approve the decision. He did. And while discussing the syndication, Seth asked Phipps if he would buy a share. For several minutes they bandied the price about while Ogden hesitated.

"Do you think I ought to go?" he asked Seth.

"Well, Mr. Phipps, Bold Ruler was *your* horse and this is his greatest son. It would be a kind of slap in your horse's face if you didn't."

Bold Ruler raced in Mrs. Phipps's colors, but Ogden managed much of the stallion's career as a stud horse, arranging the coin flips and building the bloodstock, and finally, ordering the dying horse put down. At his mother's death, Ogden ascended to the leadership of the most powerful racing family in America, a family with bands of the finest bred mares in the world and stables at Belmont Park filled with their sons and daughters.

The $190,000 for a share gave him only brief pause.

"Yes, I better go," Ogden said.

By the time he walked into his office early that February morning, Seth had already recorded Phipps as the first shareholder in the Secretariat syndicate. He was about to start working the telephones when he glanced outside and saw the blue 1973 Fleetwood cruising by. It was seven-forty-five. Dr. William Lockridge eased his Cadillac to a stop near the office, shut off the engine, and picked up a copy of the *Daily Racing Form*. It was a cold morning in Paris, and Bill Lockridge sat bundled against it in his quilted duck-feather coat, pearl gray, waiting for the van that was trailing him from his Walmac-Warnerton Farm in Lexington. Lockridge was a modest but successful market breeder, selling at auction the young horses he bred and raised himself. He was a regular customer at Claiborne Farm, breeding his mares to Claiborne stallions. In fact one of his mares had an appointment with Reviewer, a young Bold Ruler stallion, that morning. The breeding shed opens at eight o'clock, so Lockridge killed the engine and sat back with the racing form. He had fifteen minutes. His eye caught a story about Secretariat. He became engrossed in it.

Lockridge's opinion of Secretariat had changed considerably since he first saw him in a picture on the front of the *Thoroughbred Record* that past summer. At the time, the photo reminded him of something his New York trainer, Jimmy Picou, had told him earlier. Picou had seen Secretariat run, and he told Lockridge that the colt was a son of Bold Ruler who ran as if distances wouldn't bother him. When Lockridge saw the picture, when he noticed the Nearco sloping rump and the thick muscles packed along his neck and shoulders, he concluded that he was looking at a Bold Ruler sprinter and nothing more, a prototypical dashman.

Lockridge followed Secretariat closely through the autumn, through the extremely fast mile of the Champagne Stakes, through the stakes-record clocking in the Laurel Futurity at a mile and a sixteenth, and finally through the victory at Garden State Park. And he saw what Picou had seen as far off as Saratoga.

What most compelled his interest in the colt, what made the colt so attractive to Lockridge as a stud horse, was the male line to which he belonged.

Seth Hancock opened the door of Lockridge's Cadillac, startling the doctor, and slipped in next to him.

"I'm getting ready to start syndicating now. What do you think?" asked Seth, and quoted the price.

"That's the retail price," said Lockridge, but he didn't hesitate.

"Do you want in?"

Lockridge, considering it briefly, was convinced that the red horse would do well in stud, and the better he did the more he would be worth. "This horse had to do well because he was from the most genetically prepotent male line in the history of American thorough-bred racing. That line gets a higher percentage of high-class horses than any other male line in the breed."

"Do you want in?"

"I certainly do," said Lockridge.

1. Secretariat being led to the track at Belmont Park for a workout. Photo: N.Y.R.A. – Paul Schafer

2. Field of five breaks from starting gate for 105th Belmont Stakes. Secretariat is in #2 post position. Photo: N.Y.R.A.—Bob Coglianese

3. Secretariat rounds turn for last quarter-mile in the 1½-mile race at Belmont. Photo: N.Y.R.A.—Bob Coglianese

4. It was a record that still stands: Secretariat winning the Belmont by
31 lengths in a time of 2:24. Photo courtesy of *Thoroughbred Record*

5. Passing in front of the grandstand, Secretariat is all alone as he
nears the finish line. Photo: N.Y.R.A. – Bob Coglianese

6. Ron Turcotte checks his record-shattering time as he crosses the finish line. Photo courtesy of *Thoroughbred Record*

Chapter 19

So the first day has begun, not behind the desk but outside the office, where Seth is shaking hands with Lockridge, climbing from the Cadillac, and ducking back inside to search the world for twenty-six more.

Seth tells Patti Tompkins, his secretary, who is working in a nearby office, to start making calls to breeders at the top of the list, to those Penny has asked him to call, and to those he believes are most likely to buy a share. For he is moving early and quickly to lay a strong foundation for the syndicate, something he regards as essential, playing to the psychology of the marketplace as he understands and anticipates it. He knows the price and the speculative nature of the investment could create conditions for a flourishing stock market mentality, in which what *appears* is as vital as what *is,* and it is imperative to keep up the appearances.

Seth believes that speed is important to ultimate success, that the longer the syndication takes to complete, the more suspicious of the goods becomes the marketplace.

"See if you can get Walter Salmon for me," Seth tells Patti.

Tan and still vigorous, nearing seventy, Walter Salmon, Jr., has just returned home to New York from Florida, where he has heard that a Meadow Stable syndication is about to begin.

He has already thought about buying a share in Secretariat, anticipating since hearing of Chris Chenery's death that the colt might have to be sold to raise cash for inheritance taxes. So when Salmon picks up the phone in his Roslyn, Long Island, home—a renovated stable set back off the sound—he knows the instant he hears Seth's voice that he is calling on the syndication of either Secretariat or Riva Ridge. It is his business to know and anticipate such things.

Salmon's father started him in the business of raising and selling thoroughbreds more than fifty years ago, and to that work he has applied himself ever since. At the time Seth calls, Salmon is the head of a large and diversified real estate and farming enterprise that fixes his energies on his sixty-story office building at 500 Fifth Avenue and his thirty-two-story office building at 11 West Forty-second Street, both in Manhattan; on his Hiram Walker, Coca Cola, and Canadian Club signs that wink and nod above Times Square; on Saint Thomas in the Bahamas, where he owns 120 acres of land on the top of Fortuna Mia Mountain; and on his 3500-acre showplace of a farm, called Mereworth, in the heart of the Blue Grass country, where his father bred and raised Discovery more than forty years ago. Walter Salmon owns fifty-eight broodmares and breeds and raises yearlings for the marketplace. He runs a major commercial breeding enterprise, one of the largest and most successful in Kentucky, annually dispatching his best bred mares to some of the finest and most promising stallions in America—to Arts and Letters, Damascus, Dr. Fager, Majestic Prince, Nashua, Tom Rolfe, Creme de la Creme, Buckpasser, Le Fabuleaux, Hail to Reason, Hawaii, and Gallant Man. Salmon owns shares in numerous stallions, and he has earned a name as one of the industry's most active buyers, investing money from his considerable fortune to gain access for his mares to all the most vigorous male lines available in the country.

"And we wanted to know if you wanted a share in the horse," Seth is telling him.

"What's the price?" Salmon asks.

"One hundred ninety thousand a share."

Salmon does not leap into a commitment. He questions Seth on the terms of the contract. He wants to know, for instance, how many other commercial breeders there will be in the syndicate. Salmon always asks this. It is one of his standard questions.

Walter Salmon thinks about it, and then he says to Seth, "I'll call you back."

Walter Salmon, vigorous investor in bloodstock, will call back?

What is wrong?

For Seth Hancock this is the first disturbing moment. It is not a refusal, just a hesitation, but it gives him pause to wonder whether something might be whacky in the general American economy, something that would make a financially sensitive man such as

Salmon hesitate to check the economic barometer. Seth knows that the thoroughbred breeding and sales industry is robustly healthy. Just a month ago, at the dispersal sale of the late Fletcher Jones's Westerly Stud in California, the champion mare Typecast had been sold for a record $725,000, a whopping sum to be paid for a broodmare. Business has been booming in the bloodstock industry, yet Salmon is taking his time.

"See if you can get Mrs. duPont for me."

Allaire duPont has been a client of Claiborne for many years, a person of taste and financial vitality in the breeding of American bloodstock.

At her 800-acre Woodstock Farm in Chesapeake City, Maryland, she raises thoroughbreds, keeping thirty-five broodmares in the nursery, rides and looks after her great gelding Kelso—five times America's Horse of the Year (1960–1964), five times winner of the two-mile Jockey Club Gold Cup, and the biggest money earner in the history of the sport, winner of thirty-nine of sixty-three starts and $1,977,896. "Kelly" was foaled and raised at Claiborne.

Seth is depending on Mrs. duPont to take a share. Lately she has been breeding mares to Claiborne stallions Round Table, Buckpasser, and Herbager, among others, and Seth has her high on the list as a potential buyer for a share in Secretariat. Reaching her at Woodstock that morning, he informs her of the essentials in what has become his standard sales delivery.

"I called because Mrs. Tweedy has authorized me to syndicate Secretariat for her and I'm in the process of doing it right now. We wanted to know if you wanted a share. The price is $190,000 a share, in thirty-two shares, and Mrs. Tweedy is going to keep two under the Meadow Stud and two will be owned by the Chenery Corporation, which is a family holding corporation. The terms are 10 percent down and 40 percent when he passes his fertility test, the remaining 50 percent on January 15, 1974. He'll continue to race in her colors and anything he might win will go to her."

After thinking about it a moment, discussing terms with Seth, Mrs. duPont tells him that *that* is a sizable sum of money to ask for a breeding share and that she would have to consult her accountant before making such an investment. She promises to call him back when she makes up her mind.

Mrs. Richard C. duPont, an extremely active breeder in the bloodstock market, with close and traditional ties to Claiborne Farm, will call back later?

It *is*, Seth knows, a lot of money, but *not* too much for what he sees as Secretariat's potential worth as a stud horse. Yet now here are two active bloodstock investors hesitating over a commitment. For Seth Hancock it has suddenly become a discouraging early morning. He is shaken by the turn of things because, if Walter Salmon and Allaire duPont refuse to buy a share, who *will* buy one? They are supposed to be among the surest, the ones most likely to join. It is as if he is trying to put a twenty-eight-piece orchestra together while the lead musicians are sitting around tuning their instruments. It is especially troubling because time is crucial. Seth soon finds they're hardly alone.

"People were saying, 'Well, I don't know, that's an *awful* lot of money. I'll call you back.' "

"See if you can get E. V. Benjamin for me," Seth asks Patti Tompkins.

An old friend of Bull Hancock, a well-known horse breeder and bloodstock agent and the master of Big Sink Farm in Versailles (that's *Ver-sales*, not *Vers-eye*), Kentucky, E. V. Benjamin is another of the breeders that Seth is counting on to buy a share.

At the moment Benjamin is working in the library of his home, where he has his offices, and he is at the desk when Seth begins to lay out the terms before him, just as he had done with Mrs. Du Pont.

Hearing the price, Benjamin blanches.

Benjamin, a successful commercial breeder, has not been a timid spender for shares in stallions. He paid $65,000 for a breeding share in Horse of the Year Damascus, $65,000 for a share in European champion Sir Ivor, $20,000 for one in Drone, and $35,500 for a share in grass specialist Hawaii, all Claiborne stallions. And now Seth is asking him to buy one share in Secretariat for $14,500 more than he paid for those four shares combined. It gives Benjamin pause.

"I paid all kinds of money for shares in horses, but never a $190,000 deal," Benjamin says.

Benjamin, having been close to Seth's father, wants to help Seth on his first major undertaking as the president of the farm. But first he has to make some calls, to find others who will share the risks with him.

"I don't know, Seth," says E. V. Benjamin, squirming. "I might go, but *that's* an *awful* lot of money."

Hanging up, Benjamin asks his thirty-seven-year-old son, E. V. (Tony) Benjamin III, if he wants a share in the red horse. Together they share ownership of Chou Crout, America's champion sprinter of 1972, a five-year-old mare they are about to retire and send to Damascus. She could be sent to Secretariat in 1974. Tony is noncommittal, so the elder Benjamin turns to sources outside Kentucky, to New York and Ohio, looking for backers to share the cost of a share with him, finding one buyer in New York, a banker. At one point, Benjamin calls Seth back, one of two or three calls he makes during the day to Hancock.

"I'm 75 percent sure," he tells Seth.

Not much later he calls back again. "Put me down for sure—and with a question mark."

It is still a cold February morning in Paris, and Seth is discouraged waiting for Salmon and Mrs. duPont to call, waiting for Benjamin to try to round up support. News that he is syndicating Secretariat has begun to leak out from those he has called, and down in Florida bloodstock agent Jim Scully has heard the rumor and is slipping into a phone booth near Hialeah.

Among others, Jim Scully represents Zenya Yoshida, the leading breeder of thoroughbreds in Japan, the owner of 200 broodmares there and an expansive tract of real estate in Kentucky known as the Fountainebleau Farm. It was Zenya Yoshida's cousin, Shigeo Yoshida, who staggered the galleries in California when he bid $725,000 for Typecast.

It is past midmorning. By now Seth is taking calls as well as making them, fielding them from all over. Then he hears Scully's voice. Scully, a wiry, thirty-two-year-old former racing magazine writer, gets 5 percent commission on every dime Yoshida spends on bloodstock in America, 5 percent of the millions Yoshida has been pouring into the purchase of American bloodstock.

"What are you doin', Seth?" Scully asks.

"Jim, I'm awful busy now." Hancock has a sense of humor.

"Wait a minute. What are you doin'? I'm here in a phone booth in Miami and there's a lot of talk goin' around."

"What do ya hear?"

"I hear you're doin' Secretariat."

"You want one?" Seth asks him. Scully leaps. "Put me down for one," he says, "for Yoshida." Scully pauses, then adds quickly, "Put me down for maybe two. There's another client of mine who might want one."

"One to a customer. But if I need any more help I'll call you."

At the Big Sink Farm in Versailles, E. V. Benjamin is reaching Susan Proskauer at her home in Akron.

They are old friends, and Benjamin is asking if she would like to be a partner in a share.

Mrs. Proskauer was born Susan Sternberg in Breslau, Germany, and she remembers the day in 1938, when she was almost twenty years old, that her father took her on a three-hour automobile ride to the base of the Sudetenland in Czechoslovakia. There he put her on skis and watched her escape from Germany. Her parents didn't survive the holocaust. She later fled Czechoslovakia, when the Axis powers overran it, and finally found her way to America. Her first job was as a maid in Brooklyn, where she learned English, and even today her accent is distinctly German but with a trace of Flatbush Avenue in it. She became a dressmaker in Manhattan, later still a dress designer. Then in 1945, she married an Akron pathologist, Dr. George Proskauer, then fell in love with Chris Chenery's Hill Prince in 1950, went into racing herself in the 1950s, and soon was involved in breeding horses. She met Benjamin, who introduced her to Bull Hancock.

"What do you think?" Susan asks Benjamin.

"I think we ought to buy a share," says Benjamin. She agrees.

Benjamin, with two partners and himself paying a third, dials Claiborne for the third time that day.

"Erase the question mark."

So the day grinds on for Seth, the first and the slowest of them all, the longest and the most difficult.

He is still waiting for Salmon and Mrs. duPont to call back. John Finney is still waiting, too, wondering what is going on in the matter of Claiborne syndicating Secretariat. And Tim Rogers and Jonathan Irwin are in Europe, waiting for word on their proposal.

Seth calls the Greentree Stable of John Hay Whitney and Mrs. Joan Payson. He doesn't talk to Mrs. Payson, though she is a partner in the racing farm and stable. Veteran Greentree Stable trainer John Gaver, who once trained the great Tom Fool, confers with John Hay Whitney on the offer, and Gaver recommends that Greentree decline the share.

"You're paying a hell of a lot of money for an untried three-year-old," John Gaver says.

Greentree then calls Seth back. They decline.

Not all breeders are so hesitant as Salmon, Mrs. duPont, Benjamin, and Greentree. Like Jim Scully, the enthusiasts add a sense of relief to Seth's day. They are those who buy almost without question, without having to think for hours about it. On that first day the enthusiastic buyers are Milton (Laddie) Dance and Richard Stokes.

They call Laddie Dance at his condominium on a glittering swath of beach in Boca Raton, Florida, where he and his wife Jean, heiress to an Oregon lumber fortune, are spending a part of a winter.

The Dances are only small market breeders, moving to build slowly upon their band of mares at their 320-acre Taylor's Purchase Farm in Maryland, but Laddie is well connected in the industry and he has made known frequently his wish to be part of a Secretariat syndicate. He is Fasig-Tipton's auctioneer, possessing one of those pneumatically deft larynxes out of an old Lucky Strike ad, and a wooden gavel to punctuate his fervent spiel.

Lucien Laurin trains the Dances' horses, and for weeks Dance has been telling Lucien he wants a share in Secretariat.

Laddie has seen the colt run at Saratoga, has seen him, too, around the barn at Belmont Park, and he has already approached Penny seeking a share. He has written her a letter to make the request official, and she has included Laddie's name on her list for Seth. The horse meets all of Laddie's standards as a prospective sire.

Seth discusses Penny Tweedy's plans for Secretariat—all prospective buyers are asking him about that—and Seth says she is aiming him for the Triple Crown, by way of the Bay Shore, Gotham, and Wood Memorial, and later the Travers and Woodward. No one can take exception to that. Seth would recall Laddie as the first person he has reached who doesn't say, "That's a lot of money." Laddie says nothing of the sort. He says, "I'm in."

Nor does Richard Stokes dwell hours on the question.

Seth doesn't know Richard Stokes, in fact has never spoken to or seen the man, but he is calling him at home now because Penny has him on her list. Stokes, a Virginian, had met Penny during a recent visit to The Meadow, at a time when she was still hoping the colt might one day stand at stud in Virginia. She had asked him if he would like a share in the horse if he were syndicated.

Stokes, forty, a former gasoline station attendant who married the heiress to the Johnson and Johnson pharmaceutical fortune, runs a modest commercial breeding establishment at the 750-acre Shenstone Farm in Leesburg, a small town in the idyllic horse country of northern Virginia. Stokes has ten broodmares, one a daughter of Native Dancer that he thinks would fit Secretariat well.

Stokes is at home on the farm when Seth reaches him, sitting in his modernistic library on his gingerbread tan leather short-backed chair looking out the glassed-in room toward the paddock. He hesitates only momentarily.

"That's a lot of money," Stokes says to Hancock. "But I'll have one. I like the horse."

For Seth, the day stumbles on as he waits for key breeders to call back.

It is noon. Seth asks Patti Tompkins to stay with him at the office to answer phones for him. At times there are two or three people waiting to talk to Seth, idling on hold. Hanging up on one, he picks up on another. A worker in the office drives into Paris, to Overby's Restaurant on Main Street, and buys lunches to go for Patti and Seth, who has a sixty-five-cent cheeseburger, french fries, and a Coca Cola. He eats his lunch between calls.

It has been a long morning.

At one point, as a courtesy, Seth calls the Cincinnati office of Dr. Eslie Asbury, the surgeon to whom Bull sold a share in Nasrullah for $10,000 in 1949. Asbury made a $700,000 profit on that purchase, by his own estimate. Now, almost a quarter of a century later, Seth calls Asbury to ask if he would buy a share in Nasrullah's finest grandson for $180,000 more than the original investment. Dr. Asbury is not in, and Seth leaves a message relating details and asking Dr. Asbury to return the call.

Arriving at his office, Asbury receives the message Seth has left and hardly thinks about it.

"Bold Ruler just hadn't had any record of horses that went on to win the classic races," he would say. "The amount of money they were asking was based on the premise that he was going to be a great three-year-old."

Asbury isn't sure of Secretariat. He decides not to return Seth's call.

"See if you can get Taylor Hardin for me."

It has been seven months since breeder Taylor Hardin, owner of Newstead Farm in northern Virginia, turned to Penny Tweedy at Saratoga, just minutes after the colt beat Russ Miron, and told her he wanted a breeding share in Secretariat.

Hardin is now on the phone, and Seth is asking him if he wants a share. Taylor objects at the price, saying it is far too high. He says to Seth, "I heard this horse is sore, I heard he's about to break down."

Seth bristles, listening to the old rumor. "Mr. Hardin, if you think he's broke down, I wouldn't ask you to go into the syndicate," Seth says. Hardin declines the offer.

It is nearing the end of the first day, and Seth Hancock has sold only six shares—to Phipps, Lockridge, Benjamin, Yoshida, Dance, and Stokes. It is still too early to assess the level of one share in Secretariat for $190,000, to know for sure whether there are twenty-two more out there. The offer *has* been turned down, but it has been accepted with alacrity, too, and there are still a number thinking about it.

Among them are Walter Salmon and Mrs. duPont.

What's keeping them? To Seth they remain pivotal, weather vanes and barometers of the industry's intent, indicators of acceptance among potential buyers. Their hesitation has weighed down Hancock's end of the day, causing him concern since early morning when they told him they would call him back. He's still wondering which way they plan to move, in fact, when Patti Tompkins tells him Mr. Salmon is on the line. Answering, Seth hears Walter Salmon tell him: "I'll take a share."

Thus a major commercial breeder, a businessman owning seven breeding shares in various stallions, has decided to pay more for a share in Secretariat than he has ever paid for a single share in his life.

"Thank you, sir. I sure do appreciate it."

Four o'clock Friday afternoon the outlook has brightened.

"How are you doin'?" Penny asks. He has just called to let her know.

"I have seven positives. But I have a lot more to call me back."

His tone is matter-of-fact about the course of the day. Waiting for prospective buyers to call him back, Seth spends his evening working, casting about for more.

For several hours Seth has been trying to track down Will Farish III, the breeder and owner of Preakness winner Bee Bee Bee. Farish's family, his grandmother and aunt, have known the Hancocks for years, boarding mares at Claiborne. Will Farish is in the investment business in Houston, chiefly mining exploration for hard-rock minerals. He is a member of the Jockey Club, owns a racing stable, and has a ranch in Texas.

Will Farish has told Seth months earlier, after seeing Secretariat run at Saratoga, that he would like a share in him if he ever were syndicated, and his enthusiasm for the youngster grew over the winter. He had been visiting his barn at Belmont Park and watching him go to the track in the morning.

It is Friday evening when Seth finally makes contact with Farish in Florida, where he is staying at a friend's house. Seth reads the terms to Farish—the number of shares, the plans, the price.

"That's certainly awful full," Will says. "A heck of a price."

Yet Farish, discussing the upside and downside potential of the colt, feels that the price is justified given the booming nature of the bloodstock industry. "He had so many things about him that took the gamble out of it—being already the two-year-old champ and the Horse of the Year, and he'd already won an extraordinary amount of money and he was a beautiful individual and a son of Bold Ruler, and Bold Ruler is the phenomenal sire of sires. You could probably get your money back by selling sons and daughters of Secretariat in the first two years."

Ten minutes into the phone call, Farish owns a share.

He makes eight, leaving twenty, and Hancock begins closing in. He goes to bed that evening still not knowing which way Allaire duPont plans to move on the deal, but the pressure is lifting, and he's far more optimistic than he was twelve hours ago. Salmon has given considerable relief, and Hancock is especially buoyed over Farish's purchase because Farish is young, compared with others Seth has spoken to, and he is seeking rapport with breeders close to his age, with those he might know and do business with for many years to come. Now what of Mrs. duPont?

She doesn't keep him waiting long.

Early on Saturday she rings Paris from Chesapeake City and sends Seth on his way at last, giving him the final boost he needs, the confidence that what remains is within reach and that, if he just keeps at it, it's only a question of time. "I knew when Mrs. duPont said yes that I had it."

Through the next three days, working to tie it together, Seth keeps mining the richest and most productive veins of the industry. Among those who bought shares in the first day are men who represent all the most powerful breeding groups in the country, and from them he continues to gather support, share by share—from those with foreign gold such as Zenya Yoshida, from Kentucky breeders such as E. V. Benjamin and Bill Lockridge, from the few superrich and the old rich such as Ogden Phipps, and most especially from the American businessman-as-breeder, such as Will Farish. Seth reaches out to them over the weekend, picking up one after another, confident as time passes that he is launched, inevitably now, upon a world-record bloodstock syndication.

Among the Midases of the sport are Mellon as well as McKnight, who raised the Minnesota Mining and Manufacturing Company from a modest adhesive tape and sandpaper firm to a $1 billion empire.

Seth speaks to their representatives.

Mellon is in his room at Claridge's, in London for a week on business and to see his colt, Mill Reef, when he receives a telegram from his New York office telling him the terms of the Secretariat contract.

Paul Mellon, sixty-four, is the son of financier Andrew Mellon—secretary of the treasury under presidents Harding, Coolidge, and Hoover, ambassador to the Court of Saint James, and the original benefactor of the National Gallery of Art, which he built for $16 million and adorned with his $50 million art collection: Rembrandts, El Grecos, Botticellis, Goyas.

Paul never shared his father's interest in finance, preferring William Blake to Pittsburgh banking, but he did acquire his father's enthusiasm for philanthropy and art collecting. He has given millions to conservation projects, such as Cape Hatteras State Park, millions more to Yale, his alma mater, and even more millions to the gallery, of which he is the president and chief benefactor.

"Giving away large sums of money nowadays is a soul-searching problem," Paul Mellon has said. "You can do as much damage with it as you do good." Mellon writes poetry, rides to hounds, owns a rare book collection of numerous volumes, and is the owner and head of the 4600-acre estate in the Blue Ridge Mountains of Virginia, with a whitewashed stone farmhouse with French windows.

Reading the cable in his room at Claridge's, Paul Mellon cables back that he accepts the terms of the syndication, authorizing purchase of a share pending the approval of Elliott Burch, his Yale-educated trainer.

"It's too much money," Burch complains, talking to Seth from his Florida home near Hialeah. But yes, he says, Rokeby will buy a share.

The Rokeby acceptance is valuable and important to any syndicate, especially to commercial breeders such as Salmon, for Mellon's presence will ensure that one of Rokeby's superbly bred mares will be sent to Secretariat once a year. His is a private, not a market, venture. Mellon breeds to race, seeking intrinsic excellence in his horses, not commercial quality.

Ars gratia artis.

If Secretariat fails as a stallion, he will manage to fail on his own, not through the lack of depth in the mares that Rokeby sends him. For a commercial breeder, then, Rokeby is the perfect colleague on a breeding syndicate: Rokeby yearlings sired by Secretariat will not be offered competitively at yearling sales, where they would depress demand for his progeny, but their success on the racetrack will serve to drive up the value of shares in the stallion and his offspring sold commercially.

The Mellon acceptance is part of no pattern. No dominant theme of acceptance or rejection emerges among the owners of large private farms in America, such as Rokeby, though there is a tendency toward rejection among members of this class of landed wealth. John Hay Whitney of the Greentree Stud is only one. Seth experiences his severest disappointment during the days of syndication when he reaches Robert Kleberg, owner of the King Ranch of Texas, at his small farm in Florida. Kleberg presides over a colossus legendary in its size and scope, the very symbol of Texas itself—over giant herds of beef cattle, over quarter horses, over 650 oil and gas wells, over enough land to embrace all Rhode Island and parts of Massachusetts, and stables of horses that race under his brown silks with the white running *W.* The King Ranch bred and owned the great Assault, the 1946 Triple Crown winner and Horse of the Year, among other lesser lights.

Seth offers and Kleberg declines; the colt does not fit into his breeding program. Much traditional money fails Seth. Michael G. Phipps, sixty-three, who would die two weeks later of a heart attack, also declines the offer when Seth calls. Seth calls the Calumet Farm, reaching farm manager Melvin Cinnamon, who also turns down the offer. Some of the richest are the most reluctant of all.

"That's too much money!" Nelson Bunker Hunt, son of billionaire oilman H. L. Hunt, tells Seth. "You act like he's won the Triple Crown already."

The winds are warmer in Florida, where Seth contacts trainer Johnny Nerud at William L. McKnight's Tartan Farm. There Nerud manages McKnight's growing thoroughbred holdings.

"I am in the breeding business, and I'm breeding horses for Mr. McKnight, and he wants the very best horses I can get him," Nerud would say. "So I have to buy the best available—and at all times. It has nothing to do with how much money they are. But it's: 'Do I like 'em?'"

McKnight can buy anything Nerud likes. At eighty-five, he's one of America's wealthiest men, a powerful industrialist who went to work for 3-M as an assistant bookkeeper in 1907, when it was making sandpaper, became its president in 1929, when its sales were $5 million, and rose to become its chairman of the board in 1949, when sales were $1 billion. Retiring in 1966, McKnight went home with more than $200 million in stock.

John Nerud has invested in mares and stallion shares for McKnight, with his patron giving him wide latitude in decision making. Nerud has just finished morning training hours at the farm in Florida when Seth calls him.

"A hundred and ninety thousand."

"Well." Nerud thinks about it. "For that kind of money, I'll have to ask Mr. McKnight. But I'm sure it's all right." The latitude has its limits. "When I spend two hundred thousand dollars of Mr. McKnight's money, I think I'm obligated to tell him."

Nerud quickly reaches his patron, who is at home in Florida busy running his empire.

"I bought a share of a horse."

"Well, that's good. Who'd you buy?"

"Secretariat."

"That's good. How much did you give for him?"

"Probably better if I don't tell you," says Nerud.

"I'll find out anyway."

"Well, I gave $190,000."

"That's all right," says William McKnight.

Among the acceptances by Mellon and McKnight, among the refusals by Kleberg and Phipps, Whitney and Calumet and others, Hancock seeks out foreign bloodstock breeders and their agents, finding them in Europe, Canada, and America. The devalued American dollar has enriched the value of their currency in America—their pounds, yen, dollars, and francs, both Swiss and French—and they've been spending them hungrily on American bloodstock. In 1972, 25 percent of all select yearlings sold in America were bought by foreign interests. Among the foreigners, then, Seth finds enthusiastic investors in Secretariat. That Yoshida's agent, Jim Scully, is the first buyer actually to seek out a share in the colt is evidence of this.

It is eleven o'clock in Zurich, Switzerland, when the telephone rings in the modernistic fourth-floor office suite of Walter Haefner, who is working at his desk. Through the window Haefner can see the Lake of Zurich, dotted now and then with sailing ships, and beyond a rim of small mountains. On the telephone is Murray McDonnell, Haefner's representative in America, calling to tell him he now owns a share in Secretariat.

Haefner is a Swiss banker, a member of the board of the Union Bank, the biggest bank in Switzerland. He is the sole distributor for the Chrysler Corporation in Switzerland, the owner of that firm's Swiss assembly plant, and the sole distributor for Volkswagen there. Haefner is a wiry, engaging man of sixty-three, the owner of two frosty gray eyebrows that jump up and down when he speaks. A continental sportsman in the best tradition, he loves the sports of speed, bobsledding in Saint Moritz—ninety miles an hour down an icy track—and riding racehorses. Speed is what attracted Haefner to racing, when he first had a chance to ride a racehorse in Paris in 1959. "I loved it, the sensation of speed on the horse."

He has been an active buyer of bloodstock in America, and he has been waiting for McDonnell to call him since he was told a week ago that Secretariat might be syndicated and he might have a chance to buy a share.

"Don't hesitate!" Haefner had told him then. "That sounds too good. Don't tell me about figures, don't worry about that."

Haefner picks up the phone and hears McDonnell's distant voice. He looks at his watch, sees it's eleven Zurich time, and figures it's five in the morning in New York.

"What are you doing up so early?" Haefner asks him.

McDonnell tells him that Seth has offered him a share and that he took it for him, for $190,000, and he wants to tell him about it.

"Murray," Haefner tells him. "We have done many good things together, but this is the best ever."

The search for foreign gold goes on.

Seth reaches French trainer Alec Head at his training quarters, Villa Vimy, at Chantilly. Head is part of a long line of French horsemen reaching back to William Head, an Englishman who started as a jockey in England, crossed the channel in 1880, and settled in La Croix Saint Oven, where he established himself as a trainer. Alec is the grandson of William Head and the son of Willie Head, for decades a leading horseman in France and the father of Freddie Head, France's leading jockey. Their business ties to Claiborne Farm are numerous. When Seth calls Alec at Chantilly, business between them goes on. Head buys a share in Secretariat for Jacques Wertheimer, one of his owners.

Seth now moves to contact E. P. Taylor, the Canadian thoroughbred giant whose fortune is in forestry, mining, real estate, farm machinery, and thoroughbreds. He is the owner of the Windfields Farms in Canada and America. In Maryland it's a 400-acre tract of land where he stands stallions Northern Dancer and Royal Orbit at the stud. Taylor is in Nassau, the Bahamas, so Seth speaks to a representative in Canada, asking him to contact Taylor. Taylor is almost certain to buy a share.

He is among the world's foremost market breeders, America's fourth leading breeder in money won during 1972, when horses bred by him won 308 races at $1,433,489. Every year from 1960 through 1969, horses bred by Taylor won more races than the horses bred by any other breeder. He has been an enormous shaping force in Canadian racing—the father of the sport there—and a participant in America, where he won the Derby and Preakness with Northern Dancer. His activities have been felt most strongly in the bloodstock industry—he buys and sells yearlings, buys mares, stallion shares, and land.

Reached by his man in the Bahamas, Taylor takes no time to make up his mind. "I thought it was a good buy," he says. "If you're a breeder, it's a matter of simple common sense: you have a good chance of getting your capital costs back in two, three, or four years."

As Taylor's acceptance is no surprise, neither is that of insurance millionaire Jean-Louis Levesque. "And will you please put the share in the name of my son Pierre?" he asks.

Across the Atlantic, meanwhile, the market for Secretariat is alive with hope and money in the British Isles.

Hugo Morriss, the prominent English breeder, buys a share from Seth. And through Charles Kenney, one of the three members of the Claiborne advisory committee, Mr. and Mrs. Paul Hexter of Ireland and Miami buy a share. They are prominent in European racing, and through Mrs. Hexter they have powerful ties to Claiborne Farm. Her father, Rent-A-Car and Yellow Cab king John D. Hertz, owned and bred the great Triple Crown winner Count Fleet. Hertz, whose Stoner Creek Stud adjoins the Claiborne Farm, was a long-time friend of the Hancocks, both Seth's grandfather and father.

Kenney is the manager of Stoner Creek, and through him the Hexters have entree to the horse. They have told Kenney already that they want a share in him. Seth calls Kenney, knowing he represents them, and asks him to contact the Hexters and find out if they want a share. Kenney does; and they do.

So the Paul Hexters own a share.

On to Ireland.

Captain Tim Rogers, still waiting for Finney to call, is relaxing in an easy chair in his country home outside Dublin, in a sitting room hung with paintings of horses, a window facing a hedge and lawn in front and, beyond that, fields running flat under oaken post-and-rail fencing. Though he regards the chances of importing Secretariat as "problematical," Rogers has taken home with him a feeling of excitement over the possibility.

"We might have done it," he has told his wife. "There is a chance."

Seth reaches Rogers in the sitting room.

"Captain Rogers, this is Seth Hancock. I'm calling because Mrs. Tweedy has authorized me to syndicate Secretariat, and I'm in the process."

Rogers listens on in silence.

"And we wanted to know if you would like to take a share. The price is $190,000 a share in thirty-two."

For Seth, the call is innocent of any meaning beyond the selling of Secretariat; he does not know about Rogers's offer made to Penny through John Finney. So he doesn't know he's telling Rogers, for the first time, that Secretariat will not be standing in Ireland and there will be no international bloodstock coup, no world-record $6.5 million spectacular. Rogers, curiously, is also of two minds at the moment—bitterly disappointed yet somehow relieved—ambivalent, as Finney was ambivalent. For Rogers, it has to do with how he feels toward Bull.

Rogers and the elder Hancock had been friends as well as business acquaintances. Rogers had bought the stakes-winning Dike from Bull, importing him to Ireland, and his fondness for the American had run deep: "A man I admire more than anybody else," Rogers would say. Rogers believes that Bull, were he alive, would never have permitted a foreign syndicate to purchase and export Secretariat. "I knew that if Bull Hancock had been alive, there would have been no chance of buying this horse." So making the quiet but powerful move to buy the colt, Rogers is "desperately keen" on succeeding, but he feels vaguely guilty about it, feels that if he pulls it off, if he succeeds as a thief in the night, he will have somehow taken advantage of Bull's son, while he is trying to establish himself—in effect, parlaying Bull's death into a major Irish bloodstock coup. He buys a share.

Hanging up, Rogers quickly calls Jonathan Irwin, who is in Dublin, and he tells him what has just happened.

"If you want a share in the horse, you better ring him straightaway," Rogers tells Irwin.

It is getting late, for Irwin almost too late.

Irwin calls Seth, asking for a share, and Seth tells him, "I'm sorry, Jonathan, it's blocked out. Unless someone else drops out."

"What?"

Irwin can hardly fathom it. He is flabbergasted. "Miserable. Bloody miserable. One minute I had a chance to buy the whole horse, and the next minute I couldn't even get a damn share in him!" He's crushed until the next day, when Seth unexpectedly calls him back. Someone has backed out, and Irwin grabs the share for the Meiwa Stud of Japanese industrialist Tadao Tamashima.

In America again, Seth has been working Kentucky bloodstock breeders and agents, and among them the offer has been both accepted and turned down.

Seth tries the Hurstland Farm of the Nuckols brothers, a successful thoroughbred nursery with more than fifty mares and almost 1000 acres of land. Charley Nuckols declines the offer, advising Seth that they are in the process of buying up bloodstock owned by a close relative. So Seth moves on.

On Saturday he calls the Delray, Florida, home of Warner Jones, Jr., the seventy-ninth member of the Jockey Club, a close friend of Bull since boyhood, his traveling companion when their parents sent them to Europe to study the breeding business, the great grandson of the founder of Frankfurt Distilleries.

Jones is gray haired now, lean, athletic, and wearing a perpetual tan. He is sixty-one, he smokes unfiltered Camel cigarettes and has a bullfrog deepness in his voice.

Jones has been a thoroughbred market breeder since 1937, the year he sold the first yearlings he ever bred at his 800-acre Hermitage Farm in Goshen, Kentucky, east of Louisville. He bred Dark Star, sold him to Captain Harry Guggenheim for $6500 as a yearling and watched him win the 1953 Kentucky Derby in a tight finish with Native Dancer. He has bred almost thirty stakes winners in his life.

"Life is a game and money is what we keep score with," he has said.

At the moment now Warner Jones is keeping score.

"I'm a market breeder, Seth. I'd like to buy one but I'd rather buy a mare." What Warner is thinking is that he could buy two mares, for $95,000 each, for the price of one share in Secretariat, and breed and sell their foals.

"That's good," Seth says, piqued. "You know, I don't need you."

"Am I going to be able to breed to him if I don't take a share?"

"No."

"That's a lot of money," Warner says. Seeking time to think about it, though he says he's already made up his mind to buy a share, Warner says he'll call Seth back on Sunday. He wants time to drive to Hialeah and see the colt just one more time. He calls Lucien, who's at Hialeah, and asks him if he can drive over to see the colt at the barn and off goes Jones, along the highway from Delray to Hialeah. "I wanted to confirm my mental picture of the horse: that he was the best lookin' horse I'd ever seen." Arriving at the Meadow Stable at Hialeah, he asks the stablehand to lead the colt from the stall. Jones studies him methodically, as Charles Hatton studied him at Saratoga the summer before, looking at the straightness of the hindleg, the hindquarters, the head. "He's got a beautiful head and he's wide between the eyes. That's an indication of brains in a horse, and he's got a real beautiful jaw that you want in a stallion, just the kind you want. You don't want a stallion to have a narrow little head like a mule's head. This horse doesn't. He has a strong, masculine jaw."

He has seen what he came to see. Warner Jones is the only buyer to steal a last-minute peek at the goods.

On Sunday, Seth is taking it easy, relaxing in front of the television set in his home. He has the syndication nearly wrapped up. He is watching a sports special as he dozes. The phone awakens him. It's Warner.

"Seth? I think this is the best lookin' horse I ever saw. I also think it's too damn much money. But you put me down for a share anyway."

Among the Kentucky market breeders, as it turns out, only Lockridge doesn't put off buying a share when he is asked. They are a reluctant group compared with the others, shrewd in the ways of all horseflesh. Benjamin, Salmon, and Jones all need time. So, too, does the firm of J. B. Faulconer and Hillary Boone, bloodstock agents.

Hancock reaches J. B. Faulconer at the firm's offices in Lexington, and for a moment Faulconer thinks that Seth is calling on some military matter. Seth Hancock is a private first class in the 100th Division of the Army Reserve. Major General Faulconer commands the division.

"I think we'll go in," Faulconer finally tells him. "But I'll have to speak to my partner first."

"Christ," says his partner. "That's a lot of money."

The two men are relative newcomers to the breeding business. Faulconer is the former publicity director at Keeneland Race Course in the Blue Grass country and Boone is one of the founders of Extendicare, a corporation that builds and acquires hospitals throughout the United States. Seth is calling them because they are on Penny's list of names. Ordinarily, Seth would not have contacted them so soon, if at all.

Faulconer advises the firm to buy. Boone winces, figuring not only the $190,000 outlay but also the loss of 12 percent of that going into the deal: money is worth 8 percent, the prevailing interest rate, and "it takes 4 percent to insure the horse." Boone provides most of the money in the partnership, Faulconer the advice.

"If you think that's the thing to do, well, go ahead," says Hillary Boone.

And Faulconer does.

With these breeders in the business who buy shares come businessmen involved in breeding. They form an important, powerful segment in the bloodstock industry, bringing to it money made in oil, automobiles, real estate, fast foods, and paper manufacturing, and among them Hancock seeks and finds customers such as Will Farish and young Dan R. Lasater, Richard Brooks and Howard Brighton Keck.

Keck is the president of the Superior Oil Company, a Houston-based giant whose sales in crude oil and natural gas ranged between $100 million and $200 million last year. Keck has been associated with Claiborne Farm as a client and owner for many years.

"What do you think?" Keck asks Seth.

"Well, you've got a lot of mares that will suit the horse. And you don't have any Bold Ruler blood, Mr. Keck. I know it's a lot of money, but if he wins the Triple Crown he's going to be worth a lot more than this. If he doesn't, well, he's still going to be a hell of a stud horse."

And Keck is in.

Brooks and Lasater buy it up as quickly.

Brooks is the owner of Brooks Buick, a successful auto dealership in Baltimore. He and his wife raise thoroughbreds at their 126-acre Hillstead Farm in Glyndon, Maryland, a mile down the road from

Sagamore. They are small market breeders, owning only a few mares. Seth doesn't know David Brooks. Penny knows them because Lucien happens to train their horses, and she has them on her list. At the barn one morning, they had mentioned to Penny that they would be interested in owning a share of Secretariat.

Brooks is at his Florida home in Lost Tree Village, a swanky, sporty, fenced-in resort community set on a golf course. Among his neighbors are Perry Como and Jack Nicklaus. In fact, Brooks has just finished playing eighteen holes of golf with Laddie Dance, who has already bought his share, when Seth calls. David Brooks, a distinguished looking man who bears a resemblance to TV commentator Howard K. Smith, has already thought about the price and is delighted with a chance to have access to such a prospect for his mares. He's in, too.

Dan R. Lasater is living in a rented chalet on Lake Hamilton in Hot Springs, Arkansas, where he spends winters watching his horses race at Oaklawn Park. He has just returned from the racetrack, where he goes mornings to watch the horses work, and decides to call his office.

"Have you gotten a hold of Seth Hancock yet?" a secretary asks.

"No. Why?"

"He's been trying to reach you."

"Did you give him my number here?"

"No."

Lasater fumes. "Look," he snaps, "anytime somebody like that calls, be sure to give them the number down here. Someone calls like that it's usually important."

Off the phone, he quickly calls Claiborne, but Seth is out to lunch. Lasater is frantic. He rushes down a pathway to the cabin of his general manager, John Fernung, and bounds through the front door, telling him about the message, "I think he's calling about Secretariat."

In fact, Seth has been calling everywhere to reach him. Dan Lasater is young, personable, landed, and extremely rich, a newcomer to thoroughbred breeding but just the kind of breeder Seth wants in the syndicate. For Lasater, this would have been unthinkable just ten years before.

Lasater grew up in a poor family in Kokomo, Indiana, living in an eight-by-twenty-four foot trailer until he was nineteen years old, the son of an employe at the Delco Radio Corporation. After graduating from high school, Lasater got a job with a McDonald's hamburger outlet, sweeping a parking lot for sixty cents an hour. But Lasater quickly worked his way up, becoming a manager of a store, a reader and disciple of McDonald's *Wonderful Training Manual,* with chapters on hamburgers, milk shakes, and french fries. He turned workers into perfectionists, doling out responsibilities to the milk shake and the french fries makers. He was nineteen. Then he got bored. So he sought and found a financial backer for a fast-food restaurant in Kokomo, and he made that a success, underselling McDonald's. With the same backer, he then helped found the Ponderosa Steak House chain, offering a nine-ounce steak, an eight-ounce potato, a salad, and a roll for $1.39. The company prospered and survived hard times. In 1972 Dan Lasater decided to retire as the executive vice-president in charge of Ponderosa Systems operations.

He was twenty-nine, and he had $30 million.

Now Lasater has four farms, including a 480-acre nursery in Goshen, Kentucky, that is devoted exclusively to raising thoroughbreds. He has thirty-four mares, a flourishing multimillion dollar investment in land and horses, and he wants a chance for a share in the red horse. Returning the call, Seth offers him one and Lasater takes it.

Not all businessmen and foreigners jump for shares. That they don't, in fact, leads to the selling of one share to the only practicing professional in the syndicate, George Strawbridge, a thirty-five-year-old Latin American history teacher from Widener College.

This begins when Seth traces English bloodstock agent George Harris to an apartment in New York. Working out of the Heron Bloodstock Agency in London, Harris has just arrived in America. Harris promises to call Seth back and starts to contact clients, the first one overseas.

Failing to reach breeder Henry Berlin at his business in Barcelona, Spain, Harris makes contact with him finally in Normandy, France, where he owns and operates a stud farm. Berlin, hearing the price and the plea that he has but a couple of hours to make a decision, complains to Harris that the urgency is *so* typically American.

"I can't make up my mind in a couple of hours," Berlin tells Harris. "I'll need a chance to think about it."

Sorry. There is no time. Harris needs a commitment from his client now. So he calls Peter Fuller, a Cadillac dealer from Boston, but he declines, too. "Not at this time," says Fuller, owner of Dancer's Image, the disputed winner of the 1968 Kentucky Derby.

So Harris then calls Strawbridge, reaching him at his Augustin Stable in Chesapeake City, Maryland. Strawbridge, an heir to the Campbell Soup fortune, not only teaches history in Chester, Pennsylvania, but rides to hounds and in steeplechases and races a string of fifteen horses, jumping and running on the flats.

"How do you evaluate him?" he asks Harris.

"He's got spectacular breeding. He's a bit high but I think it's sound. If he runs like he did as a two-year-old, he'll be a buy."

Strawbridge regards the offer as an excellent speculative opportunity. "I'll go," George Strawbridge says. The call lasts no more than three minutes.

And John Finney? Well, he's still waiting for word, either from Penny on the Irish offer or from his Hialeah operative. Finney is leaving the clubhouse of the golf club one morning when, passing by the first tee, he hears his name ring across the fairway.

"Hey, John!"

Finney looks up. There, standing at the first tee 100 yards away, standing there and waiting to tee off for a round of golf, is his connection, who is leaning on his golf bag.

"I got the phone call!"

Finney gallops over to the tee. He listens as his operative explains the details: "$190,000 a share. Thirty-two shares. She races him for a year." John dashes to a telephone.

Quickly now, trying to organize his forces, sensing he is fighting time, Finney calls an associate at Fasig-Tipton, Larry Ensor. John is now hunting shares for American clients such as Bertram Firestone, a Manhattan real estate developer, and Howard Gilman, chairman of the board of the Gilman Paper Company in New York.

Finney reaches Ensor, explaining to him the details of what he has just heard. "Look," Finney says. "I'm calling Firestone; you call Gilman and see if he wants in. I don't know if I can get him or not, but if we're gonna do it, we're gonna have to move fast."

Before he contacts Seth, Finney wants to reach his clients, so he calls Firestone at his Connecticut home, advising him of the terms of the deal.

"He's a hundred and ninety thousand a share," Finney says at one point in the discussion. "Do you want in?"

"That's a lot of money," Firestone says.

"Well, I've already told you that I was a consultant to the estate and I advised them to sell. By definition it can't be a good time to sell and a good time to buy. If this is the best risk for them, obviously they're passing the risk as a potential buyer on to you. But I don't think the horse's value can ever diminish to less than $100,000 a share. If Secretariat falls on his ass, he could be worth only $100,000 a share. Maybe $125,000. If he wins the Triple Crown, the upside potential is only $20,000 to $30,000 to $40,000. I'd say that if he wins the Triple Crown, he'll probably be worth $230,000 a share. The downside potential is much greater than the upside potential."

"What do you think?" Bert says.

"You're on a 60 percent value trip and a 40 percent ego trip. But, if you're building a stud and want the very best, and if you want to take a chance on what I think is the best prospect combining pedigree, conformation, and ability that I've seen in twenty years, then go ahead. He has that downside potential if he doesn't run up to snuff in the Triple Crown. But if the horse succeeds, there will not be a second chance. This is it."

Suddenly Firestone's wife, Dariel, an heiress to the Avon cosmetics fortune, picks up an extension phone. She has been hearing part of her husband's side of the discussion. "What are you two men doing?" she asks. "It sounds very exciting."

"Yes it is," says Finney, "but it's a little scary."

Once again Finney runs down the colt's upside and downside potential, the terms of the contract, and the urgency of this matter at hand. The Firestones hedge.

"It's obvious you haven't reached a family consensus," Finney says. "I'm going to hang up the phone and stay off. Call me when you've decided. But *don't* take more than ten minutes."

Precisely twelve minutes later—Finney glances up at the clock— the phone rings. It's Bert.

"We're in," he says.

Larry Ensor, meanwhile, is speaking to Howard Gilman at the offices of the Gilman Paper Company in New York. Ensor tells Gilman that a decision is urgent. Asking for time to consider it, Gilman calls his brother Charles on the office intercom, telling him the details of what Ensor has just told him.

"How much?" asks Charles.

"A hundred and ninety thousand a share."

"How does that pay out?"

"You can't make a business analysis of that kind of thing," says brother Howard.

Ensor holds as the Gilmans talk it over on the intercom.

"Well, what kind of *investment* is it?" asks Charles.

"You can't make an analysis. You're figuring human things, you're figuring genetics, you're figuring health, and these things can't be put on a balance sheet."

The Gilmans are relatively new to bloodstock breeding. They own the 5500-acre White Oak Plantation about forty miles north of Jacksonville, Florida. Most of the land is planted in southern pine trees, the principal wood for making paper, though they do have about 100 acres under grass and sixteen mares nibbling at it. The Gilman Paper Company breeds for the marketplace, and Howard Gilman sees the share as a sound commercial gamble.

"If it works out, we'll do extremely well," Howard says. "There should always be a salvage value in any case. We're not buying a complete pig in a poke."

"If you think it's all right, then go ahead," says Charles.

"Try to get it for us," Howard tells Ensor. "You've convinced me."

Ensor now calls Finney, telling him that the Gilmans want a share. Armed with the two commitments, John calls Claiborne. He holds the phone for forty minutes, unable to get through, and he imagines Seth fielding calls from all over, picking up one voice after another, calling and answering and calling again. Finally, still not having spoken to Seth, John calls his father Humphrey, for years a close confidant of Bull, and asks him to "put in a good word for Firestone and Gilman." Humphrey calls Seth.

"John has been trying to reach you and hasn't been able to," he says to Seth. "He's very much interested in a share or two. He's down in Florida. Bert Firestone is interested in a share and so is Howard Gilman. Will you please call John?"

"I'll call him," Seth says.

Reaching Finney in Florida, Seth tells him he has one available share and will give it to Firestone. Seth knows Firestone, the owner of Chance Hill Farm, has been an active bloodstock buyer and has acquired quality mares for breeding.

"He's getting the first shot," Seth tells John.

Finney adds, "If you can get a share for Gilman, I'd very much appreciate it."

"Who's Gilman?" asks Seth.

Finney outlines the Gilman breeding program, telling Seth that the Gilmans would also be sending high quality mares to Secretariat.

"There isn't a share available now," Seth says. "But there might be one later."

Seth tells Finney that John Galbreath, owner of Roberto, is considering the purchase of a share. If Galbreath declines, says Seth, the vacant share will go to Gilman.

At least, thinks Finney, Firestone has a share.

It's Monday, and Seth is trying to tie it all together.

For days he has been working to track down F. Eugene Dixon, calling his office in Philadelphia and places where he might be found in Florida. Dixon is a fifty-year-old sportsman, philanthropist, and horse breeder, and Seth can't reach him now because he is living on his fifty-six-foot yacht *Wayfarer*, with a permanent crew of three, somewhere off the Florida coast. But Seth keeps trying. Dixon has been an active buyer of bloodstock, purchasing $1 million worth of horses at the dispersal sale of his late uncle, George D. Widener, from whom he inherited part of his fortune. "I pride myself on being one of the few members of the Widener family who has ever held a job," says Dixon.

On Monday, Dixon is sitting at the Bath Club in Miami Beach when he hears his name being called by a page. Sitting at poolside, he sips a daiquiri on the rocks, and picking up the phone talks briefly to Seth. He takes a share.

On Monday there is one more share to sell, and Seth is talking to John Galbreath, trying to sell it to him. Galbreath owns the 618-acre Darby Dan Farm off the Old Frankfort Pike in Lexington, one of the nation's most prosperous private thoroughbred nurseries. For years Galbreath has been a leading importer and buyer of running horses at retail prices. He purchased Swaps for a record $2 million in 1956, the year that magnificent chestnut broke four world's time records and equaled a fifth. He later imported Ribot, sire of Graustark and Roberto, from Italy.

It is the second time Seth has spoken to Galbreath about buying a share, and Galbreath is telling Seth that Roberto and Good Counsel are at stud and he still has Graustark at Darby Dan and he already has enough stallions for his mares.

Then he adds, "But I'll do it for you."

Seth backs off. He does not want to be his daddy's son at Claiborne Farm. "No, Mr. Galbreath, thank you but I don't need the help; I just thought I would give you an opportunity for a share."

Calling back Fasig-Tipton, Seth reaches Larry Ensor—John Finney is out of the office—and tells Ensor that the Gilman Paper Company owns the final share in Secretariat.

At the moment, at least, Seth believes the job is done. He tells a reporter from the *Daily Racing Form* that the syndication of Secretariat, for a world-record $6,080,000, has been completed in thirty-two shares. And the next day, Tuesday, the *Racing Form* prints a brief announcement of that, though it reveals nothing of the makeup of the syndicate. Sitting in his office at Aqueduct, Alfred Gwynne Vanderbilt sees the story, and he wishes he had been invited to buy a share. For months Vanderbilt has been one of Secretariat's most ardent cheerleaders, telling people that the colt is the finest racehorse he has seen since Native Dancer. Now he has been left out of the syndication, hasn't even been called to join the syndicate. He was never close to Claiborne, so Vanderbilt calls Kenny Noe, Jr., the racing secretary for the New York Racing Association and asks him to contact the Meadow Stable. He wants it to be known that he would buy a share in Secretariat if one became available, if there were any vacancies. He does not want to contact Penny personally because he does not want to put her in the position of having to say no.

It is an enormous syndicate, and the weights of it are still settling when word of Vanderbilt's interest reaches Hancock. Vanderbilt knows someone might drop out at the last minute, if not through second thoughts, at least through something else. And so it happens, as if magically for the breeder of Miss Disco.

Hugo Morriss, the English breeder, has tried to make his 10 percent down payment of $19,000, but the English government has refused to allow him to send the money out of England. The deal involves a large foreign investment, and the government refuses to permit it. So Seth has a sudden and unexpected vacancy on his syndicate. And he has the name of Alfred Vanderbilt in front of him. So he calls Vanderbilt and asks him if he still wants the share.

Alfred says, "Sure."

Vanderbilt was shareholder twenty-eight. With him, Hancock was done.

In four days he had sold the most expensive animal in history, disposing of the available twenty-eight of thirty-two shares for $5.32 million in what was the most ambitious solicitation of its kind on record. If the lay reader of the sports pages didn't do double flips at breakfast over Secretariat's record-breaking victory in the Laurel Futurity, he set down his spoon seeing that America's Horse of the

Year, still heading for the Kentucky Derby, had already been sold for more than $6 million as a stud horse. And he was still a virgin. To the initiated Jets, Blackhawks, or Lakers booster, Secretariat must have seemed the reductio ad absurdum of the bonus-baby mentality—the strong, silent farm boy who signed for $6 million before anyone even knew if he could play.

The syndication story played prominently in a number of major American newspapers, and reporters and columnists diligently mined and explored the stalagmites and stalactites of this engaging phenomenon. They wrote about his height, his beam, his physique, his power, his burst of speed, his record, his sire and his dam, his training, his diet, his state of celibacy, his eventual love life on the farm, his value exceeding $325 an ounce—more than three times the value of gold—his jockey, his groom, his owner, his trainer, and his chances of winning the Triple Crown. It is a rite of spring among journalists to seek and write about the favorite for the Triple Crown, a subject that has grown into a body of mythology for turfwriters. For journalists who had loved and written of the sport since 1948, who had seen endless combinations of horses beat each other year after year in the Derby, Preakness, and Belmont stakes, covering racing was like being involved in a marriage that had never been fully consummated. It had been a quarter of a century since Citation won the Triple Crown. Twenty-five years!

"God, don't mention the Triple Crown to me," Lucien told *Newsday* columnist Ed Comerford in Florida. "I hate that, especially when these people say he's got it in the bag. I'll tell you something that might surprise you. I'll be glad when I get done with him. It worries me the way they talk about him going back to Man o' War. He's such a handsome horse. Everyone falls in love with him. That's the whole deal. But he hasn't done anymore than Riva Ridge."

Furthermore: "I'm getting an ulcer."

Finally: "I can't sleep."

Comerford was but one of a parade of journalists to visit Lucien and the red horse after the syndication. Among others was the inimitable Red Smith, who spent part of a morning watching groom Eddie Sweat turn a rub rag on the colt. Red, noting that the horse had filled out, duly reported his findings in a March 4 dispatch to *The New York Times:* "At three he is a strapping dude, magnificently muscled, giving him a sense of controlled power even in repose."

From the beginning of the year through the syndication and the flight to New York, Secretariat had been working in the fashion of a Derby favorite, showing great gusts of speed at Hialeah. The splint cleared up in January, when Lucien started breezing him, and on January 22 Lucien told *Daily Racing Form* columnist Joe Hirsch, "He's doing very nicely and is on schedule. As you know, we fired a splint in early December. That situation has cleared up perfectly, and he's ready to go."

He never did compete in Florida.

Less than three weeks later, on February 7, the colt drilled a brisk five-eighths in 0:58 $^3/_5$, more than a second under a twelve-clip, and galloped out in 1:12.

Three days later, the Chenery family convened its meeting in Tucson, and it was decided there to syndicate the colt and not to take the risk of racing him until it was done. Lucien continued putting the horse through heavy training in the morning hours.

On February 12, he zipped through a brilliant six-furlong drill in 1:11 $^2/_5$. Five days later the colt went seven-eighths in 1:25 $^2/_5$, another fast move. Six days later, on the day the process of syndication began, he went another seven-eighths in 1:26. Five days later he worked seven-eighths in 1:23 $^2/_5$, his farthest and fastest move of the year.

He was coming to the new year with the wind at his back.

Penny had already told Joe Hirsch that the colt could not be ready for the mile and an eighth of the $100,000 Flamingo Stakes March 3, but after the syndication was announced February 26, she shifted direction. She called Lucien, told him the syndicate was wrapped up, and asked him to run the red horse in the race, the nation's first major three-year-old event.

"Penny," Lucien protested, "I can't get him ready."

She insisted. But so did he. Finally she gave in, unable to budge him.

"I still say that *that* stubborn man wanted his share and wanted to make sure he was syndicated before he would risk racing him."

"No," Lucien said later, "I couldn't get him ready."

He was suddenly the trainer of the world's most valuable racehorse, and there were a number of investors, shareholders in the colt, who were wondering already how the colt was doing, what Lucien planned to do with him now. He was preparing to send the horse north to New York one day when he received his first telephone call from Seth, who asked Lucien about the horse. Lucien spoke to him, not knowing at the time about the "rule," as Penny called it, governing his relationship with members of the Secretariat syndicate. The rule was that it was no one's damn business what Lucien was doing with him, that the syndicate was not supposed to take an active interest in the horse's program.

The second time Seth called, Penny happened to be at the barn at Hialeah, and when she heard who was calling Lucien she asked to speak with him.

"Seth, the arrangement is that the horse races under my direction, the contract specifies that he will race under my direction until November 15 and that there will be no interference from the syndicate."

"Well, ma'am, there were some people, myself included, who didn't feel you used good judgment taking Riva Ridge to Hollywood Park last year, and we'd sure hate to see you do something like that to Secretariat."

Penny admired his bluntness. "I would hate to see me do it, too," she said. "In retrospect, I think going to California *was* hard on him. But if I decided to, I would have the right to do the same thing with Secretariat."

"Yes, ma'am."

The new year had begun.

Chapter 20

At seven-thirty in the morning on Long Island, among the chilled breaths and overcoats at Belmont Park, Secretariat first took shape gliding through the churchlike dimness of Barn 5.

The metal lids of cameras' eyes blinked once, then successively, as the shape expanded toward the center of the paddock, while reporters scribbled notes on pads. Penny Tweedy, standing next to Lucien Laurin, said brightly, "He looks wonderful, Lucien. And he feels good, too. He's got a hump in his back."

Everyone watched a moment as groom Eddie Sweat led him round the walking ring adjacent to the barn. Whether by inference or action, the red horse seemed not so much to walk as to drift through the silver light. His shoulders fluted where the ligaments tied his bones together, his neck and quarters lined in packs of muscle over which his coat seemed drawn too tight—perhaps a half size too small, as if he were outgrowing it—while his neck was bowed and his chin drawn up strict beneath its mass, and there was a trace of white around the outskirts of his eyes. Lucien, looking him up and down, carefully, walked over to Ron Turcotte, who was waiting to get on the colt.

It was March 14. For Laurin, Turcotte, and Penny Tweedy, the four-month wait was almost ended.

The red horse hadn't run since the Garden State Stakes in mid-November, and now he was just three days away from his first start as a three-year-old. He was to race five other colts in the $25,000-Added Bay Shore Stakes at Aqueduct March 17, Saturday, a seven-furlong sprint. There was less than half an hour to his final major workout for the Bay Shore. Most of the serious roadwork had been done in Florida, where Lucien had been building a deep foundation, called "bottom," on the horse's physical condition. Since that last seven-furlong work, Secretariat had gone a mile in 1:40 ⅗ on March 7. He walked for his exercise the next day, as he always did after he worked, and galloped the next. On March 10, he was flown from Miami to Queens, vanned to the stable area at Belmont Park, and bedded down in Stall 7, his permanent home in Barn 5 for the remainder of the year. Riva Ridge, and ten other horses, came with him on the two-and-a-half-hour flight north. At Belmont Park, he walked the next day, then galloped two days in a row. Now he was ready for the final drill.

The schedule called for speed, and Lucien decided to send him out under Turcotte for a three-eighths-of-a-mile sprint over the blazing fast main track at Belmont Park. A short, fast sprint on the eve of a race is known as a "blowout" or "sharpener" among horsemen; others refer to it as a "zinger," backstretch slang connoting a work designed to grind any dull edges off a horse's speed.

Secretariat thrived on such speed work three days before a race, as it turned out, and the faster the better.

In a moment Turcotte was astride him, tucking a whip under his arm, fitting his feet into the stirrup irons, and gathering up the leather of the reins. A security policeman stopped traffic as the red horse headed across an access road leading through the stable area.

"That him?" he asked.

"Yeah, that's him," someone said.

Moving for the racetrack near the clocker's shed, Secretariat came to within twenty yards of the gap and stopped, pricking his ears, raising his head, and staring, motionlessly, toward the racetrack. Horses galloped past, singly and in sets, and he watched the movement, listened to the hooves slapping and the sound of riders' voices.

Turcotte let him look, then clucked to him. The big horse strode off without hesitation, through the gap in the fence, turned, and galloped away. Penny, Lucien, and Penny's personal secretary, Ellie Disston, made off toward the ground-level ramp near the finish line. Lucien took out his gold watch, the one presented to him for Riva Ridge's victory in the Kentucky Derby a year ago, and looked across the track for the red horse.

Far across the racetrack infield, Secretariat turned and galloped into the backstretch. Turcotte was standing in the irons. The figures moved slowly around the mile-and-a-half oval toward the far turn, bouncing on the outside as horses raced past them on the rail. As Secretariat circled the far turn, galloping slowly, Turcotte drew him to a halt. The three-eighths pole was just ahead. Ron let the red horse walk, looked around for traffic a moment, and then clucked to him, urging him again into a gallop.

Nearing the three-eighths pole, 660 yards from the finish line, Turcotte reached down and grabbed the lines, dropping to a crouch. Secretariat accelerated suddenly, pounding at a dead run past the pole, still picking up speed, gathering momentum, as he raced around the turn for home and leveled out. Lucien snapped his watch as the red horse drove past the quarter pole. He glanced at it, saying nothing, swallowing. Toward the three-sixteenths pole, racing through the stretch, Secretariat reached out his forelegs and folded them into the racetrack as he made the straight, passed the eighth pole, passed the sixteenth pole, and raced for the wire. Turcotte's jacket was billowing out like a parachute behind, and the colt's ears were pinned flat. They drove under the wire, Turcotte standing up, his hands resting on the colt's neck. Lucien clicked the watch. He looked at the dial.

"Oh my God," he said.

"What's wrong, Lucien?" someone asked.

"He went 0:33 ³/₅." For a moment he said nothing more. The time was sensational, faster than a twelve-clip by :02 ³/₅ of a second, even over the Belmont track. It is unusual for horses to break 0:34 in a three-furlong workout. Lucien continued to watch in silence as Turcotte pulled the red horse up toward and around the bend, trying to bring the youngster to a walk. The two galloped past the pole a quarter mile beyond the wire. "He must have pulled up five-eighths in a minute," Lucien said quietly. To check his clocking of the work, he headed straight for the racetrack telephone inside the vacant ticket-sellers' booth of the clubhouse. The phone reaches the clocker's shed upstairs, on the roof of the grandstand. There, clocker Jules Watson, for one, times all the workouts on the main track at Belmont. Lucien slipped inside and called him.

"Hello there, Jules. How fast did you get him?"

There was a pause, which lengthened like a shadow on Lucien's face, and then, "Thirty-two and three-fifths? Right. Up in forty-four and four-fifths?"

Lucien's clocking, fast as it was, was a full second slower than Watson's official time, which other clockers quickly confirmed as accurate. Lucien took down the fractions by eighths, then read them back slowly to Watson: "Eleven and one-fifth, twenty-one and four-fifths, thirty-two and three-fifths."

It was startling. The colt had sped through the second eighth in 0:10 ⅗, the third eighth in 0:10 ⅘.

Off the phone, Lucien announced, "Thirty-two and three-. . . ."

"Well," said Penny. "That ought to open his pipes."

It was almost eight o'clock when Secretariat came off the racetrack and headed for the barn. By eight-fifteen the news had already spread throughout the stable area, and it was setting off flights of hyperbole and incredulity among the armies of swipes and clockers, trainers and outriders and hot walkers on shed row.

Turcotte, off Secretariat and up on another horse, was heading back to the racetrack when syndicate member Alfred Vanderbilt spotted him.

"Say, Ron," Alfred called, "I heard you burned up the racetrack this morning."

"No, I just dried it out a little."

A stable area is an open classroom without partitions, and news moves very quickly through it. The word reached the wooden clocker's shed at the training track—someone yelled it through the window. In seconds pony boys and exercise boys were taking it with them at a gallop around the racetrack, back to their barns, spreading and respreading it to grooms and jockeys' agents, who hustled it word of mouth.

The workout seemed to set a tempo for the rest of the morning at Barn 5, where Lucien and Penny spent time talking amiably to the press. Eddie Sweat slipped quickly in and out of Secretariat's stall, pitchfork in hand, and stable workers talked about the move, and Jimmy Gaffney walked the colt around the barn to cool him off.

Gradually the morning wound down and in the office by the barn, Lucien hung up the telephone, rubbed his eyes, and sat for a moment on the chair by the desk near the office door.

"I'm amazed," he said. "I wanted him to work fast but I don't know if I wanted him to work that fast." So the work had given him some pause. It was designed to hone the edges, not break them off. "For him it was just a blowout. It makes a difference if he comes back with his head between his legs. But he didn't. For him it was a blowout."

Then Lucien went out the door and down the staircase toward the shed. "I want to see if he's done eatin'," Lucien said. He walked briskly up the aisle four stalls down. Approaching, he saw Eddie Sweat.

"How's he doin', Mr. Sweat?"

"He's okay, boss."

Lucien ducked under the blue and white webbing, peeked over the top of the feed tub, and ducked out again, grinning. Standing at the back of the stall, Secretariat regarded Lucien suspiciously, raising his head as Laurin came and went.

"If that work had bothered him, he'd have backed off his feed. Look, he licked the tub. You come by tomorrow and he'll be jumpin' sky high. We'll have to put the saddle and bridle on him and put a boy on his back. That's the only way we can quiet him down. Put the tack on him and let him think he's goin' to the racetrack."

Yet the work gave Lucien some reason for concern: he was wondering whether the colt had made the change from two to three. "Our three-year-olds sometimes don't come back as good as they were." He would not know for sure until the Bay Shore. A workout is no definitive guide. Only a race, and the competitive instincts in a horse it draws upon, is the true measure of form, the only way of determining whether Secretariat brought everything with him over the new year.

"He knows he's back in business," Lucien said. "I'm dyin' to get that first one over with Saturday."

Dressed in a shiny blue trench coat, puffing a cigarette in a box seat, Lucien Laurin sat down and waited for the coming of the seventh. "I took a tranquilizer last night for the first time in my life," he said, "and I slept like a baby. I figured, why should I be walking the floors all night?"

It was 3:42 in the afternoon, March 17, and the Bay Shore was less than an hour away. Lucien had the look of a doomed man. He was quiet, reflective, and considerate, as he always was, but the day was bearing down on him. He wore his anxiety visibly. Nearby, Penny was greeting friends, cool as the mint green coat she wore, Elizabeth Ham with her, arrayed in a bright red coat and a brown fur hat.

Heavy rains had fallen earlier in the day, turning Aqueduct into a mire, but by four-fifteen the sun was out and the gulls were dipping and sailing overhead. Beyond the long chute that joined the backstretch, Eddie Sweat was walking with Secretariat down a pathway toward the paddock. The sixth race had just ended, and Lucien made his way slowly down the winding staircase to the saddling area. The crowd was moving in front and behind him, the bettors draped across the paddock fences, owners and trainers looking on. Walter Salmon, for whom Seth had waited through his longest day, was there. So was Vanderbilt, and Eddie Arcaro, the master horseman of his time, winner of five Kentucky Derbies, two Triple Crowns with Whirlaway and Citation, the rider of Bold Ruler. They all gathered—some forty owners and trainers and visitors.

Trainer Johnny Campo, the man who had bounced all his finest two-year-olds off Secretariat the year before, was in the doorway leading from the tunnel to the paddock when Secretariat walked by.

"Look how big he got," said Johnny, shaking his head.

Suddenly, through the large doorway beneath the clubhouse, Sweat and Secretariat appeared, turning into the paddock amid whispering. The horse had grown up and filled out, in height by an inch and a quarter from the ground to the withers since September, from 5 feet 4.75 inches to 5 feet 6 inches, and measuring a massive 78 inches now around the belly. He weighed 1154 pounds, at least 200 pounds heavier than the average thoroughbred.

"Here we is," muttered Eddie Sweat. "Here we is." The groom turned the colt into a saddling stall, bringing him around to face the front, while Henny and Lucien moved closer. No one was at ease, not even Secretariat, who was usually the calmest of them all. Standing there, Secretariat defecated, emitting washy feces, and Lucien turned to Henny and said, "He's a little loose. I hope he's all right."

"He'll be okay," said Henny. "He's probably just a little anxious, a little nervous, heh?"

Secretariat, his head up and brown eyes luminously large, shifted the bulk of his body from left to right as he waited there. Once he raised a hindleg and lashed it into the dirt floor, chopping up cinders and spraying them against the wooden boards behind. Sweat spoke quietly to him.

"Easy now, Red."

Arcaro walked to the stall and looked in on him.

"He's got to get going," Lucien told Arcaro. "He's getting awfully on edge right now. He's like a fighter." Once again the red horse shifted his feet. Dipping his head, he rolled and chewed at the bit in his mouth, biting into it. Arcaro seemed intrigued. He walked to the left side of Secretariat, stood back and looked him over for a long minute, his eyes flicking over the hindlegs, the quarters, up along the back and neck and shoulders, then to the head.

"God, he's a grand lookin' son of a bitch," said Arcaro.

Lucien beamed, nodding. "Isn't he, though?"

"He's too good lookin' to run!" Arcaro said.

From the tunnel leading to the jockeys' room, holding a whip in one hand while adjusting the leather number strapped to his arm, Ron Turcotte emerged wearing the blue and white blocks of the Meadow Stable. He was chewing gum, and he appeared resigned. He walked directly to Lucien and the two men huddled.

Ron Turcotte had not felt such pressure since he started riding thoroughbreds at age nineteen, after he hitchhiked from Toronto to nearby Woodbine Race Course. Someone picked him up at the stable gate and deposited him that morning at the barn of Edward Plunkett Taylor's Windfield Farm. He walked in and got a job working as a hot walker for a month, cooling out horses after exercise, then grooming for a time. He finally went to Taylor's farm and learned to break yearlings under tack. He was on his way to becoming one of America's leading riders, but he had had an unlikely beginning.

Turcotte was born in Grand Falls, New Brunswick, on July 22, 1941, one of fourteen children supported by a lumberjack in the small community of Davis Mill, in the New Brunswick parish of Drummond. While growing up, he saw his father infrequently. Alfred Turcotte spent many weeks of his summers lumbering in the woods. Ron left school in the eighth grade, to help support the family when their home burned down. He harvested potatoes and went to work as a lumberjack himself. He cut trees and hauled logs behind a team of horses and worked in a lumber mill. When he was eighteen, with a purse of fifty dollars saved, he went to Toronto to look for a job in construction. He was lonely and still looking, in fact, when his Toronto landlord told him he should try riding the runners at Woodbine. So he hitched that ride out of town.

He was extremely powerful, and he learned to use his strength to push and bounce a racehorse through the lane.

So he became known as one of the strongest riders in the game, steady and durable, and he earned early on a reputation for honesty, as a rider who would scrub and shove as hard with a $5000 claimer as with a stakes horse like Riva Ridge. He rode his first winner in 1962, two years later his first stakes winner. In 1965, he won the Preakness Stakes on Tom Rolfe. He rode Northern Dancer, too, and champions Arts and Letters, Fort Marcy, Damascus, Dark Mirage, and Shuvee in the years leading up and down to Riva Ridge. Yet Turcotte remained, despite the wealth and fame his riding brought him, utterly without pretensions. He never forgot that he grew up poor. When he made a name in riding in America, he returned to Canada, married a girl he'd known from childhood—Gaetane Morin —and bought a three-bedroom suburban split level in Valley Stream, Long Island. They had three kids and a Datsun station wagon; he came home at night, and Gae fixed him dinner.

Turcotte had been earning almost $200,000 a year even before he rode Riva Ridge. The horses he rode won $1,904,175 in 1970 and $1,989,306 in 1971. His finest year was 1972, when he was riding both Secretariat and Riva Ridge. His mounts earned $2,780,626, a figure that made him the third leading jockey in America in money won.

Yet through the years, too, he was the object of sharp criticism in the press, and he did not react well to it, growing sensitive and defensive. For months he held personal grudges against writers whom he thought had criticized him unfairly and thoughtlessly, and in one case he actually manhandled a reporter. He seemed to ride without confidence at times, without a sureness in himself, but the sharpest and most persistent criticism of his riding was that he had a way of getting a horse into traffic problems. He had come under especially sharp attack for his rides on Tom Rolfe in the 1965 Kentucky Derby, in which he finished third when many thought he should have won; on Damascus in the 1968 Charles Strub Stakes at Santa Anita, in which he had Damascus bogged down in heavy going on the rail while the inferior Most Host, the winner, was racing in firmer footing outside; and on Riva Ridge in the Everglades.

Lucien told him quietly how much the race meant to them and the colt. "I don't care how far he wins by," said Lucien. "I don't care if he wins by fifteen. And I don't care if he wins by just a length, just so he does it right. Ride him like you did last year. Give him some time. When you finish, I want you to work out a mile. If he's not too tired. You're on him, so you decide. And warm him up real good."

They were speaking in the walking ring as newsmen gathered around them. A television crewman, wearing headphones, squatted down beside them holding a microphone shaped like a fungo bat. He held it up directly between Lucien and Turcotte. Nearby, Alfred Vanderbilt glanced over and frowned. Undaunted, Lucien and Turcotte swung into French Canadian, as they frequently did when they wanted to talk privately—in public.

"Use ton propre jugement," Lucien said. In English, "Use your

very own judgment." And added, *"Use le pas pour rien."* That is, "Don't make excessive or wasteful use of him."

"Riders, up!" called Lucas Dupps, a paddock judge.

Lucien bent down and grabbed Ron's left boot, raising him aboard. As Turcotte gathered up the reins, Lucien reminded him, "Don't forget to warm him up real good, Ronnie. He's a little muscle tight."

In front of them, trainer Woody Sedlacek lifted jockey Mike Venezia on Champagne Charlie, a roan son of E. P. Taylor's Northern Dancer. He had just won the $25,000 Swift Stakes at Aqueduct two weeks before, a six-furlong sprint that was the first in the New York series of races leading to the Triple Crown. Venezia believed his roan horse was improving, and he believed he had a shot to beat Secretariat going seven-eighths. The Swift had been Champagne Charlie's first race since November, and in it he had beaten Actuality, who had nearly broken a track record at Hialeah in the Hibiscus Stakes on January 20. In the Bay Shore, Actuality was back for more. The horseplayers were not as high on Champagne Charlie as Venezia, sending him off as third choice at $8:60 to $1.00. They were busy making Secretariat the prohibitive choice at $0.20 to $1.00.

As the post parade began, the file of six horses stepped up the ramp and toward the racetrack, and Lucien and Penny and the crowd around them headed for the box seats.

"Mrs. Tweedy, he's the most beautiful horse I have *ever* seen," someone said.

"He sure is a grand lookin' horse," said New York Racing Association president Jack Krumpe.

Penny, laughing, stopped at the foot of the stairs rising to the clubhouse, held her hands a foot in front of her chest, and said, huskily, "I keep thinking of him as a large, well-stacked girl."

Sweep, Jules Schanzer's nom de plume in the *Daily Racing Form*, didn't go as far as that, though he liked the red horse, too:

> What more can be said for Secretariat after the reams of copy that have followed the Horse of the Year 1972's doings since his return to training in Florida? The outstanding colt appears to have chosen an ideal spot for his seasonal debut and should enjoy an easy romp over moderate opposition in this renewal of the Bay Shore Stakes.

And so did Charles Hatton, as high as ever on his red horse: "Except for a few paddock provocateurs, nobody can imagine his

Bay Shore rivals heading him off, unless they started last night."

Lucien, climbing the two flights of stairs to the box seat section, passed by trainer Syd Watters, who smiled at him, reached as if to embrace him, and patted him on the arm.

"Good luck, my man," Watters said. Watters had learned something in his life about luck. Two years ago he was the trainer of the three-year-old Hoist the Flag, the Kentucky Derby and Triple Crown favorite who won the Bay Shore Stakes in record time, then broke a leg before the running of the Gotham Stakes, the third race in the New York series. Hoist the Flag was saved to stand at stud at Claiborne Farm, but Watters never got over the blow. "You get one of those once in a lifetime," he said. "I don't think I'll ever get over it."

Lucien slipped into a seat. His hands shaking slightly, he raised his binoculars to his eyes. Nearby, Penny and Elizabeth settled into their seats, while on the infield the lights of the tote board flashed and Secretariat held at 1–5. The horses were at the gate. The red horse stepped into Post Position 4, Actuality on his left, and Turcotte could feel his anxiety and eagerness. Hundreds in the crowd of 32,960 were lapping up against the rail along the homestretch, craning necks. It was post time, and starter George Cassidy hit the switch.

They bounded from the gate, legs driving and whipping up the racetrack, hooves and metal plates slipping and splattering, jockeys pumping, goggles down.

Secretariat broke alertly, just as he had done last year, and Turcotte gave him time to collect himself. On his own, the red horse went to work setting his bones in motion. He had not changed in that. He was next to last within the first few jumps out of the slip, taking mud in the chest and face, while up on the lead Close Image charged up on the leaders and went to the front, racing for a daylight lead down the backside. Actuality tracked the pace from the outset. Impecunious lay third, Champagne Charlie near them on the outside. The red horse was just getting with it, through the first sixteenth of a mile, when an accident occurred. It took place unexpectedly, about 100 yards out of the gate, and it nearly ended it all for Secretariat.

Torsion, who had broken badly, sailing in the air, came down racing with Secretariat on the outside. He was racing down the backside when he shied from the stands on his right, moving over and slamming sharply into the red horse. Secretariat grunted, absorbing the blow. For an instant Turcotte thought he might go down.

"Thank God he's built like a bulldozer. He might have slipped and fell." Secretariat wavered off stride for several jumps, then found himself again, and set out for the far turn in chase of the leader.

Close Image was a length and a half in front, dragging the field through an opening quarter mile in 0:22 ⅕. Secretariat, bounding along six lengths behind, was running it in 0:23 ⅖. He was moving and acting like the Secretariat of 1972. He had taken a hard shot from Torsion, then shaken him off and picked up the momentum of his stride again. And he was grabbing the bit, too, as he had done the year before, and he was pounding at the racetrack and barreling along almost as heavy-headedly as ever. Yet Ron had decided not to ask him for too much, not to risk riding him as if he were the same Secretariat of the year before. "Not after the syndication, the firing of the splint, the chance of the change between two and three. He was still maturing."

Turcotte didn't want the blame if Secretariat was beaten. So racing for the turn, having the choice of going either outside or inside of Champagne Charlie—of saving ground and risking traffic on the rail or taking the high ground and losing lengths, as he would have done last year—Turcotte decided to save the ground. "I didn't want to run a mile while the others were going only seven-eighths." He was also looking out for himself, so no one could accuse him of losing the race because he lost too much ground, of asking a $6.08-million racehorse to do too much his first start of his three-year-old year. So he risked the rail, keeping the red horse on the inside of the roan.

"I was protecting my ass," Ronnie said. And that's how he almost lost it.

Moving to the inside of Champagne Charlie, racing about ten feet off the gooey rail, he thus made the most serious mistake he ever made on Secretariat, an error that would lead to raised eyebrows and to a recounting of the old accusations that he knew how to put a good horse in a bad spot.

In seconds Turcotte saw his mistake unfold around him, but by then there was nothing he could do about it, for the moment nothing at all. Midway of the turn the colt was rolling, drawing up to three lengths behind Close Image while charging the second quarter in 0:22. He was flying. And Champagne Charlie was moving with him, staying outside of him. Venezia saw he had the red horse in a blind switch—that is, inescapably trapped on the rail—and he was determined not to let him free if he could help it. Turcotte's dilemma grew clearer, more urgent, as the horses swept around the bend and moved for home. It was reminiscent of the Sanford Stakes, when the colt was faced with a wall of horses.

Turcotte couldn't drive him through and he couldn't lean on Champagne Charlie, illegally carrying him out and interfering with him. So Turcotte was on America's premier racehorse, all dressed up with no place to go.

There was one chance, thought Turcotte, to shake free of the switch. And he thought he would try it.

He could ease Secretariat back and go around Champagne Charlie, losing a few lengths but not too many. So he took the red horse back at the turn. Venezia took back with him.

"Every time I eased back, Venezia eased back with me. It was the best race I ever saw Mike ride. I would have had to sacrifice six lengths to get around him."

Turning for home, with Close Image having dropped out of it, Actuality was in front on the rail under jockey Bobby Woodhouse, Impecunious was on his right under jockey Jim Moseley. Venezia was outside of them, trying to keep them together in a three-horse wall blocking Secretariat's path. The red horse, meanwhile, was breathing on Actuality, and Turcotte was hoping for an opening. The crowd knew Secretariat was in trouble, and they were already screaming on their feet as the horses neared the stretch. At the top of the straight, Venezia tried but couldn't keep Actuality and Impecunious together any longer. His wall was crumbling. "I was trying to keep the hole closed but Impecunious was trying to get out," said Venezia. "I had been keeping him in till the quarter pole. Then I couldn't keep him in anymore."

The three leaders—Actuality, Impecunious, and Champagne Charlie—drove through the upper stretch, heading toward the three-sixteenths pole with 330 yards to run. The breach began to open. Impecunious started to drift away from Actuality, opening a hole between them. Secretariat started to lunge for it, Turcotte pushing and clucking. As the red horse started to drive through, beginning his surge, Woodhouse suddenly reached back and strapped Actuality, left-handed, driving Actuality to the right, closing the breach.

Woodhouse heard Turcotte screaming, "Bobby! Bobby! Bobby! Bobby! Straighten up! Straighten up! Straighten up!"

The breach stayed open briefly. And Secretariat plunged through it near the eighth pole, brushing Impecunious and busting off for the wire 220 yards ahead. Quickly, he opened up three and a half lengths, then raced under the wire widening the margin to four and a half in a clocking of 1:23 ⅕ after running free for only one-eighth of a mile.

Up in the box seats, Roger Laurin shouted, excitedly, "He's too much horse! They can't stop him! They can't even stop him with a wall of horses!"

Penny Tweedy looked up and lifted her hands in the air, as if in supplication.

Lucien lit another cigarette, accepting congratulations, beaming, with Penny and Miss Ham standing with the colt in the winner's circle. Secretariat was blowing hard, his nostrils flared. Suddenly the inquiry sign flashed on the tote, and it sent a mumbling through the crowd. Jim Moseley, Impecunious's rider, was claiming a foul against Secretariat for interference in the stretch drive. The crowd stayed draped around the winner's circle, cheering the winner anyway.

Turcotte, jumping off Secretariat, told Lucien about the hole opening and then closing in midstretch. "Woodhouse, that son of a bitch, he came out and closed the gap. He hit his horse left-handed and came over on me." Turcotte headed downstairs to change, his mouth crusted with part of the turn for home. Down in the jockeys' room, Woodhouse was telling about hearing Turcotte's voice at the three-sixteenths pole. "I heard Ronnie yellin' for racin' room, for some help. He was in trouble. He yelled my name, but I ain't goin' to give him no money . . ."

Then over the loudspeaker, as Turcotte and Moseley waited, Dave Johnson announced that the foul had been disallowed, that Secretariat had won the Bay Shore—officially.

But Turcotte knew he had almost blown the Bay Shore foolishly. "I realized I had made a mistake, taking excessive chances on the rail instead of using the horse to go around," he said later. "I was stupid to take the chance when I was on Secretariat, stupid because he was the same Secretariat I knew as a two-year-old. As it turned out, I should have gone around."

He didn't go around, and it became the longest seven furlongs of his life. "I never thought six million bucks could be so heavy," he said.

But the colt was back and running in his old form, and now Lucien moved to crank him up again, this time for the $50,000-Added Gotham Stakes, over one mile at Aqueduct April 7. After the Gotham Stakes, if all went well, came the $114,900 Wood Memorial at one and one-eighth miles at Aqueduct, and after that the Kentucky

Derby at one and a quarter miles on May 5. Secretariat had made it through the winter with his speed intact, his late charge and his old instincts as an alley fighter.

Charles Hatton was back, too, watching Secretariat smash through the Bay Shore field like O. J. Simpson plunging the line, like a hawk scattering a barnyard of chickens. Sitting down to compose his March 20 column, Charlie wrote: "Confronted with a seemingly impenetrable wall of horses, he came smashing through like Kung Fu."

Chapter 21

I don't know if you can print this, but I call him sexy.

Penny Tweedy

A light rain fell through the morning of April Fools' Day, Sunday, rapping on the roof of Barn 5. The lights inside the shed were dim, plunging the figures, the horses, and the men with them, into shapes that wavered ghostlike in the bluegray air.

The rain drew pungent aromas from the bales stacked in the loft above the stalls—of clover, timothy hay, and straw. It danced off the shingles, forming puddles in the yard, and ran in rivulets down the windowpanes that lined the shed row walls. Grooms moved in and out of straw-bed stalls, sticking and probing the blades of forks for mats of urine and manure. Hot walkers cooled out horses by walking them around the indoor shed. The shed was a row of nineteen box stalls looped by a walking path ten feet wide. The hot walkers, moving counterclockwise, circled it every two or three minutes. They led files of horses by chain and leather lead shanks—one man at the head of each horse—talking to the horses, sipping coffee, smoking, looking up at the clock. They would earn enough for grub and cigarettes, perhaps enough to bet the double, perhaps not. A radio played faintly and a pregnant cat padded from stall to stall, sniffing at one, then moving on.

"She was raped at Hialeah by the old Tom," Eddie Sweat said sadly. "I tried to stop it but I was too late."

At either end of the shed sets of horses stepped to and from the racetrack, their metal shoes clicking down the paths and paved roads that wound loosely among the barns of the stable area. It was nearing midmorning, according to the clock by the feed room door, and inside the work went on. Leaving the rear of Stall 7, Secretariat appeared momentarily at his open doorway, thrusting his head outside, his ears forward, and for several minutes stared across the aisle toward the windows blurred by the rain. Then he sank back again, his head receding very slowly.

Into the shed, walking from his office across the yard, came Henny Hoeffner. He was striding hastily about his morning work, as if shooing the morning from one moment to the next, harnessing and organizing time and motion on the clipboard he was holding in his hand. Rain dripped off the brim of his hat, a blue golf hat with a wrap-around brim. Hoeffner was Lucien's assistant trainer, second in charge, the man who conditioned and supervised the stable of horses in Lucien's absences, which had become frequent in the last few years. Riva Ridge and Secretariat had already spent weeks out of town—at tracks in Kentucky, New Jersey, California, and Maryland—and Laurin went with them.

In fact Laurin hadn't been at Belmont Park for at least two days. He was still in New Orleans, at the Fair Grounds, where he had saddled Ed Whittaker's Angle Light on Saturday for the $50,000 Louisiana Derby at one and one-eighth miles. The bay came to the eighth pole two lengths in front, but he weakened in the final yards and finished third, beaten a length by Leo's Pisces. Lucien would return soon to resume supervising the training of the red horse. Now work went on without him, in a tempo as casual as the comings and goings of the horses.

"Okay, Ed Sweat, get the big horse ready. He'll be goin' out next," said Henny Hoeffner.

For Edward (Shorty) Sweat, April 1 would be a morning of established rhythms, too, cadences to which he'd grown accustomed in the years of his life since leaving school in his sophomore year and finding work with Lucien Laurin.

Sweat was born on August 30, 1938 in a small farmhouse on a 15-acre farm in Holly Hill, not far from the coast of South Carolina, the sixth of nine children of Mary and David Sweat. They were a poor black family of tenant farmers, mostly, though David Sweat had a reputation as a crack shot, a backwoodsman, and a hunter of small game: squirrel, rabbits, possum.

Ed started early to help support the family, working after grade school on surrounding farms, picking cotton at twenty-five cents a day, digging sweet potatoes and harvesting corn and soybeans and watermelon. At the age of eight he was doing a man's work.

As a child he took an interest in horses. On the school bus he would pass the thoroughbred horse farm down the road owned by Lucien Laurin. He ran a thoroughbred training center, and Sweat asked for and got a job from him, and walked the two and a half miles to work. He started by digging fence holes and planting fences, making fifteen dollars a week. By 1955 he was walking hots and grooming horses on the farm, beginning as Turcotte began up north, as most grooms and jockeys begin. Sweat tried to ride, too, but already he was too heavy for a life as an exercise boy: he was nearing 170 pounds. The plowing and the laying of fences had left him with no weight to lose. As a groom he learned fast. Those who saw him work would say he had what southern blacks call mother wit—like Yankee ingenuity, a quick and ready insight into the best and most efficient way of doing any job. Peers respected Sweat. He was serious about his work, manifestly reliable and responsible. Within three years after Laurin took him to the racetrack, he had developed into his ablest and most trusted groom. He rubbed and cared for most of Laurin's finest stock, and he learned how to handle the van. Thus he became the stable's chief van driver, too, chauffeuring the horses cross country—to Detroit, Chicago, New England, and New Jersey.

For Sweat April 1 was among the last days of ease, ordered calm, and small certainties—more than a month before the beginning of the Triple Crown. He had already felt the tension on the day of the sensational workout prior to the Bay Shore. And April 1 began the week of the Gotham Stakes, the final month of preparation. The Wood would be run April 21. Then he would be off for Louisville, if all went well enough, and for weeks nothing would be the same again.

There was a heady excitement about running a racehorse in the three most celebrated races in America. It was racing as spectacle, and those in it were a part of it. If Secretariat won at Churchill Downs, Sweat would probably be the first groom in history to win two Kentucky Derbies, certainly the first to win two consecutive runnings of the race. Yet, considering his chances, he remained skeptical. Like many others, Sweat was suspicious of the Bold Ruler blood that ran in Secretariat. He was uncertain that Secretariat could carry his speed a mile and a quarter in May. But there was nothing he could do about it, and Sweat never seemed one to worry about things over which he had no control. Yet he did do one thing to ward off the devil. Racetrackers are creatures of superstition: Sweat owned a khaki hat with a wrap-around brim and a flat top, and in time he decided he would wear it whenever he took the red horse to the post. He had worn it in the Bay Shore Stakes, first of all, and decided he would wear it in the Gotham, too.

Eddie Sweat slipped into Stall 7, a brush and a rub rag in his hands, and began the practice of his artistry, raising his arms and putting himself in motion, gyrating slightly as he cleaned the colt. His hands worked as those of a schooled boxer on the small bag, sweeping and flicking rhythmically up and down the coat, the rub rag following the jab of the brush, the brush following the rub of the rag, the rag flapping and the brush skipping off in quick, clean strokes. First he drew the brush across the back, sending dust in the air, then polished off with the rag, all the while moving around the horse and working his hands together, in unison, the implements complementing one another, and all the while talking inflectively as Secretariat kicked and frowned in protest, curled his lip and shoved.

"Stop it now! C'mon, Red. C'mon, Red. I'm gonna brush you now. Come over here, Red. You're steppin' on my toes. What's the matter with you? You tryin' to put a foot in my pocket? You've got to stand there now! I got to get you ready. C'mon. I want to brush you off a little bit."

The horse did a two-step with his hindlegs, swinging to the left toward Sweat, and then he whisked his tail and twisted his neck, closing his eyes and flipping his nose in the air, and from the stall Sweat's voice seemed reproachful. Secretariat bowed his neck, reached over and nipped at the brush in Sweat's hand, grabbing the bristles of the brush between his teeth, then turned to face motionlessly out the door, as if pacified. Then, Sweat took the brush from the horse's mouth and swung into work again. It was nearing time for Secretariat to gallop. Horses were coming back in sets from the racetrack now, coats slicked by the rain, which was still falling lightly.

There was heightened activity now around his stall. Jim Gaffney appeared with the saddle he had engraved with the name "Secretariat," the pommel pad his mother had knitted for the colt, and the blue girth and the blue saddlecloth. Sweat went to the rear of the stall and tied the horse's tail in a knot, as he had tied it in a knot for the Bay Shore. The two men moved in and out of the stall quickly, efficiently.

Gaffney picked up the saddle and lifted it carefully over Secretariat's back. "When I first put this girth on him, it used to tighten up to here," he said, showing a worn hole in the leather strap. "Now you've got to drop it two holes just to get it around him." His barrel, already enormous, was still expanding. In fact, his size had been the subject of some comment following the Bay Shore Stakes. In his March 27 column just four days ago, Charles Hatton had printed a set of statistics comparing the sizes of Secretariat, Man o' War, and Triple Crown winner Gallant Fox, three large animals:

Man o' War—Height 16 hands, 1 ⅝ inches; girth 71 ¾ inches; weight, 1,050 pounds.
Gallant Fox—Height 16 hands, 1 inch; girth, 73 inches; weight, 1,125 pounds.
Secretariat—Height, 16 hands, 2 inches; girth, 75 ⅕ inch; weight, 1,160 pounds.

Secretariat was larger than the other two horses in all particulars, and two days earlier he'd just turned three by the calendar.

Gaffney drew up the cinch, tightening it, as Secretariat kicked again. "Hey, you big bum, stand there now!" said Sweat.

Then, the groom took a steel pick from his pocket and started moving from hoof to hoof on the colt, cleaning out the muck caught in the bottom of his hooves. Finally they led the colt to the gap in the fence on the west side of the yard. It was still raining. Water ran off Henny's hat.

"Jimmy, gallop him once around and then jog him all the way back. Don't wait out there."

Trainers, waiting by the gap in the fence, saw Secretariat coming and studied him as he stopped and looked at the racetrack. The gap was by the clubhouse turn, the first turn, at Belmont Park, where the horses in the mile-and-a-half Belmont Stakes still had more than a mile and a quarter to run. Horses drilled by through the mud. Trainer John Rigione called out to Hoeffner.

The figures grew larger through the lane. Secretariat galloped by, Gaffney standing in the stirrups, the reins loose, talking to the colt. Around the turn, Gaffney pulled him up, turned him around and jogged back toward the gap. He emerged through the gap in the rain.

The horse was breathing lightly. His legs were splattered with mud, his body wet.

Secretariat danced back to the barn, on his toes, his neck arched and eyes glaring. Back at the barn Eddie Sweat was waiting for the colt with a bucket of hot water and a large sponge. Sweat put a blue blanket across Secretariat's kidneys, then crouched at the colt's side and moved from one leg to the other sponging the horse's legs, one at a time. The colt didn't like it, lifting his legs, menacingly, while he nibbled at Gaffney's hand. Sweat washed the colt's face, methodically, pressing the sponge on the forehead, letting the water drain down between the eyes and along the jowls. Then Sweat brought the sponge down between the eyes, over the wide spread of the brain pan, then over the eyes themselves, down the nose and around the lips, then into the nostrils. When he finished Sweat tossed a red wool blanket over the colt's rump, back, and neck. Then he fastened the leather straps in front, drawing them closed, and went around to the back and untied the knot in Secretariat's tail.

Gaffney led the colt away, serving now as a hot walker, and Eddie went to work. It was past nine, and the morning was leveling off. As Gaffney took the colt around the shed, Sweat picked up a fork and worked again inside Stall 7, dressing it up with fresh straw and thrashing the straw with the fork blades. Motes of straw dust rose from the floor. Sweat worked the fork lightly across his fingers, lifting and tossing the straw bed, turning from corner to wall to corner again in the fifteen-by-twenty-foot cubicle. Above him were two sprinklers attached to a pipe.

Now the rain was letting up. At nine-thirty Hoeffner turned into the shed, saw Gaffney leading Secretariat toward him up the aisle, and said, suspiciously, "Hey, Jimmy, is that pony botherin' him?"

The pony, an Apalloosa named Billy Silver, was just becoming involved in his long and unrequited love affair with Secretariat. In back at the west end of the barn Billy Silver lived in a jerry-built wooden stall over which he could hang his head and sniff at horses and hot walkers angling past him.

Gaffney shuttled past again with Secretariat, who was walking docilely, his head down and neck straight. They had been walking about thirty-five minutes.

"One more time around, Jim," said Sweat.

It was almost ten when Gaffney nosed Secretariat back into his stall. By then his bed had been made—a fresh, foot-deep mattress of golden straw—and the water bucket had been filled and hung inside.

Sweat, with Gaffney holding Secretariat at the front of the open door, once again picked out the colt's feet, which had collected cakes of sandy loam soil from the racetrack, brushing each foot, all around it. Then he dabbed a brush into a tin can filled with a dark, butterlike salve with a not unappealing odor. With the brush, he painted the salve around the hoof, as if lacquering it—hoof dressing, to keep the feet from drying out.

For the horses it was nearing early lunch. Secretariat had already eaten about four quarts of oats that morning, and now Sweat was cutting two gargantuan carrots into inch-thick discs. Meanwhile the feed man had just ladled four quarts of dry oats into the tub and a quart of sweet feed mixed with molasses. Sweat unclipped the tub from the wall across from Stall 7. It was feeding time, and the stable was alive with the nickers and whinnies of the famished. Heads stuck out of stalls, eyes rolling, nostrils flared and fluttering. Secretariat pawed lustily. He bobbed his head when Sweat approached him, crossing the aisle, and backed up as Eddie dipped beneath the webbing of the stall. Then he came forward, as Sweat straightened up in front of him and started to fasten the latches of the tub, holding it with both hands and trying to fasten it to the rings on the corner. Secretariat pressed forward, nudging into Sweat, pushing and leaning over his shoulder. Sweat fumbled with the latches. The horse pressed in again, edging into Sweat. The latches rattled on the tub.

Sweat shouted finally, turning his head and glaring at the colt, who pricked his ears and nickered back.

Lucien was back at Belmont Park the following morning, April 2, planning his moves and taking time to watch Secretariat roll in his stall and kick his feet in the air. Lucien was now measuring each step to the Triple Crown, considering all the possibilities, anticipating and adjusting to and for whatever might affect the health, happiness, well-being, and peace of mind of the red horse. The stress on Laurin fluctuated, alternately easing and intensifying in these closing weeks.

A serious cold or illness on the eve of a major prep race for the Kentucky Derby could force a change in plan, throwing off the schedule leading to Louisville. The New York series, if followed as Laurin planned to follow it, would not leave a horse unfit at Churchill Downs on Derby Day—not for lack of racing. The Swift was six furlongs, the Bay Shore was seven, the Gotham eight, and the Wood Memorial nine. One race led naturally to the next, building a horse's conditioning. A cold, forcing Laurin to suspend important training or to bypass one of the races, would then require him to improvise and try to make up for time lost. That was a dangerous game. The Derby was May 5, less than a month after the Gotham Stakes, and it left little time to lose. Laurin had to work and race Secretariat to reach a physical peak for the Derby, then hope he could sustain that for both the Preakness and the Belmont stakes. He was involved in an orchestration of the horse's energies, a heightening and intensifying of them.

On the morning of March 23, he sent Secretariat through a half-mile workout in 0:48. It pleased him momentarily. Back at the barn, he was at the door of the shed when Secretariat walked past. Then the red horse coughed once, twice, hollowly. Laurin did a double take. Turning, he said something to a stable worker, who told him that the colt had been coughing off and on for about five days.

No one had told him of this, and that morning he'd worked the horse a half at a twelve-clip. Laurin was beside himself, twirling once around, pointing his finger in the air, raising his voice and saying, "I want to know every time he farts!"

His regular veterinarian, Mike Gerard, stopped by the office later that morning and said there was a cough going around. He then suggested something for it, and Lucien jumped as if a gun had gone off behind him.

"No shots!" he said. "I don't want no shots for him, Mike. *No shots!*"

The cough disappeared that week, on its own, and Lucien had Secretariat out blazing a mile in 1:35 ⅖ on March 28, five days later, galloping out an extra eighth of a mile in 0:13 ⅖ for a full mile and an eighth in 1:48 ⅘, sensational time even on that fast Belmont track. The 1:48 ⅘ was time that equaled the Wood Memorial Stakes record set by Bold Ruler in 1957. Three days later Laurin was in Louisiana for Angle Light's race at the Fair Grounds. Two days later, on April 3, he was supervising Secretariat's final workout for the Gotham Stakes, but it fell short of his hopes. Thirteen seconds into the move, Turcotte and Secretariat were running past the half-mile pole. Laurin caught the next eighth in 0:13, for a quarter in 0:26.

"That's too slow," Lucien said. Secretariat had breezed through the first three furlongs in 0:39, a thirteen-clip, hardly enough to draw from him a deep breath.

They picked up speed through the lane, running the fourth eighth in 0:12 ⅕.

"Now he's letting him fly," said Laurin. The colt went the final eighth in 0:11 ⁴/₅, going the five-eighths in 1:03, the final quarter in 0:24. Lucien didn't appear pleased. Shrugging, he sighed, and headed back to the barn to gather with newsmen. There were just four days to the Gotham, and the name Secretariat was stirring interest in the media. A television crew was in the yard, for the first time, as well as the newspaper reporters. The slow workout drew only mild notice. The red horse, not the workout, was the event that they came to see.

"What about these advance notices that he's a superhorse?" the TV man asked Laurin, who answered without hesitation, "I don't believe there is such a thing as a superhorse. But he has done everything beautiful."

Around the walking ring outdoors, with Turcotte on his back, walked Riva Ridge, still months away from the races. Secretariat, walking inside the shed, was cooling out.

"What chance does Secretariat have in the Triple Crown?"

Seeing Riva Ridge, Laurin said, "Last year I thought *he* had the shot of his life. This horse has a good chance. You never know from one day to another, to be honest with you." Nearby, Penny was talking to someone of the pressures they had felt in the Bay Shore Stakes—since that was the horse's first start—and then was trying to explain what Lucien had in mind with the red horse. As usual, she was articulate and informative. "He's aiming the horse to reach his peak for the Triple Crown," she said. At one point, looking at Riva Ridge, she told a reporter, "There's a *real* Derby winner." He was still her golden boy.

"A horse has to prove himself," Laurin was saying. "They're going back years when they compare him with Man o' War."

"Can you compare Secretariat's temperament with Riva Ridge's?" someone asked him.

"They're both very intelligent horses."

"Why does Secretariat insist on coming from the backstretch to win?"

"Horses are different. Riva Ridge was a frontrunner, and this horse comes from behind."

"Aside from the bloodlines, what makes Secretariat great?"

"I wish to God I knew."

The media were moving in. And so, too, were the odds makers, bringing Delphi to Reno, Nevada. Later in the morning, Laurin came into the office kitchen wearing an overcoat speckled here and there with mud, pulled it off and walked to the stove. Turcotte, his coffee cup half filled, smoking a cigarette, sat intently reading the front page of the *Daily Racing Form*, specifically a one-column story headlined: "Secretariat Even Money For Derby."

So the odds makers were at work again. Five days earlier, on March 28, the *Form* had carried a story saying that the Reno Turf Club had made Secretariat the 6–5 choice to win the ninety-ninth running of the Kentucky Derby. Now they had shaved him another point, making him even money.

Turcotte read the last paragraph of the story aloud: "As an added fillip, North Swanson, operator of the Future Book, posted Secretariat at 5–2 to capture the Triple Crown—the Derby, Preakness and Belmont stakes."

There was a silence in the room.

"Jesus Christ," Laurin said. "Can you imagine 5–2 to win the Triple Crown?" His words measured, he added, "I wouldn't bet him if he were 10–1. I wouldn't bet $2. No . . . sir!"

Lucien walked toward the door, as if the thought were gradually dawning in its entirety on him: he was the trainer of a son of Bold Ruler who was worth $6.08 million as a stud horse, who had never run farther than a mile and a sixteenth, who was 6–5 to win the one-and-a-quarter-mile Kentucky Derby and 5–2 to sweep the Triple Crown, including the one-and-a-half-mile Belmont Stakes.

The red horse walked the next day, Wednesday, and Gaffney galloped him Thursday and Friday, letting him stretch out through the lane the day before the race. Hopping off, heading into the tack room, Gaffney said, "I let him gallop out a little through the stretch to blow him out for the race tomorrow. He'll win. I don't know who could beat him. He's absolutely super. That track is going to be lightning fast. If he gets rollin' and no one gets in his way, he could shoot for a record." Gaffney entered the tack room. Cleaning off the saddle, he said, "You haven't seen the best of Secretariat yet. Believe me. I think he's much better now than he was for the Bay Shore. He's just gettin' sharp and good. I have known him a year this month, and I know him like a book."

Secretariat, with a hot walker at his head, turned the corner at the top of the shed and moved powerfully down the aisle past the stalls. Ed Sweat, standing at the door of the colt's stall, watched him pass, leaning on the fork. "He trained real good for this race. He's edgy. The Ridge was the same way when he was two and three. But The Ridge has settled down quite a bit. He's already been through the hard campaign."

Eddie Sweat was awake before five the next morning, and he was at the barn by five-thirty, pulling up to the shed in his car, buying his usual cup of regular coffee, and walking down the shed in the half dark.

Sweat ducked inside the stall and checked the feed tub and the pail. All was as he wanted it. The colt had been fed several quarts of dry oats at three o'clock that morning, and he had finished it, always a sign of good health. Then Sweat cleaned the stall, and so tipped off the red horse that the day would not be an ordinary one —that, in fact, it would be a racing day: he didn't replace the dirty straw with fresh.

"He knows what's happening now," Sweat said later that morning. "He ain't got no hay in the back and he ain't got no fresh straw in the stall. I didn't change it this morning. I never do on a day he runs. He won't eat dirty straw. He's a smart rascal. He knows what's happening. Look at him. He's quiet now. He don't want to be bothered." As always on a day he raced, Secretariat hung morosely about the back of the stall.

Outside the sun was up, dappling the ground in shadows. The pregnant cat was lying on a red and black trunk inside the tack room. The morning had an edge to it: the colt was running that day. The front page of the *Racing Form* read: "Secretariat 1–5 In Big A's Gotham."

In the office, Laurin had just gotten off the telephone when Marshall Cassidy, the assistant track announcer, appeared at the door of the office. Cassidy bowed his head, as if reporting for duty, and said, "Lucien, I have a group of students with me from New York University who would like to see Secretariat. Is there any chance?"

"You know it's not a good day," said Lucien.

"Okay, if you don't, . . ." Cassidy started to leave.

"No, no. It's okay," said Lucien, who was always too nice to refuse a friend. "Just don't let them stay too long."

Cassidy made the formal introduction for the group of students: "This," he said, "is Secretariat."

There was a rush of murmurs.

Then a formal farewell and the group was gone. "I'll never get my work done here," said Sweat. "He wants to be left alone. Everybody's coming by this morning."

They were harbingers all. More and more was being said and written about the colt and the Kentucky Derby, even more now of the Triple Crown. It was a refreshing turn for those involved in the sport. Racing scandals had recently rocked political foundations in Illinois, ruining former governor Otto Kerner, while allegations of horse drugging had been made in a widely publicized congressional inquiry. Racing needed a hero, a symbol and a standard of the game as sport. It needed a horse to fire the imagination of the nonracing public, a winner of the Triple Crown—the most glamorous of racing's accolades—and the red horse was nearing odds-on.

Near noon that morning of the Gotham, Laurin jumped into his car, zipped out of the stable area, and drove off to Aqueduct, about ten miles southwest of Belmont Park, to meet for an interview with television producer Tommy Roberts. He sped down the Cross Island Parkway like a jockey, pulled into Aqueduct, and came to a halt near the barns along the backstretch. There, waiting at the mouth of the chute, where it joins the backstretch of the Big A, were Roberts, cameramen, jockey Turcotte, and the old master, Eddie Arcaro.

"Hi, Eddie," said Laurin, beaming.

"Hi, Lucius," said Arcaro, who always called him Lucius.

The day was bright and blue at the seven-eighths pole of the racetrack, 220 yards down from the end of the chute, where the one-mile Gotham would begin later that afternoon. The conversation dwelled on Secretariat. Arcaro, known as old "Banana Nose" to every horseplayer who ever made a bet at old Aqueduct, old Jamaica, or old Belmont Park, looked snappy in the sunlight in his red pants and a striped sports coat and a tan that spoke of fairways and putting greens.

"Secretariat is one of the prettiest horses I ever saw," Arcaro said. "In fact, going back in my memory, the only horse I ever saw any prettier was Eight-Thirty. Remember Eight-Thirty?" Turcotte shook his head, Laurin nodded, acknowledging the generation gap. "Eight-Thirty looked like a show horse," said Arcaro.

He presided for the moment—articulate, informed, recalling the past with clarity and relish, talking about the 1948 Kentucky Derby and the Calumet Farm entry of Citation. He talked about Nashua, the brilliant son of Nasrullah on whom he had won the Preakness and Belmont stakes in 1955, and of Swaps, the colt who beat Nashua in the Kentucky Derby. "Oh, Swaps was a great horse," said Arcaro. "I'll never forget the Washington Park Handicap in Chicago. I was on Summer Tan and we went to the half-mile pole in 0:44 ⅕, and around the turn I looked over at Swaps next to me and Shoemaker had Swaps's neck bowed. I couldn't believe it. And he looked like he was running easily. When I got off, Sherrill Ward—he was training Summer Tan—he said to me, 'What the hell were you running so fast for so early?' We'd done six furlongs in 1:07 ⅘. I said to Sherrill that Swaps was next to me and his neck was bowed. Sherrill said, 'No!' I said, 'We'll go look at the films!' Swaps was probably the worst managed horse in history. There is no telling how great Swaps would have been if he'd been managed right. No telling."

"They scratched a good horse today, Step Nicely," said Laurin at one point.

"If I had your horse, I wouldn't worry about anyone," said Arcaro.

"I don't like all the talk of superhorse," said Laurin. "I really don't."

Tommy Roberts organized the Arcaro and Turcotte filming. Roberts would ask a question about Citation and Secretariat; Arcaro would answer for Citation, Turcotte for Secretariat.

Leading the men through rehearsals, Roberts asked how the horses worked.

"Citation was a super workhorse," said Arcaro. "He was a gentle horse in the paddock."

"Secretariat's a super workhorse," said Turcotte.

"How about in the starting gate?" asked Roberts.

"Citation was a very fast break horse," said Eddie.

Roberts then asked about running style.

"Citation could do anything," Arcaro said. "He could go to the front or come from behind."

"I never asked Secretariat for speed," said Turcotte.

No, Turcotte had never asked the colt for speed. He'd always let him settle down and let him run when he wanted to run. Turcotte had never sent him, as they say, never rushed him to the front early. That morning, answering Tommy Roberts's question, he knew he was standing near the spot on the racetrack where all would end in several hours.

Earlier in the barn at Belmont Park, Turcotte and Laurin had sat together in the tack room and talked about the strategy for the race. They agreed that the Gotham was a good time to send Secretariat to the lead near the start, to let him get himself together and race him on the front end. In the Gotham they would try a tactic that would serve a larger strategy. If Secretariat went to the lead and won, the colt would have a new dimension to him, another capability that opposing trainers would have to fear and consider in their tactics against him. The running style of the colt would have an element of unpredictability, a capacity for surprise. It was wiser to experiment in the Gotham than in the Kentucky Derby. A horse accustomed to racing off the pace, as Secretariat had done in all his races, might react sourly if he were sent to the front before the turn. It might confuse him. If the colt reacted adversely to it in the Gotham, only money would be lost. At Churchill Downs they would lose the Derby and any hope to win the Triple Crown. There is only one chance in Louisville, as Vanderbilt had learned with Native Dancer, and no going back.

"I think we should send this horse today," said Lucien. "Let's see what he can do up there. I'd hate like hell to put him on the lead on Derby Day and see him quit with you. We'd kick our ass back to Canada."

Five hours later Turcotte was walking Secretariat past the seven-eighths pole and toward the starting gate 220 yards away. The wind was blowing off Jamaica Bay as the horses stepped into the gate. Secretariat was going off at 1–10 on the tote, with the second choice, the frontrunning Dawn Flight, off at $5.90 to $1.00.

Two stalls down, sitting on Champagne Charlie, was Mike Venezia. Two weeks had passed since the roan had finished second to Secretariat in the Bay Shore Stakes, a race that had not undermined Venezia's belief in his horse. Despite the Future Book and the talk of the Triple Crown and Secretariat as a superhorse, Venezia held fast to the thought he had a chance to beat the red horse with the roan.

Secretariat moved into the three slip. Then Flush. Then Champagne Charlie, who was stepping into the five hole at 11–1. Venezia believed that Turcotte might send the red horse to the front, keeping him free of such traps as were laid for him two weeks ago. "Secretariat had an inside post in the Gotham and everyone was looking to trap him," said Venezia. Before them now, stretching out like a furrowed field ready for planting, were the thousand yards of the backstretch straightaway. They would not have a chance to trap the colt that day.

Secretariat wobbled breaking from the gate, battering the sides as he powered away from it, so Turcotte waited and let him regain his balance. He held the colt together, giving him the chance to assemble himself, but that didn't take long. He chirped to him, and as the field headed down the chute, the colt was lying in third, the closest he had ever been to the lead at the start of a horse race. Turcotte gathered him up, and Secretariat leaned into the bit, as Turcotte coaxed and moved rhythmically on him. Dawn Flight dashed to the front. Harrison Kid lay second. Champagne Charlie was right there, Venezia waiting and giving him time. Secretariat was tracking them down the chute when Turcotte tapped him once and clucked to him, dropping him to the inside. He could feel Secretariat pick up speed.

As the horses bounded from the chute, Secretariat was racing near the lead. Swipes and hot walkers and Pinkerton guards stood draped across the rail as the horses passed them at the end of the chute and raced across the backstretch. Turcotte was still not asking him through the first quarter, though he was keeping him near the pace. The colt was leveling out beneath him. Turcotte could feel him. Dawn Flight raced through the opening quarter in 0:23 $\frac{1}{5}$, a gentleman's opening gambit, with Secretariat just a length behind him in third on the inside in 0:23 $\frac{2}{5}$.

Passing the pole Turcotte sent him to the front, clucking and asking him to move, and the red horse picked it up and took off in a rush, sprinting through a gap between the rail and Dawn Flight and charging up to the lead.

The tempo of the race accelerated. The red horse dashed an eighth in less than eleven seconds. He was applying the cruncher. He was racing down the backside about a head in front, with Dawn Flight right beside him on the outside.

Turcotte was trying to get the colt to settle down as they charged down the straightaway for the turn. He had roused him, and now he was trying to calm him down. Turcotte didn't like the way Secretariat was breathing. It was irregular. He was racing and breathing like a human sprinter dashing out of the block, almost holding his breath as he accelerated, burning tremendous amounts of oxygen quickly. Down the backstretch the horse felt rank to Turcotte, and he was having trouble getting the red horse to relax. Jockey Angel Santiago, riding Dawn Flight, was not helping any at all. He was yelling and chirping to his horse and popping his whip and whistling, keeping Secretariat's eyes open and his blood up.

Secretariat raced the half mile in 0:45 $\frac{1}{5}$, sprinting the second quarter in a sensational 0:21 $\frac{4}{5}$.

Dawn Flight began disintegrating as Secretariat rushed the turn, and within a few jumps the colt was two lengths in front. Passing the three-eighths pole, midway of the turn, Turcotte decided to let him go, to turn loose his head. Perhaps then he would relax, Turcotte thought. He was afraid the horse would burn himself out, he was trying to get him to breathe right.

As Dawn Flight staggered rearward, meanwhile, Venezia had dead aim on the red horse and was tracking him in second. Venezia hadn't let him get away, letting the roan ease up around the turn. He sensed he had a chance to win it, and he was waiting for the moment to make his move. Secretariat was racing the third quarter in 0:23 ^{2}/s, around the turn, backing off slightly as he turned for home at the top of the straight. There he began to tire, after racing six furlongs in a torrid 1:08 ^{3}/s, time which tied the track record for the distance. But Turcotte wasn't concerned.

Banking into the straight, Venezia was closing the margin between them. Unknown to Turcotte, Venezia had begun to make his run at the three-eighths pole, 660 yards from the wire. "I decided to make one charge with my horse, at the three-eighths pole, I decided Secretariat had been going too long on the lead and I had to try to win it. I wanted to make some kind of run at him because Secretariat had never really been challenged, and I figured that maybe—if he were challenged—he wouldn't want to go on. I thought maybe if he backed up a little I'd get by him. If my horse ran big, I'd swallow him. But now I had to go get him."

Venezia asked the roan for more speed, and he responded at the bend, edging up toward Secretariat as they made the turn and set off down the lane. He could feel Champagne Charlie close the gap. He reached, asking for more. The roan responded again, shaving the margin to a length and a half, then to a length. Turcotte, at first unaware as Champagne Charlie came to him, suddenly heard the immediacy of the crowd—a reboant roar that grew in intensity as Champagne Charlie came to Secretariat.

"I could hear the crowd and I thought the stands were coming down."

They were passing the three-sixteenths pole now, with 330 yards to go, and announcer Dave Johnson's voice boomed out: "Secretariat now in front by a length and a quarter. Champagne Charlie on the outside up to challenge. Down the stretch they come! Secretariat on the rail. Champagne Charlie on the outside."

Turcotte, hearing the crowd and aware that something was unfolding behind him—something of an alarming nature—glanced to his right. He could hardly believe it, after that pace he had been setting with the red horse.

By now, as the two raced for the eighth pole, Secretariat had had the breather he needed, and he had finally relaxed, easing off between the quarter pole and the three-sixteenths pole. "I still thought I had that closing run," said Turcotte. "When Champagne Charlie came to me at the three-sixteenths pole, I set my horse down again, and I could feel Secretariat start to pick up the momentum again."

The roan never got his nose to the front, though the crowd was frantic as he edged to a neck away. Turcotte struck Secretariat twice, deep in the stretch, and the red horse moved away again. In the last 200 yards he rushed off to win by three.

Secretariat raced the mile in 1:33 ⅖, tying the track mark set by an older horse five years before, and up in the stands there was another sustained breath of relief following that long drive through the lane, as there had been after the Bay Shore. Laurin was almost as excited as he was after that race. "I thought he was beat at the three-sixteenths pole. I almost had a heart attack."

Chapter 22

All seemed within their grasp after the Gotham. Secretariat appeared virtually invincible, emerging without a peer among the three-year-olds, bounding along as if inexorably destined to win the Kentucky Derby, Preakness, and Belmont stakes. Historically, all this was in the harshest defiance of the odds. Only eight horses had ever won the Triple Crown, and never in history had the same team of owner-breeder-trainer-jockey won consecutive runnings of the Kentucky Derby, much less all three. Never had a son of Bold Ruler won any of the three, so star-crossed were the sire's progeny for the three-year-old spring classics. Yet never had a two-year-old son of Bold Ruler come to his three-year-old year with such speed and promise.

For Laurin, Turcotte, and Penny Tweedy, the press was on to win the second Kentucky Derby, to take another crack at the Preakness Stakes, and to try to win the Belmont the second year in a row. Following the Gotham they radiated confidence, swelling with hope. Penny's feelings of pessimism about Secretariat had dissolved almost entirely since the Bay Shore Stakes. The race had convinced her that the colt had experienced safe passage through the transition period over winter, and it set her to thinking that she had a shot to win the Derby again in 1973. The Gotham simply reinforced that notion in her mind, filling her with optimism. The colt was running heavy-headedly, battering at the ground, but not so much as he had at the age of two. He was giving signs that he was learning to run, to carry himself more smoothly. Turcotte felt a change between the Bay Shore and the Gotham stakes—a greater airiness in stride. The colt had done everything asked of him and had done it well. He had blown by horses on the outside. He had rushed past them on the rail in the Gotham. He had busted between horses. He had come from behind and had gone to the lead. He had run over fast and sloppy racetracks. He relished turns—the sharper the better—and worked willingly in the morning. He had no limiting flaws, at least none that had surfaced yet.

After the Gotham, Laurin turned and aimed him for the final prep race before the Kentucky Derby, the $100,000-Added Wood Memorial, one mile and an eighth at Aqueduct on April 21. To that race the colt brought a lengthening list of nicknames—Superhorse, Big Red, Big Red II, Red, the Big Red Machine, the Red Horse, and Super Red. He was hailed already as the ninth Triple Crown winner, the peer of Man o' War, and the greatest heir of the greatest sire in American history.

But at least one major question had arisen in the last several weeks, one major threat to Secretariat's dominance of the spring classics. There were no outstanding three-year-olds tracking the red horse through Florida, as Arcaro had said, and there was nothing of critical note training in either Louisiana or Kentucky. But out west in California, a big horse had emerged in full scale, growing up and filling out that winter in the foothills of the San Gabriel mountains at Santa Anita Park. He was Sham, and he had classic dimensions to him.

Sham had become one of America's most accomplished three-year-olds since Pancho Martin started training him at Santa Anita that winter, just weeks after his patron, construction magnate Sigmund Sommer, paid $200,000 for him at the Bull Hancock dispersal sale at Belmont Park. He had won that first start for them in December at Aqueduct, breaking his maiden, and had come back New Year's Day at Santa Anita and won that allowance race by fifteen.

"This is my Derby horse," said jockey Laffit Pincay, Jr.

Pancho shipped Sham across the Rockies following the Santa Anita Derby, bringing him to Long Island and a stall in the Sommer barn at Belmont Park, at the opposite end of the stable area from Secretariat. It was a fighting move—a move that said that Secretariat's reign as champion of his generation had endured too long, that vowed Sham would go out of his way to meet him on his own turf.

Proud, defiant, angry, and confident, Martin came looking for a scrap, for the chance to send his Sham against the red horse. The Kentucky Derby could wait.

He would battle him first in the Wood.

Pancho had deviated from the traditional course: other Santa Anita Derby winners—Swaps, Lucky Debonair, and Majestic Prince —went directly to Kentucky from California, doing their final tuning up at Churchill Downs or Keeneland. Now Martin was gearing up for the race at Aqueduct. "The Wood is the way I wanted to go, that's all," Martin said one day at the barn. Trainers, like fight managers, often speak for their horses in the first person.

While Martin was grabbing hold of the bit on his way to Kentucky via Aqueduct, it was not unanimous in the Sommer camp that the colt should even go to Churchill Downs. When Sommer saw Sham in the Santa Anita Derby, his thoughts turned to Kentucky. He had never run in a Derby.

Martin had never even been to Churchill Downs, much less had a horse in the Derby, and the challenge of winning it and beating the red horse began to consume him. The two men decided that Sham would run in the ninety-ninth Kentucky Derby. But they had to overrule Viola Sommer, Sigmund's pleasant, cherubic, unobtrusive wife, who shared her husband's interest in the racing stable and had definite ideas of her own concerning the Kentucky Derby.

Viola Sommer thought there were too many unqualified horses causing too much traffic in the Derby and that a good horse could get hurt in it too easily. The Kentucky Derby, in fact, was known for its large fields and the unqualified horses entered in it by owners willing to pay the $4100 in entry fees for the privilege of saying they had a horse compete in it. Martin believed Sham could win, but that, to Viola, was beside the point. Even if Sham were better than Secretariat, that didn't justify risking injury to their horse.

But the plans were laid, against her wishes, to ship the bay colt to Kentucky following the Wood.

Martin and Sommer had been together for eight years. Martin had a reputation as a brilliant conditioner, a peer of the inimitable Allen Jerkens and Hirsch Jacobs, and Sommer, a self-made construction millionaire, had strong ambitions. Sommer sought out Martin after Martin claimed a horse from him, won several races with the horse at a higher claiming value, and then lost him in a claiming race himself, though not before making a large profit for the owner. He hired Martin to train for him exclusively.

By 1971, Sigmund Sommer was America's leading owner in money won, the horses owned by him winning a world's record $1,523,508 in prize money. Sommer broke his own record in 1972:

his horses won $1,605,896. He owned a high-class operation, with Martin orchestrating the stable operations like a major-general, buying and selling horses at the races. They lost a number of exceptional horses, however, to illnesses and accidents. Sommer's Autobiography, voted the leading handicap horse in America in 1972, broke a leg at Santa Anita and was destroyed. Dust the Plate, a promising two-year-old, broke a leg that summer past and had to be destroyed. Stakes-winning Hitchcock collapsed and died one morning of a heart attack. While being loaded on a plane bound for Europe, stakes-winning Never Bow fell from the loading ramp and broke his neck.

Autobiography died in March, while Sham was emerging as the leading three-year-old in California, and the death left Martin and Sommer crushed. In that emptiness rose Sham, a rangy, elegant looking bay horse with a leggy leanness to him and a dappling coat. Pancho soon came to regard Sham as the best horse he'd ever trained, better than Autobiography, and toward him became as solicitous as a father toward his gifted son. There was honor involved in all this, too—and pride and faith. All these needed defending during battle. As it turned out, Martin would have a better chance to win the Wood than he ever imagined then, for events in mid-April began conspiring to bring the race within his reach and shape the course of things for weeks to come.

Laurin eased off Secretariat's training following such a fast mile in the Gotham. He sent him out an easy half mile in 0:49 on April 13. Then he said, "I'll work him once again and then try to catch Sham." On April 17, he boosted Turcotte aboard the red horse for that second work, a one-mile breeze around the main track at Belmont Park. Laurin told Turcotte to let the colt run the mile in about 1:38, two seconds slower than twelving it. Turcotte, after warming him up through the stretch, took Secretariat to the mile pole past the clocker's shed and got ready to break him off. The colt grew anxious. Ahead of him, at once, Turcotte saw a loose horse galloping toward him, clockwise. So he waited. The loose horse came charging past him and up the homestretch, reins flapping and riderless, going the wrong way. Secretariat was getting edgy as Turcotte waited. Then he lost sight of the loose horse, and decided to send the colt on his way.

Turcotte picked up speed and galloped toward the mile pole, then sat down on Secretariat and took off around the turn and into the long Belmont backstretch, all the while letting the colt run and watching ahead for the loose horse. Down the backside and around the turn Turcotte watched for trouble. The fractions were agonizingly slow: 0:13 ⅕, 0:26 ⅕, 0:52 for the half, 1:17 ⅘ for the three-quarters. "He's thirteening it pretty good," Laurin said, grimly.

The red horse accelerated through the final quarter in 0:24 ⅖, finishing out the mile in 1:42 ⅖, about five seconds slower than Laurin had wanted him to go. It was a dismal move, the slowest and least impressive of all Secretariat's workouts.

But Laurin was a master at last-minute improvisation, and what he planned was a quick blowout to bring the colt to his toes.

Sham, meanwhile, had his second sharp workout since arriving in New York. Martin sent him a mile in 1:37 ⅖ on April 12, and five days later wound the watch with a sizzling five-eighths in 0:58, the fastest move of the day. It may have been too fast.

Nor were Sham and Secretariat the only runners aiming for the Wood to appear on the racetrack that morning. Laurin sent Edwin Whittaker's Angle Light a mile in 1:42 for his final Wood Memorial prep. It is a common and legal practice for trainers to run two horses of different owners in the same race. Angle Light was getting sharp. The same day Sham worked his mile, Angle Light worked a brisk six furlongs in 1:11 ⅖. Meanwhile, Laurin was still assuring Penny that there was nothing to worry about with Angle Light, as he had assured her the last fall; yet she remained concerned about him, seeing him as a real threat to Secretariat.

Angle Light was the best horse Whittaker had ever owned. Whittaker had bought him for only $15,500 at the 1971 Keeneland summer sales, and he'd already won $89,006 as a two-year-old, and had finished second in the Garden State to the Horse of the Year. That winter, while Secretariat was idle, Whittaker nearly won the $100,000-Added Flamingo Stakes at one and an eighth miles with him. The colt just missed for all the money, finishing a neck behind Our Native in third. Whittaker's enthusiasm grew. After Angle Light raced to a ten-length victory at Aqueduct on March 21, according to *The New York Times,* Whittaker said, "This colt is going to the Kentucky Derby *with* Secretariat because they're both trained by Lucien Laurin. As to who will win, I can't say, but they'll run one-two." Laurin thought the colt would run sharply in the Wood, and he also believed Sham's long journey from California might adversely affect him.

The problems began sometime before the Wood Memorial, perhaps even before the slow mile workout. Jimmy Gaffney jumped on Secretariat on Thursday morning, two days before the Wood, and took him to the track to gallop him. The horse wasn't acting himself. Gaffney started to gallop him and sensed there was something wrong. He went a mile and a half open gallop and had to kick the colt a little bit to do it.

This puzzled Gaffney because Secretariat was a horse who worked so willingly in the morning. When he brought the colt back to the barn he told Sweat about it.

The next day was even more alarming to Gaffney. On Friday, Hoeffner told Gaffney to gallop the red horse a "two-minute lick" —that is, a mile in two minutes, which is not a flat-out run but it is faster than a normal gallop. Gaffney took him to the track, and again he had to kick the colt to keep him going. Worse, when he brought Secretariat back to the barn, the colt was blowing—a sign of distress fatigue. After Turcotte brought Secretariat back to the barn following the slow mile on Tuesday, the colt was blowing and his nostrils were flared.

Gaffney never told Laurin of the need to kick the red horse. Lucien's father-in-law had died the week of the Wood, and Gaffney didn't want to upset him further. He was under more strain than usual by the close of the week. He had two horses coming to the Wood Memorial, the final Derby prep race, and there was a death in the family. In the confusion of those final days, things weren't meshing at Barn 5, and whatever plans there were to give the colt a blowout never materialized. The source of the problem remained hidden and unknown until the morning of the Wood Memorial, concealed under Secretariat's upper lip, just to the right of center.

Dr. Manuel A. Gilman, the examining veterinarian for the New York Racing Association, discovered a swelling abscess under the lip. Gilman arrived early at Barn 5 that morning to give Secretariat the routine prerace physical examination and to identify Secretariat *as* Secretariat by checking his tattoo number—Z20669. All horses have a tattoo number as part of the universal horse identification system, which is designed, in part, to ensure that horses competing in races *are* the horses their handlers claim they are.

The number is tattooed inside the upper lip. Gilman lifted the lip to look at it.

He was the first to notice the abscess. It was blue, about the size of a quarter, and was sore and getting sorer. Gilman went to see Laurin about it, and brought Lucien back to the stall to show it to him, referring to it at the time as an abscess.

"I don't think it will bother him," Gilman was heard to tell Laurin.

So Secretariat would go to the post that afternoon with what appeared to be a harmless abscess inside his upper lip. But the morning brought a combination of things that would bear upon the Wood Memorial that afternoon. Pancho Martin and Sommer read Charles Hatton's column for the day, and it compelled Martin to rashness. Through the week, Martin planned to run three Sommer three-year-olds in the Wood—Sham, Knightly Dawn, the colt accused of bothering Linda's Chief in the Santa Anita Derby, and a speedy colt named Beautiful Music, who had just won his only start by ten lengths at Santa Anita. There was talk that Martin might be ganging up on Secretariat and still talk of the Santa Anita Derby, with intimations that Knightly Dawn had lain on Linda's Chief deliberately, despite the stewards' ruling to the contrary. Hatton sat in Secretariat's corner, and he was clearly concerned about the entry. Through the week his column implied that there might be skulduggery afoot in the Wood Memorial. He accused no one of plotting foul play, but the slant of his column made it clear that he believed the three New York stewards—Nathaniel Hyland, Francis Dunne, and Warren Mehrtens—might have to settle the outcome of the Wood by arbitrating foul claims. Hatton came to racing in an era when jockeys rammed one another, grabbed saddlecloths, and recklessly cut each other off—before the film patrol—when anything went if you could get away with it.

Fearful that the Wood might develop into a donnybrook, Hatton wrote on Thursday: "The Wood is supposed to decide who has the most horse, not the most horses."

On Friday Hatton criticized several horses being pointed for the Wood:

> There ... were indications the stage would be cluttered by a lot of spear carriers when the protagonists, Sham and Secretariat, make their appearance. The eyes of turf fans everywhere, as well as the sharp optics of the stewards, will be focused on the $100,000 added nine furlongs. We shall not be surprised if the tote board lights up with foul claims like Times Square on Saturday night. Our best advice is to hold all mutuel tickets.

Martin had entered the three horses, and Hatton quoted Lucien Laurin as saying: "The only way they can beat him is to steal it."

There was nothing intrinsically inflammatory about that. In racing, the stealing of a race is an old tactic, probably dating back to the days of Ben Hur. A horse steals a race when he goes to the lead, sets a leisurely pace unchallenged, and then has enough left to hold off superior horses when challenged in the lane.

But Hatton gave "stealing" a darker dimension when, after quoting Laurin, he wrote: "Stewards Dunne, Hyland and Mehrtens are assurance that nobody is going to purloin the race." With that he implied foul play and added: "It is not as if horses have not ganged up on Secretariat before, if it comes to that, and he is the best alley fighter of his species we have ever seen."

Growling with anger, Martin scratched both Knightly Dawn and Beautiful Music, leaving Sham to do it all himself.

The scratches changed the makeup of the Wood, taking two speed horses from it and leaving the pacesetting to the only other consistent speed horse in the race—to Edwin Whittaker's Angle Light.

Less than an hour to post time for the Wood—the seventh race —the race for which everyone had been waiting, in stall 16, next to Secretariat, stood Angle Light. Sweat gave Secretariat a final cleaning with a rag and brush.

Exercise boy Charlie Davis took the halter as Sweat moved around the horse and swept a brush and towel down the back and rump, down the Nearco croup, and across the flanks and shoulders and down the legs. Secretariat bit at Davis and kicked at Sweat, who was working quickly.

The speakers in the barn crackled with a metallic voice.

"Get your horses ready for the seventh race. Get your horses ready for the seventh race."

That was the Wood. Sweat moved to bridle the colt. Secretariat had always been sensitive around the ears, but the colt never shied when Sweat put the bit in his mouth.

Now, as post time neared, Sweat couldn't bring the colt to open his mouth. Sweat had touched the abscess earlier in the day, after Gilman left the barn that morning, and Secretariat had flinched. He applied hot towels in order to bring it to a head. First Sweat put the blue frame of the bridle over the colt's head, fastening that, and then put the bit in his left hand and stood on Secretariat's left side and tried to open the jaws.

Secretariat raised his nose, backing away. Sweat paused, talking to him. He brought Secretariat forward again, and tried to insert the bit. The colt again resisted. Minutes passed. Sweat had never had such trouble putting the bit in Secretariat's mouth. That afternoon it took Sweat about five minutes to put on the bridle, finally coaxing the horse to take the metal—gently. Sweat picked out the dirt from Secretariat's feet, moving from leg to leg as Davis held him. At 4:20 Sweat picked up a blue wool cooler and unfolded it. Stepping into the stall, he tossed it across the horse's back and buckled the front leather straps.

"That's it," said Sweat. "Nothing more to do but wait." And wait.

Secretariat threw his head repeatedly, tossing his nose in the air as they waited for the signal to go to the races.

The voice over the loudspeaker broke out harshly again.

"Bring your horses to the paddock for the seventh race. Bring your horses to the paddock for the seventh race."

It was 4:23. Davis unfastened the webbing and Sweat took Secretariat from the stall and down the aisle of the receiving barn for the Wood Memorial. Nearby, leaving his stall, was Sham. Sweat stopped and waited. Behind him was Angle Light.

Out the door they marched through the sunlight of the afternoon —Secretariat, Angle Light, Step Nicely, Champagne Charlie, Sham, Flush, Leo's Pisces, and Expropriate: the seventh race, the forty-ninth running of the prestigious Wood. Up the ramp from the barn to the racetrack, the horses crossed the chute and stepped down a two-lane walking path outside the clubhouse turn. Now and then a jet roared overhead, while the wind from Queens scalloped the waters of the infield ponds and the flags pointed toward Jamaica Bay, as if giving directions to the gulls. Beyond them rose the grandstand of Aqueduct, its back to the city, and beneath it the crowd of 43,416 horseplayers.

Secretariat stopped on the path beyond the chute, raising his head to see the distance. "Nothin' but people over there, Red," said Sweat. "Now come on." Bowing his neck, Secretariat bounced two jumps and settled to a walk. He seemed nervous, flighty, stopping and starting and looking toward the grandstand. Nearing the end of the path, where it joined the racetrack, the starting gate rolled by and stopped, ready to be wheeled into position near the finish line in front of the grandstand. Aqueduct is a one-and-one-eighth-mile oval. The red horse jumped as he approached the starting gate, then stopped and snorted, pricking his ears forward and looking at it.

"Wait now," said Sweat. "That's the gate. You're not getting into that for a while."

The paddock was filling with owners and trainers and newsmen. Among them were Robert Kleberg of the King Ranch, who turned down a share in Secretariat; Walter Salmon, oil executive Howard Keck, and Johnny Nerud, who didn't. Seth Hancock was with Keck. The trainer of Citation, H. A. (Jimmy) Jones, was there talking with Sam Renick, a former jockey who rode in the wake of the days of the Handy Guy.

"That horse," said Jimmy Jones, looking at Secretariat, "he's as big as a four-year-old."

"He's bigger than Citation ever was," said Renick.

The crowd draped over the apron of the paddock fence and applauded as Secretariat walked into the circle. Laurin met Turcotte in the walking ring, and they conferred briefly there. They had already decided that Turcotte should ride the colt as he usually had ridden him.

Nearby in the paddock, Martin talked to Jorge Velasquez, who would ride Sham. Laffit Pincay had another commitment that day, and Martin had picked Velasquez as a substitute.

Up the steps walked Jacinto Vasquez, a heady Panamanian jockey with a sly grin and a tough, swaggering way about his walk and talk. Laurin had chosen Vasquez to ride Angle Light, and while Laurin greeted Turcotte, Vasquez walked over to Edwin Whittaker, who was wringing his hands.

"Nervous?" said Vasquez, as if about to slap him on the back.

"Yes," said Whittaker.

"Don't be," Vasquez assured him. "It's just another race."

The crowd was buzzing in the post parade, clapping for Secretariat as he walked up the ramp to the racetrack. They were busy sending the Secretariat–Angle Light entry off at $0.30 to $1.00, and making Sham the second choice at $2.60 to $1.00. There were fewer than ten minutes to post as Laurin and Penny Tweedy climbed the stairs to the box seats. The Sommers were waiting in their seats, too. Racing Secretary Kenny Noe, Jr., who wrote the conditions for all the races and weighted horses for the handicaps, moved into his seat up front, near Vanderbilt and Ogden Phipps, who was there to see Bold Ruler's greatest son try to get the nine furlongs of the Wood.

Down on the racetrack, meanwhile, assistant starters led Sham to Post Position 2, just inside of Champagne Charlie. Number 2 was a favorable post that would give Velasquez a chance to establish position before the turn, without using Sham, and to save ground around it. Secretariat stepped into Post Position 6, with Angle Light on the extreme outside, in Post 8. There are only 330 feet from the finish line at Aqueduct to the first turn, and Vasquez would let Angle Light bounce the first 300 feet to get position for the run into it. He didn't want to get caught outside on that bend and lose ground. He couldn't afford it. Laurin's orders to him had not been difficult.

Vasquez knew that speed was Angle Light's game, so he decided to gun the bay the first 100 yards into the turn, then try to get him to relax on the lead. Vasquez respected Angle Light. He had ridden Our Native against him in the Flamingo, beating him by only a neck.

When the gates slammed open, sending the field of eight thorough-breds barreling toward that turn, Vasquez saw the open space in front of him and sent Whittaker's bay rolling for the lead, sprinting quickly from Post 8 and crossing over to the rail.

Several strides from the barrier, Step Nicely came over toward Secretariat, and Turcotte eased the colt back, taking a hold of him through the first sixteenth of a mile into the bend. The red horse dropped back to seventh, next to last, in the dash for the turn. Taking advantage of his post, Velasquez let Sham roll into the curve. He broke second and let Sham settle in behind Angle Light. Velasquez was not afraid of Angle Light and through the run to the first turn he sat still and began his long wait for the horse he feared, waiting and waiting as Angle Light cruised on the lead in front of him.

Turcotte steered Secretariat clear of trouble going into the first bend, swinging him to the outside and keeping a hold on him around the turn—"A slight hold," Turcotte said. By now he was not afraid of losing ground with Secretariat, not afraid of going wide with him.

The race was on. Or was it?

Banking into the backstretch, passing the chute, there he was—Angle Light. He was running along unchallenged on the front end, galloping through the opening quarter mile in 0:24 ³/₅. Angle Light had stolen the opening quarter. Sham, a length behind him, went it in 0:24 ⁴/₅. Secretariat, with Turcotte sitting tucked on him, ambled along in 0:25 ³/₅, barely fast enough to force him to a deep breath when he was fit. No one moved to counter Vasquez's gambit. He was breezing Angle Light on the lead, and he was feeling the bay relax beneath him as they turned and moved down the 500-yard back-stretch straightaway. Velasquez was still waiting for the red horse. He was not going to send Sham to the front to fight it out with Angle Light and set it up for Secretariat's paralyzing final burst of speed. Velasquez would continue to track Angle Light and wait for the red horse. The timer was catching Angle Light in twelves to the eighth, too, too slow. With each relaxed and easy stride, Angle Light thus became more dangerous. Hunched over him, Vasquez began to look like a kid playing with matches.

Turcotte had already sensed trouble as Angle Light swept into the backside. Secretariat was carrying his head higher than he usually did, Turcotte thought, and he seemed to be climbing around the first turn, his front legs not striding out level. More troublesome, though, was what Turcotte felt through the lines in his hands: The colt wasn't running up against the bit. Turcotte had picked him up around the turn, after he swung him to the outside, but the colt didn't grab the bit and lay against it, as he did whenever Turcotte shortened his hold and asked him. Racing past the seven-eighths pole, following that slow first quarter, Turcotte chirped to Secretariat, urging him to take hold and get with it. He chirped several times, making a kissing sound with his lips, but there was no response.

Up front, Angle Light barely picked up speed as he raced through the second quarter down the straight. He was running now against the wind, moving the quarter at the rate of 0:23 $^3/_5$. He opened up a length and a half on Sham, who was still tracking him while, patiently, Velasquez waited for Secretariat.

So Angle Light breezed the half in 0:48 $^1/_5$.

He was twelving them to death.

The Wood unfolded beautifully for Angle Light that opening half. Glancing at the teletimer, which blinked excitedly on the tote board, the crowd seemed to sense it, for there was a stirring of voices as the fractions flashed on it—0:24 $^3/_5$, 0:48 $^1/_5$. Getting no response when he chirped to Secretariat, Turcotte tapped him on the shoulder with the stick. They were racing past the three-quarters pole. The colt moved up, picking up the beat, but he didn't take hold. Turcotte's concern now deepened to dismay.

Angle Light raced into the far turn and started sweeping around the bend for home. No one had moved to him down the backside, and he was still running very easily under Vasquez, who was sitting as still as a statue on his back. Velasquez waited for the red horse. And Turcotte, growing desperate as the horses made the turn, knowing that time was running out, cocked his whip, reached back and strapped the colt. He was empty as a jug.

Angle Light raced to the three-eighths pole still a length and a half on the lead, and he was still drumrolling to the beat of twelve. They were midway of the turn, with only 660 yards to go. Velasquez, having waited long enough, decided to wait no longer. He roused

Sham and asked him to move to Angle Light, who dashed past the three-eighths pole in 1:12 ⅕ for six furlongs, almost a perfect twelve-clip. For an instant Sham closed the gap. But Vasquez, who had yet to ask Angle Light to run for him, let out a notch. Responding to him, Angle Light eased away from Sham. Turcotte, meanwhile, was pasting Secretariat around the turn for home, lashing into him with the whip. He was going nowhere. Velasquez went to the whip, too. Now Angle Light came into the straight more than a length in front of Sham. The Wood Memorial had begun.

At one point, as the horses made the turn, jockeys Larry Adams on Expropriate and Chuck Baltazar on Leo's Pisces were drifting to last. Secretariat came past them on the outside, then edged away from them. Seeing Turcotte in trouble, Adams yelled to Baltazar, "Hey, Chuck, look at him. He ain't gonna make it today!"

"It don't look like it!" Baltazar hollered back.

In the box seats came the echo. Seth Hancock told Keck, "He ain't gonna make it today, Mr. Keck." The two men suddenly left the box, off to catch separate planes, and Hancock watched the stretch drive over his shoulder, heading toward the door.

What he saw was Sham moving to Angle Light at the top of the stretch.

There Vasquez went to work on Whittaker's bay, urging him to ease away from Sham again. Driving to the eighth pole, he had almost two lengths on Sham. Velasquez rode furiously, pushing and bouncing him down the lane, while Vasquez did the huck-a-buck on Angle Light to keep him on the lead, shoving and driving the colt toward the eighth pole. The crowd moiled frantically. Secretariat was fourth on the outside passing the eighth pole, a full two lengths behind Sham. He was gaining only slowly, struggling with Step Nicely for third. The big money bettors who came for Secretariat had only Angle Light in the final 200 yards.

He was tiring through that final furlong, beginning to feel the twelves. He had run the mile in 1:36 ⅘, and he was still a length and a half in front of Sham. For all he was doing, Velasquez couldn't cut Vasquez's lead through the whole of the upper straight. Then suddenly he began. Passing the eighth pole, Sham gained on Angle Light, each stride cutting into Angle Light's lead. Sham sliced it to a length, then three-quarters of a length, then a half, then a neck. Vasquez pushed Angle Light. He rode with the horse, using his weight and strength in rhythm with him. He did everything but jump off. Still Sham came to him. But Angle Light hung on. Twenty yards from the wire, heads were bobbing almost together, and Sham was gaining with each jump, though he was tiring now himself. Just as he was come to swallow Angle Light, the wire flashed by.

Angle Light won it by a head. Sham was second. Secretariat was third, four lengths behind Sham and a half length in front of Step Nicely.

"Oh, my God! What have I done now?" Edwin Whittaker said, as the horses hit the wire.

"What do you mean?" asked Jack Wainberg, a friend of Whittaker's.

"I just buggered up the Kentucky Derby," Whittaker said.

Chapter 23

In the box seats, Lucien Laurin looked around toward Penny saying, "Who won it?"

"You won it," she yelled.

"Angle Light," someone called to Laurin. "Angle Light won it."

"Angle Light?" It was a howl of incredulity, and the expression he wore said all the rest, that he'd just won the Wood Memorial but with the wrong horse, that he'd won it with a horse he'd been insisting to Penny and everyone could not and would not beat Secretariat. Down the aisle between the box seats now, strolling toward Laurin, his white hair climbing in waves above his spectacles, came fifty-nine-year-old Edwin Whittaker. He was the center of triumph in a spectacle of gloom. Whittaker never really expected or believed that Angle Light would ever beat Secretariat. It seemed simply beyond hope. In most any other barn Angle Light would have been the big Derby horse, but in Laurin's barn the colt was but a second-string stablemate of the most publicized and illustrious horse in America. Whittaker understood that. He was simply pleased that Laurin had brought the horse as far as he had, farther than any other trainer had ever brought a horse for him. Angle Light was a contender. Actually, Whittaker did harbor one strong hope whenever Angle Light raced against Secretariat, one more poignant than any illusory dream he might have had of victory, that *maybe* Angle Light might stand up to him.

Penny saw him coming toward her, and she took a breath, as if to inflate her cheeks with a smile, and reached out saying; "Congratulations."

"Thank you," said Whittaker. "I'm sorry."

"I'm glad for you," she said.

Penny Tweedy never liked Whittaker, but she would keep up all the appearances of gentility and gracious good-sportsmanship. Inside she was growing furious with Laurin, and at one point leaned over the railing of the box seat and said to him, "You and I have got to talk."

Whittaker felt sorry for Laurin, and he didn't want to cause him further anguish in public.

Laurin, his features grimly set, moved off on the long walk down the stairs and across the formal apron to the winner's circle ceremony. Whittaker's head rose and dipped as he walked along, acknowledging the salutations.

Crowds of people had gathered by the paddock fence. Many of them had come expecting to witness the flight of superhorse—Pegasus redivivus, a Man o' War, a Gladiateur. They did not like what they had seen. That Angle Light had saved the hour for those who bet heavily on Secretariat, that no one who bet on the red horse actually lost money on the Wood, didn't seem to make all the difference. Their expectations souring to bitter disappointment, they turned their derision on Laurin, Turcotte, and the red horse, who was galloping back to the unsaddling area as Laurin and Whittaker walked across the circle.

Voices cried out.

"You bum, Turcotte. You got $6 million worth of horse and you ride him like manure."

"Whatsah mattah, Ronnie, you fall asleep out there?"

"That's the last time you'll ever ride that horse."

"Where are the stewards?" said another. "A 1–5 shot runs like he's 50–1."

Ed Sweat led Secretariat down the racetrack, back toward the receiving barn, his face expressionless amid the taunts and boos that followed him. Henny Hoeffner led Angle Light into the winner's circle. Pictures were snapped, and Vasquez hopped off. Laurin walked immediately to Turcotte, who had just weighed out at the scale. Turcotte's brow was furrowed, his eyes wide open as he talked to Laurin. He looked like a man who was genuinely amazed.

"He just didn't fire," Turcotte said. Turcotte walked across the paddock for the jockeys' room, descending the staircase below a crowd of bettors that jeered him raucously.

Laurin, talking to reporters, said he couldn't explain it. "Ronnie says the horse didn't fire," he said. "Didn't have his usual punch. I think they lost the race on the turn, going wide. That and the slow pace."

Awkwardly, somewhat sheepishly, Vasquez stood around a moment as if waiting to apologize to someone, to anyone for winning the Wood. He had ridden brilliantly, with understanding and insight, engineering the most artful upset in New York racing in the last year. Vasquez reached out his hand to Laurin.

Sitting nearby on the bench in front of his locker, a towel wrapped around him, Turcotte was listening to Vasquez expound upon the race. "I always thought Angle Light was a good colt," Turcotte said quietly. "Never as good as Secretariat, but a good colt. I always knew he was as good as those other horses."

The race had plainly baffled and worried him, and he was trying to make sense of it.

What puzzled him was the colt's uncharacteristic dullness throughout the race.

That afternoon and evening—in fact for the next several days—Turcotte would examine a whole range of explanations for Secretariat's race in the Wood, turning each one over in his mind. He was reaching for something to hold on to, for some clue to explain the staleness, for something that might make sense to him. He knew Secretariat well by then. He had ridden him in most all major workouts and in all races since the summer past, and the race in the Wood simply didn't figure in any pattern that he knew. The Derby was only two weeks away, which left him no time to fool himself.

Turcotte considered that Secretariat, as a son of Bold Ruler, might be out of his depth in races beyond a mile, despite the colt's rompings in the Laurel Futurity and Garden State Stakes and the records of the several Bold Rulers who had won at a mile and a quarter. It was known as the "invisible shield" theory, and it was trotted out whenever a Bold Ruler ran brilliantly in the sprints and then stopped at nine or ten furlongs, as if running into something unseen. Turcotte also rejected a correlative belief that Secretariat, as a scion of the temperamental Nasrullah tribe, resented being taken back and rated off the pace, finally refusing to run when he asked him. Bold Ruler had resented Arcaro's exertions in the 1957 Kentucky Derby, and he came up sulking down the backside. Penny Tweedy, among others, came to believe this theory to explain away the Wood.

Turcotte summarily rejected it. Never had Secretariat shown any tendency to sulk. He was not a moody horse. In all those workouts and races, Turcotte could not recall any problems of temperament. Secretariat never quit, never spit out the bit and refused to run. In fact Turcotte had come to regard him as a kind of model of tractability. He could do anything with him. Several days before the Wood, recalling races on the colt, Turcotte said he thought he had ridden him poorly in the Garden State Stakes. He took him back sharply after the break, falling many lengths behind. Secretariat didn't sulk then.

Why suddenly now?

It made no sense to him. The colt hadn't given off what Turcotte regarded as a vital sign of a sulker: a resentful hardening of the neck and body muscles.

Nor had he acted sickly or weak. Nor had he been walking sore. He didn't feel limp and tired. In fact, because Secretariat didn't feel especially "short" or tired under him, Turcotte didn't take too seriously those who blamed the slow workout. If the work had been inadequate, which it no doubt was, at least the colt would have made his run and then tired. But he didn't do that.

Reluctantly, for want of a more compelling explanation, Turcotte, who still didn't know about the abscess, finally settled on the notion that the record-tying mile in the Gotham Stakes probably sapped more out of Secretariat than anyone had realized, dulling his edges severely.

The impact of the Wood was felt at once, and reaction to it ran from the anger of Pancho and Penny to the alarm and concern of syndicate members, even to a cause for hope among owners who'd been conceding the Derby to the dominant shape of Secretariat. All bets were off. The Wood threw open wide the Derby doors—buggered it up, as Whittaker said. But more, it colored the days leading to May 5, setting the frantic pace, dictating the tone of things at Churchill Downs, and heightening the tension of rivalry between Secretariat and Sham. The Derby had become a horse race.

Word of Secretariat's defeat spread swiftly from Aqueduct that day—from New York to Kentucky and Texas and Ireland and France. Telephones started ringing that evening, and they continued ringing for weeks. Many of those who had invested $190,000 in the red horse were troubled deeply over the loss. Others were not.

Meanwhile, the Blue Grass country was rampant with rumors about Secretariat physically breaking down. The rumors said the colt was walking wide in front, a sign of bad knees, though walking wide was a characteristic of many Bold Rulers. They said he had bone chips on his knees, bad ankles, more splints hurting him, and bucked shins. The place was a nest of speculation and hearsay.

In the stable area at Belmont Park, where just a month ago news of that sensational workout swept among the sheds, the Wood had vastly tempered enthusiasms for the colt. The change in attitude was swift, and it stunned syndicate member Vanderbilt, who spent his mornings in barns, coffee shops, and clockers' sheds there. Listening to the talk, he heard knowledgeable horsemen no longer giving the colt a chance at Churchill Downs. He couldn't believe it. In all his years at the racetrack, ever since his mother took him to Pimlico as a child, Vanderbilt had never seen such a wholesale abandonment of faith in a racehorse, or an abandonment executed with such suddenness, and all on the basis of just one race.

The Wood Memorial began something that only the Derby could end.

The evening of the Wood, Penny Tweedy and Laurin returned to Barn 5 at Belmont Park, and there gathered with friends and family with whom they had a dinner date at the Tweedy home in Laurel Hollow. The mood was subdued, even somber. Ron Turcotte, done working for the day, joined them as he usually did following a race. Secretariat and Angle Light, fed and cooled out, were in their stalls. Turcotte and Penny spoke briefly of the race, of his timing and even of how hard he had been working. She never told him that he ought to take time off, that perhaps he had been working *too hard*, but that was what Turcotte understood she meant.

"I don't think you were sharp in judging the pace," Penny told him. "Your timing could be off."

She reminded Turcotte of Secretariat's last workout and of an error in judgment he made while working Riva Ridge the same day. "You worked Secretariat too slow the last time you worked him a mile, and then you broke off Riva Ridge an eighth of a mile too soon in his last work," she said. Riva Ridge was supposed to work seven-eighths, and Turcotte erred and broke him off at the mile pole, though he realized his mistake en route and compensated for it by pulling him up at the eighth pole instead of at the wire. He had no excuse for the lapse.

Turcotte agreed that he had messed up the workout; all week he had been assuming blame for it, and he would continue to take responsibility for it. Then he added, "I thought he might blow out

233

before the race," but he decided not to press the point. He didn't want to imply criticism of Lucien: Laurin worked for Penny and Ron was riding the colt because Laurin put him there. Diplomatically, it would be unwise for Turcotte to criticize Laurin to his boss.

"The horse just didn't run his race," he told her. "I don't feel I took too much hold of him. I got him in the clear and he just didn't respond. I started nudging him at the three-quarter pole and there was no response."

She believed Turcotte had misjudged the pace and let Angle Light steal away with it. In fact, she wanted to take him off Secretariat and find another jockey, but they were coming to the biggest race of all, and it was too important to switch jockeys.

She, too, knew nothing of the abscess on the upper lip.

Penny expressed no displeasure with Laurin while they gathered in the office at Belmont Park. She would not make a scene. But when the guests left for the drive to Oyster Bay, Penny and Lucien climbed into his Mercedes and drove out the stable area and through the iron gates, then up the Cross Island Parkway north toward the sound. The drive usually took about forty-five minutes, but that evening it took them longer.

It was a "terrible fight," beginning before they reached the stable gate, and Penny started and controlled it, setting whatever thrust and intensity it had. She gave him little chance to speak in defense of himself.

For that hour, Penny vented upon Lucien all the fear, suspicion, frustration, and confusion that the running of the Wood had aroused in her. She felt he had humiliated her in public. She was chagrined, but it really went beyond chagrin. She felt she had a moral obligation and responsibility to all those people who had an interest in Secretariat—to the family and her father's estate, to Claiborne Farm and to the syndicate members—not to put the colt in the position of embarrassing himself and harming his value. She felt they had invested their faith as well as their money in the red horse, and now her trainer had beaten him with another horse.

The ultimate chagrin was that Lucien had just told Charles Hatton the only way they could beat Secretariat was to steal the Wood. Then he up and stole it himself. And Penny was hopping mad at him. So she reproached and rebuked him the hour long, and he in turn became so furious with her that he refused to follow her directions on getting to her house.

She even wondered whether Lucien felt some obligation to Whittaker, as one Canadian to another, and then she remembered all the times she told Lucien how she feared Angle Light, and she remembered all the times he told her there was nothing to fear, and she remembered all the easy assurances of the autumn and winter past. She knew Lucien had spent his early years bumping about the leaky-roof circuit trying to win a pot to pay the bills. She thought he had entered Angle Light in the Wood as a kind of insurance—a backup in case the red horse didn't fire.

"You got greedy . . ." she told him that evening in the car.

"I couldn't tell the other man not to run his horse in the race," Lucien protested.

"No you couldn't. You're a public trainer. Each man has his shot. But you should have warned Ronnie that this could happen. *You* had a special responsibility. Not that you shouldn't have let Angle Light run, but *you* should have made sure that Ronnie understood your fears about him . . . *You* should have been super careful with Secretariat. We gave you a free service to him just to make sure you were careful with him. You should have taken Angle Light seriously and made sure Ronnie knew this was a real threat."

"Blame Ronnie!" Lucien cried.

"No! I blame you because every other jock figured you weren't going to get Secretariat beat by Angle Light. So they all took the cue from what Ronnie did! The other jocks figured, 'Angle Light's supposed to be a rabbit, he's supposed to back up. Certainly Laurin won't let this expensive horse get beat. So this must be a phony, and even though it's a phony pace, Angle Light's going to die, it's all right.' And that's how Angle Light just stole the Wood! You've embarrassed yourself, you've embarrassed me and you've embarrassed a good horse. And for nothing! Because Angle Light is never going to be any more than he was today. And if I didn't have so much faith in you and weren't so fond of you, I would throw you out now. I would have reason to change trainers tonight! And instead I'm going to give you hell."

They ended up lost in the old whaling community of Cold Spring Harbor. By the time he pulled into the Tweedy's driveway, the fighting had subsided, and Penny was feeling better.

"We really had a knock-down, drag-out fight and it was really so good," she said. "By the time I got here I was pleasant. Lucien was very silent."

So they were Derby bound.

On April 22, the day after the Wood, Laurin was already preparing to ship Secretariat and Angle Light by plane to Louisville. He had decided to send them the following day—Monday—accompanied by Ed Sweat as groom and Jimmy Gaffney as exercise boy. When the red horse traveled to Laurel and Garden State the autumn past, Charlie Davis took Gaffney's place as exercise boy for Secretariat. Gaffney had his family in New York and his job behind the mutuel machines at Aqueduct, and he didn't want to give up the money to go with the red horse then. But Secretariat in the Kentucky Derby and Preakness Stakes was something different. Thus he decided to sacrifice his mutuel clerk's pay and accompany the colt out of town, prevailing on Laurin to send him instead of Charlie Davis.

There would be that triumphant sweep through Louisville and Baltimore, a tour de force: he had it all dreamed out in his mind. On the day of the Belmont Stakes, the day he saw Secretariat winning the Triple Crown, he would fit himself out—tails, top hat, and cummerbund—and lead Secretariat to the starting gate on Billy Silver. Secretariat would win, and Gaffney would step down in that warm flush of victory, full of good memories. It was his wish to retire that way, and all dressed up for the occasion; he had it all worked out. Now it was the morning of April 22, in the somber wake of the Wood.

"Are you ready to go?" Laurin asked Gaffney.

"I've wanted to talk to you about that," said Gaffney. "I've changed my mind. No one around here wants to talk dollars and I just can't afford it."

Laurin said he understood. But Ron Turcotte was not as understanding. He remembered Gaffney had been telling him for weeks how much he was looking forward to going to Kentucky with Secretariat. So he was caught off guard.

"I'm not going to the Derby," Gaffney told Turcotte.

"Why?" he asked. Turcotte would remember how disappointed he was thinking that Gaffney—of all people!—was so let down on the colt after the Wood, and after boosting him for so long.

So Laurin sent Charlie Davis, a long-time friend of Sweat from Holly Hill, South Carolina, for years Laurin's most trusted journeyman exercise boy, the regular rider of Riva Ridge. On Monday they flew to Louisville out of Kennedy, vanned the short distance from the airport to Churchill Downs, and unloaded the two colts, Billy Silver, the trunks, and the suitcases at Barn 42, the main Kentucky Derby barn. They bedded Angle Light in Stall 20. Sweat took Secretariat to Stall 21, the same stall occupied by Riva Ridge the year before.

And there the final drive to win the Kentucky Derby began—the last two weeks of feast and fever played out in an old riverboat city on the Ohio, with its racetrack, a graceful flight of wood and spires overlooking a mile oval. The rumors of Secretariat's unsoundness persisted and increased in the closing days; pressures intensified and bitternesses surfaced while, oblivious to most of this, thousands flocked to Louisville to see Secretariat do battle with Sham.

The abscess had worsened since the Wood, and Sweat was clearly troubled by it. The colt was not himself. The day after their arrival in Louisville, Dr. Robert Copelan came by the barn and Sweat spotted him. Copelan was the regular veterinarian for Laurin's horses when they were in Kentucky.

Copelan lifted the lip, looking under it. By now the abscess was larger than on Saturday, and it was growing more painful as it matured. It was sore and puffed up and there was an actual swelling on the outside of the lip, but Copelan was not alarmed about it. It wasn't serious. The upper lip was not an uncommon place for a horse to get an abscess. Copelan thought it might have been caused by a hay briar or an ingrown hair. But it was something that had to be watched and cared for. Copelan decided to treat it conservatively. He instructed Sweat to bathe it with hot towels in hopes of bringing it to a head on its own. He would lance it on Thursday if it failed to break open by then.

So the bathings became a part of Sweat's routine the next two days, Tuesday and Wednesday. Sweat would fill a bucket with hot water from the faucet—as hot as his hands could tolerate—dunk and wring out a towel and press the steaming cloth to the lip. The colt's eyes would widen and Davis and Sweat would mutter to soothe him.

Early Thursday morning, Sweat climbed out of bed and went into Stall 21 to check the abscess again. Raising the lip, he saw it had a pimple on its peak and it was festering, with pus and blood oozing from it. Grabbing a wet, clean sponge, Sweat wiped it off, then called Davis. Sweat quickly prepared another hot-towel application, and Davis held Secretariat as Sweat dunked and wrung and pressed the steaming towel to the lip, squeezing it gently, working to force the seed of the abscess from it and reduce the swelling and hence the pain. The abscess continued to drain. Doc Copelan, prepared to lance it, arrived at the barn shortly after noon on Thursday and examined it.

"Well, Eddie," said Copelan, looking at it, "that's good. This thing has already ruptured on its own and I don't think we're going to have any more trouble with it."

So things were breaking for them just in time, and it wouldn't be the last time.

That evening—Thursday night—Jacinto Vasquez and Turcotte flew together to Louisville to work Secretariat and Angle Light the following morning. Signing into the Executive Inn not far from the track and airport, Turcotte received a message telling him to meet Laurin and Penny for a conference in her room. He went upstairs immediately. Walking into the suite, Turcotte could feel that the moment had an edge to it—sharp with emotion and tension. The Wood had been a horror show and Penny was still agonizing over it. Laurin had already spoken to friends about retiring if the colt lost the Derby. For her part, Penny knew she would seriously have to consider retiring Secretariat if he ran as poorly as he had in the Wood. She had no legal obligation to retire Secretariat, but the moral commitment was firm and unmistakable. She had told Seth that if Secretariat lost once, she would wonder why; if he lost twice, she would consider stopping him and sending him to Claiborne. She knew the colt would have to run big in the Derby. It was crucial. They could not tolerate another Wood Memorial. So they had reached a juncture together, and the future was as uncertain for them as the immediate past was bleak.

Penny said, "Ronnie, do you really think the horse can go a mile and a quarter?"

Lucien broke in; "Do you *really* deep down in your heart believe it?"

Turcotte thought a moment. And nodded. And then he said, "I really believe he can go the distance."

The next morning, Laurin boosted Turcotte and Vasquez on the colts and sent them out to work six furlongs together. They worked it in 1:12 3/5 in company, not a bad move at the Downs. But Turcotte didn't like it. Secretariat kept throwing his head, for one thing, still smarting from an abscess about which Turcotte knew nothing. It had broken the morning before, but was apparently still sore to the touch. He again refused to grab the bit, and at one point in the workout Turcotte actually threw the lines away, riding with slack reins. Turcotte remained troubled. After returning home to New York, he told a friend that the colt was still not himself and that he didn't like the workout, that something was wrong, that the colt seemed dull and listless. The problem was still something he not could figure out. Revelation came just days later. One afternoon at Aqueduct, as he was lounging in the jockeys' room between races, an official of the New York Racing Association—a friend of Turcotte's who had connections in the examining veterinarian's office—took him aside and told him about the abscess, about how it was found the morning of the Wood, where it was located, the probable effect it had on him, and for Turcotte it all came together like a vision, so sudden was the realization.

It explained why the horse never took hold at any time and why he threw his head at Churchill Downs and why he didn't tire or sulk or flatten out in the Wood. Ron felt he understood it all. Relieved, he felt almost euphoric. Now he had an answer for all the questions the running of the Wood had raised. It was a physical problem, not a head or attitudinal problem. Turcotte felt a sudden swelling of confidence.

Down in Kentucky Eddie Sweat felt no such thing. Through the days leading to the Kentucky Derby, the man who knew the red horse best remained disturbed about the way he was acting and carrying himself. The colt seemed dull and lifeless all the time, unlike the Secretariat he had known in the winter and spring and through those two sharp races in New York. The colt was playful then, but not now. He would bounce only occasionally when he walked. The change was subtle, barely noticeable to anyone but the man who had been around the colt constantly. He looked well, his eye was clear, but he was missing his jaunty alertness. Daily, Sweat watched for a change, but saw none. Periodically Sweat would think the horse was getting sick and he would take his temperature: it was always normal. Sweat conveyed his fears to Charlie Davis. Unshaken, Davis worked to shore up Sweat's confidence, to assure him that all was well.

So the April mornings and afternoons breezed by, breaking off at the May pole into Derby Week, while the town filled with gamblers, hustlers, visiting businessmen, college students, and racing people and their Derby horses. They came in by car and by train, by plane and thumb, filling the rooms of all the inns in town, sleeping in parks, playing the horses by day and cards by night, the whoring and the chaste, the drinking and the temperate.

The horsemen's world is a morning watch. That week they rose and went to the racetrack in the mornings as usual, grabbing coffee on the way to sip and a paper to read while honing their horses for the Derby.

Among them this year were Jimmy Croll with Royal and Regal, winner of the $100,000 Florida Derby at nine furlongs; Sherrill Ward with the giant Forego; trainer Bill Resseguet with his little iron horse, Our Native, who'd already run twenty-three times in his life; and young Don Combs with the long shot, Warbucks. From Louisiana and Florida came trainer Lou Goldfine with My Gallant, winner of the important Blue Grass Stakes at Keeneland April 26, and the speedster Shecky Greene, winner of three stakes in 1973. Also from Florida came the winner of the Everglades Stakes, Restless Jet with Jimmy Jones, and Johnny Campo to try the red horse again, this time with Twice a Prince. From California came trainer Randy Sechrest with Gold Bag—the colt who used to work out with Secretariat at Hialeah in the winter of '72, the colt who beat Secretatiat by fifteen lengths the first time they worked a quarter mile together. Now the two were back again, and facing each other. Laurin had sold Gold Bag in January, and Sechrest took him to Hollywood Park and won the Coronado Stakes with him. Then Secretariat lost the Wood, which opened it up for all of them.

The week of the Derby started on Monday, April 30, and Laurin began it with a countdown. That morning he put on a blue-striped overcoat, left his suite at the Executive Inn, and made off hurriedly to the racetrack. He hadn't been eating or sleeping well since the Wood, and he looked drawn and weary, alternately pinching the bridge of his nose and wiping his chin.

Out of the car, Laurin entered the shed of Barn 42. The security guard, stepping forward, recognized him immediately and let him pass.

"How is he?" he asked Sweat. The red horse was in his stall and looking out the door from the back of it.

"He's all right," said Sweat. "All he want to do is eat."

"Good, let him eat," said Laurin.

He was still counting.

Down the shed, seven stalls away from Secretariat, was the leggy Sham, and just twenty feet beyond him and blocking the doorway of the tack room stood Pancho Martin. Sham was bridled and saddled for a three-quarter mile workout. As they took the bay from his stall, Martin preceded him to the racetrack between barns and ma-

240

nure bins and groups of newsmen. Pancho stooped to pick up pebbles and stones in Sham's path, tossing them aside. Later in the week he hired a man with a broom to walk in front of Sham whenever he went to the racetrack, and the man would briskly sweep the stones away. Pancho was taking no chances.

Martin climbed into the clocker's shed on the backstretch as Sham started his warm-up gallop to the three-quarter pole. Beyond were the twin spires, the emblem of Churchill Downs, the empty stands, and the infield that would be filled with more than 125,000 people in five days. Many horsemen stopped to watch the workout, sitting on ponies and leaning on the fence rails as word spread that Sham was on the track.

Exercise boy Pedeo Cachola galloped Sham toward the shed and down the backstretch. Nearing the pole he sat down, and Sham broke off quickly, accelerating for the turn. He ran the opening quarter in 0:23 ⅘, then made the bend and drilled the half in 0:47 ⅕, sharp time for the Downs. Cachola stayed hunched over him through the lane, sending him the next eighth in 0:11 ⅘. That gave him five-eighths in 0:59. Sham was rolling. He finished out in 1:11 ⅕ for six furlongs. It was a brilliant move over the track. Sham would appear for the Kentucky Derby off a powerful workout—his final major workout—and Pancho sensed victory.

"He has never been better," he said, leaving the clocker's shed with a flourish. "Never! That was a *big* move!"

Sham's work seemed to inspire and embolden Martin, for it coincided with his sudden launch into a week-long run of soliloquies denouncing Laurin and extolling the manifest gifts of Sham.

Twirling a Mexican cigar with Havana tobacco, leaning against the cinder block of Barn 42, sipping a demitasse (against doctor's orders), and wearing a hat with a feather in it, Martin held forth among the crowds of newsmen gathered there to hear him. He was cocky, brash, and self-assured, confident of victory. He excoriated Laurin in an oratory of disdain, sarcasm, and ire.

"All you hear from Laurin is excuses, excuses, excuses, excuses. He's got more excuses than China's got rice, and China's got a lot of rice. Cryin' like a little baby. That's not my game." Smiling wryly he said, "It's very coincidental that the only time Secretariat ran a bad race is the one time he met Sham. We are going to run four times against one another: the Wood, the Derby, the Preakness, and the Belmont stakes. We'll see who's the best out of the four. If he beats me, I'll say he's better. We'll see who's the best. If he beats me more than I beat him—if he beats me three out of four—I'll take my hat off and congratulate him and say, 'You got the best horse.' "

Martin took off his hat and put it back on. "In my estimation, I got the best horse. My horse is in top condition. He loves the track. And I got Pincay. What more do I want? I have the best horse in the country. But the only way we can find out is running over there."

Pancho jabbed his cigar toward the racetrack in the distance. "And I ain't gonna have no excuses."

Chapter 24

It was the evening of Tuesday, May 1, for Turcotte the close of a long and nervous day, and he was hoping to relax. He had just arrived in Kentucky from New York, following a five-hour journey that left him frazzled and edgy in his room at the Executive Inn. He had ridden all morning at Belmont Park and all afternoon at Aqueduct. When the last race was over, he showered hurriedly, climbed into a pair of jeans, a work shirt, and his Meadow Stable jacket and took off with his agent for Kennedy where he had to catch a helicopter shuttle to Newark Airport. Nothing went easily on that trip: Kennedy was under a heavy fog when Turcotte got there, and all chopper flights had been grounded. He rented a limousine to take him across the two rivers to Jersey and brooded all the way about missing his flight and being stranded in New York.

Turcotte was going to Louisville to ride Secretariat in his most important workout so far that year, the colt's final major drill for the Kentucky Derby. Turcotte hadn't liked that first workout at Churchill Downs, and now he was anxious to try him again, hoping he had returned to what he had been. The work would give some indication of the kind of colt he would be riding Saturday.

The limousine deposited him at Newark on time. Then the plane was late. Restless still, he glanced at his watch and paced the terminal. It was raining. By the time he arrived in Louisville and checked into his room, he had a headache and felt uncomfortable. He took a sleeping pill and went downstairs to have a cup of tea, something to settle him. He crossed the lobby where he met Eddie Arcaro.

They sat down at a table by the window overlooking a fountain, a statue, and a waterwheel. Arcaro settled into his chair with a martini, Turcotte with a brandy on the rocks. Arcaro was good company—Turcotte was feeling better already. Arcaro asked about Secretariat's race in the Wood, a race he'd won on Bold Ruler sixteen years ago. Arcaro, like many horsemen, had doubts about Secretariat and the whole three-year-old crop, and he expressed them publicly before the week was out: "There isn't a standout horse in the field. This is not a good three-year-old year. It's hard to explain why it happens this way. No one knows if Secretariat can go a mile and a quarter."

"This horse doesn't have to go a distance, you know," Arcaro continued to Turcotte. "Bold Ruler wasn't a true distance horse. I remember a horse I never thought could go the distance in the Derby: Whirlaway. When Mrs. Markey asked me to ride him, I didn't want to. Ben Jones told me, 'Don't worry about the horse. He'll go the distance. But for God's sake ride him the way I tell you.' " Arcaro told Turcotte the story of Whirlaway and how Ben Jones said no one could beat him sprinting and the idea was to save Whirlaway's speed and let him gallop along easily for the first part of the Derby and then bust him loose in the late stages. Turcotte paid close attention to the master as he sipped his brandy, and he got the strong feeling that Arcaro was trying to tell him something about how to win a Kentucky Derby with a horse who didn't want to go that far.

He had already given much thought to how he was going to ride Secretariat on Saturday. Among Laurin and Penny and others there was some sentiment for sending the horse early—right out of the gate —and lying close to the front from the start. But Turcotte mulled over what Arcaro told him. He believed Secretariat could go the distance, but he wasn't absolutely certain of it—no one was, because he hadn't done it yet.

"I know he can beat any horse in the country going a mile," said Turcotte. "It's that extra quarter. But, I really think he can go on."

"I sure hope you're right," said Arcaro. "I got him in a pool in Florida."

At 5:47 the next morning the rows of sheds were coming alive at the Downs. Television film crews patrolled between the barns and racetrack. Newspaper reporters trundled from shed to shed.

Down the shed from Barn 42, horses were grazing on the strips of grass beside their barns. Handlers held them by leather shanks. It was already Wednesday, only three days from the Kentucky

Derby, and stable hands could feel it coming, the gathering bustle and the stirring of hope.

Lucien Laurin and Penny Tweedy arrived by 7:25 that morning, and Laurin approached the stall holding part of the bridle and the blinkers, putting them under Secretariat's nose and saying, as if peeking into a crib, "If you're a good boy, you'll let me put this on." Turcotte helped him, and the two men huddled talking in the shed.

Whatever Lucien Laurin was—excited or strained or tired—he was not confused about how to train the red horse for the ninety-ninth Kentucky Derby. He had his back against the wall. He appeared as if he had it all to do, and more. He was at his finest when the crunch was on, when he was under the severest pressures, for he seemed to train then with the sharpest insight and perception. He appeared harassed, and often angry and worried. At times he seemed frantic, trying to put down the stories of unsoundness. But he never lost hold of what he was doing.

The rumors of unsoundness exasperated Lucien, following him from New York to Louisville to Lexington, and wherever he went people asked him if it were true that the colt was standing in ice or had a bad knee.

If the condition of Secretariat's knees had been discussed sotto voce at the racetrack, after the Wood it became an open debate. Newspapers and wire services gave space to the circulation of the rumors, adding substance to their otherwise vaporous shapes. Hearsay was juxtaposed with fact, without any attempt at verification from a primary source. The Associated Press, for instance, ran a widely circulated story on April 26 in which the reporter interviewed the noted Las Vegas odds maker, Jimmy "the Greek" Snyder, and quoted Nevada's leading expert on Secretariat's knees as follows:

> I just don't like Secretariat—I don't know why, I just don't like Secretariat. I said before the Wood Memorial that this horse had no right to be a 1–5 odds-on choice. The race bore me out. . . . I've said it before and I'll say it again—I still think they're putting ice packs on Secretariat's knees.

Jimmy the Greek had never been to the barn at Belmont Park, and he was handicapped by a somewhat limited grasp of horseracing, as witnessed by his immortal explanation for Secretariat's defeat in the Wood: "Maybe the pace was so slow Secretariat thought it was just a workout."

In Louisville, the day before the workout, the estimable *Louisville Courier Journal* ran a story on the front page of its sports section in which the Associated Press reporter quoted H. A. (Jimmy) Jones as saying:

> It doesn't measure up as a good field. There are some good horses running, no great ones. No superstars . . . I don't know about Secretariat. He has good breeding and his record was good coming into the Wood Memorial. But he ran as if something was pinching him. I keep hearing reports that there is some heat in his leg somewhere and he is being treated with ice packs, but Lucien denies it. Some people around the stables insist it's true.

Laurin came to Kentucky in an announced search for Secretariat's redemption, and if he worried privately about the colt's ability to go the distance, publicly he remained confident.

On Wednesday morning, preparing for the redemption and convinced he was bringing the colt to the Derby off the right workouts, Laurin gave Turcotte the same instructions he did before the colt worked the sensational three-eighths of a mile that day before the Bay Shore. Wednesday was the end of a four-month program of races and workouts, all aiming ultimately for this Saturday.

"Let him bounce, Ronnie," Lucien told Turcotte under the shed. "Don't punish him, but let him roll."

They had put blinkers on him as a signal to Secretariat that serious work was at hand, and Laurin raised Turcotte aboard. As Turcotte gathered up the reins, Lucien and Penny left hastily for the clubhouse to watch the workout from the homestretch side of the oval, rather than the backstretch clocker's shed. They did not know the clubhouse doors were locked.

The newsmen and stable hands followed Secretariat into a drizzle to the racetrack. Cameras whirred as men walked backward, while Billy Silver pricked his ears and swipes and hot walkers stopped work as the entourage passed. Secretariat ground the bit in his mouth —his eyes flicking, rimmed in white—and turning to the touch, he galloped off on the sloppy track. Turcotte warmed him up well, while Laurin and Penny went from one entrance to the next, trying frantically to hail a guard to let them in. All the gates were locked.

Turcotte galloped Secretariat past the clocker's shed, where a large group of reporters gathered, and then took the colt to the five-eighths pole and aimed him toward the far turn. Coming to the pole, Turcotte took a hold and clucked to Secretariat and then Turcotte's blue and white jacket started billowing out in back and as he passed the pole he chirped again and again and felt the red horse accelerate.

He plunged for the far turn, Turcotte sitting quietly on him, and raced for the bend in an opening quarter of 0:23 ⅘. Now he started picking it up, faster and faster, as they raced for the quarter pole and the turn for home. They went the third eighth in 0:11 ⅕, and the fourth in 0:12 for a half mile in 0:47. He was pounding for the wire, while in the clubhouse Laurin and Penny rose just in time to see him work the final eighth. Turcotte sent him through a final 220 yards in 0:11 ⅗. He finished out the five-eighths in 0:58 ⅗. Turcotte stood straight-legged at the wire, and Secretariat galloped out another eighth in 0:13 ⅖ for a six-furlong clocking of 1:12.

At the clocker's shed a man came walking past on a pony. "Man," he said, "that big son of a gun went around there like a train. What did you get him in up there?" he asked.

"Fifty-eight and two," someone shouted. A fifth of a second fast.

"See," he said to a companion. "I knew that son of a gun was rolling."

Turcotte pulled the red horse up around the turn and came past again, slowly, then to a stop. He was smiling.

Secretariat was back again, and Turcotte knew it.

Laurin and Penny missed the workout, and when they returned to the barn and got the report they were visibly aggravated that they hadn't seen the show.

Like Sham, Secretariat was coming to the Derby off a sharp final drill, the kind on which the red horse thrived. He was eating sixteen quarts of grain a day, seven more than the average horse, and most of it in noncrushed oats, and he needed hard work to burn it off and keep him fit. With age he could endure more and even harder work than ever, far more than most horses. That was not so with Angle Light. He ran better off slower works, not needing such tighteners before a race. Angle Light was training for more than the Kentucky Derby on that Wednesday morning. Whittaker was aiming him for a larger pot.

In the wake of the Wood Memorial, the price of Angle Light soared from an estimated $200,000 to more than $1 million—all because he beat the Horse of the Year, the Derby favorite, the $6.08 million stud horse. For Whittaker this was the time to sell and he began considering offers of as much as $1.5 million for Angle Light. He had the colt shipped to Kentucky, meanwhile, though he was convinced he wouldn't be running him in the Derby. Whittaker believed the bay would be sold by then. One of the offers was for $1.25 million, and Whittaker was seriously entertaining it. Under the proposal Whittaker would sell the colt to a breeding syndicate of seven members, and he would receive the money in three payments, with the last two installments payable at 6 percent interest: $400,000 on May 5, 1973; $425,000 on May 5, 1974; and $425,000 on May 5, 1975.

Penny Tweedy's feelings of enmity toward Whittaker, which the Wood Memorial aroused, had not subsided in the week following the race. They didn't spring from anything substantial. Whittaker had never said or done anything to hurt her. Laurin took charge of Angle Light's training in the winter of 1972 at Hialeah—about the same time he started training Secretariat—at the urging of Ron Turcotte, who was Whittaker's friend and a fellow Canadian. Penny resented Laurin's taking Angle Light, and she came to feel that Whittaker had somehow "wormed his way in" to the Laurin barn. She was offended by Whittaker's deferential manner, for another thing, and regarded it as insincere.

None of this, though, went to the root of why she was coming to feel such hostility toward Whittaker, who was unaware that he was the object of such powerful emotion. She was still wondering where Lucien's loyalties lay and wondering what, if any, feelings of obligation he had to Whittaker. She was still grappling with the anxieties that had surfaced in the wreckage of the Wood, and she felt strongly that she had to remove Whittaker from the scene.

Knowing generally how she felt, Laurin saw the potential for conflict if Whittaker were to arrive at the barn while she was there. If it was any consolation to him, at least Secretariat and Angle Light got along, eyeing one another docilely from their adjoining stalls.

Laurin sought to avoid clash and confrontation. One day following the Wood, when Penny was at Belmont Park to watch Riva Ridge work out, Lauren asked Turcotte to head Whittaker off at the Belmont stable gate and arrange to keep him occupied until Penny left the barn.

Whittaker talked to Laurin alone in the racing secretary's office. Laurin told him he thought he could sell Angle Light. "Would you take a million and a half for him?"

"Sure," said Whittaker.

"I'll know by Tuesday."

With that, Edwin Whittaker flew to Kentucky. He went to work on the $1.25 million syndication deal while Laurin moved to sell the colt for $1.5 million. Events moved quickly in Kentucky as the Derby neared. By Wednesday morning, the day of the workout, Laurin's efforts to sell the colt had failed, but Whittaker was still in touch with the Kentucky syndicate. The deadline for the sale was that night. There had been delay in putting the syndicate together, and some of the prospective members of the syndicate wanted to watch Angle Light work that Wednesday morning. Turcotte was given to understand that he was working Angle Light for the benefit of prospective buyers, and he later recalled telling Whittaker that a fast workout would knock the colt out of the running for the ninety-ninth Kentucky Derby.

"Don't worry about it," Whittaker said, according to Turcotte. "He's not going to be in the Derby."

So Angle Light, with Turcotte hitting him surreptitiously a couple of times around the turn, drilled five-eighths in 0:59 on a track he did not like, an extremely sharp move for him under the circumstances. After getting off Angle Light that morning, Turcotte was more certain than ever that Laurin did not plan to run him in the Derby.

In Louisville, meanwhile, the center was not holding for Edwin Whittaker. He spoke to Laurin by telephone and told him the details of the syndication offer. Laurin told him that he didn't think it was a good deal. "Don't sign anything," Lucien said.

It didn't matter. The syndication failed. The deal fell through later that night. Whittaker then tried to reach Laurin, and finally found him at the Executive Inn. There was no answer from his room, so Whittaker had Laurin paged and arranged to meet him in the dining room.

Soon after, Whittaker and his attorney, who was in Louisville to represent Whittaker on the sale of the horse, came into the dining room. Whittaker spotted Laurin, and across the table from him he saw Penny Tweedy. She was in a sour frame of mind. For the moment, she was angry at Lucien. She had flown to Kentucky the day before, on Tuesday, specifically to attend the social functions—but Lucien hadn't been in the mood. By the time Whittaker arrived, she had had a couple of drinks, and when she saw him approach the table, she thought: "Here he is, worming his way in again."

Whittaker sat down on Laurin's left and on Penny's right, and they began talking. At one point, she would recall, "Whittaker pulled this same wormy act of, 'Oh, I don't know whether I'm going to run in the Derby; my horse isn't worthy of it.' " Penny Tweedy didn't believe Whittaker.

They spoke of the syndication that had fallen through, and Penny Tweedy listened to Whittaker explain the details.

Then Whittaker, with only limited experience as an owner, said deferentially, "Well, I don't know much about horses."

"Mr. Whittaker, you know a lot more about horses than you make out to know," Penny told him. "You're a sneak."

Whittaker's back came up. "Well, thank you very much. I've never been called a sneak before, but there's always a first time. How do you think I'm a sneak?"

"Well, you sneaked in with Angle Light."

"I'll tell you what," Whittaker said. "Why don't you buy Angle Light?"

They did not raise their voices as they spoke. Their tone was calm and conversational, but it was borne on the back of its meaning to other tables nearby, where patrons of the Executive Inn picked up on it. In fact directly behind Penny, unknown to her but listening to the conversation, sat veteran jockey Walter Blum, who was in town to ride Royal and Regal in the Derby.

Penny accused Whittaker of worming his way into the barn, of talking out of both sides of his mouth, of not giving Laurin any direction.

"I'm not having anything to do with this," Lucien said at one point, as Whittaker would recall it. "I'm going to let you two fight it out between you."

"If you have to choose between Mrs. Tweedy and myself," said Whittaker, "you've only one choice, Lucien. Why don't you make it? Just give me up. There's no way I'm going to buy horses for you like the Meadow Stables are buying for you. You've spent your whole life to get where you are now. Why give it up?"

"Nobody's going to tell me who to train for."

Some who heard the conversation thought Penny was worried that Angle Light might cause interference in the race and compel a victorious Secretariat's disqualification. It would have been a legitimate concern. But later Penny said that was not what provoked her that night. "I don't understand yet why I had to get rid of Whittaker," she would recall. "I don't know why. I think I was worried about Lucien's loyalty." She was not worried about Angle Light's interfering with Sham. In fact, at one point, she insisted to Whittaker that he enter the colt in the Derby. "You owe it to me to put Angle Light in the Derby," she said to him. "You owe it to me."

"The only reason you want Angle Light in the Derby, Mrs. Tweedy, is so that when you win the Derby, which you will, you will have Angle Light in there and then you can say that Secretariat beat Angle Light. But that's a foregone conclusion. What Angle Light did the other day in the Wood, you've got to be realistic about it. Angle Light didn't beat Secretariat. Sham beat Secretariat."

Whittaker fell silent now. Laurin listened silently, too, while behind Penny, Walter Blum was listening unabashedly.

"You and your smooth talk," she said to Whittaker. "Why don't you pick up your marbles and go home?"

She was angry now, and at one point she looked around and sensed that someone was behind her, so she turned her neck further and saw the face of Walter Blum about six inches away from hers. He smiled. She knew there was no hiding what she'd done.

"Isn't this interesting?" she asked.

"Yes," said Walter Blum. "It's *very* interesting."

Whittaker had had enough. "I don't mind picking up my marbles," Whittaker told her. "But I'm not going home, Mrs. Tweedy. I think I've had enough of this, Mr. Laurin. Mrs. Tweedy." He started to rise. "I think we've discussed this quite far enough. I think I'll go to bed."

"Why don't you sit down and discuss it?" she said.

"There is no point of it. If I do, I'll probably put myself down to somebody else's level here, and I don't want to go that low tonight. Mrs. Tweedy, if it will make you feel any better to have Angle Light in the race, after you win the Kentucky Derby and you get up there in the winner's circle, just remember that Angle Light was in the race."

Whittaker had already made out a check to cover entry fees for Angle Light. The entries were to be drawn in the morning, and now he set the check in front of Lucien. When Whittaker came to the table that evening, he wasn't sure whether Angle Light would be in the Derby. Laurin had already told him that Angle Light didn't care much for the track at Churchill Downs.

"There's no sense running him if he doesn't like the track," Laurin told him.

But now it was late Wednesday evening in the dining room of the Executive Inn and he had just been tongue-lashed by a woman in a public place. If it wasn't pride, then perhaps it was because he had always wanted to run a racehorse in the Kentucky Derby—it was his great ambition—and now time was running out and the syndication had fallen through and he had to act now. "I suppose all the time I wanted to enter the horse in the Derby," he later said. Whatever it was compelling Edwin Whittaker, he had made up his mind by the time he decided to leave that table to its inhabitants.

"Lucien," said Whittaker, "enter Angle Light in the Kentucky Derby."

"Who should I put on him?" asked Laurin.

"John LeBlanc is here . . . Put him on."

Whittaker said goodnight and turned and left, moving now toward the end of one of the most aggravating experiences of his life.

On Thursday morning, Whittaker answered the telephone in his motel room. It was Lucien.

"I want to have dinner with you and Mrs. Whittaker," Lucien told him. "Mrs. Tweedy wants to apologize. I'm insisting she apologize."

"Lucien, you're a very foolish man," Whittaker told him, as he recalled it later. "You should never tell a woman to apologize to a man. It's against their egos."

But Laurin insisted on it, and that evening he met the Whittakers for dinner in the same dining room where the incident had occurred the night before, though they sat at a different table. Laurin kept fidgeting as he waited for Penny Tweedy, watched for her to come in. She was late. When she finally arrived, she went to Whittaker's side and stood there.

"Mr. Whittaker," she told him, "I want to apologize for last night."

"Mrs. Tweedy, it's not necessary. Mr. Laurin had no business asking you to apologize."

For some, then, Derby Week lurched to a close.

Secretariat walked that Thursday morning, as he usually did the day after a workout, with Davis leading him around the shed.

Davis galloped Secretariat on Friday, and he thought the colt moved well under him. "Don't worry about it, Baby," Davis told Sweat. "Everything's gonna be all right."

On Friday, too, Penny Tweedy drove to Claiborne Farm to have lunch with Bull's widow, Waddell, and Seth and Ellen Hancock. They ate in the big house across and down the road from the main gate of the farm. After lunch, Mrs. Hancock said, "Penny, I'm sure you know I'd be thrilled if you won the Derby, but you must understand that I'll be rooting for Sham. Bull wanted to win the Derby more than any other race, and he could never win it in his lifetime, but if he could do it after his death, well, I still wish he could."

Turcotte relaxed that night, for him a pleasant Derby Eve. At ten o'clock he bought a *Racing Form,* and went upstairs to his room. He spread out the *Form* and its *Derby Supplement* and read it in bed.

There was a story on Lucien headlined, "Laurin Keeps Cool Despite Pressure Level," and in the facing column a story on Turcotte pointing out that only two jockeys—Isaac Murphy and Jimmy Winkfield, two brilliant black riders of years ago—had ever won consecutive runnings of the Kentucky Derby. Turcotte fell asleep with the light on and the paper spread out in front of him. He was having no trouble sleeping.

By Friday evening thousands of people were arriving and reveling in Louisville. They spent the night in swank motels and hotels. They parked their cars in double files on Longfield Avenue, waiting for the main gate to open, while others slept the night in pup tents pitched along the side of the road. They slept in sleeping bags, in cars. The Derby was still the old country fair come to town, a race born in the days when the feed and grain dealer from Paducah could match his bay mare with the banker's roan across the river, and all the live-long day. Now the week of revels had ended. The fair was about to begin. It was passing midnight, Saturday.

At four o'clock Secretariat was awake and peering from his stall in search of breakfast, his two quarts of oats. Derby Day had begun. Turcotte awoke early, too, dressed and turned off the light that had been on all night and left his room. He joined Laurin and Jack Tweedy and Ed Whittaker for breakfast and the drive to the barns. Because he had no mounts before the Derby, Turcotte wanted to take a ride around the racetrack on Billy Silver, to get a feel of the texture of the track.

Sweat and Charlie Davis got Secretariat ready for a walk around the shed. It would be his only exercise until Sweat took him to the paddock for the ninth race. Davis then led him from the stall, at the end of a chain and leather lead shank. As Secretariat started around the shed, he suddenly jumped and danced a few steps, sashaying here and bouncing there.

Nearby, Sweat saw Turcotte saddling Billy Silver, and he told Turcotte that he thought the red horse might be back again, as he had been in the days of the Gotham. In fact, Sweat told him, Derby

Day was the first day since the Wood Memorial that he thought Secretariat was himself again, and he was back just in time.

Outside the shed, Lucien and turfwriter Joe Hirsch stood talking. Laurin was wearing a fedora, tinted glasses, and a topcoat. The temperature had risen to forty-one degrees by six o'clock, and it was growing warmer as the sun mounted a cloudless sky. But it was still cool at eight o'clock, and Lucien stood shivering with his hands in his pockets. Events of the week had hounded and pursued him. He had lost seven pounds in the two weeks before the Derby, and through the final week he appeared increasingly harassed and harried. Yet he never lost his sense of wit and humor.

Churchill Downs opened at eight sharp, and the thousands began moving across the brick-lined walks through the marigold and tulip gardens and through the white mansion of the clubhouse and grandstand. The weather grew balmy, reaching toward a cloudless sixty-nine degrees. All morning, the crowd flowed steadily off Fourth Street into the Downs. The 45,000 seats had already been sold long ago, so most of those arriving early came to settle on blankets in choice locations on the infield. The crowd spread across acres of greenery stretching from the clubhouse to the far turn, swelling in size from 25,000 people at nine o'clock to more than 50,000 people at ten. Endless lines filed through the tunnel connecting the grandstand and the infield. By early afternoon there were more than 75,000 people in the infield. With them, the population of Churchill Downs climbed to a record 137,476. They were an active but not unruly crowd.

The infield was a tropical fish tank of colors and bodies of divergent and often lovely shapes. They wore cut-off blue jeans and pink and yellow halter tops, lime-colored pantsuits and avocado jumpsuits. There were hotpants of pale pink and almond brown and fiery orange, shirts of burnished gold, and hats from which ribbons flowed rich with ivory lace, and bare legs and bare feet everywhere. Among them drifted maxidresses and miniskirts and sunglasses tinted green and blue, round as insect eyes, and taffeta bows and Bermuda shorts.

Frisbees rose and dipped through the late morning, sailing into noon. Radios played rock. Off to the side a group of young men, holding the corners and sides of a blanket, threw a woman ten feet in the air, then fifteen feet, while crowds gathered cheering her higher and higher. A man climbed a flagpole near the center of the infield, and crowds raised their hands and chanted him on and on.

Beyond the gamboling, meanwhile, greeting customers of Churchill Downs on Derby Day, a woman stood outside a gate and handed out religious tracts: "Bet on a winner. Bet on Jesus."

Barn 42 was quiet through the afternoon, quieter than it was the year before, thought Eddie Sweat, who sat on a beach chair outside the barn and waited.

Lucien and Penny stopped by at two-forty. Laurin went inside the shed and peeked in at Secretariat. The red horse spent most of the afternoon hanging morosely about the back of the stall. Sweat said the colt wanted to be left alone, didn't want to be bothered with anything, and that was an encouraging sign. Laurin spoke briefly to Eddie, then left in the car again with Penny. At the racetrack, rumors were circulating that both Angle Light and Secretariat were going to be scratched.

Penny Tweedy and Elizabeth Ham were talking in the box seat section. They were laughing, and Penny seemed more relaxed than she had been all week, as if she'd come to terms with whatever might happen in the ninth. She was greeting friends and smiling handsomely and wearing a white pleated shirtwaist on whose left lapel she wore her mother's gold pin—a horse and jockey in flight. Penny always wore it for luck. She was in fine spirits, but she didn't expect Secretariat to win.

Down the row of seats was Viola Sommer. She hadn't wanted Sham in the Derby, and her attitude was skeptical, a curious contrast to Pancho's gusty rhetoric.

Up the stairs, darting and weaving through the white suits and white bucks, came Lucien Laurin. He was in no mood for conversation now. "He's coming to the race good," he said, heading toward the box. "He's coming to the race as good as the horse last year." He waved a hand. "I won't have no excuses. If he gets beat, I won't have no excuses."

Below, in the jockeys' room, Ron Turcotte lay down on a cot and slept through part of the afternoon. He woke up with a start, his heart pounding, when he heard from another room an announcer calling the Wood Memorial. Churchill Downs was playing it on its closed-circuit television. For a moment Turcotte thought the Derby had been run and that he finished third. Turcotte got up later and sat with a visitor in the jockeys' lounge. He seemed relaxed and said, "He'll beat these horses today if he runs his race. You'll see." Turcotte returned to his locker and got dressed.

It was five o'clock. Sweat had been working around Secretariat, brushing him off and getting him ready, fitting on the bridle and checking the blinkers, when the call echoed through the stable area: "All right, bring your horses to the paddock. Bring your horses to the paddock at once for the Derby."

Moments later Sham and Secretariat and Angle Light started for the track, between the barns and out the gate and toward the paddock, around the clubhouse turn. From the box seats and the dining room and the ground floor, owners and trainers descended on the paddock. They shook hands, called out names, and waited for the horses. Crowds pressed against the outside fence, television cameras beamed down on the tanbark ring, horses came in down the tunnel from the racetrack one by one, in file.

"Hey, Frank," a reporter whispered to him. "Es la hora de la verdad?"

Pancho looked up. He grinned. His voice was huskier now, more gravelly from the extensive use he'd made of it, and he raised his right hand to his face, as if holding a baton to it, and sang in his Cuban bass:

"When you're smiling

"Keep on smiling,

"The whole world smiles with you."

All the horses were in the paddock now. Eddie Sweat was leading Secretariat around the ring and into one of the saddling stalls. Lucien fitted Turcotte's saddle to Secretariat, drew up the cinch, and fastened it. All was done. The jockeys started moving down the stairs, the cameras following them. They joined the trainers. Turcotte's expression was severe. Then a stoical Pincay came into the paddock, wearing the green and yellow silks of Sigmund Sommer. He was restless and uneasy, and the same thought kept turning over and over in his mind; "Get position and don't get in traffic trouble on the turns."

Both men were nervous. Pincay approached Martin, whose instructions were terse and to the point, "You know the horse. Lay close to the pace. Don't be too far off it. Don't worry about Secretariat. Last time we did we got beat."

Turcotte had already thought all those hours about how he was going to ride Secretariat. Many people, horsemen and friends, had given him advice on how to ride this son of Bold Ruler. They advised him to go to the front, they told him to lay second, to lay third. They told him to run with Sham. They told him to come from off the pace. He knew what he would do, had known all along what he would do. Laurin agreed that the wisest plan would be to let Secretariat run his own race through the first part of it. There would be no gunning him through the stretch the first time—no hollering, no chirping, no using the stick to get him rolling early.

Crossing the paddock, Turcotte saw Laurin and he went directly to him. Lucien had set a lighted cigarette on the stall board next to him, and he was leaning against it when Turcotte joined him there with Secretariat. The cigarette was making a hole in Lucien's jacket, and Turcotte saw it, "Lucien! You're burning your jacket."

Lucien wiped at the charred hole. He hardly seemed to notice. "You know the horse, Ronnie. Just try to keep clear. Don't worry about a thing. Ride the race the way it comes up. *Use ton propre judgment.*"

The time had come. A paddock official called the order to mount, and Turcotte held his stick in one hand and moved to Secretariat's left side, raising his left boot behind him at the knee. Laurin reached down, grabbed under the boot and raised Turcotte up. Lucien patted the boot and said, "Good luck now, Ronnie."

They walked in file to the racetrack, Angle Light and Secretariat as the 1 and 1A entries, through the tunnel to the wide open door debouching onto one of the world's most celebrated bridle paths. Bettors called to them along the way. The horses stepped through the tunnel, one by one emerging into the warm sunlight of the late afternoon. They walked across the racetrack, turned right, and headed down the homestretch past the clubhouse. The colt felt composed to Turcotte in the post parade. He danced sideways in time to the music as the brass band started playing and the thousands came to their feet singing Stephen Foster's anthem of nostalgia, "My Old Kentucky Home."

There were yells, howls, and then applause. The rituals had ended. The horses had turned around in front of the clubhouse and started making their way back through the long stretch, moving clockwise toward the starting gate parked at the turn for home. As Turcotte passed the eighth pole, heading toward the upper stretch, he yelled to the pony boy accompanying him, "Just go alongside of me and follow me whatever I do."

Turcotte chirped to Secretariat and sent him into a slow gallop to the upper stretch into the turn. He let Secretariat gallop off around the turn and continue his warm-up to the half-mile pole. Secretariat felt smooth and limber to Turcotte around the turn. At the half-mile pole by the far turn, Ronnie eased the colt to a stop, feeling he had warmed him up enough, and turned around. It was quiet at the far turn. Turcotte glanced to his left, to the infield, and later remembered seeing the bare backs and beards of youth and the thousands of blankets and faces clustering at the rail near the racetrack. These people would see the Derby clearly only as the horses pounded into the far turn, past the half-mile pole, with about 900 yards to go, and they would see the horses make the bend before they lost them in the drive. They and the thousands more had been making Secretariat and Angle Light the 3–2 favorites, with Sham second choice at 5–2, betting a record $3,284,962 on the Derby alone.

They neared the starting gate, a jungle gym of green and white slats and bars and doors pulled by a tractor. Turcotte eased the red horse to the outside of the track and waited for the loading to begin. All the horses were converging directly behind the gate. One by one the assistant starters took the horses to their stalls—Restless Jet, Angle Light, Warbucks, and Sham. Navajo was loaded in six, then Twice a Prince and Our Native. As they loaded, Twice a Prince suddenly went up and almost over, hanging his front legs over the stall. Turcotte saw it happening. There were shouts. An assistant starter moved to Secretariat, reaching out his hand to take the bridle and lead him into the stall. Turcotte pivoted Secretariat to the left and walked away from the starter. He did not want to stand in the gate while they were trying to unravel Twice a Prince from it. Turcotte walked Secretariat about twenty feet back, then stopped him, and watched the starters work to free the horse. The delay lasted several minutes. The red horse relaxed. When Twice a Prince was on his feet again, Turcotte took Secretariat back toward the gate.

He reached to his helmet and pulled a pair of plastic goggles over his eyes.

A starter came to him again, reaching out.

Secretariat stepped into the starting gate. The doors slammed shut behind him. Locked inside, he pushed forward and threw his head in the air. Adroitly, like a mountain goat, an assistant starter slid in over the bars beside him. He reached for the bridle to hold him. Turcotte yelled, "Take it easy with him. He's anxious. Handle him easy now."

The starter's hand gently touched the extension of the bit. Feeling the hand, the colt settled down at once.

The last horse—Gold Bag—moved into the gate on the far outside.

It was 5:37.

Turcotte reached down and grabbed a full handful of Secretariat's mane, holding it to keep his balance at the break, and he bent forward in the fallen stillness.

Chapter 25

Secretariat rose on his hind legs from the gate, his forelegs rising and falling once, grappling like pistons on a piece of heavy machinery, while Turcotte clutched the mane and then released it, bouncing to a crouch. Sham had rapped his mouth sharply on the iron bars of the gate, tearing loose two teeth, and within a dozen strides of the barrier he drifted suddenly to the right, as if careening to the taste of blood, and ricocheted off Navajo. Around him seven tons of horses veered through the straight toward the first turn. Hooves walloped at the ground amid stentorian snorts, clods of dirt flying, and at once the crowd came roaring to its feet.

Turcotte sat quietly at the break. Beneath him he could feel the red horse struggling to set his mass in motion, and he gave him all the time he needed for it, not rushing him a step. Glancing right he saw Shecky Greene take off with Larry Adams for the lead. To the left Pete Anderson settled down on Forego. Secretariat worked to stay with them at the start, digging in as always, but they all outran him from the slip. In a moment he was running last. On the inside, then, a whole wall of horses pulled away, leaving him more than a length behind but giving Turcotte room to maneuver more freely for position. Looking for a spot to settle him in the run for the first turn, Turcotte eased back on the left line, swinging the colt toward the rail, and drifted left to join Warbucks there. In front of them the field of horses raced through the tunnel for the first time, scrambling and sorting themselves out for position. Around him Turcotte could hear the sounds begin to vibrate in the light of the late afternoon, growing rich in intensity, while in the upper stretch he began to sense that all was well with Secretariat again. He was striding fluidly, not climbing but leveling out as he gained speed, and something else, too, that gave him a sudden rush of relief.

"He was running against the bit. I took a snug hold of him and he took a hold of me, but he was relaxed and not fighting me. I let him go on his own and I was very happy with the way he felt. He was comfortable and so relaxed, so I was very confident in the straight. I knew he was the old Secretariat."

The race evolved quickly, without hesitation, through the first eighth past the stands. Shecky Greene raced to the lead, sprinting clear of horses on his left and right. Adams knew that speed was Shecky's trump, so he was leading with it. He angled Shecky to the rail, crossing the path of ten horses. Sitting folded on the colt, Adams went to work trying to nurse his speed, to save what he could for the last half mile. Behind him Walter Blum sent Royal and Regal dashing from the gate. He broke fast, and at once started tracking Shecky in the run to the turn. Blum was sitting tucked, too, leaning forward this time, and so was Earlie Fires on the impetuous Gold Bag, who cut across the track from Post 13 to range alongside Royal and Regal. LeBlanc sat tight on Angle Light, racing fourth on the rail just inside Blum, while Pincay tracked them all on Sham. They were bunched. Pincay was running in search of position. He had sent Sham fast from the gate, and now he was steadying him in traffic.

The cavalry charge strung out as they neared the wire. Shecky opened a length and a half on Gold Bag, who was running head and head with Royal and Regal. The traffic suddenly thinned, and now Pincay sent Sham past Angle Light, from fifth to fourth as they raced into the bend. Sham was well placed now, within range of Shecky Greene and lying just off the rail out of trouble. Secretariat was still last. He was more than ten lengths behind Shecky Greene and running head and head with Warbucks. Turcotte thought he was still running effortlessly, his strides measured, his teeth clamped on the bit, running relaxed and in no particular hurry at the moment.

The crowd was cheering Shecky into the turn, as if he were flying the flag of the Seventh Cavalry. He raced through the opening quarter in 0:23 ⅖, keeping them honest behind him, while Sham trailed him by three in 0:24. Farther back, Secretariat was lopping along in 0:25 ⅕ for the first 440 yards, averaging thirty-six miles an hour, not much faster than he ran the first quarter in the Wood. Coming to the wire, he drifted into Warbucks, seemed to graze him, and Turcotte heard the voice of Bill Hartack screaming at him: "Hey! Hey! I'm here!"

Turcotte eased back on the right line. Shecky swept into the clubhouse turn. Up in the box seats, Lucien and Penny were staring at the spectacle as it unfolded below them, at what appeared to be a second act in the horror show of the Wood. His hands set on the railing in front of him, Lucien looked like a man who'd just been sentenced to watch the rest of it. Penny stood horrified, a hand to her face.

"My God! Not another one of these," Lucien exclaimed. "I'm getting out of here."

"You'll stay here and face this with me!" Penny said.

Together they faced the clubhouse turn, where the colt was just beginning his move, if that was the word for it, for it had no definable limits, no distinctive beginning, and no distinctive end. It occurred gradually. Secretariat would race no single quarter mile shading 0:22, as he'd done in the Gotham, deliver up no spectacular cruncher that would power him to the lead. This was finer and rarer than that, a move artistic in scope and conception, relentless in the manner of its execution. And into the turn it began, unspectacularly, with Turcotte sitting chilly. This was what he had been waiting for and now he let it unfold without interference, providing only guidance to the colt. Turcotte had felt Secretariat picking up speed passing the wire. There he had edged past Warbucks into twelfth place. Into the turn he let the colt move to Twice a Prince, who was running wide, slipping inside of him into eleventh place.

He continued to accelerate around the bend, moving faster and faster as Shecky swept them toward the backstretch. As he went by Twice a Prince, Turcotte saw a flight of three horses directly in front of him—Forego on the rail, Navajo on the extreme outside, My Gallant between them. Turcotte glanced to the rail. It was clogged and full of potential traps, a dangerous place to move past ten horses. He would avoid the rail, he thought, and sacrifice the ground for open space. He had to move somewhere, had to keep the momentum of the run. The flight of three horses was moving too slow, Turcotte thought, too slow for the colt who had been building a tempo and was now moving to their heels. Still snugging him, Turcotte tugged gently on the right line, moving his hands only slightly, and eased Secretariat outside Navajo. Now he was four horses wide on the turn, losing ground but free of trouble. Now he sat still as stone again.

That was all he did, nothing more. He didn't make a sound, didn't cock his whip. On they went.

Secretariat never dropped a beat. Swinging out, he switched leads like a machine, from right to left, and then took off again. He might be awkward leaving the gate, but in full flight Secretariat could move like a fine male dancer, and in the Kentucky Derby he was moving with more grace than Turcotte had ever felt with him before. Gone was the heavy-headedness, the battering at the ground. "It was the first time he ever put everything together—the clumsiness had gone out of him. The Derby was the first time. He seemed to gain the strength to carry himself, and it was like he was flying through the air." He moved to Navajo with the characteristic way he had, snapping out his forelegs at the knee and folding the ground under him, his hind legs propelling him forward, his forelegs reaching and snapping at the ground.

He went past him in bounds. Midway of the turn he charged past the flight of three and headed for the backstretch picking up speed, moving from eleventh to eighth. And Turcotte kept riding laissez faire, letting him move on his own and feeling as he continued to accelerate. "I could feel him picking up momentum, going a little faster around the turn."

Ahead now were Restless Jet on the rail and Our Native outside him, forming a second flight of two, and Secretariat had them measured as he swept past Navajo. He went after them in the accelerated drumroll of his stride, staying on the outside and rushing to the flanks of Our Native. He cut his margin to a half length as they raced to the three-quarter pole into the backstretch. Turcotte was struck by the ease with which Secretariat was moving to his horses. "He was going so effortlessly—just picking up horse after horse on the turn." As Secretariat went to Our Native, Shecky Greene dashed past the three-quarter pole with a half-mile clocking of 0:47 ^{2}/s. Breezing by the pole, he was in front by three. Adams sat motionless on him. Behind him Sham stayed close, ranging into third and running head and head for second now with Gold Bag.

Secretariat continued to advance. Into the backstretch he drove past Our Native and Restless Jet. He moved from eighth to sixth, and raced the half in 0:49 ^{1}/s. He was still nine lengths behind Shecky Greene, but he cut into the margin as he measured Angle Light and moved to him down the backside. He gained inexorably on him. He ranged to his side nearing the five-eighths pole midway of the backstretch. As he came to swallow Angle Light, Pincay eased Sham past

Gold Bag into second behind Shecky Greene.

The Derby began to unfold rapidly at the turn.

Sham reached out for Shecky Greene, shaving his lead from three to two lengths, while Secretariat advanced past Angle Light in bounds at the five-eighths pole. The winner of the Wood Memorial did not resist. Now Turcotte saw Gold Bag and Royal and Regal ahead of him, another flight of two, and beyond them Shecky Greene and Sham. That was all that was left. Secretariat now lay fifth. So far his move had carried him from last to fifth, and it left him only six lengths behind Shecky as they went to the half-mile pole at the far turn. Shecky had a length and a half lead on Sham, racing the six furlongs in 1:11 ⅘, almost six twelves in a row. He had not let up a moment since the break. Adams kept sitting tight and nursing him along, trying to spread thin his speed. Secretariat raced the first three-quarters in 1:13, which put him four lengths behind Sham. He had dead aim now, Turcotte felt, and he was still running powerfully beneath him, breathing well at the turn, inhaling and exhaling rhythmically.

Turcotte's only hope now was that the colt would have something left for the final quarter mile down the lane. If he keeps running like this, Turcotte thought, I won't have to ask him until the quarter pole.

In front of him, now, Sham began to move to Shecky Greene. The crowd quickened. Pincay decided to wait no longer. He had been lying within quick reach of Shecky since the first turn. Down the backside he had seen Shecky spooking from shadows on the rail, and at the turn he feared the colt might shy from the rail in front of him and force him to check Sham. He did not want to risk losing momentum now. Pincay felt confident of victory. The race had broken right. Sham was running well for him. He had saved ground on the turn; he had moved to Gold Bag and Royal and Regal as he pleased. Sham had done everything Pincay had asked of him. Pincay was on a Cadillac. All that remained in front of him was a sprinter who was dashing through the seventh furlong and already was going out of his depth. Pincay knew that. And now he lay a length and a half away. So Pincay let out a notch, and Sham picked up the beat at once. He cut into Shecky's lead as they made the turn. In an instant he was at his throat, then head and head with him.

Turcotte saw the move. But still he waited with Secretariat. It was not time, he thought. He could loosen his hold and chirp to the colt and tap him on the shoulder with the stick and move right now to Gold Bag and Royal and Regal. But it was too soon, he thought, too soon to ask him to do more than he had been doing so generously on his own. The timing had to be right. On his left Turcotte heard the crowd sounds building in the distance, making a sound like the sea, and he could hear the drumbeat of the stride and below him see the snap of the forelegs in front. Turcotte pumped his arms in rhythm to the thrust of the colt's stride. They raced in unison around the bend. Secretariat had been running on his right lead down the backside, and now he switched again, machinelike, to his left lead at the turn. Turcotte kept him on the outside, ready to make his move and sacrifice more ground for open space. He had already given several lengths away. Sham and Shecky pulled to the three-eighths pole, their noses bobbing together, Adams conceding nothing to Pincay. Shecky raced with Sham for more than 100 yards. They battled as a pair. Two lengths behind them Royal and Regal and Gold Bag raced as a team, and two lengths behind them Secretariat was alone in fifth but coming to them now, gathering more speed around the turn, building more momentum, his mane blown back and his forelegs snapping out, and then it all seemed to happen at once, in the rush to the three-eighths pole midway of the turn.

Sham inched away from Shecky Greene, shaking him off and taking the lead for the first time.

Royal and Regal coasted along beside Gold Bag in fourth, and Walter Blum began thinking what a fine spot he was in, racing just off the pace and not yet having asked his horse for speed, and so it began to occur to Blum that he actually had a shot to win his first Kentucky Derby.

As Secretariat came in a rush to Gold Bag, who had just chucked the bit and started drifting back, the red horse drove to the side of Royal and Regal, blowing past him as Blum glanced to the right and saw him go by.

Secretariat now lay third, joining battle. He was still running on his own, faster now than he had run since he left the starting gate, the move having swept him through ever faster quarters. Now they came to the five-sixteenths pole. Adams saw the red horse coming on the outside ("He looked like the Red Ball Express") and Pincay was now a length in front. He did not see Secretariat coming.

Pincay thought he had won his first Kentucky Derby. Before him stretched the emptiness of the racetrack. He was in front and hand-riding, his whip still uncocked and at his side. As they all came to the five-sixteenths pole, Turcotte looked ahead and saw Sham and thought he was running very easily and wondered for a moment if he could catch him. Already the move had lasted three-quarters of a mile, and in it Secretariat had run every quarter mile faster than the preceding quarter—the first in 0:25 ⅕, the second around the clubhouse turn in 0:24, the third down the backside in 0:23 ⅘, and now he was rushing through the fourth quarter at the rate of 0:23 ⅖. Through it all, Turcotte had remained a figure of patience in a whirl of motion, his actions deliberate, his timing precise, his earliest instincts sound. He had ridden with an insight into the momentum of the race and the way the colt had been responding to it, sensitive to the scope of the move and to the possibilities it implied if it were left alone to run its course. And that was what he had done —he was confident it would leave him close to the lead at the turn for home—and now they were racing past the five-sixteenths pole and he measured Shecky Greene, saw Sham, and decided he had waited long enough. He was hand-riding, pumping on the colt, when he first chirped to him. Nothing happened, so he chirped again. Nothing happened again. Turcotte cocked his stick, turning it up, like the stave of a picador arming himself, and flashed it in front of Secretariat's right eye, and that was when he felt the surge of power, suddenly, as if there'd been a change of gears.

"He really took off with me," Turcotte said.

Secretariat moved to Shecky Greene in a rush.

They all swept for home, Sham scooting along the rail, saving ground and banking toward the straight more than a length in front, according to the films, cutting the corner and pricking his ears. Turcotte came to the corner on the outside, already wide with room to spare between him and Sham, but Turcotte wanted to race down the middle of the racetrack. He wanted more room for error, more space to straighten out the red horse if he bore in, as he had done in the Wood Memorial behind right-handed whipping. He did not want to be lapped on Sham in the stretch. So he swung the red horse wider at the corner, and for a moment the colt seemed to lose momentum. Turcotte raised his stick and lashed him once right-handed.

Secretariat moved to Sham at the top of the lane.

This was what the thousands had been waiting for. They were all on their feet—deafening and growing louder as Secretariat and Sham raced through the top of the straight. Turcotte pumped and pumped again. He was riding hard. He threw all his weight and strength into building the colt's momentum, driving his arms and torso forward at the forward thrust of Secretariat's reaching stride. Sham was in

266

front by a length beyond the quarter pole. Pincay had still to draw his stick. He had been hand-riding Sham, and he was confident passing the quarter pole and into the upper stretch, which is where he thought he felt something on his right. He did not hear or see it; rather he felt it there, and so he looked under his right arm and all he recalls seeing were the blue and white checked blinkers and the massed brown of Secretariat's neck. He was about a half length away.

Pincay drew his stick.

Secretariat then changed leads for the fourth time in the race, from left back to right at the top of the lane, and now he moved to Sham picking up momentum again. He cut the margin to a half length and then a neck as they drove to the three-sixteenths pole. Turcotte and Pincay rode furiously, alternately pumping and going to the whip. They switched their sticks from the right to the left hand. They muscled Sham and Secretariat down the stretch, two of America's strongest riders leaning and lifting together, while the dome of the grandstand rocked with noise at the sight of it. Slowly, digging in relentlessly, Secretariat gained ground on Sham through the upper stretch, and by the three-sixteenths pole he had come to Sham to swallow him and then they were nose and nose. Together they drew away from the field. Churchill Downs vibrated to the spectacle of it.

Down near the finish Eddie Sweat grabbed his khaki hat and waved it as he saw the two colts battling toward him.

"Come on with him, Ronnie! You got 'em! Come on with him, Ronnie! It's all over now!"

And it almost was. The two raced as a team for 100 yards, between the three-sixteenths pole and the eighth pole. There Secretariat had Sham in trouble and Pincay knew it. He continued using the stick as Turcotte reached and flashed his whip in front of Secretariat's left eye, warning him not to lug into Sham. Then Turcotte went to hand-riding him again, scrubbing on him. Past the eighth pole Secretariat was still reaching out. Even now, despite the fatigue, his form never deteriorated. Slowly at first, then methodically, he pulled away. He opened a length and then two lengths as they drove to the wire. The red horse was drawing off in the final yards, in command now, when they raced past the finish line.

Secretariat won by two and a half lengths, and as he crossed the wire there was a welling of strong cries, rebel cries from the southern crowd, while all over hands began gesturing to the infield board.

The board was flashing 1:59 ⅖, a new Kentucky Derby record by three-fifths of a second. It had been a magnificent performance.

The whole place seemed to erupt at once. In the box seats Penny and Lucien and Jack and Elizabeth grabbed hands and kissed jubilantly, while in the press box two wage slaves ran into one another, colliding and clasping arms, and spun dancing past the mimeograph machine. The Downs entered into a state of ecstatic turmoil, with many horsemen and horseplayers stirred by what they'd seen.

The crowd on the lower level cheered in volleys as Turcotte pulled Secretariat to a stop and started riding him back past the clubhouse. Turcotte was standing high in the saddle, and the clapping followed him as he made his galloping way around the clubhouse turn to the front of the grandstands. For the second year in a row, too, Penny and Lucien descended together toward the winner's circle, traversing the racetrack and waving to acknowledge the ovation. Eddie Sweat, with his beige hat back on his head, met Secretariat as he had met Riva Ridge the year before, on the racetrack near the gap that led to the winner's circle.

All Sweat would recall was looking up and seeing Turcotte gesturing above him. By nature Turcotte was not a person given to theatrics, but he reached for his riding helmet and doffed it in his right hand, like a matador, and the crowd rose howling for more. The flourish was eloquent, saying that Secretariat had answered all the questions—he had redeemed himself, as Lucien would say—and that he was all horsemen had been saying he was since Saratoga. Reporters and photographers and television men jostled around him.

"One more time!" the photographers yelled to Turcotte. So he doffed his helmet again. And again.

Around him jockeys steered their horses to the unsaddling area in front of the grandstand. Pincay rode Sham to the mouth of the paddock tunnel and Martin met him there, grabbing the reins. Martin's face was white and severe, pulled as tight as a mask. Pancho had been right. He had been right all along. Sham was ready to run a tremendous race, the race of his life. Sham, too, had broken the Kentucky Derby record, finishing eight lengths in front of Our Native in 1:59 $4/5$. He would have won most any other Kentucky Derby. His fate was to be born in the wrong year, the year of Secretariat. Martin spoke briefly to Pincay, who went to the jockeys' room.

"He ran perfectly," said Pincay. "He just got tired, I guess. He wasn't really that tired, he was trying, but you know, the other horse. Maybe next time. When the other horse came up on my horse, my horse gave him a good fight. I switched my stick to the left and I could see he really wanted to come on. But he slowed a little. He showed a little sign of tiredness at the sixteenth pole."

In the clubhouse Sigmund Sommer appeared dazed. "Secretariat beat us fair and square," he said.

Down on the racetrack, Secretariat was breathing heavily, and a detailed map of veins and capillaries crisscrossed the rolling landscape of his neck and shoulders. His fingers working excitedly, Sweat unfastened the blinkers and clipped a chain and leather lead shank to the bridle. He took the colt to the gap in the fence leading to the winner's circle. Prematurely, someone came forward and draped the blanket of roses on Secretariat's withers, while behind Turcotte saw someone reach out and touch the colt in the flanks. Secretariat jumped at either the touch of the hand or the blanket, driving Sweat into a hedge. In the excitement and confusion of the moment, Sweat felt he was being strangled in the retaining rope being manned by the troops of the National Guard. Extricating himself, though suffering painful rope burns on the back of his neck, Sweat settled Secretariat down quickly.

The Meadow Stable party was collecting in the winner's circle. Mrs. Carmichael was there, among others, and above them all towered the lanky Hollis Chenery, his face wreathed in a smile reminiscent of his father's. Turcotte and Sweat took Secretariat into the circle for pictures, and following the ceremonies Turcotte slid off the colt and moved to Penny Tweedy. He leaned forward and kissed her on the right cheek, and she wrapped a long, braceleted arm around his shoulders, drawing him forward. Lucien grabbed Turcotte's right hand with his right hand and patted it happily with the other. For a moment there it looked like the reunion of a family that hadn't been together for a long time, and in a way it was.

As Sweat led Secretariat away, returning up the racetrack to the barn for the routine urine and saliva tests, the crowds lining the route started up again as they went by. Sweat returned the salute. Holding the lead shank and checkered blinkers in his right hand, he thrust his left fist high in the air. Even in Kentucky they cheered. Behind him, the victory celebration, as portable as the glasses of champagne in their hands, began ranging all over Churchill Downs; in the hours to come it would move from television cameras at the winner's circle to the directors' room and to the press box and thence out to Barn 42. Lucien and Penny came to the box with drinks in their hands, and they appeared gratified yet curiously subdued, as if living a dream that was anticlimax to the nightmare.

"Well, that's one Bold Ruler that can go a distance," Penny announced to laughter. "Oh, I feel marvelous, and I have a lot of happy co-owners. They were all saying, 'Go-go-go-go.' Lucien's done a fantastic job getting this horse ready—to withstand the pressure of everything that's been said since the Wood and just to keep his cool and do his job and get his horse ready and just stick to that one objective. Lucien's a perfectionist, a man who cares intensely about his work. Yet he's a very tough fellow inside. He has tremendous strength." Penny spoke well in public. She understood what newspapermen needed—clarity and color dressed up in complete sentences —she knew how to say clearly what was on her mind.

"Ronnie rode him beautifully," she said. "My! He did. Of course Ron took some heat after the Wood, but he didn't lose the faith. I thought he rode a magnificent race. He just kept his horse out of trouble, saved ground on the first turn, and only got into him when they hooked Sham."

No, said Lucien, standing with her and Jack Tweedy before the gathering of reporters, the outcome was no surprise to him. "I thought he was going to run good because he trained good for the race. Naturally you do worry because of the last race. I had more pressure on me than I ever had in my life. Everybody was scaring me to death with that Bold Ruler stuff." He told reporters he thought the colt had a "good chance" to win the Triple Crown the second time around, and said he thought he would bring a sharper Secretariat to the Preakness Stakes. "I hope to go there and win it this time. I think he'll be even finer for the Preakness."

Actually, the race seemed to impress Turcotte more than it did the others in the Meadow Stable. Though he was not saying it publicly, Turcotte believed following the Kentucky Derby that Secretariat was the greatest horse he had ever ridden or seen. Asked by a reporter to compare Secretariat and Riva Ridge, he declined to do so as a matter of personal policy. Most of the good horses Turcotte had ridden—Arts and Letters, Tom Rolfe, Damascus, and Northern Dancer—were standing at the stud, where one day Secretariat would be competing with them for the breeding dollar and the best broodmares in America. A jockey could only stir ill will, and profitlessly so, by proclaiming publicly that one man's horse was superior to another's. So he held his opinions on such matters to himself.

"He broke good and dropped back on his own," Turcotte said at the press conference. "At the first turn I didn't want to steady him behind those horses so I eased him to the outside. He picked up those horses on his own. He felt from the start as though he was running well enough to win. He did all the running on his own until we challenged Sham. Then I asked him. When I saw Sham at the turn for home, I was concerned because he was running easy and I didn't know if we could catch him. When I asked him to run there, he really got down to business. They were rolling but I was flying."

Turcotte's public thoughts and comments shielded his feelings of wonder at what he had seen and experienced in the Derby. Seeing the teletimer and the fractions and thinking about the way that Secretariat had won it, he was awed by the performance. He could not recall having known anything quite like it. The colt had always been prodigal of his gifts, showing great speed, intelligence, and a high sense of fearlessness and competitive drive. So Turcotte had decided long ago that Secretariat was a very good horse, but on this May afternoon he glimpsed an even more extraordinary dimension, something that set Secretariat distinctly apart from all the other horses he had ever known. There was great strength and stamina underlying the speed, and a rare depth of it, and beyond that there was method in the way he used it all and put it all together. He could race to the front in a burst of speed. He could come off the pace in a sprint around the turn. And in the Derby, he demonstrated how to cut up a field of horses with precision, one at a time, and grind them down slowly. All around the clubhouse turn and down the backside, as Secretariat gained speed and picked up horse after horse, Turcotte kept wondering how long this could last, thinking the colt might run himself empty by the turn for home. Yet, as he measured and moved past the horses, he felt Secretariat doing it so easily. So he let him do it some more. What made the deepest impression on Turcotte was that there was never a loss of form at any time, coordination remained perfect, the action of the legs synchronized and never rubbery, even under the severest stress of the final drive.

Analysis of the fractional times and Secretariat's position throughout the race merely reinforced Turcotte's original conception of the way the colt had run, though more dramatically than he had imagined. Not only had he shaved three-fifths off Northern Dancer's two-minute mark, but he came to Sham and drew away from him through a final quarter mile timed in 0:23. Thus Secretariat raced every quarter mile in the Kentucky Derby faster than the preceding quarter. His final splits were 0:25 ⅕, 0:24, 0:23 ⅘, 0:23 ⅖, and 0:23. No one could remember when a horse had ever done that over a distance of a mile and a quarter. Secretariat literally went faster and faster from start to finish, traveling thirty-six miles an hour down the stretch the first time, more than thirty-nine miles an hour the second. All the important fractional records became his, too, after that slow first quarter. He stood all the old notions of pace on their ears. After passing the finish line the first time, he raced the last mile of the Derby in 1:34 1/5, two seconds faster than the first mile of the Derby, and the last three-quarters of a mile in 1:10 1/5, almost two seconds faster than Shecky Greene raced the first three-quarters. The final half mile in 0:46 2/5 was a full second faster than Shecky ran the opening half, and the final quarter was two-fifths faster than Shecky's first quarter. For thirty-two years, ever since Arcaro followed Ben Jones's orders, Whirlaway had the record for the fastest closing quarter in Derby history, 0:23 3/5. Only two Derby winners had ever run the final quarter mile faster than 0:24—Whirlaway and Proud Clarion, who ran 0:23 4/5 in 1967, a record that stands as testimony to the fact that racehorses usually slow down through the final 440 yards of a mile-and-a-quarter event, not sprinting faster and faster through it.

Secretariat ran the last half in 0:46 2/5. Perhaps that was the most extraordinary of all the records set that afternoon. That time would put him near the lead in the *first* half of most sprinting races.

Early Sunday morning Ed Sweat was sweeping rose petals from the front of Secretariat's stall. Empty bottle of champagne and the broken stems of glasses were lying on the grass outside the shed. Secretariat was wide awake and standing in the doorway of Stall 21, and Sweat set down the rake and picked up a fork to clean the stall. He was moving jauntily, playfully, bantering with Secretariat, who was blockading the doorway and refusing to budge.

Through the morning horsemen came to the barns, to Barn 42 especially, to check on their Derby horses. They had already studied the charts and a number of them felt, as Henry Forrest felt, that they had seen something rare in this Kentucky Derby. As Secretariat's performance in the Wood Memorial threw the Derby wide open to them, his performance in the Derby closed the Preakness Stakes at Pimlico. Secretariat was leaving for Baltimore the next morning.

However the race had not convinced Martin that Secretariat was superior to Sham. Sham would be leaving Louisville by plane the following morning, flying to Baltimore for the Preakness, the second leg of the Triple Crown. So the rivalry would be renewed there.

Lucien, Turcotte, and Kenny Noe came to the barn together that morning, and Turcotte and Noe stopped in the stable kitchen for a sweet roll and a cup of coffee. Turcotte had won 10 percent of

$155,050 in prize money for his ride on Secretariat, and he was in jaunty spirits as he spoke about the race and the horse between bites.

"All I did was fasten the seat belt," he insisted.

The Wood had created problems that only the Derby could resolve, and there were resolutions in its aftermath. One of the problems would not follow Lucien to the Preakness Stakes: Angle Light would not run at Pimlico. The Derby and the campaign before it had taken much out of him, and he would be shipped back to Belmont Park. There was never open trouble again between Penny and Whittaker. What the coming of the Derby had created, the running of it resolved. But Whittaker would not forget what had happened to him in Kentucky, and it would leave some bitterness in its wake. For all the turbulence of Derby Week, it all ended very quietly. There was a party in Barn 42 after the race, and Whittaker went to it. He met Penny under the shed. Whittaker was disappointed not because Angle Light had not won the Derby, a possibility he had regarded as extremely remote, but because the bay hadn't made a race of it. After Secretariat swept past him down the backside, Angle Light faded to tenth.

"You never had any worries to start with," Whittaker told Penny at the barn. "You don't have any worries now. You're goin' to win the Triple Crown. There's not another horse like him. And good luck to you." Then Penny picked a rose from the victory blanket and pinned it to his lapel.

Chapter 26

Lounging in his room at the Warren House in Baltimore and speaking long distance to his wife Juliette, Lucien Laurin was the picture of a man vindicated by a horse redeemed. He had just kicked off his brown moccasins and folded into a chair by the desk with the telephone next to him. His bed was rumpled, a sheaf of newspaper clippings scattered across it, but his manner was composed. Talking to his wife, he wandered back and forth between French and English. There were only four days left to the Preakness Stakes, and in the accelerated pace of his existence, working to bring a $6 million horse through the most difficult and challenging series of races in America, he was enduring almost as well as Secretariat, even enjoying himself at times. His wife was scheduled to join her husband in Baltimore soon.

He certainly had been having a better time of it in Baltimore than he'd had in Kentucky. Once again there was the interminable waiting, but this time with a difference: it was without the taste of chalk that lined the mouth of Derby Week, without the feeling that there was no more time, no more room to maneuver, no more chances. In a way, the Derby had altered the tone and direction of Lucien's life. He would not retire now, for one thing. And by Tuesday of the week before the Preakness, he seemed almost a different man from what he'd been the two weeks before, during Derby Week, and on the day of the Derby itself. His color had improved, as if he were resting more fully, and he appeared less harried. He was eating better and relaxing more, a man clearly more at ease, at times happy to the point of being content. If anything was missing, it was enthusiasm for

Secretariat's performance in the Kentucky Derby—as if Lucien were still reserving judgment.

He was training a racehorse whom Charles Hatton was proclaiming the greatest Kentucky Derby winner of his time—greater even than Old Rosebud of 1916, who was Ben Jones's standard, too. Other horsemen were enthusiastic, also, such as the conservative and cautious trainer Sherrill Ward, who said, "Secretariat has the potential to be as good as Count Fleet and Citation." Others were saying that, too, but Laurin was making no point of it, and that was in strong contrast to the year before when Riva Ridge won the Derby and Lucien promptly compared him to Citation and Count Fleet, causing snickers.

Laurin was at least certain that he had the best three-year-old in America, so he could relax, train his colt at Pimlico and spend a casual few hours eating crab cakes, reading in the motel room, and going to the barn to admire his red horse. Lucien was superstitious, and the Preakness plainly spooked him. He had tried but failed three times to win it, with Amberoid and Jay Ray and Riva Ridge, and the race made him leery. Turcotte and Penny had teased him because he was the only one of the three who hadn't won the Preakness. Hill Prince won it in 1950 for Chenery, Tom Rolfe in 1965 under Turcotte. Lucien wondered whether the race was his jinx. He wanted very much to win the ninety-eighth running. On his way to the barn that afternoon, sitting shotgun in a Plymouth Fury, he read a press release from Pimlico dated May 15. It said, in part:

> The probable field for the ninety-eighth running of the $150,000-Added Preakness Stakes at Pimlico Race Course Saturday swelled to seven today with the addition of Our Native, third in the Kentucky Derby, and two lightly regarded rivals for the awesome twosome of Secretariat and Sham.

One of the two was a horse named The Lark Twist. The final paragraph read:

> The Lark Twist has won only one of his 14 starts this year and finished sixth, beaten some five lengths, in a 1 1/16-mile allowance race Monday at Garden State.

Lucien grew angry as he thought about what it could mean, thinking the worst. "Jesus Christ almighty, that horse could bump into horses leaving the gate. You don't know what the hell a horse like that is going to do. It's dangerous."

By the time the Fury was slipping past the guards at the gate and winding through the quiet of the stable area, Lucien had calmed down, and never brought the subject up again that afternoon. Climbing from the car, he walked through the russet-colored stakes barn, Barn EE, turning the corner of the shed and passing the guard and walking directly to Stall 41. Billy Silver was in Stall 40. Guard Bill Vernon nodded hello. Lucien spoke to Sweat, who was washing bandages in soap and water. On the stall a halter was hanging. A brush and currycomb lay on the fence. A blue and white checked shield, looking like a Meadow Stable coat of arms, decorated the front of the stall. Billy Silver was standing at the doorway, his perpetual duty station, and waiting for Secretariat to join him. The red horse was lying down. Security had grown tight since Louisville.

Lucien grinned, standing in front of the stall door. Secretariat had just awakened from his noontime nap and came to his feet with a deft, assertive shift of his considerable shoulders. He came to the door and looked at Lucien. Outside the barn, twenty feet from the breezeway of the shed, was a thirty-foot-wide strip of grass that ran the length of Barn EE. In the back, the strip was enclosed by a steel fence acrawl with vines and in front by a dark brown wooden fence, as on a corral, to which had been nailed, at intervals between fence posts, signs bearing the names of all eight Triple Crown winners, from Sir Barton to Citation. Lucien had his hands in his pockets. He was dressed casually—wearing his yellow hat, moccasins, and brown tweed pants—and somehow suggested a suburban father outfitted to mow a lawn or replace the storms with screens.

"Do you think we should graze him out there a little, Edward?" he asked. "The poor son of a gun is in his stall all day. Must be dull."

Sweat took the leather halter off the stall hook and slipped it over Secretariat's nose, fastening it with the buckle at the left side.

"Are you going to put a chain over his nose, Edward?" asked Lucien.

"Nahhhh, he'll be all right."

"If you can handle him in the Derby with those roses, Edward, you can handle nim here." Lucien had seen the red horse drive Sweat into the ropes when the blanket was put over his withers. "People were so crazy that day in the winner's circle," said Lucien. "They were all around him. I thought he was going to kick somebody's brains out."

276

Sweat led Secretariat out the door and through a gap in the wooden fence to the deep carpet of grass. Lucien walked to the gap, too, and leaned back on the fence and beamed with pride at his Preakness horse. "Ten minutes of this is like a dozen vitamins, Edward, a dozen vitamins," Lucien said with relish. Secretariat reached down and started tearing up the greenery.

Then Billy Silver hollered from the doorway of his stall. He was standing with his neck thrust over the webbing and his ears pricked forward. "Listen to him!" said Lucien. "He likes this horse. He wants to be out there with him, Edward. Should I get him?"

Lucien trusted and respected Sweat and was quick to defer to him on some matters. Sweat appreciated the trust. Lucien went to fetch Billy Silver.

"I never saw a pony so crazy about a horse," Lucien said, bringing Billy Silver to the side of Secretariat on the grass.

"Yeh," said Sweat. "But he don't care nothin' about the pony."

Thus together, side by side now, the two horses grazed, raising the aroma of freshly cut grass. The grass was four inches deep and Secretariat buried his nose in it, sniffing and biting off thick tufts. Mechanically, he folded and baled it with his lips, worked it along the sides of his mouth, shredding it with his teeth, then conveyed it down the great grain elevator of his neck.

The year before Lucien used to graze Riva Ridge at the same place on the grass, thinking then that he would go on soon to win the Triple Crown. The race was a nightmare and now he was back again, in precisely the same place and situation, only now with a much bigger gun. The thought struck him of the odds against such an occurrence, and he mused at the luck involved.

Secretariat stood for a moment at the stall door and stared outside. Billy Silver was looking at him, as were Sweat and Lucien. It was growing late in the afternoon and the horses were clean and ready to be fed, and the barn was suddenly suffused with the smell of clean straw and fresh grass and horses. Lucien looked more content for this ten minutes than he had looked all spring, childlike in his enthusiasm for what he was doing. He padded about in his green coat and yellow hat and Indian moccasins helping Sweat with the chores and stopping now and then to admire his horse.

Behind him Secretariat nickered. "He feels so good," said Lucien. "You should have seen him jumping and playing after he worked fifty-seven and change the other day." Lucien trailed off and looked down the shed. From Stall 32, Sham was watching a man prepare his dinner.

The serious training was behind Lucien and the red horse, and the colt had been doing brilliantly. He was coming to the Preakness dead fit, with his eyes wide open. As Lucien had predicted in Kentucky following the Derby, he was bringing Secretariat to the Preakness with an even finer edge. He had the red horse walk three days after the Derby, then boosted Charlie Davis aboard to gallop him four days—from May 9 to May 12. On Sunday, Turcotte was in from New York and Lucien told him to let Secretariat bounce through five furlongs. And he bounced.

They had not seen such morning speed at Pimlico for years. The colt raced through five-eighths in a spectacular 0:57 $^2/_5$, by way of a half mile in 0:45 $^1/_5$, and after Turcotte stood up and eased him back at the wire the momentum sent him through an extra eighth in 0:12 $^3/_5$, which gave him six furlongs in 1:10. Clockers blinked. The week before, one of the fastest sprinters in America, the older Leematt, won a six-furlong sprint race at Pimlico in 1:10. By eighths, the splits were startling: 0:11 $^2/_5$, 0:11 $^1/_5$, 0:12, 0:10 $^3/_5$, 0:12 $^1/_5$. They measured his stride that day at about twenty-five feet, comparable to the stride of Man o' War. The work left the red horse staring. That was Sunday. He walked on Monday, then he galloped daily through Friday, when Turcotte was at Pimlico to let him blow out a quarter mile.

Sham had come to the Preakness off sharp workouts, too, and Pancho remained confident. Yet something had changed since Louisville. It was painfully visible. Pancho was a good deal more subdued at Pimlico than he had been at Churchill Downs. The Derby had stunned and crushed him, and he was not over it yet. He had been so right about Sham, and so wrong about Secretariat. In the Derby aftermath, he had not made an excuse for Sham's defeat, but by the time he'd arrived at Baltimore that had changed, as if it had taken that long to talk himself into what went wrong. He had acquired the notion that the loss of the teeth had beaten Sham, not Secretariat, and that all he needed was a fair fight to prevail this second time in the classics. He had ceased criticizing Laurin, and instead was focusing all his creative energies as a trainer on the race May 19. He personally fulfilled Sham's needs. He threw himself into the job with care and patience and even a touch of passion.

Finished with his day's work, Pancho was about to slide into his rented Coupe de Ville and head for breakfast when he stopped, as if catching himself, and looked into Stall 32. Sham was lying on a bed of straw, his legs folded under him.

"Let no one here!" ordered Pancho, in a suppressed, emphatic whisper.

His brother Isadore nodded.

Then Pancho clamped a cigar between his teeth and strode off to the car. "I want no one bothering this horse. He needs all the rest he can get."

More, he sought to exercise as much control as possible over Sham's environment. Pancho was overlooking nothing. From New York he brought the theater ropes. They were red, with a decorative dip, and they were set up majestically in front of the stall to keep visitors at a distance. One afternoon he became agitated when he saw Sham looking out his stall at a filly grazing on that grassy strip outside the shed. Pancho walked half the distance of the barn and protested to the security guard about it. "I don't want that filly grazing in front of my horse." The guard told the man grazing her to take her away.

"I want his mind *only* on running," growled Pancho.

On Thursday morning, two days before the Preakness Stakes, Pancho was in the office and making his way among the fifteen jugs of mineral water on the floor, each containing five gallons of Sham's only beverage. "It's the best water there is," said Pancho. He read the label out loud! "Mountain Valley Mineral Water from Hot Springs, Arkansas." On a wall nail was impaled the $142.53 bill for it.

"If I don't win, I'll be very, very, very, very disappointed," Pancho said. "Not disappointed—very, very, very, very disappointed. I think Sham is going to win easy, believe me! In his workout here he finished strong as a son of a gun. It was a terrific work. I don't think the Derby was a true race. If everything goes right for everybody in the race, we'll beat him."

Whatever hostility Pancho felt toward Lucien Laurin or toward the Meadow Stable seemed to vanish at Pimlico by the middle of the week.

Penny had asked a reporter friendly with both her and Martin to introduce them. After the Derby, she sought to break the ice. The reporter, seeing the opportunity, escorted her to meet Martin one morning at the barn. Pancho brightened noticeably when he saw her coming toward him.

As Penny walked up to him, Pancho reached out a hand. "Very

nice to meet you, Mrs. Tweedy," he said. He seemed delighted.

"I've heard so many nice things about you," Penny said.

"Thank you!" Pancho invited her to meet Sham, and so they walked together to Sham's stall and talked about the incident at the starting gate. Pancho lifted the lip and showed her where Sham had lost two teeth.

She patted Sham's chocolate nose and told Pancho what a nice horse he had and he thanked her again.

"He's a kind horse, too," Pancho said. Penny held her hand out again and Sham nuzzled the palm of it.

"Yes, he is a kind horse," she said. Then they chatted pleasantly a few moments, and Penny turned to leave.

"Well, thank you," she said. "It was so nice to meet you."

"It was nice to meet *you,*" said Pancho.

"Let's hope we both have racing luck in the Preakness—a good race," she said.

Smiling among his jugs of mineral water, Martin nodded his head and said, "Yes—good luck."

It was four-thirty the morning of May 19. Eddie Sweat awoke in the fold-up bed in the tack room at the end of the shed, the door open but the screen door shut, and he rolled his feet out of bed and sat at the edge of it. He had dreamed that Secretariat had been beaten by Sham, and it felt real.

There were twelve hours to post time, then ten. Lucien arrived at the barn bleary eyed from the night before, a magnificent bacchanalian evening put on by the Maryland Jockey Club, which dispensed hundreds of pounds of roast beef and lobster and shrimp and oysters Rockefeller.

"Hey, Lucien?" someone asked. "How did you digest your lobster?"

"The lobster went down fine," said Lucien. "It was the whiskey that has stayed with me." Looking around and seeing Secretariat, Lucien said quietly, "I hope he had a better night than I had."

Laurin spent more than an hour relaxing at the barn and talking with newspapermen and television commentators, among them CBS's Frank Wright, a trainer by profession, and Jack Whitaker, who was resting his chin on the palm of his right hand and looking at the red horse.

Outside the steel fence, as the morning light grew harsh toward noon, cars edged bumper to bumper for the parking lots, and on narrow streets the processions of Bermuda shorts and T-shirts moved to the grandstand gates. The running of the Kentucky Derby had been widely celebrated, having riches, rivalry, and redemption as its elements, and the Preakness was a renewal of the same gaudy combat. The talk of Secretariat as a superhorse, set aside discreetly following the Wood, was renewed with more vigor than ever in the wake of the Derby. There was heightened public awareness that this might be the year of a Triple Crown winner. So through the morning Pimlico was filling with a record crowd of 61,657 persons, almost 13,000 more than had ever come to see a race at this historic race-course. They were much like the Kentucky Derby crowd, many of them young and exuberant. Those who spread their blankets on the infield lay listening to the rock band near the far turn, while overhead the sky was a dogfight of Frisbees borne on winds that blew off what, in better times, H. L. Mencken called the "immense protein factory of Chesapeake Bay." It was a Secretariat crowd.

But Lucien Laurin had lost with odds-on favorites too many times to speak as if he had a lock on any race, especially one he'd lost three times in the last seven years. Earlier in the week, when someone had innocently suggested that the Preakness appeared to be a match race between Secretariat and Sham, he snapped, "They thought it would be a match race between Riva Ridge and Key to the Mint last year, and we were lucky to be third and fourth." So on Preakness Day Lucien spoke in modified expressions of certainty. In the clubhouse he paced nervously between dissolving points of interest, from the box seats to the knots of well-wishers in the clubhouse to the bar in the rear. Total strangers grabbed his hand, wishing him the best, as did those he knew—owners and breeders, trainers and racetrack operators, journalists.

In the press box the scholarly Andrew Beyer of the *Washington Star-News* was making bold assertions, predicting that Secretariat would run the fastest Preakness in history. The young handicapper out of Harvard had already concluded that Secretariat had run a far faster Kentucky Derby than even the record-smashing final time suggested. Beyer had been trying to bring some scientific method to bear on the quality of a horse's performance, in a sport that tried to pick winners by a variety of methods, from astrology to numerology to the Ouija board. The method involved first determining the speed of a racetrack—how fast it is—and assigning a "speed figure" to the horse's performance, a figure reflecting his running time relative to the surface over which he ran. Secretariat's speed figure for the

Derby—his running time relative to the speed of the racetrack that day—was an unprecedented 129, according to Beyer's calculations, the highest he had ever assigned a horse. Curious, he employed the method to determine the quality of Secretariat's Derby performance relative to the quality of half a dozen other Derby winners' performances.

Beyer studied the results of all the races run on the half dozen Derby Days in the past, and he discovered that there were similarities between the distances and conditions of the races run year after year. On Derby Days there was always, say, a four-and-a-half-furlong race for two-year-old maidens, a $15,000 claiming race at seven furlongs, a one-mile allowance race for three-year-olds. These were constants. By comparing the running times of horses of similar class on different Derby Days, Beyer was able to determine how fast the racetrack was for one Kentucky Derby relative to another. When he compared the times of all races run on Derby Day in 1964, the year Northern Dancer ran his record mile and a quarter in 2:00, to all the races run on Derby Day in 1973, he decided that the track in 1964 was X times faster than it was in 1973—that is, the two-year-old maidens were running X times faster, as were the $15,000 claimers and the allowance horses. And so on.

Applying this finding, Beyer concluded that, at a distance of a mile and a quarter, the racetrack at Churchill Downs was a full second faster in 1964 than it was in 1973. Thus he concluded that while Secretariat beat Northern Dancer's track record by three-fifths of a second—a margin equal, roughly, to three lengths—Secretariat would have actually run a full second faster than that in 1964, or 1:58 ²/₅, and would have beaten Northern Dancer not by three lengths but by eight. In 1969 he would have defeated Majestic Prince by eleven. Even further back were Canonero II and Riva Ridge.

Now Beyer was at work to determine the speed of the Pimlico Race Course on this May 19, 1973. He studied the running times of the day's races as they were run, the maidens and the claimers and the allowance horses. Beyer found that the track was about as fast as it was at Churchill Downs two weeks before. Assuming Secretariat would perform as well in Baltimore as he had performed in Kentucky, Beyer figured he would run the same speed figure of 129 over the one and three-sixteenths miles of the Preakness.

"How fast will he run, Andy?" a reporter asked him.

"1:53 ²/₅," said Beyer, without hesitating. Canonero's track record was 1:54.

Behind the grandstand of Pimlico Race Course it was quiet at Barn EE. At four-forty, exactly one hour to post time, Eddie Sweat was at work methodically, ducking in and out of Stall 41. Barricade ropes had been set up around the barn and security guards were manning them. The curious had gathered, speaking in whispers, to see Secretariat. The red horse was in the rear of Stall 41, remote and sullen as usual, moody and in a bad humor as the afternoon wore on. There was an increasing sense of restlessness. A plane circled overhead pulling a banner reading: "Win the Million Dollar Lottery." A kind of reverential stillness had descended at five o'clock. Sweat had already changed into clean clothes and now he was in the stall with brushes and rags. Davis stood outside nearby. In and out, Sweat emerged from the front of the stall and walked to the wall of the shed, retracing his footsteps, then crossed the aisle again. This time, before dipping under the webbing, he took the blue bridle and white nose band off a nail by the door. Billy Silver hollered. It was 5:10, half an hour to post.

Moments later, from down the shed, came the leggy and dappling Sham. A retinue was at his side—Isadore carrying the blinkers, Lalo Linares moving blockily, like a bodyguard, the pony and the pony boy and groom and Pancho, who was striding along with a cigar in his mouth, his arms swinging, his shoes polished to a sheen, his hair brushed back, and his face wearing a look of unusual intensity. They walked by Secretariat's stall, where Sweat was standing with the colt, but no one looked over at him, and no one spoke. They walked with an air of solemnity, hooves and heels clicking, heads down and then up, faintly military in the bearing they affected into battle, proud and defiant and intense as they passed the barn and angled left down the walking path.

"*Vaya con Dios,*" someone said to Pancho.

He looked up and nodded gravely. He was attending the vindication of the finest racehorse he had ever trained. Behind Pancho, Sweat stood at the head of Secretariat. He joined them in a file down the walking path behind the stable area leading to the racetrack about a quarter mile away.

They passed behind the rows of barns, Secretariat about six lengths behind Sham, down the sandy pathway along the side street roaring with the sound of engines. A motorcycle dashed in and out of traffic, the engine backfiring in a rapid, fiery explosion, while horns honked up the street.

On they walked. Secretariat had his neck bowed, turned into

Sweat, rolling the steel bit in his mouth, then nibbling at Sweat's hand, which was holding the lead shank. The blue and white checked blinkers trailed after him. Davis rode nearby on Billy Silver, looking back now and then to check Sweat and the colt. Stable workers from Pimlico lined the route.

Leaving the path at the end of the row of sheds, they all rose flush against the roaring blue afternoon, turning right and passing along a line of buses. Secretariat and Sham walked past them to the race-track and the gap in the fence at the top of the straight. Coming to the gap, Secretariat stopped. He looked at the racetrack, as he usually did, at the infield and the footballs soaring and the flags snapping and the shirtless at the fence watching for him. Secretariat waited another moment, raising his head to see the distance, and Sweat didn't rush him. He waited, too, looking at the colt and talking to him. Then he stepped off through the gap and turned right for the long walk down the homestretch, in front of the grandstands. They headed for the wire and the saddling area laid out nearby it on the infield turf course.

On the right crowds of people four-deep lined the fence of the grandstand, pressing against it. They spotted Secretariat immediately, saw him coming around the corner, and the applause began there, the cries of support and exclamation, while along the way cameras snapped and clicked incessantly.

In the grandstand people were on their feet, the applause moving toward the eighth pole as he made his slow way down the stretch. This crowd had come to see him run. A man opposite the three-sixteenths pole, draped alcoholically over the fence, pointed to him and announced, "The best horse in the world. The best horse in the world."

Everything Secretariat did, every move he made, had a kind of flourish to it. Near midstretch the red horse suddenly stopped, raised his golden tail and defecated, and the crowd in the grandstands erupted in cheers and applause. Then he strode off imperiously down the stretch again. Seconds later he wheeled to the left, pivoting and bucking slightly, and that, too, drew more howls of delight. He was a fighter robed in a magnificent fur coat, walking down the center aisle to the ring.

At the finish line, Sweat turned him left and walked him across the racetrack to the infield, where the saddling area of each horse was staked out by a large yellow sign on which was printed his number. Lucien and Penny were there, waiting. Lucien looked Secretariat over as Sweat took him to the sign marked 3. Straining on his tiptoes, Lucien began to saddle Secretariat for the Preakness.

Penny laughed looking at Lucien stretched to fit the saddle on Secretariat's back. "We're still going to have to get Lucien a stool to saddle him," she said. Cameramen moved around the colt, and Secretariat pricked his ears at the shutter clicking. "Look at that ham," Penny said. "Look at that ham put up his ears."

Lucien lit a cigarette and waited for Turcotte. Ron, chewing gum, came across the track and met Laurin by the horse. They had already spoken about the race and the horses in it that morning at the barn. They had decided on no specific strategy. There were five other horses in the race—The Lark Twist had been scratched—and two of them had early speed. One of the two, Ecole Etage, had recently shown sharp early foot and was expected, like Shecky Greene before him and Angle Light before him, to go to the front and set the pace. Turcotte had also figured that Pincay and Martin might want to send Sham to the front, for Pimlico favored horses with early speed. Turcotte and Laurin laid no elaborate plans. Turcotte wanted to leave Secretariat alone, as he had done in the Derby, and react to the race as it developed. The turns at Pimlico were supposedly sharper than those at Churchill Downs, but Turcotte was not concerned about that. He felt he knew the racetrack. He had been leading rider at Pimlico in the fall of 1963, when he first started riding, so he was not intimidated by the so-called sharpness of the turns and the narrowness of the course.

"I wasn't worried about the turns because he always goes around them like a hoop around a barrel," Turcotte said. There was that spectacular run around the turn in the Hopeful Stakes at Saratoga, and he had handled the turns well on the one-mile oval at Churchill Downs.

Pincay spoke with Martin in the paddock, and he would recall thinking that Pancho's belief in Sham had not diminished one whit since the Derby. Pancho had told Pincay he thought Sham was beaten at Churchill Downs because of the incident at the starting gate. But somehow the explanation didn't sit well with Pincay. It did not convince him because, he thought at the time, it was difficult making an excuse for a horse who'd run a mile and a quarter in 1:59 ⁴/₅. He never disagreed openly with Pancho, but he remained suspicious of the excuses. Pincay was no longer as confident as he had been prior to the Derby, yet he felt Sham had a strong chance at Pimlico. He believed the colt had been improving steadily, getting more and more fit race after race. Moreover, the Preakness was the shortest of the Triple Crown classics, and he thought that could be a problem for a horse like Secretariat who finished strongly. Of the last twenty-five winners, beginning when Citation raced to a front-running victory in it, thirteen had been no worse than third going to the first turn, and most of the remaining dozen were close behind and in quick reach of the pace. Eight horses in history had won the Derby, lost the Preakness, then won the Belmont Stakes. The Preakness had been a spoiler in the Triple Crown series.

Pancho raised Pincay to Sham's back, and Laurin boosted Turcotte. The post parade began. Owners and trainers and officials scurried across the racetrack to the clubhouse, settling into seats and elbowing through the crowd that went to and from the betting windows. A chorus sang "Maryland, My Maryland." Lucien and Penny and Jack Tweedy settled at once into a box seat near the jockeys' veranda at the finish line. On the racetrack below, Turcotte started warming up the colt, galloping him to the upper stretch with Billy Silver running next to him. Applause tracked him everywhere, a fluttering of hands and programs.

A bell rang three times loudly.

"Three minutes left," said the loudspeaker. "Three minutes."

The crowd started drifting to the rail. Turcotte felt Secretariat warming up well, very loosely, so he stopped him around the turn. Sister Yvonne, a Catholic nun and long-time friend of Lucien, put her arm around him. Laurin lit a cigarette. Jack Tweedy leaned over and said something to his wife, and Penny nodded and popped a Rolaide tablet into her mouth.

"Post time two minutes."

In the upper stretch the horses moved toward the starting gate. Billy Silver paraded next to Secretariat. The calisthenics were finally over for the day. Lucien's face had grown suddenly weary. Turning, he sighed. Several seats behind him sat Senator Hubert H. Humphrey. A man, apparently drunk, had been haranguing Humphrey for some time, but through it all the senator smiled patiently. "I think Secretariat is going to win, but I have my money on Sham and Our Native," Humphrey said.

"Post time one minute."

The horses were nearing the gate. All around the oval, in the grandstand and infield, crowds thinned out by the fences to see the race. Heads craned up. Horseplayers rushed to make final bets. Owners and trainers of Preakness horses went to their seats. Seth

Hancock was there and E. V. Benjamin. So was Howard M. Gentry, who had come north to Baltimore from The Meadow to see the red horse run. It had been almost thirty-eight months since he rushed off that night to the foaling barn in the field.

The crew at the starting gate brought the horses forward. They took Sham in Post 1, then the 35–1 shot Deadly Dream, then Secretariat to Post 3. Turcotte had pulled down his goggles and now he waited in the gate. He was more confident in Secretariat than he'd ever been. He was coming off that powerful Derby and a sensational workout, and he believed there was no way they could beat him if all went well. He took up a lock of mane and leaned forward again, waiting.

"It is now post time."

It was over in less than thirty seconds, in the time it took him to apply the cruncher.

The latch sprang and Turcotte felt the red horse having trouble with the track, floundering as the surface chipped and broke away beneath him, while in the midst of his struggles to leave the gate he hopped a tractor print in front of it. Turcotte, unalarmed and sympathetic to what the colt was going through, simply steadied and folded up on him, giving him time to settle into stride. It didn't take long.

The field took off around him.

On the inside Sham broke drifting right and bumped into Deadly Dream, but Pincay hauled him off and sent him up to challenge for the lead. He would have to fight for it: on the far outside George Cusimano was gunning Ecole Etage, asking the son of Disciplinarian for speed, and he was responding in a charge down the middle of the racetrack.

Secretariat, as if back on his feet and straightening his tie, dropped back to last in the first few jumps. Sham and Deadly Dream pulled away on his left, and as they cleared him Turcotte angled Secretariat toward the rail. Thus the Preakness began as the Derby, and there was a stirring from the stands as Secretariat galloped trailing past them down the lane. He was a stretch runner by reputation now, and nothing excited a race crowd more than that.

Turcotte already sensed victory. The colt had found his footing and was leveling out beautifully, and Turcotte felt at once that he was running with the power and the rhythm he had in the first run through the straight at Churchill Downs. So he left him alone and waited for the Preakness to develop.

It was developing up front. There, racing by the eighth pole and making his first pass at the wire, Ecole Etage was outrunning Sham. Pincay had wanted the lead if he could get it, but now he was declining to make an issue of it, letting Ecole Etage set sail on his own. It was too soon to go to the well. Besides, Pincay had been concerned since the break about the way Sham was running. He'd detected a small hitch in Sham's stride, a kind of unsoundness of motion, as if something were bothering him, and as they raced past the wire Pincay was worrying about it. Then, as quickly as it came, it went, vanishing as Sham settled into stride as he neared the turn.

Clearing the field of horses on his left, Cusimano eased Ecole Etage toward the rail, then opened up two lengths in the run past the wire. Heading for the first turn, Cusimano started sitting tight on Ecole Etage. So far there would be no hesitation waltz.

Behind Ecole Etage was Torsion, racing a head in front of Sham. The Sommer colt was racing in close quarters on the rail, hugging it too tightly, now caroming off it as he raced into the clubhouse turn. But in a moment Pincay had steadied him and was going on again. Sham was running as well as he had two weeks before.

Behind them Deadly Dream was racing inside Our Native.

And behind them, bounding happily along two lengths astern of Our Native, came Secretariat. He was gaining speed, as he had at Churchill Downs, picking up momentum. He was moving gazellelike to the first turn.

Ecole Etage was a length and a half in front of Torsion as they banked into it. Tracking him, Torsion had a half length on Sham. Sommer's bay was four in front of Our Native and Deadly Dream. Those two were still lapped on each other. Secretariat raced directly behind them. They moved to the bend. Secretariat was relaxing and running effortlessly, taking deep breaths as he galloped within himself, and Turcotte felt the colt was ready at any time to run. Then it all began. Coming to the turn, Turcotte looked up front to check the pacesetting Ecole Etage. The leader was running alone. Looking, Turcotte thought he saw Ecole Etage's head rise up, and one connection came to his mind: Cusimano is trying to slow down the pace.

He reacted instantly, almost by instinct. He reached and shortened his line in a quick flicking of the wrists, a movement of the hands so subtle, barely noticeable, yet a signal to the red horse that it was time. He felt Turcotte take a hold of him, and in turn he grabbed the bit, and when Turcotte took back slightly on the right line, tugging gently on it, Secretariat swung outside of Our Native. All this was in a set of motions interlocked as one, a kind of chain reaction started by the hands: the flicking of the wrists, the grabbing of the bit, the pulling on the right line, the swinging outside, and then the first thrust forward, with dancer's grace, when Secretariat raised his forelegs in a single stride that lifted and swept him across the hindlegs of Our Native and set him down sprinting three horses wide on Pimlico's tight first turn, like a hoop around a barrel, and through all this Turcotte sat still, having moved only his hands, and that was all he did.

Secretariat sprinted past Our Native and Deadly Dream, while in the clubhouse seats Lucien thought he'd lost the Preakness and yelled to Penny, "He blew it!"

Leaving Deadly Dream and Our Native, Secretariat sprinted after Sham. He came to Sham in a rush, cutting the margin between them to three lengths, then two, then one, then bounded past him just midway of the turn. Still sprinting, Secretariat raced to Torsion and went past him and then set out for Ecole Etage. They were turning into the backstretch. He had come from last place in less than a quarter mile, and as they went into the backside he was at the throat of Ecole Etage. Cusimano saw him coming and he let out a notch on him. But it was too late. Secretariat powered past him and took the lead. Behind him the field was a shambles. Turcotte had caught them all, including Pincay, by surprise, and now he was setting sail on the lead and waiting for a response. It never came.

Secretariat opened a short lead as he raced to the five-eighths pole, gaining a length on Ecole Etage. Pincay had taken Sham outside Torsion and was in pursuit of Secretariat.

Secretariat widened his lead past the five-eighths pole. He opened a half length on Ecole Etage, then a length, then a length and a half, then two lengths as he raced past the half-mile pole into the far turn. Sham pursued. Pincay thought he had a chance to catch the red horse. He thought the move around the turn was too fast, and he thought the colt would falter on the turn for home. Turcotte, racing past the half-mile pole, looked under his right arm and saw the Sommer colors. Yet he sat quietly. Sham was racing two and a half lengths behind him, the crowd roaring for battle.

Midway of the turn for home, Turcotte heard the lashing of Pincay's whip. So he eased his hold on the red horse, letting out a notch of rein, and felt a surge of power. Sham was running from Pincay's stick but gaining nothing on Secretariat. They wheeled past the quarter pole and into the homestretch. There were still two and a half lengths between them. The final drive was on. The crowds in the stands were leaping on the rail and on the seats, while youths in the infield leaped the fences and swept down to the rail on Secretariat's left. Hands went up. Turcotte saw them five feet away and turned Secretariat's head to the right. Unconcerned at the tumult he was creating, Secretariat raced toward home. Pincay was still working on Sham with the whip, pushing and scrubbing on him, and he was looking for Turcotte to ask Secretariat for reserves.

But Turcotte hand-rode him, feeling at any time he could have opened another five lengths on Sham, but never asking him for more than he was giving on his own. At the eighth pole he was still two and a half in front. Pincay began to see it was no use, but he rode Sham hard for the wire, many lengths in front of Our Native but unable to gain ground on Secretariat.

They came to the wire that way, Secretariat winning it by two and a half lengths, Sham second, eight lengths in front of Our Native— in a finish identical to that of the Kentucky Derby. The reaction was spontaneous. Horseplayers and fans shaking hands, slapping backs, raced onto the track by the finish line.

The infield and the winner's circle developed into a mob scene as the jockeys pulled up their horses and dismounted. People scurried around Secretariat as Turcotte rode along on him. The colt remained a center of calm among them, walking quietly, unmoved by the moilings around him, by the voices, by the garland of daisies, painted to look like black-eyed Susans, they draped across his withers. Lucien, who had howled when he saw the move on the first turn, was marveling at it now, congratulating Turcotte for sensing a slowdown of the pace and acting so decisively. If that move had failed, Turcotte would have come under a sharper and more unrelenting attack than he'd ever been under in his life, but Secretariat had won under a hand-ride, without strong urging, so the move began to take on all the aspects of a masterstroke. It was a sharp variation from the way horses are supposed to run around the first turn at Pimlico, containing the brilliance of surprise.

In one sweep around the first turn at Pimlico, Turcotte had muted the critics who thought he lacked confidence, that he could get a good horse in a bad spot. He had ridden Secretariat with rare confidence, and he'd done it with everything at stake: all the responsibility was his. The safe decision was to sit and wait. Yet Turcotte gambled, and he drew gasps from the crowd, and fooled every jockey in the race, among them Laffit Pincay, Jr., who was admittedly caught off guard. "I was really surprised. I didn't think Turcotte would ride him that way. He went by me very fast. I was hoping from the early effort that he would get tired, but. . . ."

The general reaction in the jockeys' room was awe. "I never seen anything like the horse," said Tony Black, who rode Deadly Dream, "to move so early and have so much left. I was on the inside, with Secretariat on the outside—next thing I know, I look over, and Secretariat was gone. He's unreal."

In the press box, too, there were exclamations of disbelief, and they involved the running time as much as they involved the manner of the running. The final time posted on the tote board teletimer was 1:55, making Secretariat's Preakness a full second slower than the track record of Canonero II, and 0:1 ⅗ slower than Andrew Beyer had predicted with a flourish of his red felt-tipped pen. What puzzled Beyer most, making him suspicious of the electric timer, was that the margins between the first three finishers were identical to those in the Derby. That meant, to Beyer, that all three horses had tailed off identically in their form, a coincidence the handicapper refused to accept. More, the electric timer—in which horses break a beam of light across the track—showed the speedy Ecole Etage running the first quarter mile in a very lackluster 0:25, and Cusimano was gunning him out of the blocks.

So Beyer didn't believe the teletimer, and it wasn't long before his suspicions were vindicated. Word of the discrepancy spread quickly, first coming to light when veteran clockers for the *Daily Racing Form,* including the paper's chief of clockers Gene (Frenchy) Schwartz, and the paper's chief clocker at Pimlico, Frank Robinson, told Joe Hirsch they had timed the Preakness, from different vantage points, and recorded the identical time: 1:53 ⅖.

That, precisely, was what Beyer had predicted, a track record by three-fifths of a second. The discrepancy would never be resolved, though the proof would be overwhelmingly in favor of the faster clocking. Pimlico officials, conceding that the electric timer had malfunctioned, would later accept the time belatedly reported to them by the track's official timer, E. T. McClean, who claimed he had timed Secretariat in 1:54 ⅖. Later still, behind the impetus of handicapper Steve Davidowitz, the Maryland Racing Commission held a hearing on the matter and listened to testimony presented by CBS-TV, among others, that Secretariat had beaten Canonero's track record. The television network ran videotapes of the two Preaknesses, showing that Secretariat defeated Canonero by about two lengths. The network thus claimed it had technical proof of a track record. But despite the time reported by two veteran *Racing Form* clockers, and despite the evidence presented by CBS-TV, the racing commission would finally decide to keep McClean's time as official. The *Racing Form* would forever note its disagreement in its official charts, citing Schwartz's and Robinson's time in a footnote.

Most were conceding Secretariat his second track record. More, they were already conceding him Horse of the Year, and there were not a few already conceding him the third and most difficult of the Triple Crown races, the one hundred fifth running of the Belmont Stakes, scheduled for June 9. At least one man, though, was conceding nothing. Pancho Martin had been twice shattered by the turn of things. After the race, he spoke of Sham's hitting the rail going into the first turn, as he had spoken of Sham's knocking out two teeth in the starting gate at Churchill Downs. But Pincay gave the colt no excuse in either race, not in the Derby and not at Pimlico. Sham, too, had broken the track record, as he had done at Churchill Downs, and excuses remained hard to find under those circumstances. Pincay had come to terms with Secretariat's superiority. But he said nothing to Martin of his feelings. So the drama was played out, and Pancho must have known it then, even as he prepared to ship the son of Pretense north to Belmont Park. They couldn't turn back now. Even Sigmund Sommer, a realist who had made his money in the New York construction world, kept chasing the old dream. He had a few drinks with a New York racing official following the Preakness, and with each drink Sham cut into Secretariat's margin of victory in the impending Belmont Stakes. "If I'd stayed another five minutes, Sham would have beaten Secretariat by five," said the official.

Of the three in the Sommer stable, only Viola Sommer, who hadn't wanted to begin the campaign at Kentucky in the first place, appeared suspect of all the excuses. At the barn following the Preakness, Pancho was again talking about Sham hitting the rail.

The Preakness reaffirmed Secretariat's Derby form, and it also served to inflate his value even more. John Finney had advised The Meadow that the colt would be worth perhaps $250,000 a share if he did only what he was supposed to do—that is win the Triple Crown. The estate had decided to syndicate Secretariat rather than gamble with the government's money, and they had all underestimated him.

"I wish we could syndicate him over again," Penny said. "But I'm grateful that people had the confidence to go with us before he started racing again. I still think we have a good deal."

At the time the colt was syndicated, Lucien did not think the price was high enough, and now the form had borne him out. "He was cheap at $190,000 a share," he told reporters at the barn. "They should have syndicated him for $250,000 a share."

But all that, for the moment, was peripheral to what was coming up in three weeks. Secretariat had successfully made it through the first two races of the Triple Crown, and now there was but the Belmont Stakes to run, and Penny was eagerly looking forward to it. As she, Lucien, Jack Tweedy, and Howard Gentry walked into the press box following the Preakness, she repeated, "We have two down and one to go. It's up to Lucien, Ron, and the horse."

Chapter 27

By ten o'clock Sunday morning Eddie Sweat and Charlie Davis had almost finished loading the van, piling the interior with feed tubs and buckets, lawn chairs and unopened bags of feed, fold-up beds and suitcases and trunks laden with bridles, blinkers, and bandages. They had already led three horses onto the van, too—Billy Silver and the speedy Spanish Riddle and In Trust, an unraced two-year-old filly that Laurin had agreed to take back to New York. Others in the stakes barn, including Sham, had been shipped off earlier, and most of the stable workers had cleaned and drifted off to lunch. A radio was playing soul music, it was raining steadily, and there was a sense of desertion in the air.

Down the aisle of the shed, his victory hat tipped askew, whistling and swinging a lead shank in his hand, came Eddie Sweat. He went directly to Stall 41, patted Secretariat on the neck, rubbing his fingers through his mane, and led him out the door. He whispered, "Now this time, Red, we're goin' home."

They were heading north to Long Island and to the stable area at Belmont Park, to Stall 7 of Barn 5. Only four weeks had passed since the Monday following the Wood, when they flew Secretariat and Angle Light to Kentucky for the Derby, but in that time Secretariat had remade and glossed his image. He had performed beyond all reasonable expectations, shattering track records in two of America's oldest and most prestigious races, and he'd done it in shows of versatility and style.

He had left New York as a vaguely discredited son of Bold Ruler —and was returning as racing's reigning prince of the blood, a commanding victor at a mile and a quarter, America's classic distance. He had left Long Island one race away from being retired, and was returning on the threshold of what passes in this sport for immortality. He had left New York worth a tenuous $6.08 million to more than a score of uneasy and sometimes panicky syndicate members, and he was returning worth as much as $10 million to men who were patting each other on the back. He had left town known largely by those who had read the sports pages and heard of the record syndication, and he was returning a national figure, a culture hero. The nation was beginning to suffer the effects of Watergate, and the news was filled with names such as Haldeman and Mitchell and Dean, Ehrlichman and Liddy and Hunt, McCord and Strachan and Magruder. Though oblivious to all but the sensate world within his immediate grasp, Secretariat represented everything that they did not—honest, generous, simple, and incorruptible. More, he was coming to a historic meeting place, to the last and most challenging of the Triple Crown races, in recent years the most difficult of all to win for Triple Crown candidates.

In the last fifteen years, six horses had won the Kentucky Derby and Preakness Stakes, then failed in the Belmont. They had come to the race either lacking the stamina to go the route, tired or worn down by the first two races, poorly or inadequately trained. For one reason or another, the Belmont was one too many, and they had come up short. Tim Tam had broken a sesemoid bone at the top of the stretch in 1958, wobbling home on three legs, though there was some doubt whether he could have handled victorious Cavan that day on all four. Carryback was not himself in 1961. Northern Dancer tired in 1964. Two years later, so did Kauai King. Majestic Prince and Canonero, both of them sore, were not the horses they were at either Churchill Downs or Pimlico. Neither should have run in the Belmont Stakes, but the historic pressures forced their owners' hands. It had been so long since Citation! There had been so many failures, so many near misses.

Now the red horse was returning to Long Island, the soundest and most brilliant of all the candidates in history, and he generated crackling excitement in and out of the sport of racing. He had a presence to him that the others did not have, a sense of greatness, what horsemen used to call the "look of eagles." Sweat knew he had it.

He walked Secretariat through the shed to the loading ramp, waited a moment out of the rain, and then walked him quickly to the foot of the gentle incline and up into the wide open door. Turning the colt, Sweat backed him into a narrow stall, then clipped chains to each side of his halter. On Secretariat's right was Spanish Riddle, while facing across from him, about ten feet away, was the melancholy Billy Silver. Sweat quickly fastened the hay rack to a post between Secretariat and Spanish Riddle, and the two reached and tore at it voraciously, nervously.

Davis moved to Secretariat's head, patting him and talking softly. He climbed quickly into the cab, and moments later the engine fired up, raucously, the van shook with tremors and Secretariat spread both fores to brace himself. Sweat let out the clutch, sending the van pitching and teetering slowly through the stable to the gate. The red horse tossed his head sharply as the van hit bumps and wobbled left and right. He pawed at the floor and strained forward on the chains that held him. Davis talked to him above the engine noise.

The van picked up speed, passing the manure bins, and Secretariat pounded violently at the rubber matting on the floor, beating and scraping it with his left fore.

As they neared the stable gate, Davis picked up the leather end of the lead shank and put it, like a lollipop, into Secretariat's mouth, and the colt grabbed it at once, settling down. Sweat waved to the guards at the gate—"Good luck," one of them yelled back—and took a right on Winner Street for home.

"As soon as we start moving, he'll settle down," said Davis. "He ships beautiful. No trouble. No trouble at all."

Sweat turned off Winner Street and headed up Northern Parkway toward the superhighways skirting Baltimore. He stopped at a light, outside the gates of the track, and motorists gazed up indifferently at the chestnut with the blaze of white down his face. It was still raining steadily, drops running down the glass, and his ears played constantly as he looked across the streets of Baltimore. Horns honked. A small child waved to him. He sniffed at the window pane.

At three o'clock in the afternoon, Sweat came to a halt at the Belmont stable gate, turned left inside with the light and edged slowly through the doors, parking under a mass of leaves dripping with rain. Leaves were sticking through the windows, and Secretariat sniffed at them. It had rained all the way. The cab door slammed and Sweat walked toward the office for the paperwork.

Moments later he emerged from the office and took off in the truck through the stable area, turning left at Ogden Phipps's barn and past

296

Paul Mellon's barn and the stable of the Calumet Farm. He edged past Barn 5, and there were grooms and stable workers and racing officials and photographers waiting for him, newsmen from the Associated Press and United Press International and the *New York Daily News* and *Newsday.*

Sweat led Secretariat down the ramp and toward the barn, and everyone greeted him as he crossed the road, slapping him on the back and shouting encouragement to him.

Cameras were clicking as photographers ducked around to get pictures. Horses' heads popped out of stalls and regarded Secretariat as he walked past. Among them were Angle Light, Voler, Capito, and, further on down the aisle, there was Riva Ridge. Almost a year had passed since Riva Ridge had returned from Pimlico, the latest of the Triple Crown hopefuls who had failed. Riva Ridge stuck out his nose as the red horse passed, sniffing at him. The photographers hovered for pictures. Sweat grew annoyed. A cat sneaked out of the tack room and Secretariat reached down and nibbled at him.

"You can't come in here with all those cameras," said Eddie Sweat finally. But they all came anyway. Sweat turned the colt in Stall 7, freshly made with straw, unclipped the lead shank, and left. Photographers hovered, wild with delight as Secretariat made two quick turns of the stall, sniffing at the bedding, and then collapsed to his side, rolling on his back and kicking his feet in the air. They loaded film and snapped pictures of the red horse, urging him to prick his ears, which he frequently did at the sound of shutters snapping.

Thus Secretariat came home to Belmont Park, and those first few minutes were but an augury of the weeks to come. The day after his return, a full nineteen days before the Belmont Stakes—a day that he didn't even leave the shed—at least sixty reporters, photographers, and film crew members turned up at Barn 5, some wandering into the shed, others standing in the paddock adjoining it. Secretariat was now clearly an object of national adulation and curiosity, a source of intense interest that grew as the Belmont neared. CBS-TV was estimating that 28 million saw the Kentucky Derby, and that as many saw the Preakness Stakes. The impact of that exposure was just beginning to be felt.

The colt became the cover boy for three national weekly magazines—*Time, Newsweek,* and *Sports Illustrated*—and the topic of features and news stories in newspapers throughout America. The two wire services had men covering the red horse daily, and television and film crews tramped to Barn 5 periodically, taking film and tape of him grazing, walking, and working on the racetrack. The traffic was so heavy, in fact, that Penny and Lucien sought to establish some kind of controls. Reporters were not allowed inside the shed, first of all, and then they were not allowed inside the paddock adjoining the barn. Then interviews were granted largely by appointment. Penny had her home phone number changed and unlisted. Secretariat was a media happening, an event whatever he did, a celebrity.

Through the weeks leading to the Belmont Stakes, Penny became a familiar voice on radio, a face on news and talk-show television and in glossy magazines, a name in print. She was frequently referred to as the "First Lady of American Racing," a title she would protest, but she was certainly the sport's most engaging, visible, and energetic spokeswoman. People stopped her on the street and approached her in supermarkets. And she loved all the fame and attention. She lived the hectic eighteen-hour days leading to the race, at the barn early watching the colt exercise and giving interviews most everywhere, seated and on the run—in the paddock, in the stable office complex, in the dining room of the clubhouse, in her box seat and home and in her wine red Mercedes Benz in which she scooted hurriedly from home to racetrack to the city.

On network television she expanded in her role, simplifying and clarifying for a public largely uninformed about racing and breeding. Thus she appeared on NBC's *Today Show*, interviewed by Gene Shalit, and spoke in the simplest terms, though not patronizingly, about bloodlines and the record syndication and racing generally, about the red horse in particular.

"Now Secretariat is what is known as a Bold Ruler because his sire is Bold Ruler," said Shalit. "Bold Rulers usually don't run a mile and a half, which is the Belmont distance."

"That's true," she said.

"Do you think this horse is an exception? That this son of Bold Ruler can go a mile and a half?"

"Well," she said, "I do think so. Of course, he's half Bold Ruler but he's one-quarter Princequillo, and Princequillo is staying blood."

"That's the dam?"

"That's the dam. She's Somethingroyal, by Princequillo. Her family, Imperatrice, is also staying blood; so he has an even chance and I think we might be able to do it."

"Everyone talks about Secretariat as some kind of a superhorse as a three-year-old," said Shalit. "The horse is so remarkable. Are there any more home like him?"

"Yes, he has a baby brother who is a year now, and I've taken the terrible risk of giving him an important-sounding name. He's by Northern Dancer and we've named him Somethingfabulous. I think this is the sure kiss of death. But so far he looks good."

"He's a brother or a half brother?"

"He's a half brother . . ."

"Then there's another horse, called Capito, who made his debut just a few days ago. That's Riva Ridge's half brother. How did he make out in his first race?"

"He won! It was very satisfactory."

"So you've got two horses coming up that you have your eye on. One a half brother to Secretariat, one a half brother to Riva Ridge. How soon can you predict that a horse is going to be a great race-horse? When he's a colt? Can you tell when you're looking at him running 'round The Meadow?"

"With Secretariat, he's *so* good-looking that we always had high hopes for him, but you really don't know until you see him run his first race. People say, oh, he had the look of eagles and so forth, but I think that's romance. I don't think real horsemen believe that."

"Some of the big news lately was the syndication of Secretariat," said Shalit. "You sold him for something over $6 million. What was it, about a hundred and eighty thousand a share?"

"A hundred and ninety."

"A hundred and ninety thousand dollars a share. You have four shares, the others have the others. Now, that was before a lot of this attention and excitement came to Secretariat. Suppose you had waited, suppose you had bitten your nails and said, 'I'm going to hold off until after the three races, to see what he does in the Triple Crown.' Or even after the Kentucky Derby and the Preakness. What do you think he would be worth now in syndication?"

"This is a gambling game and we had to take a gamble. We had a tremendous obligation to Uncle Sam, and I didn't feel we could gamble with Uncle Sam's money. We had to pay those inheritance taxes whatever the horse did, so we took a gamble. Perhaps you hadn't heard of him in January but he was Horse of the Year as a two-year-old; it had never happened before. So he had quite a lot going for him then. I think probably if we were to syndicate him today we could get a quarter of a million dollars a share. That sounds terribly greedy. But if he wins the Belmont I just don't know, we haven't had one in twenty-five years!"

"Citation was the last. Are you superstitious, since you're a gambler? Since you're in horseracing? I mean, do you always wear the same pair of shoes when you go to the track?"

"Well, I always wear this little pin."

"Can we see that on camera?" The camera dollied in. "It's a jockey," said Penny. "It was my mother's. A jockey riding a horse. It was given to her by old friends of the family and whenever we have a horse in a race I have that on. That's about the only consistent thing I do, and I try not to bet too much on our horses."

"Mrs. Tweedy, thank you very much, Mrs. Helen Tweedy, manager of Secretariat. We wish you good luck at the Belmont Stakes!"

Penny Tweedy enjoyed an enormously responsive and largely sympathetic press. Newsmen admired her wit, her enthusiasm, her ability to frame a sentence, and her respect for candor when she spoke of herself and how people had responded to her. So she told Jurate Kazickas of the Associated Press, in a story circulated widely: "I have not really done anything not related to horses in the last five years, but it has given me the thrill of accomplishment. I love the prestige, the excitement, and the money."

Asked about her fan mail, she said, "Most of the letters are wonderful, but occasionally we get hate mail, too. Things like, 'Oh, you rich Anglo-Saxon bitch with your roses and silver trays.'"

Several news and magazine stories depicted her as "handsome," one of them as "extremely handsome," while another called Penny "striking," as if to differentiate. She was described as "articulate and bright" and "warm and open" and as having "a sense of steely determination" and "an unabashedly competitive spirit, independence and ambition." The press loved her.

More, she always had a sense of humor and understood what made readable copy. When she might have been bland, she was not.

"Speaking of Penny, where does that come from?" Jerry Tallmer of the *New York Post*, asked.

"My mother's name was Helen, as was mine, so there was a need to differentiate. I guess it was an era when nicknames were popular. And I deplored it. Penny, Boofie, Muffie—we should all be shot."

In the crush of the publicity, authors and artists wanted to do books and paintings about Secretariat, so Penny sought the counsel of the William Morris Agency, the world's largest talent agency, among whose clients were listed Mark Spitz, Elvis Presley, Don Rickles, and Sophia Loren. "Only two things bother me a bit," she would tell Tom Buckley of *The New York Times* between dances at the Belmont Ball. "The first is that Secretariat will be retired from competition so soon, although it was unavoidable. The second is that we've had to put a price tag on a horse who should be appreciated for his good qualities alone." Yet there was more than one price tag on Secretariat, more than the $6.08 million syndication. Anyone who wanted to paint Secretariat and merchandise photographs of him, to publish the books and make Secretariat T-shirts and medallions, had to talk money and percentages with Penny or the agency. Penny liked money, as she told Jurate Kazickas, and she sought her share, not only for herself but for the C. T. Chenery estate, which would benefit from all proceeds earned by the name of Secretariat off the racetrack.

Those who sought to do Secretariat-related projects had to receive her permission or that of the agency. And she continued acting decisively and forcefully on matters involving the selling of Secretariat.

"What about the artist from South Africa?" Lucien asked her one day outside the office, as she dipped into her Mercedes Benz. "Has he been commissioned?"

"No!" Her tone was emphatic. "He's been given permission, that's all."

"Well, he keeps coming around here," said Lucien.

"Well," she said, thinking a moment. "Tell him the next time he comes, that Mrs. Tweedy hopes he has gotten enough pictures. And 'Please don't come around here anymore.' "

His stable was besieged daily by reporters and photographers, by racing officials and the merely curious. His days were consumed by work and interviews, but Lucien Laurin trained with greater insight than he had ever done before. That Lucien was now sixty years old, that he was being subjected to the cruelest pressures in the sport—those brought on by the historic quest for the Triple Crown—that trainers were quietly second-guessing his every move seemed not to shake or deter him from the course he had plotted and thought was right. He had never in his life trained so superbly, and Secretariat thrived on it. The colt had just cracked two track records, and Lucien hardly let up on him. He kept cranking him tighter, asking more and more of him, for the first time actually beginning to get

to the bottom of the colt. Between workouts, Secretariat was galloping a full two miles every morning, stretching his muscles for the
longer distance of the Belmont Stakes, measuring his stride. Those
mornings were events, with photographers and cameramen following him by the dozens to the track. Yet among them he remained
unruffled. Nothing fazed him; nothing upset him.

Lucien walked Secretariat three days after the Preakness. The first
workout was May 27. Turcotte sent him three-quarters of a mile in
1:12 ⅕, an almost perfect twelve-clip. The colt looked sharp, bouncing off the racetrack and jumping back at the barn.

As the Belmont Stakes neared, Secretariat continued training
brilliantly. The colt walked the day following the six-furlong workout, then galloped just three days. On June 1, eight days before the
Belmont Stakes, Laurin sent him out for his most critical work in
preparation for the race. He wanted Turcotte to work the colt a flat
mile in 1:36, time that would have won a classy race for stakes-
winning fillies just the day before. The winner, Barely Even, raced
the mile in 1:36 ⅘. But standards of time were beginning to have
no meaning whenever the colt performed—in the Kentucky Derby,
quarter after quarter; in the sensational workout prior to the
Preakness Stakes, when he galloped out three-quarters in 1:10; and
in the record-shattering Preakness Stakes itself.

Turcotte emerged at 9:10 at the gap in the fence, stopping to let
photographers take their pictures, and then walked the colt onto the
racetrack and to the far turn. Turning him around, he set out jogging
back past the stands and around the clubhouse turn. Then he
stopped. He looked around, left and right, then urged Secretariat into
a gallop, and coming to the red and white striped mile pole, he sat
down crouched on him.

The two took off quickly. Turcotte sat still on his back, the red
horse racing the first eighth in 0:12, the second eighth in 0:11 ⅘, for
an opening quarter in 0:23 ⅘. Down the backstretch Secretariat
picked up speed, racing the third eighth in 0:12 but then the fourth
in a rapid 0:11 ⅕, which gave him a half in 0:47. He was bounding
along airily. Keeping to the beat of twelve, he raced to the five-
eighths in 0:58 ⅘, then to the three-quarters in 1:11 and then to the
seven-eighths in 1:22 ⅘, already a sensational move. He kept to the
beat down the lane, finishing out the last eighth in 0:12.

Lucien clicked his watch at 1:34 ⅘. He watched the colt gallop
out a mile and an eighth in 1:48 ⅗. Lucien sighed heavily. It was a
marvelous workout, but was it too fast?

"He went faster than I really wanted," said Laurin. "But he did it so easily that I am very pleased." Yet there were murmurs from other trainers at the track that Laurin had worked his horse too fast.

The work hardly bothered Secretariat. The next day he was bucking and playing when they walked him up the shed, and three days later Laurin had him galloping again, limbering him up and stretching his muscles for the longest distance he would ever run. By the morning of June 6, Secretariat was ready for the third and final workout, one of those zingers to open his eyes and bring him to his toes. Laurin told Turcotte to let the colt roll for a half mile, and the red horse took off with him around the turn. It was one of those gray, melancholy mornings at Belmont Park—a chill was in the air—and when the colt appeared turning for home he seemed to emerge through the mists, grabbing at the ground and folding it under him. You could hear him breathing through all of the upper straight. For those who sought to beat him in the Belmont Stakes, that move was an omen. As Secretariat flashed past the wire, the clockers caught him in a fiery 0:46 ³⁄₅, fast enough to put him near the pace in sprints, and then he came dancing home, his neck bowed and his eyes rolling white in their sockets.

Yet, despite the brilliance of the workouts, despite those assuring him that the colt could not lose, that he was training America's ninth Triple Crown winner, Laurin spoke and moved with caution. The pressure heightened. At times he was expansive, open, and friendly, at other times tight lipped and snappy, stewing and blowing up over small things. He had been on racetracks far too long to come to any race as confident as some of Secretariat's staunchest supporters. There were too many ways to be beaten. He wriggled openly.

"I've never seen so many goddamn favorites beaten as in the Belmont," Lucien said one morning in his stable kitchen. He was sitting at the formica table over a large plate of eggs, sunny-side up, surrounded by shingles of beef and toast. A cup of coffee sat steaming next to him. Turcotte, reading the *Daily Racing Form,* sat across from him, his helmet on his lap. Turcotte looked over the top of the paper as Lucien spoke.

"I'll tell you one thing," he said. "I'll be glad when this son-of-a-bitchin' thing is over with, believe me. I just want it to end, and soon." The conversation drifted. Laurin talked a moment of the way the colt's value had soared since the Derby, to over $250,000 a share, though no one had sold out. Between bites of toast, he nodded across the table at Turcotte and said petulantly, "Just don't fuck it up Saturday or he'll go down in value again."

Staring at Laurin, whose face returned to his food, Turcotte looked for the moment as if he wanted to pick up the plate of eggs and break it over Lucien's head. But he said nothing.

For Laurin, the press to win was on. He grew touchier, more protective than ever of Secretariat's privacy. One morning, a television crew of eight men arrived at Barn 5 to take a sequence for a news show, and as the colt emerged from the barn they followed him quietly, their lenses fixed. Lucien watched them, letting them into the paddock for the pictures. Later that morning, after the day's work was done, he watched them trooping up the shed toward Secretariat's stall. He howled them out, gesturing fiercely.

And he became more sensitive to routine, to what had been working well for him in the past. George (Charlie) Davis, who had been exercising Secretariat since he'd left for Louisville and the Kentucky Derby, had remained his most trusted exercise boy, the rider of Riva Ridge, and he felt a constancy in him that he didn't feel in Gaffney. In fact, he hadn't been pleased with the way Gaffney had ridden the colt, believing Jimmy was too busy putting on a show, grandstanding when he galloped him of mornings. Now in the crunch he turned to Charlie Davis, as if by instinct. Gaffney sensed what was coming. He had been warned on the first Wednesday following the Preakness, when Lucien met him after he had galloped Secretariat.

"How did he go?" Lucien asked.

"Like a champ, Mr. Laurin. He wanted to play a little out there."

Lucien then confided in him, "Jimmy, Mrs. Tweedy doesn't like the way you ride the horse." So Gaffney knew there was a problem, yet he wasn't expecting what happened in the shed on Friday morning. Henny, who had hired Jimmy just a year ago, approached him there. Lucien was in the office.

"Jimmy," said Henny, "Lucien's taking you off the big horse."

"What?" said Gaffney. "What for?"

"I don't know."

"Well, I quit, then." Henny tried to talk him out of it, but it was no use. "I'll pick up my paycheck," said Gaffney.

Crushed and bitter that Laurin hadn't fired him himself, Gaffney left the barn with his Secretariat saddlecloths and his pummel pad, the one that his mother had knitted for him, and then drove home to tell his wife. She had sensed it coming, too, and knew what had happened when she saw him walk in the door of their Queens apartment. She saw his eyes filling. Sitting down, he said nothing.

"I can't believe it," Jimmy finally said. "I didn't believe they'd do it."

So the pressures of the Triple Crown were felt by all those around the colt. Even Eddie Sweat, while still talking freely to reporters, seemed more remote, less communicative amid the daily intrusions, more pressured as the demands on his time increased. He had come a long way from the vegetable gardens of Holly Hill, South Carolina, to the shed row at Belmont Park, to take his place with Will Harbut as racing's most celebrated groom, the doyen of backstretch swipes. Now, as the biggest moment of his life arrived, he spent more and more time at the barn, arriving earlier, going home later, making sure the colt had everything he needed—hay, water, bedding. Like Lucien, he became increasingly protective of the colt and the routine that regulated his life.

The *Time* and *Newsweek* covers appeared on newsstands during Secretariat's final week of training for the Belmont Stakes, and they gave the colt an aura of invincibility. Both labeled him a superhorse on the covers. There were few dissenters following the Derby and the Preakness Stakes. But there were a few, and among them was Pancho Martin, whose faith in Sham had never waned. It felt like months since those chilly mornings in Kentucky when Pancho leaned up against the cinder block of Barn 42 and extemporized on Sham's superiority, attacking Laurin. Now he spoke in more subdued tones of Sham's superiority in the Preakness. This time he was wearing patent leather shoes, chewing on his cigar, and sitting on a park bench beneath the trees at Belmont Park.

Pancho held a copy of *Time* magazine, with Secretariat looking at him, and he stared at it for a long time.

He muttered, "Superhorse." Then he clamped the cigar in his mouth, pointed to the front of *Time* and said, his words solemn, "If he beat me in the Belmont Stakes, *then* I'll call him a superhorse. I *know* he's a good horse—everybody knows that! If he beat me fair and square—and he hasn't beaten me fair and square yet—then I will"—he paused, poising his cigar—"I'll call him the nicest things you can call a racehorse." Then he denounced the accounts that Sham appeared washed out and tired in the first few days home from Pimlico. "He looked like a drowned rat," said Charles Hatton, who watched Secretariat and Sham train at Belmont Park, where he wrote his daily column. But Sham recovered, and Pancho with him, and he claimed that Sham had not lost confidence, that he had a chance to beat the red horse going twelve furlongs.

Pancho was also planning to enter Knightly Dawn in the Belmont. He was the colt who came into Linda's Chief in the Santa Anita Derby, but there seemed no way that Pancho could beat the red horse other than with Sham. Speed would only help Secretariat, set it up for him, so Knightly Dawn would work for Secretariat as well as Sham. The Belmont was the center of discussion at the racetrack for a full three weeks preceding it, among trainers and grooms, hot walkers and track officials. Only a handful thought Sham had a chance. One was John Parisella, a youthful trainer and a man far closer to Martin than to Laurin.

"If I was in Frank's position," Parisella said one day at the race-track, "I would say his best chance to beat Secretariat is to go to the front and dictate the pace. Lucien Laurin had better take the lead. Martin actually believes he has the better horse. All he wants is a clean-run race. If Sham goes to the front with slow fractions, Secretariat is going to have to go get him. This is a grueling distance and Sham is eligible to beat Secretariat. It's not as simple as some people might make it seem."

But Parisella and Martin were in the smallest of minorities as Belmont Day approached. Most of the intelligent trainers, such as Phil Johnson, were speculating on the length of victory rather than on the strategy.

"If Knightly Dawn goes out there and sets the pace, he'll make it a true race," said Johnson. "And if it's a true race, Secretariat will win it. Turcotte has only two things to worry about. If the pace is too slow, he has to go to the front. If the pace is too fast, he has to sit still for a while. All this psychology—whether Knightly Dawn or Sham will go to the lead—doesn't make any difference. They're not going to unnerve Turcotte, who sits so cool on a horse. If Frank was dealing with anything but that big red bombshell, it might work. But not against him." Many horsemen felt that way; that there was no fair way he could be beat. And that feeling set the tone of things.

The fact is that the Belmont Stakes was not to be a race but a coronation. All that remained to speculate was the margin of Secretariat's victory, his running time, the incidentals. However he won it, whether by two and a half lengths—as he had won the Derby and the Preakness—whether by five or by ten lengths, the important thing was that he win. And there seemed no doubt of that. Victory would be enough to satisfy a public that had waited all these years to see a racehorse win the Triple Crown.

Turcotte sensed he was riding possibly the greatest horse that had ever lived. One evening, he and Lucien had dinner at a restaurant in Valley Stream, Long Island, then drove to Belmont Park and to Barn 5. They had each been drinking. They stood together outside the barn and talked. It was very late and it was dark. Outside the shed, Turcotte said to Lucien, "He's the greatest horse that ever looked through a bridle."

"Do you think so, Ronnie," said Lucien. "Do you *really* think so?"

"If we don't win the Belmont," said Turcotte, "I might as well pack my tack and leave New York."

"You?" said Lucien. "What about me?"

So Turcotte came to the race supremely confident, talking about winning as he rarely did. At the Belmont Ball on Thursday night, Turcotte accepted accolades for his victory on Riva Ridge the year before. The winner of the Belmont is honored at the ball the following year. Turcotte told the formal gathering of socially elite from the Jockey Club: "If it's a clean race, I'll be back here next year." As he sat down at the table, his wife Gaetane whispered, "Ron! You never talk that way. I hope you didn't jinx him." Sitting back in his chair, Turcotte lit a thin cigar and sipped his drink.

Laurin, as cautious as he had been, got caught up in the air of coronation in the final days before the race. There had been speculation on the running time, some believing a record was possible. The Belmont main track had been lightning fast the week before the race, but it had slowed through the final days. The talk of a record Belmont Stakes had tailed off. Andy Beyer would predict 2:27, two-fifths of a second slower than Gallant Man's track mark, if Secretariat ran a speed figure of 129, as he had done at Churchill Downs and Pimlico. Of the winning margin there was some conjecture. Some thought the margin would be a repeat of the Derby and the Preakness. Others thought that, with the added distance, Secretariat might win by five, perhaps more.

Lucien had his own ideas. He knew the colt was at his peak in physical condition, wound up and ticking since that final sharpener in 0:46 ⅗, and the night before the race he abandoned all caution.

"I think he'll win by more than he's ever won by in his life," said Lucien. "I think he'll probably win by ten. What do you think of that?"

Chapter 28

It is four sharp on Saturday morning at Belmont Park, and Pinkerton guard Joe Fanning sits framed against the light of the tack room door in Barn 5, hunched forward in his chair and snapping off the playing cards in front of him. The Belmont Stakes is thirteen hours away, and the imminence of it pervades the silence of shed row and the world of the horses sleeping in it. The air is warm and a wind is blowing from the sound, turning the leaves on the row of trees by the street lamps of the stable area. A tire screeches occasionally along Hempstead Turnpike, which runs alongside the stable. A rooster crows. The night is cricketless. Nightwatchman Clem Kenyon has just fed Secretariat his single quart of uncrushed oats, the limited ration of grain on the day of a race, and now Kenyon is gone and Secretariat is finished with it. He is lying down again, his legs folded under him in Stall 7. Breathing deeply, his sides rising and falling like bellows, he is asleep.

It is 5:10. Secretariat, on his feet, pokes his head outside the stall and looks at Henny Hoeffner. Henny sees him, stops and looks him up and down, very slowly, and walks on. More men emerge from the doorway. Screens slam. The coffee truck idles past, stops. Seth Hancock, intense and uncommunicative, emerges from the complex of ground-floor rooms by the barn and walks down the road to another shed. Ed Sweat arrives in his Dodge at 5:25, and moments later stable foreman Ted McClain strolls by, too. They are coming to work. There is muttering, the sipping of coffee, lips smacking.

"I can hardly wait to see this day over with," says McClain.

"This is it," responds Sweat. "I'm as ready now as I can get."

Sweat ambles down the aisle of the shed, passing the rows of stalls, and on the way calls Secretariat's name. The colt sticks his head from the doorway and pricks his ears and flips his nose in the air. Setting his coffee down across the aisle from him, Sweat crosses over to see him. "Hey, Red," he says. "Let me get old Big Red ready here."

The routines begin. Sweat spreads a piece of burlap cloth in front of the stall and begins piling it with large forkfuls of old straw and moist bedding and manure, whistling and chattering with his red horse. A rake leans tipped against the webbing, and Secretariat suddenly grabs it, seizing the handle in his teeth. He scrapes it across the aisle in front of him, then pulls it back into the stall. Grooms stop, look, and laugh.

The activity at the barn picks up, the rich composts of straw and hay rising in front of all the stalls down the shed.

Davis leads the colt out of the stall and into the fresh light of the walking ring in the paddock. A thin dirt path traces the circle, perhaps 100 feet around, passing the shed and the pony stalls, passing the chain and wooden fences and the spigot where the grooms come to fill their buckets with water. Caring for the ponies in the stalls, Robin Edelstein rattles a bucket on the wall, and the effect is of an explosion under Secretariat, who leaps high on his hindlegs in the air and paws at the sky, a bronze general's horse in Central Park. He rises high above Davis, who looks up, cowering, and snatches the chain that connects them.

Floating down, Secretariat prances around the ring, his neck bowed and drawn up tightly beneath the throat, kicking dirt and cinders in the air, spraying the walls of the pony shed, jumping again, shifting left and right. He has never been so fit. In all these past three months, from the days leading to the Bay Shore Stakes, he has never seemed so sharp. Robin Edelstein rattles the buckets again and he rises up once more, towering above Davis, higher this time, his hindlegs almost straight, and coming down he dances off sideways, his nostrils flared and snorting, his eyes darting, islands of brown in pools of white. The final half-mile drill in 0:46 ³/₅ has ground him so fine at the edges, leaving him sharper than he has ever been. He moves as if on springs, bouncing when he walks, aglide, and those who pass him stop to look in wonder at the sight. Now Davis is talking almost incessantly to him, trying to calm the colt and keep him on his feet. Davis tugs on the chain. A plane flies overhead and Secretariat stops and raises his head and watches it, turning his head slowly as it passes off to Kennedy. There is noise as a set of horses passes by and he lunges forward again, up and down twice, spinning on his hooves, and kicks and then goes up once more. He comes down moving as if in dressage, his neck arched in a crest, which accentuates the power, while his back and shoulders are roped with muscles taut beneath a dappling coat that shifts with light.

Trainer Bill Stephans rides by on horseback and stops to watch Secretariat play. "Looks good, don't he?" he says.

Henny Hoeffner comes by.

"Okay, Charlie," says Henny. Davis shortens his hold on the shank and leads the red horse back inside the shed, then up the aisle and into Stall 7. He has been out eighteen minutes. He will not leave the stall again until he walks to the paddock for the Belmont Stakes.

Secretariat is back in his stall at 6:15, and five minutes later Lucien Laurin arrives in his gray Mercedes.

"He was buckin' and playin' the whole time he was out this mornin'," someone says to him.

"That's good. That's good. Means he feels good."

Henny Hoeffner has already organized the morning on his clipboard, orchestrated it through to its conclusion, and Lucien wanders about abstractedly for a moment, peering into stalls, the tack room, and finally into Stall 7 to see the red horse.

Horses are going out now in sets, and Lucien and Henny follow Capital Asset and Capito, the two half brothers, out the gate and to the track to watch them exercise.

So the morning passes in review—bays and chestnuts, grays and browns, galloping slowly past, working out.

By ten o'clock news and TV men have begun to stop by the barn. The day has grown oppressively muggy, and the last of the horses are back in the barn. In the paddock, Billy Silver, who will take Secretariat to post for the Belmont Stakes, is now limping about heroically on a sore foot. Beseechingly, Charlie Davis takes him around and around to help work out the kinks.

"Come on, Billy," says Davis. "Can't stop on us now."

Mopping his forehead with a handkerchief, Lucien looks at Billy Silver and shakes his head and flees the heat to his air-conditioned office. He sits down on the couch, his face red, and rubs his face once more. Turcotte is there talking to CBS commentator Frank Wright. Jack Whitaker asks Laurin how he is doing.

"I've done my part," Lucien tells him. "It's up to the master now. God almighty. I'm glad it's close to the end. It's getting rough and tough. It's beginning to get the best of me, so help me. Everyone expects him to do so much. That's what bothers me."

Tony Leonard, the photographer, approaches Laurin with a proposal for pictures. Lucien is beginning to fret and pace the floor. "The *Blood-Horse* is putting out a special supplement—twenty-four pages—that they're going to send to every racetrack around the world," said Leonard. "They want me to get pictures of you, Secretariat, the groom. Do you think I can get some of those?" The question is inappropriate for the moment, and Lucien's voice seems to teeter on his words, his voice dry with impatience.

"No one under the shed!" he says. "No one! I'm lucky *I* can get under the shed today."

There are still the big and small decisions to be made. Sweat knocks on the door. "Which of these nose bands do you want to wear —the blue or the white one?"

"The white," says Lucien.

The day's pressing work is done. It is 10:30. The horses eat a normal lunch, though Secretariat's is cut to one quart of dry oats from the regular regimen of three. Ed Sweat turns inward. He crushes out a cigarette.

"He's in the back of the stall. He knows. He knows and he don't want to bother. He's thinkin' about it." Excusing himself, he walks to the middle of the shed and turns on the spigot, and for the next hour sits cleaning the leather halters and lead shanks with soap and water. The morning lurches on toward noon. Lucien has borne up well under the strain, and now he is giving a tour of his barn to a visiting dignitary. Moments later he is raving about a horse he had just sold who, he has just discovered, is a cribber given to gulping air. Secretariat gazes impassively at Laurin as he passes the stall. He pricks his ears and listens, then calmly turns to his hay. Fifteen minutes later the shed is empty and cool again, and the wind is moving through it and waving the manes of the horses looking out their stalls, though Secretariat remains at the back of his. Sweat washes towels. Outside the crowd is coming to Belmont Park in endless caravans of cars and buses strung along Hempstead Avenue and the parkway. The lots fill quickly. From the shed you can hear the lot attendants hollering and directing lines of traffic.

There are 67,605 persons coming to Belmont Park—the Taj Mahal of American racing—and they come fully expecting to see a coronation. They jostle through the clubhouse and the dining rooms, among the grandstand seats and across the lawns. An oomppah band plays music at the eighth pole. Back at the barn, two years after breaking Secretariat under saddle in the indoor training ring, Meredith Bailes is back at the shed and talking to those visiting. "He was beautiful to train," he is saying. "No problem. A perfect gentleman. We thought the world of him, you know, because of his breeding. I been wrong with a lot of them, but I really felt he was special when we had him. So did Mr. Gentry. We live right off Route 95, between Washington and Richmond, and I felt we could have galloped him right down the road. Nothing bothered him."

The races begin at 1:30. Horses are now moving along the stable pavement to the racetrack, and thirty minutes later returning through the tunnel bespattered with sand and heaving out of breath. Cars are now packed bumper to fender throughout the expanses of the lots. Lucien goes to the races. And now Penny is in her box seat with Jack Tweedy and sister Margaret and brother Hollis. There is something almost monarchical about her—set off by the way she smiles and dips her head. She is standing now in the second-floor box seat above the grandstand, as if on a balcony overlooking multitudes seeking absolution. She is dressed in a blue and white dress over whose sleeveless top hangs a golden pendant, and her hair is teased and drawn in puffs in the shape of a turban. She raises her arms, and her cheeks are flushed. The crowds below her shout her name and wave and carry signs—"Good Luck Secretariat," one of them proclaims—and she beams and waves back and shouts her thank-yous to the left and to the right. The tumult builds throughout the afternoon at the racetrack, while at the barn the mood grows solemn.

There is a crowd of people—grooms, hot walkers, assistant trainers, news reporters—waiting at the barn for Sweat and Secretariat. Pigeons flutter about the eaves, roosting in the straw bales above the stalls. Every half hour, from the distance, the grandstand builds in a tremendous roar of sound as the races, one by one, are run. Minutes later, the horses who drew the roars come dripping with sweat and panting back to the barns, like gladiators returning from the Roman Circus.

It is four o'clock, and Sweat is working casually around the colt, who stands at ease, quietly.

From the tunnel, suddenly, the horses return following the fifth race on the card, a one-mile sprint for older horses. The track is not as fast as it has been. Four of the fastest older horses on the grounds —including Tap the Tree and Spanish Riddle—have needed 1:36 to run a mile. Spanish Riddle has won the race by a half length. The first four finishers are all stakes winners. Two races later, around the corner of the tunnel leading to the racetrack, comes the badly beaten Angle Light. He is puffing and moving wearily, his head down and his legs and eyes spackled with sand thrown up in his face by the eight horses to finish in front of him just moments earlier. He has not been the same colt since the Wood Memorial. He ran poorly in the Derby, and on Belmont Stakes Day he has run even worse, taking the lead early and then fading badly. For the moment he is just another spear carrier in the spectacle to come. At the age of three, he has already passed his youth and prime. Few seem to notice him as he heads up the shed toward Secretariat, and no one asks his name.

At 4:07, Charlie Davis rides up on Billy Silver and reins him quickly to a stop. The Appaloosa gelding is no longer sore. He is standing still and waiting for Secretariat. Sweat has just fitted on the bridle. Now all is set.

From the crowd, then, there is a murmuring. "Here he comes," someone says. Edward Sweat is leading Secretariat up the aisle of Barn 5, past the rows of stalls, and toward the doorway at the end. The colt's head is down, he is moving relaxed. Ted McClain walks in front of him.

"Y'all are gonna have to step back from here now," says Ted.

It is 5:10, just a half hour to post time.

Leaving the shed, Secretariat's head comes up, as if he wants to stop, but he advances next to Sweat, his eyes flicking and his neck and head turned slightly to the left, his ears not playing and his teeth chewing on the bit, rolling it with his tongue and grinding down on it. He looks almost predatory. As he turns out of the shed, Sham and Pancho Martin cross the road in front of him and head through the tunnel to the paddock. Sweat's expression is stern. He says nothing to anyone, holding the bridle with his right hand. He is wearing his victory hat.

Racing official Frank Tours is walking directly behind Secretariat, five feet away, and blocking people from stepping on the heels of the colt. There are people all around him. A ten-year-old boy, darting in and out of the moving crowd, runs into Tours, who has his arms spread out.

Stay behind!" shouts Tours.

The entourage scuffs down the rubber-floored tunnel and rises to the paddock 200 yards away. Crowds line the fences. Sweat passes through the cyclone fence by the racing secretary's office, up the top of the incline to the paddock.

He enters the walking ring, which is lined twenty-deep in a circle around it and there is applause as he makes the circuit. Owners and trainers and syndicate members cluster in the grassy paddock shaded by a giant old white pine that is encircled by a row of park benches. The atmosphere is that of a garden party—women draped in chiffons and silks. Penny has descended, too, and so has Lucien, who is rubbing his hands nervously. A television camera beams down. Secretariat makes a circuit of the walking ring. Sweat takes him to his stall for saddling. Lucien fits on the blinkers and adjusts the bridle while CBS's Frank Wright comes by. "Lucien, the heat doesn't seem to be bothering him too much, does it?"

"No, I think . . ." What follows remains unclear. Caught shifting mentally between French and English, Lucien momentarily loses his capacity for articulate speech. He speaks unintelligibly, then regains command and says, "He used to be a little on edge and kick but today he's acting very good. Very quiet and very wonderful."

The jockeys come to the paddock—Danny Gargan for Pvt. Smiles, Braulio Baeza for Twice a Prince, Angel Cordero, Jr., for My Gallant, Laffit Pincay, Jr., for Sham, and Turcotte.

Turcotte and Laurin meet in the ring. They have already discussed the race, and Laurin is going over briefly what they have already talked about. "Now don't take him back too much, Ronnie. See how they're going. I've been looking at the record and many Belmonts have been won on the lead. If he wants to run early, let him. But don't send him. Don't choke him, either. . . . *Use ton propre jugement.*"

"Riders up!" yells the paddock judge.

Laurin lifts Turcotte aboard, wishing him luck, while the crowd around the ring ebbs back to the grandstand. The horses make one circuit and turn out of the ring and head through the tunnel to the track. Secretariat appears cool and dry, even in this heat, a contrast to Sham, who is washy wringing wet with perspiration.

At once they emerge in the clear light of the racetrack.

"Here he comes!" Jack Whitaker tells 30 million people.

As he leaves the tunnel, there are boos and applause following him up the racetrack, and then the band strikes up the Belmont song, "Sidewalks of New York," and the crowd stands and sings.

Looking around, Turcotte sees that none of the jockeys are warming up their horses. They are trying to relax them, he thinks, to keep them cool. Now he feels Secretariat moving almost dully, so he taps the colt with his whip and tries to wake him up. But Secretariat responds indifferently. Turcotte taps him again. The colt again reacts without enthusiasm.

"There's something wrong with him, Charlie," says Turcotte. "I tap him and he doesn't seem to want to move."

The other jockeys continue to go easy with their horses, not warming them up in the heat. So Turcotte decides to go to the front, if no one else wants to set the pace. He decides to prompt the pace from the outset. He has been thinking that Sham or My Gallant would be trying for the lead, but now he thinks they'll be taking back. So, he decides, he will press the issue. He will let the red horse go to the front.

He gallops Secretariat around the turn and back into the stretch. The horses are now filing toward the gate. The crowds are all out on the pavement, shoulder to shoulder, and there is a crackling excitement in the air. More applause builds, rises, ebbs.

This is what they've come to see, not only those at the racetrack but those watching on television. The horses load into the metal starting gates. Starter George Cassidy stands on a green platform by the rail twenty feet in front of the gate, and watches as the horses move one by one. The assistant starter takes Secretariat into the stall gate, then slams closed the door behind him. The colt stands calmly. They load Pvt. Smiles and My Gallant next to him and Twice a Prince. Then Sham. Anticipating the start, Secretariat drops into a crouch, lowering himself about six inches back on his hindlegs. They are all ready.

It is 5:38.

The five colts vault from the gate head and head, Secretariat leaving with them in three giant strides in which his forelegs and chest rise fully four feet in the air, breaking more sharply than he has ever broken in his life. The crowd is on its feet howling. Secretariat isn't falling back today, not as he usually does at the break, but rather picking up speed quickly and running with My Gallant through the first half dozen strides. He is racing with the field from the first jump. Looking to his left quickly Cordero sees the red horse grabbing the bit and running powerfully against it, and decides not to make an issue of the pace. Taking hold of My Gallant, Cordero drops the colt behind the red horse going to the turn. Other riders follow his lead. Baeza, outrun from the gate on Twice a Prince, lets the colt settle to find his stride. Gargan drops way out of it on Pvt. Smiles. But not Sham. Pincay hustles. He has been told to try for the lead on Sham,

316

so he rouses Sham from the outside post to loom up for the lead. The Belmont Stakes develops with a rush to the turn.

Folding up and keeping his hands still, Turcotte at once takes a snug hold of Secretariat. Glancing right, he sees Sham going for the lead and Cordero taking back on My Gallant. Now he has room on the rail. A hole stays open in front of him. Seeing the space, Turcotte keeps a hold of the colt while chirping to him. Secretariat responds, surging and accelerating to the turn. Sham joins him on the outside. Slipping to the left as the others fall back, Sham comes to the flanks of Secretariat. The crowd stays on its feet. The Belmont is a match race at the first turn. Sham is a head in front of Secretariat as they race past the 1 ⅜ pole, 220 yards out of the gate, and the jockeys are letting them go. The pair draws away, racing the opening eighth in 0:12 ⅕. They appear to be on their way to the beat of twelve, to that opening half-mile in 0:48 seconds that is the throne in the Belmont Stakes.

But then they pick up more speed, gathering momentum around the turn. Pincay seeks the lead, and now he moves to make an issue of it. Chirping, he urges Sham to keep pace with Secretariat. Turcotte, seeing Sham thrusting his head in front, and responding with more speed, sits and waits on Secretariat. The battle joined, Secretariat skimming the rail with Sham lapped right on him, the two begin to pull away from My Gallant.

They drive the bend as one. The crowd senses a fight and they roar them on. They're running as if it's a six-furlong sprint: they rush the second eighth in 0:11 ⅖. Pincay knows they're going too fast, senses Sham working too hard, but he presses on. He is under orders to challenge for the lead. Martin wants the red horse to run at Sham. Sommers's bay moves up faster on the turn, challenging and probing at Secretariat. The red horse forces the pace. He is sailing beside Sham. Pincay is waiting for Turcotte to take back on the red horse. But Turcotte is conceding nothing. He feels his colt is running easily so he gives him his head and let him roll for the turn.

Together they race the opening quarter in 0:23 ⅗, sharp time.

Now is the time to take back. Now they can give the colts a breather, time to settle down through two more eighths in 0:12 for that half in 0:48. But Pincay has not given up on gaining the lead. He tries for it again around the turn, urging Sham on. He goes to the lead by a full head. Then he is a neck in front. Then almost a half-length. They power past the 1 ⅛-pole. It is Sham's longest lead, and he battles to keep it. Secretariat gives him no time to relax. He contests every step of ground. He presses at Sham, keeping the pressure on him. And presses again. He's not letting him get away. They race the third furlong in 0:11 ⅖, still a sprinting pace, far too fast for this distance.

They have nine furlongs to go and they should be galloping. At this moment Turcotte could ease the pressure, but he does not. Turning for the backside, he lets Secretariat come to Sham again. Neither lets up. Unrestrained, they are sizzling along better than twelves to the eighth down the backside. The fractions pile up. Pincay keeps looking and hoping for Turcotte to take back on Secretariat. Turcotte, for himself, looks for Pincay to take back, letting Secretariat roll. He comes back to within a neck of Sham, picking up speed, then closes to a head-bobbing nose of him.

John Finney, standing in a box seat with syndicate member Bertram Firestone, senses what is happening now. As the two colts race to the mile-pole at the head of the backstretch, following the half-mile, his eyes turn to the toteboard teletimer. Finney blinks. And so does Lucien, who grows grim as the teletimer flashes frantically its message:

0:46 ⅕.

"They're going too fast!" Finney hollers to Firestone above the din. They have rushed through the fastest opening half-mile in the history of the Belmont Stakes.

What is Turcotte doing? What is he thinking about?

He is not thinking about the clock. He is simply sitting on Secretariat. He does not know how fast he's going. He knows he's rolling, yes—but he thinks the colt is running 12 seconds to the eighth, as Riva Ridge had run the year before, galloping the first half in 0:48. Secretariat is moving so effortlessly under him, not straining but moving well and doing it all on his own. The colt is awesome in the way he runs. He has been on the left lead around the turn, and as he banks and straightens into the backstretch, Turcotte feels the hitch in Secretariat's rhythmic stride: nine jumps into the backside straight, Secretariat has switched to the right lead—machinelike in the ease with which he does it—and levels out into long, smooth and powerful strides. The pressure of the pace becomes intense. Neither colt has eased off an instant from the start.

They race in tandem for the seven-eighths pole. Ahead of them, the backstretch opens to the far turn 800 yards away, wavering in furrows in the heat, wide and flat and empty. Turcotte feels the wind rushing his face, his silks billowing out behind him. Looking to the right, he sees the wet and lathering neck of Sham, whose nose is thrust out in a drive. Turcotte thinks Sham looks as if he's under strain. And he is. Pincay feels the colt not striding well. Ten lengths behind them, My Gallant and Twice a Prince are running head and head down the backside in a race of their own. Baeza, on Twice a Prince, looks ahead and sees the hindlegs of Sham beginning to come apart, swimming and rubbery, and for the first time thinks he might have a chance for the $33,000 in second money. It is only a matter of time, Baeza thinks, before Sham will drop back to him. Cordero has seen Sham in distress, too, and now he's trying hard for second money. So Baeza hollers to Cordero, who is riding next to him.

"I'm going to be second, man!"

"Screw you, man," Cordero says to Baeza. "You gotta beat me!"

Their race is on down the backstretch.

Secretariat races the fifth furlong in 0:12, giving him five-eighths of a mile in a sensational 0:58 ⅕. That eighth begins to pry him loose from Sham. Sham is already suffering. They are still running as if in a dash, faster than Spanish Riddle raced five furlongs in the fifth that day, faster than Man o' War and Count Fleet and Citation ran the first five furlongs in the Belmont Stakes. Secretariat is almost a length in front coming to the seven-eighths pole, with 1,540 yards to go. He has just dragged Sham through a second quarter-mile of the Belmont Stakes in 0:22 ⅗, then taken him out a fifth furlong in 0:12. He cannot maintain that clip. Yet, what has been seen is still only preliminary. Now he is delivering the coup de grace, the cruncher. Secretariat rushes through the sixth furlong and under the pressure of it Sham begins to disintegrate almost visibly. The crowd can see it, clamoring and shouting as Secretariat begins to pull away from Sham, opening a length and a half. He is picking up speed again, charging down the backside, his form flawless through the twenty-five-foot sweep of his strides—forelegs folding and snapping at the ground, the hindlegs scooting far under him and propelling him forward, the breathing deep and regular, the head and neck rising and dipping with the thrust and motion of the legs. Having chirped just once to force the pace at the first turn, Turcotte has done nothing since then to bring him where he is. Yet, he is racing through the sixth furlong in 0:11 ⅗, the crunching eighth, and opening two and a half lengths on Sham. Sham is finished with that eighth. He has been asked for more than he has. Secretariat sweeps past the three-quarter pole. Eyes swing to the teletimer:

1:09 ⅘.

There are gasps from the crowd. The reaction is almost universal. Finney is stunned.

"That's suicidal!" he yells to Bert Firestone. By almost one full second it is the fastest six furlongs ever run in the Belmont Stakes, and only 0:1 ⅕ seconds off the course record for that distance. In the box seats, Lucien has seen the splits and his face is rigid. His lips are pursed. His hands are on the box-seat railing. He understands the implications of the running time. So he waits, staring at his red horse bounding around the far turn.

Down on the racetrack, racing official Pat O'Brien stands by the finish line looking at the teletimer and his mind jumps back to that afternoon of June 15, 1957, when Bold Ruler raced through the first half-mile in 0:46 ⅘ and the three-quarters in a suicidal 1:10 ⅖ and almost stopped to a walk in the stretch, finally finishing third. Remembering that, O'Brien sees the sins of the father visited on the son.

Up in the press box, CBS' Gene Petersen hollers to *Racing Form* columnist Herb Goldstein, "He's going to win big, Herb!"

Goldstein, appalled by the fraction, shouts back: *"He's going too damn fast!"*

Dr. William Lockridge, the syndicate member, looks at the time from his place in the dining room at Belmont Park and excitedly climbs up on a chair and then onto the dining room table. The beginnings of pandemonium rock the place.

What is Turcotte doing? Has he gone mad?

He is still sitting cool on the turn, listening as Sham's hoofbeats fade away behind him. Turning around once to see who is coming, he sees them dropping back. Then he turns again.

He wonders how fast he's going. He suspects he is going fast enough. He has not cocked his whip, and he's still thinking he's traveling at the rate of 12 seconds to the eighth. He thinks he has gone the three-quarters in 1:12 and that he is doing the seven-eighths in 1:24 and coming to the mile mark in 1:36. It has all been working so beautifully for Turcotte. Secretariat has killed off Sham and now he's coasting home, far in front and getting farther. The colt is bounding along on his own. He has opened three lengths on Sham. Now four, now five. Then six. Turcotte turns again and sees them all far behind him. Now he is widening the lead to seven as he races on the turn and finishes the seventh furlong in 0:12 ⅕, giving him seven-eighths in 1:22, and banks around the turn through the eighth furlong in 0:12 $^1/_5$. Once again the crowd's eyes turn to the clocks and roll in their sockets:

1:34 $^1/_5$.

It is an incredible fraction, far faster than any horse has ever run the first mile in the Belmont Stakes. Goldstein stands awed by it. O'Brien wonders how Secretariat will be able to stand up at the end. Penny clenches her hands. Lucien remains quiet, still looking solemnly at the racetrack, across the hedge and the lakes and lawns to the far turn, where Turcotte rocks on across the back of Secretariat, listens to the beat of Secretariat's hooves on the racetrack and the sound of the 70,000 people screaming and moiling and echoing 600 yards away. Finney is boggled.

"He can't stand up to this!" he yells to Firestone.

In the announcer's booth, announcer Chick Anderson's voice is rising at the sight of it. Beneath him the crowd has grown deafening loud and rich, and Anderson gropes to articulate what he is witnessing.

"Secretariat is blazing along! The first three-quarters of a mile in 1:09 $^4/_5$. Secretariat is widening now. He is moving like a tremendous machine!"

The colt is in front by eight and by ten and now he is opening twelve over Sham, who is beginning to come back to My Gallant and Twice a Prince. Feeling the hopelessness, Pincay has decided not to persevere with Sham. He feels the Sommer colt is in distress and so he coasts rearward. Turcotte wheels Secretariat around the turn. All Turcotte hears is the sound of Secretariat walloping the earth and taking deep breaths of air and then, to the right, the lone voice of a man calling to him from the hedge by the fence.

"You got it, Ronnie! Stay there."

The poles flash by, one after another, and Secretariat continues widening his lead—to fourteen and then fifteen lengths midway of the turn. Then sixteen. Seventeen. Eighteen. He does not back off. He never slows a moment as he sweeps the turn and races to ever-widening leads, battering at the ground with mechanistic precision.

Finney and Laurin and all the others are watching for some sign that Secretariat is weakening, for some evidence that the pace is beginning to hurt, for the stride to shorten or the tail to slash or the ears to lay back fast to the skull. But there are no signs of weariness. Racing past the three-eighths pole—midway of the turn for home, with 660 yards to go—Secretariat is racing faster than he was past the half-mile pole on the turn. He flashes by the pole one and one eighth miles into the race—1:46 ⅕!

Secretariat has just tied the world record for nine furlongs. He is running now as if in contempt of the clock. Those watching him begin to comprehend the magnitude of effort. He is moving beyond the standard by which the running horse has been traditionally judged, not tiring, not leg weary, not backing up a stroke, dimensionless in scope, and all the time Turcotte asking nothing of him. The crowds continue to erupt. Looking, Turcotte sees the hands shoot up in the grandstand, the thousands on their feet, hundreds lining the rail of the homestretch with the programs waving and the hands clapping and the legs jumping.

He is still galloping to the beat of twelve. Aglide, he turns for home in full flight. He opens twenty-one lengths. He increases that to twenty-two. He is running easily. Nor is the form deteriorating. There remains the pendulumlike stride of the forelegs and the drive of the hindlegs, the pumping of the shoulders and the neck, the rise and dip of the head. He makes sense of all the mystical pageant rites of blood through which he has evolved as distillate, a climactic act in a triumph of the breed, one horse combining all the noblest qualities of his species and his ancestry—of the unbeaten Nearco through Nasrullah and Bold Ruler, of the iron horse Discovery through Outdone and Miss Disco, of the dashing St. Simon through Prince Rose and Princequillo and of the staying Brown Bud through Imperatrice by way of Somethingroyal. He defines the blooded horse in his own terms.

He sweeps into the stretch through a tenth furlong in 0:12 ⅘, the slowest eighth yet, and Turcotte is still holding him together—his black boots pressed against the upper back, moving with the rocky motion of the legs, his hands feeling the mane blown back against the fingers and the knuckles pressed white against the rubber-thick reins. The teletimer flashes 1:59 for the mile and a quarter, two-fifths faster than his Derby, faster than the Belmont ten-furlong record by a full second.

He is twenty-three lengths in front. He lengthens that to twenty-four. And then to twenty-five, the record victory margin held by Count Fleet since 1943.

He is not backing up yet.

Once again he picks up the tempo in the upper stretch, racing the eleventh furlong in 0:12 ⅕, as fast as he has run the opening 220 yards of the race. That furlong gives him a mile and three-eighths in 2:11 ⅕, three seconds faster than Man o' War's world record set in the Belmont Stakes fifty-three years before. Obliterating Count Fleet's record, Secretariat opens twenty-six lengths. He widens that to twenty-seven and twenty-eight. He comes to the eighth pole in midstretch, and the whole of Belmont Park is roaring full-throatedly. The television camera sweeps the stands and hands are shooting in the air. No one can remember anything quite like it, not even the oldest veteran. No one applauds during the running of a race, but now the crowds in the box seats and the grandstand are standing as one and clapping as Secretariat races alone through the homestretch. They've come to see a coronation, America's ninth Triple Crown winner, but many are beginning to realize that they are witnessing the greatest single performance in the history of the sport. Veteran horsemen are incredulous. Eyes have turned to and from the teletimer and the horse in disbelief, looking for some signs of stress and seeing nothing but the methodical rock of the form and the reach and snap of the forelegs. For a moment in midstretch, as the sounds envelop him, even Turcotte is caught off guard by the scope of the accomplishment. Passing the eighth pole, he looks to the left at the infield tote and the teletimer, and the first number he sees is 1:09 ⅘ for the first three-quarters. He sees these numbers but they fail to register. So he looks ahead again. Then they register and he looks back again, in a delayed double take.

By now he has passed the sixteenth pole, with only seventy-five yards to run, and the crowd senses the record, too. Turcotte looks at the teletimer blinking excitedly and sees 2:19, 2:20. The record is 2:26 ⅗. The colt has a chance to break the record in all three classics —an unprecedented feat. So, keeping his whip uncocked, Turcotte pumps his arm and hand-rides Secretariat through the final yards. Sham fades back to last, and Twice a Prince and My Gallant are head and head battling for the place—Cordero and Baeza are riding all out to the wire—but Secretariat continues widening on them.

To twenty-nine lengths.

Turcotte scrubs and pushes on Secretariat and he lengthens the margin to thirty lengths. The wire looms. The teletimer flashes crazily. All eyes are on it and on the horse. Many horsemen have seen Turcotte looking at the timer and now they're looking at it too. He is racing the clock, his only competitor, and he is beating it badly as he rushes the red horse through the final yards. At the end, the colt dives for the wire. The teletimer blinks the last time and then it stops, as though it has been caught in midair—2:24.

He hits the wire thirty-one lengths in front of Twice a Prince, with Sham finishing last, forty-five lengths behind.

The sounds of the crowd have gathered in the run through the straight and now they burst forth in one stentorian howl. Secretariat has just shattered three records in the Triple Crown, this mile-and-a-half record by two and two-fifths seconds, and Turcotte stands up at the wire and lets him gallop out an extra eighth to the turn. Even easing up he eclipses records through his momentum. Clocker Sonny Taylor catches him going the final eighth in 0:13 3/5, giving the colt a mile and five-eighths in an unofficial 2:37 3/5, time that would shatter Swaps's world mark by three-fifths of a second. He has strung together a phenomenal run of eighths—0:12 1/5, 0:11 2/5, 0:11 2/5, 0:11 1/5, 0:12, 0:11 3/5, 0:12 1/5, 0:12 1/5, 0:12, 0:12 4/5, 0:12 1/5, 0:12 4/5. Incredibly, none of them is slower than 0:12 4/5.

Turcotte pulls him to a halt on the turn. Jim Dailey, the outrider who met Gaffney on the colt a year before, meets him now on the bend. He has not seen the teletimer.

"How fast you go?"

"Two twenty-four flat," Turcotte yells back to him.

"You're crazy."

"I'm telling you!" says Turcotte.

"Can't be."

Turcotte turns the horse around at the bend. With Dailey riding a pony beside him, he begins a slow gallop past the stands and the clubhouse. Ovations ripple and accompany him home. Acknowledging them, Turcotte doffs his helmet as he did at the Derby and brings down the house, prompting even more thunderous cheering and applause.

On the racetrack, Hollis Chenery greets Secretariat and Turcotte outside the winner's circle, and Chenery takes hold of the lead shank and brings them into the circle. The reception of the crowd is electric.

They lean over the flower boxes down the victory lane; long, braceleted arms reach out for him. Hands slap his glistening coat. Hands shoot up in fists. Hands are cupped over faces. Hands are holding hands and gesturing elation and awe. The clapping and the shouts of encouragement—to Turcotte and Laurin, to Penny and Secretariat—come in endless waves, and they follow them all through the winner's circle ceremony. Eddie Sweat takes the colt and walks him home, passing the crowds that line the winner's circle, the governors and racing officials, and heading back to the mouth of the tunnel. Thousands of people line the tunnel and send up cheers as

324

Sweat and Secretariat pass. Men and women of all ages holler boisterously to Sweat and clap their hands. Sweat nods his head and smiles and raises his fist in the air. As he makes his way home through the paddock, the crowds are waiting for him everywhere. The colt is sweating heavily as he slants around the walking ring of the paddock, his nostrils moist and warm and flaring. Beads of sweat trickle down his head and neck, his eyes dart left and right. The crowds shout his name over and over as he walks past them.

As Sweat leads the colt around the paddock, he passes trainer Elliott Burch, who is waiting to saddle a horse in the race following the Belmont. His patron, Paul Mellon, owns a share in Secretariat. Burch's face is flushed with excitement. His arms are folded and he turns to follow Secretariat as he goes by. He has never seen such a performance, and he calls out, "Spectacular! Just sensational!"

Burch is one of many horsemen, young and old, who would claim that they had witnessed, on a sultry afternoon in June, the greatest single performance ever by a running horse, an unprecedented feat of power, grace, and speed. The chorus is large and vocal in their claims of that, and among them are Alfred Vanderbilt and Woody Stephens, Buddy Hirsch and Sherrill Ward, P. G. Johnson and Arthur Kennedy. Charles Hatton is calling Secretariat the greatest horse he has ever seen, in sixty years of covering and observing the American turf, greater even than Man o' War.

"His only point of reference is himself," Hatton says.

That evening they all leave the racetrack rethinking their old notions and beliefs on the standards of greatness in the thoroughbred. The impact of the victory is felt everywhere. The effect of the Belmont on the value of the colt is instantaneous. As much as $500,000 is offered for a single share. Vanderbilt sells half his share to his friends, the Whitneys of Greentree—John Hay Whitney and Mrs. Charles Shipman Payson, who were offered but turned down a share originally—for the $190,000 purchase price, but only because he is their friend. All others hold on to their entire shares in the immediate wake of the Belmont, knowing that a foal by Secretariat out of a stakes-winning mare could bring $500,000 at auction. Secretariat, like his sire, is virtually not for sale.

The victors raise a thousand toasts that night. Penny and Lucien and the Meadow Stable party meet at the barn. As the colt is being cooled out following the triumph, Lucien comes through the gate into the stable paddock and is cheered lustily by the stable grooms and hot walkers who have stayed behind to greet and congratulate him. Turcotte arrives and he is cheered, too, and so is Penny Tweedy.

At Fasig-Tipton's central office, across the street from the racetrack, the company's clients are gathered over a case of champagne. They are toasting the victors. Among them is Howard Gilman, whose paper company owns a share of Secretariat only because John Galbreath turned his share down. Howard Gilman offers a toast to Fasig-Tipton for having encouraged the company to buy the share, and so the glasses are raised and the clientele sip a salute to the company for its wisdom and sagacity. And then John Finney offers a countertoast. He raises his glass and says, "The toast should properly be to John Galbreath. If he had not declined his share, you would not have gotten it."

They all agree and drink a toast to him.

"Thanks to John Galbreath."

Epilogue

The L-188 Electra banked in over Lexington, its four turboprop engines whining and vibrating loudly as it slowed for landing, and Elizabeth Ham stood dressed in her Persian lamb coat and fur hat, holding to Secretariat's stall in the center aisle of the plane. Strapped into a narrow stall directly behind Riva Ridge, Secretariat was nibbling hay.

It was November 12, 1973, and Secretariat was returning home to Claiborne Farm in Paris, Kentucky, where he had been conceived almost five years before. He may have been born to be a racehorse, the culmination and coming together of the richest and most prepotent thoroughbred bloodlines in America, but already the best years of his life lay behind him. At the age of three, he was being consumed by the industry that had raised and made him worth ten times his weight in gold. Composed and collected to the point of indifference, Secretariat waited quietly in the stall.

"It's a shame Mr. Chenery isn't here to see him," said Elizabeth Ham. "But if Mr. Chenery *were* here to see him, Secretariat wouldn't be here. He wouldn't be going to the farm. He would be racing again next year."

That was the shame of it. The Belmont Stakes, ultimately viewed by more than 50 million people during the live telecast and on countless news accounts of it that evening, had made Secretariat the most celebrated and popular racehorse of all time. He became the client of the William Morris Agency, joining all the other sex symbols of the era, and a valuable commercial property to Penny Tweedy and the estate of C. T. Chenery. He began receiving hundreds of letters, many from young girls and old men wishing him well and thanking him for the memories. And there were offers to do photos of the colt and books and statues and lithographs, records and posters and public appearances on television. Sonny and Cher, for instance, made an offer for Secretariat to appear. But that would have made it necessary to van him to Manhattan and then lead him into a studio and onto an open stage.

The idea was rejected as too risky and not in keeping with his image as a racehorse. Penny was also offered $25,000 by a Las Vegas gambling casino and nightclub for Secretariat to appear twice a day, fifteen minutes each time, in front of a nightclub audience. But that was rejected, too. Then Hazel Park Racetrack, a small oval outside Detroit, offered $25,000 if Secretariat would parade in front of the stands on a weekend—not in a race, just in a walk. But that, also, was turned down as inappropriate. There were many bizarre offers, too, such as the one to merchandise his manure by encapsulating it in transparent plastic discs three inches long and selling the discs as conversation pieces. That was also turned down.

Most of all, though, the nation's racetracks coveted him as a drawing card. His appeal was tremendous and nationwide, not only among horseplayers but among the laymen who had never seen a race. Hazel Park was but one that wanted to bring him to their grounds. There were others, and among them was Arlington Park in Arlington Heights, Illinois. Secretariat was supposed to rest until the opening of Saratoga in August, according to Penny and Lucien immediately following the Belmont, and in fact was being pointed for the Jim Dandy Stakes for three-year-olds and then the Summer Derby, the one-and-a-quarter-mile Travers Stakes. But the Arlington offer, as it would turn out, was too lucrative to pass up. So Penny opted to take him there.

Arlington offered to put up $125,000 and arrange a match race between Secretariat and Linda's Chief, Secretariat's old Sanford rival, who had been running extremely well while avoiding the red horse. It fell through when Linda's Chief was withdrawn—his trainer, Al Scotti, later said he never wanted to run Linda's Chief against Secretariat—so Arlington Park hastily rounded up three other spear carriers to meet him going a mile and an eighth on June 30, three weeks after the Belmont Stakes. In a way, it was a symbolic beginning of his career following the Belmont Stakes, a career in which his power as a celebrity and drawing card grew strong enough to affect the course of his career and fortunes as a racehorse.

328

For the Arlington exhibition, Lucien brought him out of easy training, jammed two quick drills into him and then shipped him to the Windy City track outside Chicago. Thousands turned out to see him gallop. the day before the race, and more came out to see him run. They were not disappointed. Secretariat, staying twenty feet off the racetrack rail around two turns, casually galloped to a nine-length victory while just missing Damascus's track record by a fifth of a second. The red horse ran the distance in 1:47. Returned to New York, Secretariat was kept in serious training through July, in preparation for the Whitney Stakes at Saratoga. But he failed to train sharply for it. Then the Phillip Morris Company announced that Secretariat and Riva Ridge would be meeting in a match race September 15, called the Marlboro Cup. The company was putting up the purse of $250,000. Secretariat's Belmont Stakes was beginning to draw big money to the sport. But all through Secretariat's training in July, Turcotte kept telling friends privately that the colt was not himself—his workouts through July, in fact, were the least impressive of his entire career. In the week leading to the Whitney, August 4, he was running a slight temperature and his bowels were loose and watery. Then, on July 27, he raced a mile in training in a sensational 1:34 seconds. That day, Turcotte and Frank Tours drove back to Long Island together in Tours's Cadillac. Turcotte was plainly worried.

"You're going to think I'm crazy, Frank, but I don't believe that work," Turcotte told Tours. "There's something wrong with that colt. He's just not himself."

The pressure was on Laurin and Penny to run Secretariat in the Whitney Stakes. Network television and the New York Racing Association had agreed to televise four races—the $50,000 Whitney, the $250,000 Marlboro Cup, the $100,000 Woodward Stakes, and the $100,000 two-mile Jockey Club Gold Cup—in the hopes that Secretariat would take them one at a time. In anticipation of Secretariat's arrival, Saratoga draped Main Street in blue and white bunting. It was Secretariat Month in upstate New York. Tourist trade was lively. Four days before the Whitney, Laurin had Turcotte work the colt a half mile, and 5000 persons showed up early in the morning at the racetrack to watch him. Never had so many people come to see a horse work out. Penny was getting letters from New Englanders saying that they were planning their vacations around seeing him in the Whitney. The race itself looked like a soft touch, but it wasn't. Trainer H. Allen Jerkens had his chestnut Onion ready to run the race of his life, and that was all that was needed to defeat an ailing Secretariat.

Running well out from the rail for most of the trip, Secretariat tracked the pacesetters to the far turn. When Turcotte set him down, he never fired—certainly not as he had fired in the Triple Crown races that spring. He appeared dull, and he ran dully, without the punch he had at Pimlico and Churchill Downs. He and Onion hooked in the stretch, with Secretariat on the rail, but the red horse couldn't get by him in the drive, and in the final yards Onion pulled away to beat him by a length. The next day Secretariat was running a temperature. He was in and out of training for the rest of August. Secretariat's veterinarian, Mark Girard, said that he was probably incubating a virus prior to the race.

Laurin had him walk for several days at a time. He began to recover slowly at the end of August, and Laurin worked him for the first time on August 30, sending him five-eighths of a mile in 1:00 3/s. He was not training well.

Time was running out for the Marlboro Cup. Secretariat was to face the finest racehorses in America. The match race had been expanded since the Phillip Morris Company had announced it in July. Not only had Secretariat lost in the Whitney, Riva Ridge had also lost in a turf race at Saratoga. That meant a match race would be between two horses who had both finished second in their last starts. So the two-horse match race was abandoned, and the field was thrown open to all. Now it included Riva Ridge and Key to the Mint, champions Cougar II and Kennedy Road and the winner of the Travers Stakes, Annihilate 'Em, as well as Onion and Secretariat.

Laurin worked Secretariat seven-eighths in 1:24 4/s, an unsatisfactory work at Belmont Park on September 3, and then sent him a mile in 1:37 four days later, still unsatisfactory. Riva Ridge was training more sharply for the Marlboro, and for a while it seemed that Secretariat wouldn't make it. His last major drill was scheduled for September 12, the Wednesday before the Saturday of the race. There, Laurin put the zinger into him, the sharpener on which he always thrived. With Turcotte aboard, the colt raced five-eighths in 0:57, one of the fastest workouts in New York all year, and galloped out six furlongs in 1:08 4/s, just a fifth of a second off the track record for that distance. That was all Lucien needed.

"I think he's back," Lucien said. And he was back. He returned dancing to the barn. Though elated with the move, Laurin also wished publicly that he had just one more week to get him ready. He

330

had been forced to drive four workouts into him in two weeks. They would have ruined an ordinary horse, but Secretariat improved off of each one and came to the Marlboro almost as fit as he was for the Kentucky Derby. Turcotte knew Secretariat was back, and it was only a question of how far away he was from his peak. Given the choice of riding either Secretariat or Riva Ridge, he chose the red horse.

"I think you picked the wrong horse," said Penny.

"No. I might have picked the wrong day, but not the wrong horse," Turcotte replied.

He was the old Secretariat on the day of the Marlboro Cup, though Andrew Beyer would maintain he was not as sharp as he was for any of the Triple Crown races. With Turcotte snugging down the backstretch, with Onion racing on the lead through a quarter mile in 0:22 ³/₅ and a half mile in 0:45 ³/₅, jockey Eddie Maple on Riva Ridge just outside of him, Secretariat was bounding along with his head bowed. As they came to the pole midway of the turn, Riva Ridge drove to the front through six furlongs in a sparkling 1:09 ¹/₅. Onion was still on the rail, Riva Ridge outside of him. Turcotte let out a notch on the reins, and Secretariat rushed to Riva Ridge's side. Turcotte was ecstatic with the move.

"They were a field of champions and he was just toying with them," said Turcotte.

Turning for home, ranging on the outside, Turcotte let the red horse roll. Riva Ridge could not resist. Secretariat went by him quickly and pulled away through the lane, opening two lanes at the eighth pole through a mile in a sensational 1:33, by three-fifths of a second the fastest mile ever run at Belmont Park. He opened three and a half lengths at the wire, racing the mile and a eighth in 1:45 ²/₅, lowering the world's record by four-fifths of a second.

Riva Ridge was second, two lengths in front of Cougar II.

On went the campaign. Laurin pointed Riva Ridge for the one-and-a-half-mile Woodward Stakes September 29, two weeks later, and he aimed Secretariat for the Man o' War Stakes at a mile and a half on the turf course at Belmont Park. Obviously preparing Secretariat for the grass race, he sent him over the turf at Belmont Park on September 21 in a leisurely 0:48 ³/₅ for a half mile, just to let him get used to it. Four days later, still aiming for the Man o' War on October 8, Laurin let Secretariat go a mile on the grass, this time in 1:38, for Secretariat a casual mile compared with that drill for the Belmont Stakes last June in 1:34 ⁴/₅. Then, three days later, Laurin entered both Secretariat and Riva Ridge in the Woodward. The intent was to run Riva Ridge if the track was fast, Secretariat if the track came up sloppy. Riva Ridge could not handle an off track. As fate would have it, it rained the night before the race, and the track was a sea of mud. Laurin then scratched Riva Ridge, and he sent a more vulnerable Secretariat in his place. Secretariat had not been training seriously for the Woodward—he had just gone that easy half mile and an easy mile, both on the grass. More, he was not given the zinger that was a prelude to all his greatest races as a three-year-old. Laurin had broken the pattern. Secretariat had been thrown into the breach to substitute for his stablemate. Trainer Allen Jerkens, who had brought Onion to the Whitney Stakes and was regarded as the most brilliant of all trainers of America, had the four-year-old colt Prove Out ready to run the greatest race of his life.

Secretariat set the pace for most of the way, racing through a half mile in 0:50 and the three-quarters in a casual 1:13 $^2/s$. Jockey Jorge Velasquez, riding Prove Out, stalked Secretariat to the turn for home and then drove to him with a burst of speed that swept them into the lead through the straight. Tiring through the stretch, Secretariat couldn't catch him, and Prove Out opened a length and a half at the eighth pole and almost five lengths at the wire in 2:25 $^4/s$ for the mile and a half, almost two seconds slower than Secretariat's track record for the distance.

Secretariat was blowing heavily when he came back to the unsaddling area. "He just got a little tired," said Turcotte, as he dismounted.

It was the last time the colt would ever lose. Lucien went back to the old pattern for the Man o' War Stakes. Six days after the Woodward, on the Friday before the Monday of the race, he boosted Turcotte aboard for the zinger. It was one of the fastest workouts ever seen on any turf course.

The splits were startling. He went the opening eighth in 0:11 and the second eighth in 0:11 $^2/s$, giving Secretariat a quarter in 0:22 $^2/s$. They drove another eighth in 0:11 $^4/s$ and another in a sensational 0:10 $^4/s$, giving him a half mile in 0:45, and a final eighth in 0:11 $^4/s$ for five-eighths in 0:56 $^4/s$, only four-fifths off the world's record for the distance on the grass. He went out the last eighth in 0:12 $^1/s$, giving him three-quarters in 1:09. So Secretariat was ready once again, and this time to race the best grass horse in America at a mile and a half, the four-year-old handicap star Tentam. Secretariat carried 121 pounds, 5 pounds less than the older Tentam.

He made it look easy. Turcotte was coasting on the lead, bounding along through the mile in 1:36, when Tentam started to move to him. Secretariat toyed with Tentam. As they turned for home, through a mile and a quarter in 2:00 flat, Tentam came to Secretariat, but Turcotte let out on the reins and pulled away through the stretch, winning by five lengths and breaking the track record. The pattern of the zinger held again, its final time, when Laurin and Penny decided to ship Secretariat north to Canada for his final start in the Canadian International at one and five-eighths miles, the longest distance he would ever run, on the grass course at Woodbine Race Course. Turcotte worked him five-eighths three days before the race, and Secretariat rushed through it in 0:57 ⅗, a full second faster than the track mark around a plastic fence set out twenty-eight feet from the rail to protect the turf course for the races. Canadian clockers were astonished at the move. They had never seen so fast a run at Woodbine.

It was merely a foreshadowing. In the race itself Secretariat was brilliant. It was run in a cold drizzle on October 28, just eighteen days before the syndication contract required that he be at Claiborne Farm. Only one thing would be missing in the International. Following the spectacular workout on Wednesday, Turcotte returned to New York and learned he had been suspended for careless riding in a race unrelated to Secretariat. The days of the suspension would include the day of the Canadian race. Turcotte's friend, jockey Eddie Maple, was assigned the mount on Secretariat. If it was any consolation, Turcotte got a job announcing for television at the race.

Secretariat had little trouble handling the International field. He raced Kennedy Road head and head into the far turn, and when the champion drifted out and bumped him going to the turn, he got mad. Maple had to steady him a moment, but once he was free Secretariat bounded away. He opened five lengths quickly on the turn, and by the time he turned for home—with steam puffing from his nostrils —he was in front by twelve. He rolled on under Maple through the stretch, winning by almost seven.

It was over that quickly. The victory in the Canadian International brought to a close a brief but remarkable career which many veterans —Charles Hatton and aging horse-man Hollie Hughes among them —thought greater than Man o' War's. Hatton had waited a lifetime for Secretariat, and he'd finally found him. The colt's career was an affirmation of it. Secretariat was leaving the racetrack with twenty-one career starts in which he finished first sixteen times, was second three times, and third once. He was fourth his first start, the farthest he had been behind his field.

He had won $1,316,808 in his lifetime, making him the fourth leading money-winning thoroughbred of all time, though he raced only two years. But beyond the statistical sheets and the gross income statements, beyond the track and world records and the imposing margins of victory, he left behind a feeling among those who saw him that they had witnessed a natural phenomenon. He had style, and when he was himself, he made it almost art. Many veteran horsemen, from New York starter George Cassidy to the *Racing Form*'s chief of clockers, Gene Schwartz, rated him above Man o' War among the horses they had seen. They were not alone.

"He's the greatest horse I've ever seen," said Charles Hatton. "He's the greatest horse that anyone has ever seen. Don't let anyone kid you. He could do anything, and he could do it better than any horse I ever saw. No question about it in my mind. He should never had been beaten."

"He's the fastest horse I've ever seen," said Eddie Arcaro.

"He's the horse of the century," said Hollie Hughes. "His performances are superior to any horse I've ever seen, and that includes Man o' War. Secretariat has done far more. Man o' War didn't beat older horses except for one, Sir Barton, and he was all wore out and ready for the grave by then. Secretariat is far better than any horse I ever saw. The Belmont? It astounded me. I couldn't think of anything like that I had ever seen. No one has ever seen anything like that in this century. He was the horse of the century."

They held a special formal farewell to him at Aqueduct on November 6, a crisp autumn day of bright yellow sun and overcoats drawn up above the necks. Ed Sweat and Charlie Davis, along with Billy Silver, brought him to the Big A that afternoon to parade between the races. Old horseplayers and young girls draped themselves over the paddock fence at Aqueduct and watched and listened to the ceremonies. "Goodbye, Secretariat—We Love You," said one sign. Sweat led the red horse around, and speeches were made. Vanderbilt spoke, and so did Racing Association President Jack Krumpe and Penny Tweedy, who was dressed in a dark fur coat and holding a dozen roses and speaking into a microphone. Her voice echoed throughout the clubhouse and grandstand: "Having a horse like Secretariat is something that you pray might happen to you once in a lifetime, and we've loved every minute of it."

In one way or another, Secretariat touched the lives of many people in many ways, and they were different for it. Penny had become a public figure, and she was on her way to being an ambassador for the sport, a speaker and spokeswoman. As she spoke that afternoon at Aqueduct, her marriage was almost over. Jack Tweedy had changed jobs and moved to California the summer past, following Secretariat's Belmont Stakes, and Penny stayed east with Secretariat. The days as Jack Tweedy's housewife and cocktail party companion in Denver were behind her, and she knew it then, though she would not announce the divorce until early 1974.

As they gathered in the winner's circle, as the speeches were made, Lucien Laurin stood shivering with his hands in his pockets and near tears, pale, bent over, and looking, for the first time, like a man grown suddenly old with his responsibilities. He had endured the most formidable strain of the sport, first with Riva Ridge and then with Secretariat. After forty years on the racetrack—after the years as a jockey fighting weight, after the years of disbarment and then training in the hovels of the sport, after all the years spent building up a practice in New York—he came to the races at the age of sixty and survived. If he had miscalculated in the Wood Memorial, in the Whitney and the Woodward, he did his best and most brilliant work when it mattered, through the Triple Crown, displaying a kind of genius in the weeks before the Belmont Stakes.

He remained through all of this a partisan of Riva Ridge, his first good horse, his first Derby horse, and even in the end he seemed unable to comprehend the dimensions of Secretariat's greatness. Charles Hatton once estimated that Secretariat was twenty pounds the better horse, but Lucien never seemed to recognize that. Before the Marlboro Cup, Lucien said of Secretariat, astonishingly, "The more I keep training this horse, the more I'm doing with him, the more I'm getting to believe that he's the greatest horse *I have ever trained.*" And even after the race, even after Secretariat blew past Riva Ridge with such authority, Laurin told Turcotte and Eddie Maple in the stable office, "I still think Riva Ridge can beat Secretariat." Turcotte looked at Maple, who smiled and said nothing, and told Lucien, "From a quarter mile to a mile and a quarter, you name the bet. $1000? $2000?"

Eddie Sweat waited by the fence for Secretariat, holding the lead shank as Ron Turcotte cantered the colt up the homestretch by the cheering fans. Sweat had come a long way from the rural backwaters of Holly Hill, South Carolina. In three years he had become the most famous groom in America, a symbol of Secretariat with whom many would identify. In the end, he was the one person the colt visibly responded to, the one he recognized and waited for. "I'll miss him," said Eddie, as Secretariat went past. "This is a hurting thing to me. I'm so sad I didn't even want to bring him over here. It's been a wonderful two years. Now it seems like my whole career has ended." What he had beside the memories was the victory hat, the symbol of the three-year-old campaign. The day after the Canadian International, as he sat at home in Queens with his wife, Linda, Sweat was clutching the hat and looking at the label inside of it. Linda was reading a letter when she looked up and saw him.

"You got a girl's phone number in that hat?" she asked.

"I'm gonna retire my hat," he said.

"You're what?"

"I'm retiring my hat. This hat is now retired."

"That's stupid," she said.

"It's not stupid. A lot of people retire their hats."

And so he did. Linda helped him, showing him how to press it down and fold it for a frame.

On the racetrack, as the applause followed the colt, Turcotte stood in the stirrups and went easily with him, rocking with the stride and holding fast to the reins. It would be the last time that he would ever ride Secretariat. On his back, Turcotte had come into his own in the last two years. He would not be recognized in America for his accomplishments, even in his most successful year. But he would be feted in his native Canada. Turcotte had endured the pressures of the Triple Crown—the first jockey since Eddie Arcaro to win it. Though he had ridden two other champions of 1974, Riva Ridge and Talking Picture, and was the leading rider in New York, the toughest circuit in the world, the turfwriters and racing officials chose to honor Laffit Pincay, Jr., with the Eclipse Award, the industry's Oscar, for being the first jockey in history to win over $4 million in purses. Yet, in his native land, the Queen of England would bestow upon Turcotte the Order of Canada, one of the nation's highest honors, and that to him was worth five Eclipse awards. When he climbed down from his mount on November 6 at Aqueduct, he was convinced he had had the good fortune to ride the greatest horse that ever lived.

Not all remained with memories so fond. Of the thousands who were at Aqueduct that day, one was Frank Martin. He was wearing the same hat he wore those mornings at Churchill Downs, when he was soliloquizing about Laurin and Sham. It had been a long year. The Belmont was the culmination of a four-part horror show that began when Sham failed to fire in the Wood Memorial. For the Sommers, too, Sigmund and Viola, the classics had been an ordeal. The day following the Belmont Stakes, the Sommers came to see Sham at the barn. They looked tired.

"I was humiliated," said Mrs. Sommer, standing by the car.

"I went home last night and got drunk and cried," said Sigmund Sommer. He was wearing a white shirt with the SS monogram over his heart.

Now it was five months later, and Martin had not forgotten. Sham, the colt who was to take the place of Autobiography in the Sommer barn, had fractured a leg at Belmont Park months before. He was operated on and retired to stud at the Spendthrift Farm on Iron Works Pike, off the road to Paris. Martin was leaving the paddock when the ceremonies were taking place, a cigar jammed in his mouth and his hands plunged into his jacket pockets.

"I'm just sorry it's not Sham," he said, and walked away.

Others were affected, too. Gaffney was selling mutuel tickets on the day of the farewell, still sorry at what had happened to him on that Friday following the Preakness Stakes. He had been the first to recognize the colt on the racetrack, the first Secretariat fan and booster, and he had missed the greatest glory of all. In Angle Light there was another quiet ending. Following the Wood Memorial, he never won again. Eventually he broke down. Whittaker retired him to the stud in Kentucky, and he began there with a fee of $3500 for a service. The advertisements in the breeding magazines would announce, predictably, that he was the colt who had beaten Secretariat in the Wood. That race had helped to earn him the life of leisure at the stud, giving him an identity all his own.

Whittaker's life had changed, too. He never got over the Derby experience, and the aggravation of that week ruined the game for him. He would speak, at times, as if he was still wondering what had hit him. "So I had one little horse, okay? And she had a lot of them. And here she is, has everything that she could want in the horse racing business—top friends, the publicity, the wonderful horse she had, and here she is, telling one guy, with one horse, to pick up his marbles and go home. Why?"

They played "Auld Lang Syne" at the farewell ceremony, as Turcotte galloped Secretariat up the stretch, and Henny Hoeffner and Ed Sweat met him as Turcotte rode him back.

"Eddie," said Henny, after the saddle was taken off. "Go right back to the truck with him. He don't need anything. He doesn't know what he's doin' out here with all this applause."

And Ed Sweat led him off the racetrack for the last time.

As the L-188 came into Lexington, the airport tower called to pilot Dan Neff, "There's more people out here to meet Secretariat than there was to greet the governor." To which Neff replied, "Well, he's won more races than the governor."

The cargo door opened to Lexington and more than 300 persons gathered on the grass of the Blue Grass Airport to greet them. Among them was Seth Hancock. Ed Sweat led Secretariat down the ramp and walked after Seth, who took them to a small orange Claiborne Farm van. From there the procession, with police lights blinking, began for Paris. It was a bright, chilly afternoon, and all down the Paris Pike out of Lexington the leaves were falling and the countryside was alive with change. Pregnant mares were sniffing at the fields of grass, stallions romped the pastures, the foals were weaned and the yearlings in training. There was a sense of renewal in the air.

The cars and the vans filed slowly across the railroad tracks and up the Winchester Road in Paris, which lay half asleep. The vans pulled into the stone gates and edged up Kennedy Creek, to the office and the loading ramp. By now Seth was out directing traffic. Beyond the ramp was the black creosote breeding shed. Next to the office, just fifty feet away, were the gravestones of the greatest of the Claiborne stallions, from Sir Gallahad to Bold Ruler. It had been seventy years since Arthur Hancock, Sr., married Nancy Clay and moved from Ellerslie, and these graves stood like monuments to the empire that he had built and passed on to Bull, and that Bull had passed to Seth, who was standing on the loading ramp and watching the gates come open on the van. It was there, from the same ramp, that Bold Ruler was loaded and destroyed almost three years before.

Lawrence Robinson was at the colt's head inside the van.

"Want to wait on Mrs. Tweedy?" asked Lawrence. Penny had been held up.

"No, I want to get him in his stall now," said Seth. "You ready, Lawrence? Let's go. Good, Lawrence."

In a moment, Secretariat was out of the van and on the ramp and turning and walking off, across the grassy field to the breeding shed, and then past the shed and down the path to the stallion barn. At one point he wheeled, kicked Robinson, snorted, and turned to walk off again.

At the white and orange cinder block stallion barn, Robinson led the colt inside and turned him into the first stall, freshly bedded with straw. Across from him was the stall of the aging Round Table, Princequillo's finest son and the second leading money winner of all time. He was the colt who had been born the same night and in the same barn as Bold Ruler twenty years before.

Robinson turned the colt around in the stall, and Secretariat leaned down and sniffed at the bedding, made a few quick circuits of the wood-paneled box and looked out his rear window, which faced the fields of Claiborne, and pricked his ears.

On the door was a large brass plate: "Bold Ruler." He was in his sire's stall.

Sweat approached behind Robinson and went inside. "Whoa, Big Red," said Eddie, who dropped to his knees and unfastened the bandages on the horse's legs.

"How's it goin', Eddie? Have a good trip?"

"Yeh, fine, Seth."

The men were working when Seth left the stall, filled a bucket of water and brought it back and hung it in a corner. Riva Ridge joined Secretariat in the stallion barn. They shared the place with some of Claiborne's leading stallions—Round Table, Nijinsky II, Hoist the Flag, Drone, and Le Fabuleaux. Penny and Lucien arrived moments later, and now crowds of farm workers and reporters gathered in the doorway of the stallion shed. "It's like giving up a child for adoption," said Penny, lingering in front of Riva Ridge's stall. "I know it's best, but I hate to do it."

"Well, you're in your daddy's old stall," said Eddie Sweat, looking at the nameplate on the door. "How about that!"

"If he only does as well," someone said.

"He's got a lot of wood to chop," said Snow Fields, Bold Ruler's old groom. "Yes, sir. He's got a lot of wood to chop."

The van had arrived at Claiborne at three-thirty, and two hours later the Meadow Stable party—Elizabeth, Penny, and Lucien—had left for dinner with Seth. It was growing dark at the farm. Now and then a car would roll through the gates, its headlights glinting on the trees and shrubs that lined the way, and then disappear. A night-watchman came by later. Then a family from the farm, the Logans. They turned on the lights in the shed and opened the door of Secretariat's stall. He looked at them.

"He looks like just another horse, doesn't he?" said Marion Logan.

"Yeh, just like another horse in there now," said the nightwatch-man.

And they left. The lights went out again. By the office, a farm worker sat inside the shed by the graveyard. "That's just something we took out of Bull's office when he died," said the man. He was looking at a sign in the back of the shed:

> Cows may come
> And cows may go
> But the Bull
> In this place
> Goes on forever.

"Now he's just another horse here," said the man. "Now he's a stud horse and he has to prove himself here, just like he proved himself on the racetrack. Until he does that, he's just another horse at Claiborne."

Outside the sun was down and it grew colder now by the grove of trees in the dark by the stallion barn. Leaves fell, and a faint wind strummed and turned along the trees that rose along the paddocks in the back. Then in the distance, beyond the Claiborne fields toward the home called Marchmont, the sound of a horse whinnying rose. Secretariat came to the window of his stall, and through the darkness of it you could see nothing but rims of his eyes and hear the breathing in the quiet. The sound of the whinnying rose again, and beyond that and beyond the rows of fences and the fields of grass and the salmon-colored sky, beyond the stands of trees strung out along the skies of Paris, there was the sound of horses charging the bend and the crowd on its feet roaring and the announcer calling the name of a lone figure of a horse reaching and snapping, pounding in a rush, at the turn for home.

Author's Note to
the 2002 Edition

Upon his death, Secretariat was survived by all the principal members of the small family that had surrounded him almost throughout his racing career: owner Penny Chenery, trainer Lucien Laurin, groom Ed Sweat, and jockey Ron Turcotte. Over the last thirty years of the twentieth century, Chenery served tirelessly as an ambassador-at-large for thoroughbred racing and as the most visible link to Secretariat and the decade of the 1970s, truly the Golden Era of the sport in America. While making her home in Lexington, Kentucky, the bluegrass cradle of American racing, Penny has been seen regularly at all major racing venues, from the Kentucky Derby in May through the Breeders' Cup races in the fall. "She has been a beacon for the sport," said Dan Liebman, the executive editor of *The Blood-Horse,* the industry's leading trade publication—a graceful reminder of racing's most glorious days and a bearer of the torch for the horse who most vividly represented the best of them.

Lucien Laurin retired as a trainer in 1976, came out of retirement to condition horses again in 1983, then retired permanently in 1987, ten years after he was inducted into racing's Hall of Fame. Of course, Riva Ridge opened the door to the Hall of Fame, but it was Secretariat who carried Laurin inside. Laurin spent most of his retirement at his home in Key Largo, Florida, with his wife, Juliette. He died on June 26, 2000, at Miami's Baptist Hospital from complications following surgery to repair a broken hip. He was eight-eight.

Ed Sweat, whose handling of Secretariat made him the most renowned groom in America, the man whose touch with horses was almost lyrical, died virtually penniless in April 1998 after spending the last years of his life battling a host of physical ailments, including heart problems (he had suffered a heart attack and undergone open-heart surgery), asthma, and cancer of the stomach. At age fifty-nine, in New York, Sweat lost a long and final struggle to leukemia. The man had spent, given away, or lost what money he had saved from his heyday as a groom, and in the end the Jockey Club, which administers a fund to assist racing's neediest, stepped up and paid for Sweat's funeral in Vance, South Carolina. Trainer Roger Laurin, Lucien's son and the man for whom Sweat had worked as groom of the 1984 two-year-old champion, Chief's Crown, paid the airfare for Sweat's widow, Linda, and his two daughters to fly there from New York and back. Throughout the last twenty-five years of his life, Eddie never gave up hope of rubbing another Secretariat, of finding the Big Horse again. "I been on the racetrack thirty-four years, and I ain't never gonna give up," Sweat told me in 1991. "I think they'll take me to my grave with a pitchfork in my hand and a rub rag in my back pocket. . . . I might not ever find another Secretariat, but I'll never stop lookin'." He never did.

Nor did Ron Turcotte, who searched in vain throughout his last five years as a leading rider in New York. In 1979, like Laurin two years earlier, Turcotte was fairly swept into racing's Hall of Fame—on the back of Secretariat, of course, with Riva Ridge merely showing the way.

The induction ceremonies came a year after Turcotte's career had ended tragically at Belmont Park, the scene of the most memorable ride of his career. On July 13, 1978, Turcotte was paralyzed from the waist down after his mount in the day's eighth race, Flag of Leyte Gulf, fell after clipping heels with a horse in front of her, throwing Turcotte violently to the ground. A year later, after months of rehabilitation, Turcotte and his family moved from their Long Island manse to his hometown of Grand Falls, New Brunswick, where he still resides. There he first raised cattle and later got into the business of tree farming, planting and growing thousands of red pines for eventual use as telephone poles. Turcotte became a man genuinely at peace with himself and his place in history, and he ultimately came to terms with his paralysis; with his wife, Gaetane, at his side, he has often visited America at Triple Crown time, cheerfully signing Secretariat pictures and memorabilia for the fans and horseplayers crowding around him and telling stories about his record-breaking tour de force in 1973. One day a few years ago at Saratoga, as he sat

by the paddock in his wheelchair, Turcotte ended a Secretariat solilo-
quy by saying, with the trace of a grin on his lips, "He should *never*
have been beaten. Make no mistake, my friends. He was the greatest
racehorse who ever lived, and I was the luckiest guy in the world to
be on his back."

"Pure Heart"

—*William Nack*
from **Sports Illustrated**

Just before noon the horse was led haltingly into a van next to the stallion barn, and there a concentrated barbiturate was injected into his jugular. Forty-five seconds later there was a crash as the stallion collapsed. His body was trucked immediately to Lexington, Kentucky, where Dr. Thomas Swerczek, a professor of veterinary science at the University of Kentucky, performed the necropsy. All of the horse's vital organs were normal in size except for the heart.

"We were all shocked," Swerczek said. "I've seen and done thousands of autopsies on horses, and nothing I'd ever seen compared to it. The heart of the average horse weighs about nine pounds. This was almost twice the average size, and a third larger than any equine heart I'd ever seen. And it wasn't pathologically enlarged. All the chambers and the valves were normal. It was just larger. I think it told us why he was able to do what he did."

In the late afternoon of Monday, October 2, 1989, as I headed my car from the driveway of Arthur Hancock's Stone Farm onto Winchester Road outside of Paris, Kentucky, I was seized by an impulse as beckoning as the wind that strums through the trees there, mingling the scents of new grass and old history.

For reasons as obscure to me then as now, I felt compelled to see Lawrence Robinson. For almost thirty years, until he suffered a stroke in March of 1983, Robinson was the head caretaker of stallions at Claiborne Farm. I had not seen him since his illness, but I knew he still lived on the farm, in a small white frame house set on a hill overlooking the lush stallion paddocks and the main stallion barn. In the

345

first stall of that barn, in the same space that was once home to the great Bold Ruler, lived Secretariat, Bold Ruler's greatest son.

It was through Secretariat that I had met Robinson. On the bright, cold afternoon of November 12, 1973, he was one of several hundred people gathered at Blue Grass Airport in Lexington to greet the horse on his flight from New York into retirement in Kentucky. I flew with the horse that day, and as the plane banked over the field, a voice from the tower crackled over the airplane radio: "There's more people out here to meet Secretariat than there was to greet the governor." "Well, he's won more races than the governor," pilot Dan Neff replied.

An hour later, after a van ride out the Paris Pike behind a police escort with blue lights flashing, Robinson led Secretariat onto a ramp at Claiborne and toward his sire's old stall—out of racing and into history. For me, that final walk beneath a grove of trees, with the colt slanting like a buck through the autumn gloaming, brought to a melancholy close the richest, grandest, damnedest, most exhilarating time of my life. For eight months, first as the racing writer for Long Island, New York's *Newsday* and then as the designated chronicler of the horse's career, I had a daily front-row seat to watch Secretariat. I was at the barn in the morning and the racetrack in the afternoon for what turned out to be the year's greatest show in sports, at the heart of which lay a Triple Crown performance unmatched in the history of American racing.

Sixteen years had come and gone since then, and I had never attended a Kentucky Derby or a yearling sale at Keeneland without driving out to Claiborne to visit Secretariat, often in the company of friends who had never seen him. On the long ride from Louisville, I would regale them with stories about the horse—how on that early morning in March of 1973 he had materialized out of the quickening blue darkness in the upper stretch at Belmont Park, his ears pinned back, running as fast as horses run; how he had lost the Wood Memorial and won the Derby, and how he had been bothered by a pigeon feather at Pimlico on the eve of the Preakness (at the end of this tale I would pluck the delicate, mashed feather out of my wallet, like a picture of my kids, to pass around the car); how on the morning of the Belmont Stakes he had burst from the barn like a stud horse going to the breeding shed and had walked around the outdoor ring on his hind legs, pawing at the sky; how he had once grabbed my notebook and refused to give it back, and how he had seized a rake in his teeth and begun raking the shed; and, finally, I told about that magical, unforgettable instant, frozen now in time, when he had turned for home, appearing out of a dark drizzle at Woodbine, near Toronto, in the last race of his career, twelve in front and steam puffing from his nostrils as from a factory whistle, bounding like some mythical beast out of Greek lore.

Oh, I knew all the stories, knew them well, had crushed and rolled them in my hand, until their quaint musk lay in the saddle of my palm. Knew them as I knew the stories of my children. Knew them as I knew the stories of my own life. Told them at dinner parties, swapped them with horseplayers as if they were trading cards, argued over them with old men and blind fools who had seen the show but missed the message. Dreamed them and turned them over like pillows in my rubbery sleep. Woke up with them, brushed my aging teeth with them, grinned at them in the mirror. Horses have a way of getting inside of you, and so it was that Secretariat became like a fifth child in our house, the older boy who was off at school and never around but who was as loved and true a part of the family as Muffin, our shaggy, epileptic dog.

The story I now tell begins on that Monday afternoon last October on the macadam outside of Stone Farm. I had never been to Paris, Kentucky in the early fall, and I only happened to be there that day to begin an article about the Hancock family, the owners of Claiborne and Stone farms. There wasn't a soul on the road to point the way to Robinson's place, so I swung in and out of several empty driveways until I saw a man on a tractor cutting the lawn in front of Marchmont, Dell Hancock's mansion. He yelled back to me: "Take a right out the drive. Go down to Claiborne House. Then a right at the driveway across the road. Go up a hill to the big black barn. Turn left and go down to the end. Lawrence had a stroke a few years back, y'know."

The house was right where he said. I knocked on the front door, then walked behind and knocked on the back, and called through a side window into a room where music was playing. No one answered. But I had time to kill, so I wandered over to the stallion paddock, just a few yards from the house. The stud Ogygian, a son of Damascus, lifted his head inquiringly. He started walking toward me, and I put my elbows on the top of the fence and looked down the gentle slope toward the stallion barn.

And suddenly there he was, Secretariat, standing outside the barn and grazing at the end of a lead shank held by groom Bobby Anderson, who was sitting on a bucket in the sun. Even from a hundred yards away, the horse appeared lighter than I had seen him in years. It struck me as curious that he was not running free in his paddock—why was Bobby grazing him?—but his bronze coat reflected the October light, and it never occurred to me that something might be wrong. But something was terribly wrong. On Labor Day, Secretariat had come down with laminitis, a life-threatening hoof disease, and here, a month later, he was still suffering from its aftershocks.

Secretariat was dying. In fact, he would be gone within forty-eight hours.

I briefly considered slipping around Ogygian's paddock and dropping down to visit, but I had never entered Claiborne through the back door, and so I thought better of it. Instead, for a full half hour, I stood by the paddock waiting for Robinson and gazing in the distance at Secretariat. The gift of reverie is a blessing divine, and it is conferred most abundantly on those who lie in hammocks or drive alone in cars. Or lean on hillside fences in Kentucky. The mind swims, binding itself to whatever flotsam comes along, to old driftwood faces and voices of the past, to places and scenes once visited, to things not seen or done but only dreamed.

It was July 4, 1972, and I was sitting in the press box at Aqueduct with Clem Florio, a former prizefighter turned Baltimore handicapper, when I glanced at the Daily Racing Form's past performances for the second race, a 512-furlong buzz for maiden 2-year-olds. As I scanned the pedigrees, three names leaped out: by Bold Ruler, Somethingroyal, by Princequillo. Bold Ruler was the nation's preeminent sire, and Somethingroyal was the dam of several stakes winners, including the fleet Sir Gaylord. It was a match of royalty. Even the baby's name seemed faintly familiar: Secretariat. Where had I heard it before? But of course! Lucien Laurin was training the colt at Belmont Park for Penny Chenery Tweedy's Meadow Stable, making Secretariat a stablemate of that year's Kentucky Derby and Belmont Stakes winner, Riva Ridge.

I had seen Secretariat just a week before. I had been at the Meadow Stable barn one morning, checking on Riva, when exercise rider Jimmy Gaffney took me aside and said: "You wanna see the best-lookin' 2-year-old you've ever seen?"

We padded up the shed to the colt's stall. Gaffney stepped inside. "What do you think?" he asked. The horse looked magnificent, to be sure, a bright red chestnut with three white feet and a tapered white marking down his face. "He's gettin' ready," Gaffney said. "Don't forget the name: Secretariat. He can run." And then, conspiratorially,

Gaffney whispered: "Don't quote me, but this horse will make them all forget Riva Ridge."

So that is where I had first seen him, and here he was in the second at Aqueduct. I rarely bet in those days, but Secretariat was 3–1, so I put $10 on his nose. Florio and I fixed our binoculars on him and watched it all. Watched him as he was shoved sideways at the break, dropping almost to his knees, when a colt named Quebec turned left out of the gate and crashed into him. Saw him blocked in traffic down the back side and shut off again on the turn for home. Saw him cut off a second time deep in the stretch as he was making a final run. Saw him finish fourth, obviously much the best horse, beaten by only 114 lengths after really running but an eighth of a mile.

You should have seen Clem. Smashing his binoculars down on his desk, he leaped to his feet, banged his chair against the wall behind him, threw a few punches in the air and bellowed: "Secretariat! That's my Derby horse for next year!"

Two weeks later, when the colt raced to his first victory by six, Florio announced to all the world, "Secretariat will win the Triple Crown next year." He nearly got into a fistfight in the Aqueduct press box that day when Mannie Kalish, a New York handicapper, chided him for making such an outrageously bold assertion: "Ah, you Maryland guys, you come to New York and see a horse break his maiden and think he's another Citation. We see horses like Secretariat all the time. I bet he don't even run in the Derby." Stung by the put-down "you Maryland guys," Florio came forward and stuck his finger into Kalish's chest, but two writers jumped between them and they never came to blows.

The Secretariat phenomenon, with all the theater and passion that would attend it, had begun. Florio was right, of course, and by the end of Secretariat's 2-year-old season, everyone else who had seen him perform knew it. All you had to do was watch the Hopeful Stakes at Saratoga. I was at the races that August afternoon with Arthur Kennedy, an old-time racetracker and handicapper who had been around the horses since the 1920s, and even he had never seen anything quite like it. Dropping back to dead last out of the gate, Secretariat trailed eight horses into the far turn, where jockey Ron Turcotte swung him to the outside. Three jumps past the half-mile pole the colt exploded. "Now he's runnin'!" Kennedy said.

You could see the blue-and-white silks as they disappeared behind one horse, reappeared in a gap between horses, dropped out of sight again and finally reemerged as Secretariat powered to the lead off the turn. He dashed from last to first in 290 yards, blazing through a quarter in :22, and galloped home in a laugher to win by six. It was a performance with style, touched by art. "I've never seen a 2-year-old do that," Kennedy said quietly. "He looked like a 4-year-old out there."

So that was when I knew. The rest of Secretariat's 2-year-old campaign—in which he lost only once, in the Champagne Stakes when he was disqualified from first to second after bumping Stop the Music at the top of the stretch—was simply a mopping-up operation. At year's end, so dominant had he been that he became the first 2-year-old to be unanimously voted Horse of the Year.

Secretariat wintered at Hialeah, preparing for the Triple Crown, while I shoveled snow in Huntington, New York, waiting for him to race again. In February, 23-year-old Seth Hancock, the new president of Claiborne Farm, announced that he had syndicated the colt as a future breeding stallion for a then world record $6.08 million, in 32 shares at $190,000 a share, making the 1,154-pound horse worth more than three times his weight in gold. (Bullion was selling at the time for $90 an ounce.) Like everyone else, I thought Secretariat would surely begin his campaign in Florida, and I did not expect to see him again until the week before the Kentucky Derby. I was browsing through a newspaper over breakfast one day when I saw a news dispatch whose message went through me like a current. Secretariat would be arriving soon to begin his Triple Crown campaign by way of the three New York prep races: the Bay Shore, the Gotham and the Wood Memorial Stakes.

"Hot damn!" I blurted to my family. "Secretariat is coming to New York!"

At the time, I had in mind doing a diary about the horse, a chronicle of the adventures of a Triple Crown contender, which I thought might one day make a magazine piece. The colt arrived at Belmont Park on March 10, and the next day I was there at 7 A.M., scribbling notes in a pad. For the next forty days, in what became a routine, I would fall out of bed at 6 A.M., make a cup of instant coffee, climb into my rattling green Toyota and drive the twenty miles to Belmont Park. I had gotten to know the Meadow Stable family—Tweedy, Laurin, Gaffney, groom Eddie Sweat, assistant trainer Henny Hoeffner — in my tracking of Riva Ridge the year before, and I had come to feel at home around Belmont's Barn 5, particularly around stall 7, Secretariat's place. I took no days off, except one morning to hide Easter eggs, and I spent hours sitting on the dusty floor outside Secretariat's stall, talking to Sweat as he turned a rub rag on the colt, filled his water bucket, bedded his stall with straw, kept him in hay and oats. I took notes compulsively, endlessly, feeling for the texture of the life around the horse.

A typical page of scribblings went like this:

"Sweat talks to colt . . . easy, Red, I'm comin' in here now . . . stop it, Red! You behave now . . . Sweat moves around colt. Brush in hand. Flicks off dust. Secretariat sidesteps and pushes Sweat. Blue sky. Henny comes up. 'How's he doin', Eddie?' 'He's gettin' edgy.' . . . Easy Sunday morning."

Secretariat was an amiable, gentlemanly colt, with a poised and playful nature that at times made him seem as much a pet as the stable dog was. I was standing in front of his stall one morning, writing, when he reached out, grabbed my notebook in his teeth and sank back inside, looking to see what I would do. "Give the man his notebook back!" yelled Sweat. As the groom dipped under the webbing, Secretariat dropped the notebook on the bed of straw.

Another time, after raking the shed, Sweat leaned the handle of the rake against the stall webbing and turned to walk away. Secretariat seized the handle in his mouth and began pushing and pulling it across the floor. "Look at him rakin' the shed!" cried Sweat. All up and down the barn, laughter fluttered like the pigeons in the stable eaves, as the colt did a passable imitation of his own groom.

By his personality and temperament, Secretariat became the most engaging character in the barn. His own stable pony, a roan named Billy Silver, began an unrequited love affair with him. "He loves Secretariat, but Secretariat don't pay any attention to him," Sweat said one day. "If Billy sees you grazin' Secretariat, he'll go to hollerin' until you bring him out. Secretariat just ignores him. Kind of sad, really." One morning, I was walking beside Hoeffner through the shed, with Gaffney and Secretariat ahead of us, when Billy stuck his head out of his jerry-built stall and nuzzled the colt as he went by.

Hoeffner did a double take. "Jimmy!" he yelled. "Is that pony botherin' the big horse?"

"Nah," said Jimmy. "He's just smellin' him a little."

Hoeffner's eyes widened. Spinning around on his heels, jabbing a finger in the air, he bellowed: "Get the pony out of here! I don't want him smellin' the big horse."

Leaning on his rake, Sweat laughed softly: "Poor Billy Silver. He smelled the wrong horse!"

I remember wishing that those days could breeze on forever—the mornings over coffee and doughnuts at the truck outside the barn, the hours spent watching the red colt walk to the track and gallop once around, the days absorbing the rhythms of the life around the horse. I had been following racehorses since I was twelve, back in the days of Native Dancer, and now I was an observer on an odyssey, a quest for the Triple Crown. It had been twenty-five years since Citation had won racing's Holy Grail. For me, the adventure really began in the early morning of March 14, when Laurin lifted Turcotte aboard Secretariat and said: "Let him roll, Ronnie."

The colt had filled out substantially since I had last seen him under tack, in the fall, and he looked like some medieval charger—his thick neck bowed and his chin drawn up beneath its mass, his huge shoulders shifting as he strode, his coat radiant and his eyes darting left and right. He was walking to the track for his final workout, a three-eighths-of-a-mile drill designed to light the fire in him for the seven-furlong Bay Shore Stakes three days later. Laurin, Tweedy and I went to the clubhouse fence near the finish line, where we watched and waited as Turcotte headed toward the pole and let Secretariat rip. Laurin clicked his stopwatch.

The colt was all by himself through the lane, and the sight and sound of him racing toward us is etched forever in memory: Turcotte was bent over him, his coat blown up like a parachute, and the horse was reaching out with his forelegs in that distinctive way he had, raising them high and then, at the top of the lift, snapping them out straight and with tremendous force, the snapping hard as bone, the hooves striking the ground and folding it beneath him. Laurin clicked his watch as Secretariat raced under the wire. "Oh my god!" he cried. "Thirty-three and three fifths!" Horses rarely break 34 seconds in three-furlong moves.

Looking ashen, fearing the colt might have gone too fast, Laurin headed for the telephone under the clubhouse to call the upstairs clocker, Jules Watson. "Hello there, Jules. How fast did you get him?"

I watched Laurin's face grow longer as he listened, until he looked thunderstruck: "Thirty-two and three fifths?" A full second faster than Laurin's own clocking, it was the fastest three-furlong workout I had ever heard of. Tweedy smiled cheerily and said, "Well, that ought to open his pipes!"

Oh, it did that. Three days later, blocked by a wall of horses in the Bay Shore, Secretariat plunged through like a fullback, 220 yards from the wire, and bounded off to win the race by four and a half lengths. I could hear a man screaming behind me. I turned and saw Roger Laurin, Lucien's son, raising his arms in the air and shouting, "He's too much horse! They can't stop him. They can't even stop him with a wall of horses!"

I had ridden horses during my youth in Morton Grove, Illinois, and I remember one summer I took a little black bullet of a thoroughbred filly out of the barn and walked her to the track that rimmed the polo field across Golf Road. I had been to the races a few times, had seen the jockeys ride, and I wanted to feel what it was like. So I hitched up my stirrups and galloped her around the east turn, standing straight up. Coming off the turn, I dropped into a crouch and clucked to her. She took off like a sprinter leaving the blocks—swooooosh!—and the wind started whipping in my eyes. I could feel the tears streaming down my face, and then I looked down and saw her knees pumping like pistons. I didn't think she would make the second turn, the woods were looming ahead, big trees coming up, and so I leaned a little to the left and she made the turn before she started pulling up. No car ever took me on a ride like that. And no roller coaster, either. Running loose, without rails, she gave me the wildest, most thrilling ride I had ever had.

And there was nothing like the ride that Secretariat gave me in the twelve weeks from the Bay Shore through the Belmont Stakes. Three weeks after the Bay Shore, Turcotte sent the colt to the lead down the backstretch in the one-mile Gotham. It looked like they were going to get beat when Champagne Charlie drove to within a half length at the top of the stretch—I held my breath—but Turcotte sent Secretariat on, and the colt pulled away to win by three, tying the track record of 1:3325.

By then I had begun visiting Charles Hatton, a columnist for the *Daily Racing Form*, who the previous summer had proclaimed Secretariat the finest physical specimen he had ever seen. At sixty-seven, Hatton had seen them all. After my morning work was over, I would trudge up to Hatton's private aerie at Belmont Park and tell him what I had learned. I was his backstretch eyes, he my personal guru. One morning, Hatton told me that Secretariat had galloped a quarter mile past the finish line at the Gotham, and the clockers had timed him pulling up at 1:5925, three fifths of a second faster than Northern Dancer's Derby record for 1¼ miles.

"This sucker breaks records pulling up," Hatton said. "He might be the best racehorse I ever saw. Better than Man o' War."

Those were giddy, heady days coming to the nine-furlong Wood Memorial, the colt's last major prep before the Kentucky Derby. On the day of the Wood, I drove directly to Aqueduct and spent the hour before the race in the receiving barn with Sweat, exercise rider Charlie Davis and Secretariat. When the voice over the loudspeaker asked the grooms to ready their horses, Sweat approached the colt with the bridle. Secretariat always took the bit easily, opening his mouth when Sweat moved to fit it in, but that afternoon it took Sweat a full five minutes to bridle him. Secretariat threw his nose in the air, backed up, shook his head. After a few minutes passed, I asked, "What's wrong with him, Eddie?"

Sweat brushed it off: "He's just edgy."

In fact, just that morning, Dr. Manuel Gilman, the track veterinarian, had lifted the colt's upper lip to check his identity tattoo and had discovered a painful abscess about the size of a quarter. Laurin decided to run Secretariat anyway—the colt needed the race—but he never told anyone else about the boil. Worse than the abscess, though, was the fact that Secretariat had had the feeblest workout of his career four days earlier, when Turcotte, seeing a riderless horse on the track, had slowed the colt to protect him from a collision. Secretariat finished the mile that day in 1:4225, five seconds slower than Laurin wanted him to go. Thus he came to the Wood doubly compromised.

The race was a disaster. Turcotte held the colt back early, but when he tried to get Secretariat to pick up the bit and run, he got no response. I could see at the far turn that the horse was dead. He never made a race of it, struggling to finish third, beaten by four lengths by his own stablemate, Angle Light, and by Sham. Standing near the owner's box, I saw Laurin turn to Tweedy and yell, "Who won it?"

"You won it!" Tweedy told him.

"Angle Light won it," I said to him.

"Angle Light?" he howled back. But of course! Laurin trained him, too, and so Laurin had just won the Wood, but with the wrong horse.

I was sick. All those hours at the barn, all those early mornings at the shed, all that time and energy for naught. And in the most important race of his career, Secretariat had come up as hollow as a gourd. The next two weeks were among the most agonizing of my life. As great a stallion as he was, Bold Ruler had been essentially a speed sire and had never produced a single winner of a Triple Crown race. I couldn't help but suspect that Secretariat was another Bold Ruler, who ran into walls beyond a mile. In the next two weeks, Churchill Downs became a nest of rumors that Secretariat was unsound. Jimmy (the Greek) Snyder caused an uproar when he said the colt had a bum knee that was being treated with ice packs. I knew that wasn't true. I had been around him all spring, and the most ice I had seen near him was in a glass of tea.

All I could hope for, in those final days before the Derby, was that the colt had been suffering from a bellyache on the day of the Wood and had not been up to it. I remained ignorant of the abscess for weeks, and I had not yet divined the truth about Secretariat's training: He needed hard, blistering workouts before he ran, and that slow mile before the Wood had been inadequate. The night before the Derby, I made my selections, and the next day, two hours before post time, I climbed the stairs to the Churchill Downs jockeys' room to see Turcotte. He greeted me in an anteroom, looking surprisingly relaxed. Gilman had taken him aside a few days earlier and told him of the abscess. Turcotte saw that the boil had been treated and had disappeared. The news had made him euphoric, telling him all he needed to know about the Wood.

"You nervous?" he asked.

I shrugged. "I don't think you'll win," I said. "I picked My Gallant and Sham one-two, and you third."

"I'll tell you something," Turcotte said. "He'll beat these horses if he runs his race."

"What about the Wood?" I asked.

He shook me off. "I don't believe the Wood," he said. "I'm telling you. Something was wrong. But he's O.K. now. That's all I can tell you."

I shook his hand, wished him luck and left. Despite what Turcotte had said, I was resigned to the worst, and Secretariat looked hopelessly beaten as the field of thirteen dashed past the finish line the first time. He was dead last. Transfixed, I could not take my eyes off him. In the first turn, Turcotte swung him to the outside and Secretariat began passing horses, and down the back side I watched the jockey move him boldly from eighth to seventh to sixth. Secretariat was fifth around the far turn and gaining fast on the outside. I began chanting: "Ride him, Ronnie! Ride him!" Sham was in front, turning for home, but then there was Secretariat, joining him at the top of the stretch. Laffit Pincay, on Sham, glanced over and saw Secretariat and went to the whip. Turcotte lashed Secretariat. The two raced head and head for 100 yards, until gradually Secretariat pulled away. He won by 212 lengths. The crowd roared, and I glanced at the tote board: 1:5925! A new track and Derby record.

Throwing decorum to the wind, I vaulted from my seat and dashed madly through the press box, jubilantly throwing a fist in the air. Handicapper Steve Davidowitz came racing toward me from the other end. We clasped arms and spun a jig in front of the copy machine. "Unbelievable!" Davidowitz cried.

I bounded down a staircase, three steps at a time. Turcotte had dismounted and was crossing the racetrack when I reached him. "What a ride!" I yelled.

"What did I tell you, Mr. Bill?" he said.

I had just witnessed the greatest Kentucky Derby performance of all time. Secretariat's quarter-mile splits were unprecedented — :2515, :24, :2345, :2325 and :23. He ran each quarter faster than the preceding one. Not even the most veteran racetracker could recall a horse who had done this in a mile-and-a-quarter race. As quickly as his legions (I among them) had abandoned him following the Wood, so did they now proclaim Secretariat a superhorse.

We all followed him to Pimlico for the Preakness two weeks later, and he trained as if he couldn't get enough of it. He thrived on work and the racetrack routine. Most every afternoon, long after the crowds of visitors had dispersed, Sweat would graze the colt on a patch of grass outside the shed, then lead him back into his stall and while away the hours doing chores. One afternoon I was folded in a chair outside the colt's stall when Secretariat came to the door shaking his head and stretching his neck, curling his upper lip like a camel does. "What's botherin' you, Red?" Sweat asked. The groom stepped forward, plucked something off the colt's whiskers and blew it in the air. "Just a pigeon feather itchin' him," said Sweat. The feather floated into the palm of my hand. So it ended up in my wallet, along with the $2 mutual ticket that I had on Secretariat to win the Preakness.

In its own way, Secretariat's performance in the 1316-mile Preakness was even more brilliant than his race in the Derby. He dropped back to last out of the gate, but as the field dashed into the first turn, Turcotte nudged his right rein as subtly as a man adjusting his cuff, and the colt took off like a flushed deer. The turns at Pimlico are tight, and it had always been considered suicidal to take the first bend too fast, but Secretariat sprinted full-bore around it, and by the time he turned into the back side, he was racing to the lead. Here Turcotte hit the cruise control. Sham gave chase in vain, and Secretariat coasted home to win by 212. The electric timer malfunctioned, and Pimlico eventually settled on 1:5425 as the official time, but two *Daily Racing Form* clockers caught Secretariat in 1:53⅖, a track record by three fifths of a second.

I can still see Florio shaking his head in disbelief. He had seen thousands of Pimlico races and dozens of Preaknesses over the years, but never anything like this. "Horses don't do what he did here today," he kept saying. "They just don't do that and win."

Secretariat wasn't just winning. He was performing like an original, making it all up as he went along. And everything was moving so fast, so unexpectedly, that I was having trouble keeping a perspective on it. Not three months before, after less than a year of working as a turf writer, I had started driving to the racetrack to see this one horse. For weeks I was often the only visitor there, and on many afternoons it was just Sweat, the horse and me, in the fine dust with the pregnant stable cat. And then came the Derby and the Preakness, and two weeks later the colt was on the cover of *Time, Sports Illustrated,* and *Newsweek,* and he was a staple of the morning and evening news. Secretariat suddenly transcended being a racehorse and became a cultural phenomenon, a sort of undeclared national holiday from the tortures of Watergate and the Vietnam War.

I threw myself with a passion into that final week before the Belmont. Out to the barn every morning, home late at night, I became almost manic. The night before the race, I called Laurin at home and we talked for a long while about the horse and the Belmont. I kept wondering, What is Secretariat going to do for an encore? Laurin said, "I think he's going to win by more than he has ever won in his life. I think he'll win by ten."

I slept at the *Newsday* offices that night, and at 2 A.M. I drove to Belmont Park to begin my vigil at the barn. I circled around to the back of the shed, lay down against a tree and fell asleep. I awoke to the crowing of a cock and watched as the stable workers showed up. At 6:07, Hoeffner strode into the shed, looked at Secretariat, and called out to Sweat: "Get the big horse ready! Let's walk him about fifteen minutes."

Sweat slipped into the stall, put the lead shank on Secretariat and handed it to Davis, who led the colt to the outdoor walking ring. In a small stable not 30 feet away, pony girl Robin Edelstein knocked a water bucket against the wall. Secretariat, normally a docile colt on a shank, rose up on his hind legs, pawing at the sky, and started walking in circles. Davis cowered below, as if beneath a thunderclap, snatching at the chain and begging the horse to come down. Secretariat floated back to earth. He danced around the ring as if on springs, his nostrils flared and snorting, his eyes rimmed in white.

Unaware of the scene she was causing, Edelstein rattled the bucket again, and Secretariat spun in a circle, bucked and leaped in the air, kicking and spraying cinders along the walls of the pony barn. In a panic, Davis tugged at the shank, and the horse went up again, higher and higher, and Davis bent back yelling, "Come on down! Come on down!"

I stood in awe. I had never seen a horse so fit. The Derby and Preakness had wound him as tight as a watch, and he seemed about to burst out of his coat. I had no idea what to expect that day in the Belmont, with him going a mile and a half, but I sensed we would see more of him than we had ever seen before.

Secretariat ran flat into legend, started running right out of the gate and never stopped, ran poor Sham into defeat around the first turn and down the backstretch and sprinted clear, opening two lengths, four, then five. He dashed to the three-quarter pole in 1:0945, the fastest six-furlong clocking in Belmont history. I dropped my head and cursed Turcotte: What is he thinking about? Has he lost his mind? The colt raced into the far turn, opening seven lengths past the half-mile pole. The timer flashed his astonishing mile mark: 1:3415!

I was seeing it but not believing it. Secretariat was still sprinting. The four horses behind him disappeared. He opened 10. Then 12. Halfway around the turn, he was 14 in front . . . 15 . . . 16 . . . 17. Belmont Park began to shake. The whole place was on its feet. Turning for home, Secretariat was 20 in front, having run the mile and a quarter in 1:59 flat, faster than his Derby time.

He came home alone. He opened his lead to 25 . . . 26 . . . 27 . . . 28. As rhythmic as a rocking horse, he never missed a beat. I remember seeing Turcotte look over to the timer, and I looked over too. It was blinking 2:19, 2:20. The record was 2:2635. Turcotte scrubbed on the colt, opening 30 lengths, finally 31. The clock flashed crazily: 2:22 . . . 2:23. The place was one long, deafening roar. The colt seemed to dive for the finish, snipping it clean at 2:24.

I bolted up the press box stairs with exultant shouts and there yielded a part of myself to that horse forever.

I didn't see Lawrence Robinson that day last October. The next morning, I returned to Claiborne to interview Seth Hancock. On my way through the farm's offices, I saw one of the employees crying at her desk. Treading lightly, I passed farm manager John Sosby's office. I stopped, and he called me in. He looked like a chaplain whose duty was to tell the news to the victim's family.

"Have you heard about Secretariat?" he asked quietly.

I felt the skin tighten on the back of my neck. "Heard what?" I asked. "Is he all right?"

"We might lose the horse," Sosby said. "He came down with laminitis last month. We thought we had it under control, but he took a bad turn this morning. He's a very sick horse. He may not make it.

"By the way, why are you here?"

I had thought I knew, but now I wasn't sure.

Down the hall, sitting at his desk, Hancock appeared tired, despairing and anxious, a man facing a decision he didn't want to make. What Sosby had told me was just beginning to sink in. "What's the prognosis?" I asked.

"Ten days to two weeks," Hancock said.

"Two weeks? Are you serious?" I blurted.

"You asked me the question," he said.

I sank back in my chair. "I'm not ready for this," I told him.

"How do you think I feel?" he said. "Ten thousand people come to this farm every year, and all they want to see is Secretariat. They don't give a hoot about the other studs. You want to know who Secretariat is in human terms? Just imagine the greatest athlete in the world. The greatest. Now make him six-foot-three, the perfect height. Make him real intelligent and kind. And on top of that, make him the best-lookin' guy ever to come down the pike. He was all those things as a horse. He isn't even a horse anymore. He's a legend. So how do you think I feel?"

Before I left, I asked Hancock to call me in Lexington if he decided to put the horse down. We agreed to meet at his mother's house the next morning. "By the way, can I see him?" I asked.

"I'd rather you not," he said. I told Hancock I had been to Robinson's house the day before and I had seen Secretariat from a distance, grazing. "That's fine," Hancock said. "Remember him how you saw him, that way. He doesn't look good."

I did not know it then, but Secretariat was suffering the intense pain in the hooves that is common to laminitis. That morning, Anderson had risen at dawn to check on the horse, and Secretariat had lifted his head and nickered very loudly. "It was like he was beggin' me for help," Anderson would later recall.

I left Claiborne stunned. That night, I made a dozen phone calls to friends, telling them the news, and I sat up late, dreading the next day. I woke up early and went to breakfast and came back to the room. The message light was dark. It was Wednesday, October 4. I drove out to Waddell Hancock's place in Paris. "It doesn't look good," she said. We had talked for more than an hour when Seth, looking shaken and pale, walked through the front door. "I'm afraid to ask," I said.

"It's very bad," he said. "We're going to have to put him down today."

"When?"

He did not answer. I left the house, and an hour later I was back in my room in Lexington. I had just taken off my coat when I turned and saw it, the red blinking light on my phone. I knew. I walked around the room. Out the door and down the hall. Back into the room. Out the door and around the block. Back into the room. Out the door and down to the lobby. Back into the room. I called sometime after noon. "Claiborne Farm called," said the message operator.

I phoned Annette Covault, an old friend who is the mare booker at Claiborne, and she was crying when she read the message: "Secretariat was euthanized at 11:45 A.M. today to prevent further suffering from an incurable condition. . . ."

The last time I remember really crying was on St. Valentine's Day of 1982, when my wife called to tell me that my father had died. At the moment she called, I was sitting in a purple room in Caesars Palace, in Las Vegas, waiting for an interview with the heavyweight champion, Larry Holmes. Now here I was, in a different hotel room in a different town, suddenly feeling like a very old and tired man of forty-eight, leaning with my back against a wall and sobbing for a long time with my face in my hands.

Appendix A:
Secretariat at Stud

Secretariat launched his career as a stallion at Claiborne Farm with a host of breeders expecting him to sire champions by the herd, to turn out brilliant racehorses as quickly and efficiently as he had once knocked off quarter-mile splits in the Triple Crown. His pedigree and talent notwithstanding, however, none but the most romantically optimistic of horsemen ever harbored any hope that the horse would accomplish in the breeding shed what he had achieved on the racetrack. History was against him. Fact is, not one of the indubitable giants of the American turf—not Man o' War, Count Fleet, or Citation—ever sired a horse who could have beaten him on the race course. Man o' War came the closest to reproducing himself: War Admiral, by far his greatest offspring, had flashed high and abundant gusts of speed while winning the 1937 Triple Crown, the year before Seabiscuit whipped him in their celebrated match race. But what the Admiral had to offer seemed to pale in comparison to the relentless drive and power that carried his sire to twenty victories in twenty-one starts. And neither Count Fleet nor Citation, the '43 and '48 Triple Crown winners, respectively, came even remotely close to siring a horse with War Admiral's brilliance on the courses.

Secretariat retired to stud at America's most historic commercial thoroughbred nursery, and by the end he had spent most of his career there surrounded by far more accomplished breeding stallions, including three of the most brilliant progenitors in the world—Nijinski II, Danzig, and the fabled Mr. Prospector. Yet Secretariat, first through the exploits of his own racing sons and daughters and then, more emphatically, through his influence as a champion sire of broodmares, ultimately left his enduring mark on the breed as well as the game. By the time the final numbers were in, Secretariat had sired 53 stakes winners out of a total of 663 named foals, 16 crops in all, and they had won nearly $29 million on racecourses throughout the Northern Hemisphere. If his numbers, as a sire of runners, did not measure up to those of the more celebrated Claiborne stallions, the horse certainly had his moments in the world of thoroughbred breeding. Among his offspring were two of the most gifted competitors of the 1980s—one a near–Triple Crown winner, Risen Star, and the other, one of the greatest fillies ever to grace the American turf, Lady's Secret. In 1988, Risen Star would probably have won the Kentucky Derby had he not been hung out to dry on the final turn, fully eight horses wide, while also trying to close ground behind a lukewarm pace set by the eventual winner, Winning Colors. Risen Star closed to finish third, beaten by just over three lengths. The greatest of Secretariat's sons came back to win the Preakness, and three weeks later, in the Belmont Stakes—the very scene of his sire's most memorable performance—Risen Star pounced on Winning Colors as the two sped down the back side, opened up a six-length lead on the turn for home, and then turned up the heat as he galloped home alone to win by a smashing fourteen and three-quarter lengths in 2:26 2/5 seconds. Only Secretariat had done it bigger and faster. Risen Star's margin of victory was the longest since 1973, and his final clocking was the second fastest one-and-a-half-mile Belmont in history. Risen Star retired after winning eight of eleven races and just over $2 million in purses.

If the Belmont was Risen Star's defining triumph as a racehorse, then surely the 1986 Breeders' Cup Distaff, with a $1 million purse and one and a quarter miles to cover, was the race for which that little gray bullet, Lady's Secret, will always be best known—the race in which she swept right into history. A year earlier, as a three-year-old, Lady's Secret had finished second in the same race to her stablemate, Life's Magic, and now she was back to make a run at that coveted prize and claim her right to the highest title in the sport, that of the leading racehorse in the land. She had already won an astonishing seven Grade 1 stakes through the 1986 season—these major races traditionally offer the toughest competition and thus rank as the most important events on the racing calendar—and a victory at Santa Anita would bring her total to eight, giving her a clear shot at the overall championship. The issue was never in question. Sweeping to the lead in that low, pendulumlike stride, the "Iron Lady," as she had come to be known, opened up five lengths down the back stretch under jockey Pat Day, cruised off the final turn still in front by four, and won ridden out in a gallop by two and a half lengths over Fran's Valentine. Secretariat's most capable daughter was subsequently voted the Eclipse Award as the nation's 1986 Horse of the Year. Lady's Secret ended her career after winning twenty-five of forty-five races, taking down more than $3 million in purses, and earning the ultimate accolade from no less an authority than veteran Hall of Fame trainer Woody Stephens. "I always thought Gallorette was the greatest race mare I ever saw," said Woody, recalling the great distaff campaigner of the mid-1940s, "but now I think that Lady's Secret might have been better."

Though Secretariat went to stud as the greatest son of Bold Ruler, with expectations that he would be the dominant force in carrying on that prolific tail-mail line, he actually left his deepest imprint on the breed not through his male offspring, none of whom has made any significant impression at the stud, but rather through the females that he left behind. (It ultimately fell to the surpassing Seattle Slew, the 1977 Triple Crown champion who descended in tail-mail from Bold Ruler through Boldnesian and Bold Reasoning, to keep the line flourishing into the twenty-first century, chiefly through his most accomplished son, A. P. Indy.) In the breeding shed, Secretariat turned out to be far more like his own maternal grandsire, Princequillo, the little World War II orphan from Britain via the Continent who came to these shores in steerage through submarine-infested waters and eventually established himself at Claiborne as one of the nation's greatest sires of broodmares in history. Just like him, Secretariat quickly proved himself to be one of the leading broodmare sires in America, season after season, with his female offspring coveted at studs around the world. By the fall of 2001, his female offspring had produced 4 champion racehorses and 139 stakes winners. In 1992, Secretariat was the leading broodmare sire in the nation, his 135 daughters having produced the winners of more purse money, almost $6.7 million, than the daughters sired by any other stallion. (In all, Secretariat mares have produced runners that so far have won upward of $115 million in purses.) In the best of breeding sheds, all royal blood flows together, and 1992 was the season that A. P. Indy—by Seattle Slew out of Weekend Surprise, a daughter of Secretariat—won the Santa Anita Derby, the Belmont Stakes, and America's richest race, the $3 million Breeders' Cup Classic. At season's end, A. P. Indy was named America's Horse of the Year and retired with a lifetime total of nearly $3 million in earnings.

Now a widely sought stallion, A. P. Indy is currently standing at stud for a fee of $150,000, one of the highest in America, but that is not even a third of the money commanded by the hottest of all Kentucky stallions, Storm Cat, whose roots are rich in Secretariat blood. They trace to Terlingua, who was probably the fastest two-year-old filly ever sired by Secretariat. Terlingua was out of Crimson Saint, who had spectacular speed for short distances. Trained by D. Wayne Lukas, Terlingua beat the colts in Hollywood Juvenile Championship in 1978, won the Hollywood Lassie Stakes, and ended up winning seven races and $423,896. Retired to the stud, Terlingua was bred to Storm Bird, a son of the great Northern Dancer, and out of that mating, in 1983, she foaled Storm Cat, a precocious two-year-old who won $557,080 in his juvenile year but only one race after that. Sent to the stallion barn at Overbrook Farm, in Lexington, he quickly began siring winners, one after another, and over the ensuing years he emerged as a whirlwind at the stud, a phenomenon so prolific at siring major stakes horses that in the year 2000, his 17 yearlings offered at public auction sold for $22,468,000—an average of $1,321,641 per horse. In the fall of 2001, by which time Storm Cat had already sired some eighty-five stakes winners, with progeny earnings of more than $64 million, it was announced that his stud fee in 2002 would be set at $500,000, the highest in the industry. Today the son of Storm Bird out of Terlingua, by Secretariat, is simply the most valuable stallion in the world.

In the eyes of breeders, to be sure, Secretariat had a kind of bittersweet career at the stud. "It's tough to say the word 'disappointed,'" said Edward Bowen, the former editor of *The Blood-Horse* magazine and long-time observer of the thoroughbred breeding industry, "but you'd have to admit that Secretariat didn't reach the exalted heights as a stallion that people had hoped for. But I think he was a very good sire of racehorses—a good, solid stallion—and he was and still is an outstanding broodmare sire. There his influence continues."

Secretariat

ch. c. 1970, by Bold Ruler (Nasrullah)–Somethingroyal, by Princequillo

Own.– Meadow Stable

Br.– Meadow Stud Inc (Va)

Tr.– L. Laurin

Lifetime record: 21 16 3 1 $1,316,808

28Oct73-8WO	fm 1⅝Ⓣ	:472	1:373		2:414	3↑	Can Int'l-G2	12	2	21½	15	112	16½	Maple E	117	b	*.20	96-04	Secretariat1176½BigSpruce1261½GoldenDon117¾	Ridden out	12
8Oct73-7Bel	fm 1½Ⓣ	:47	1:113	2:00	2:244	3↑	Man o' War-G1	3	1	13	11½	13	15	Turcotte R	121	b	*.50	103-01	Secretariat1215Tentam1267½Big Spruce126½	Ridden out	7
29Sep73-7Bel	sly 1½	:50	1:132	2:014	2:254	3↑	Woodward-G1	5	2	2½	1hd	21½	24½	Turcotte R	119	b	*.30	86-15	ProveOut1264½Secretariat11911CougarII126½	Best of rest	5
15Sep73-7Bel	fst 1⅛	:453	1:091	1:33	1:452	3↑	Marl Cup Inv'l H 250k	7	5	51¼	3½	12	13½	Turcotte R	124	b	*.40e	104-07	Secretariat12431½Riva Ridge1272Cougar II1266½	Ridden out	7
4Aug73-7Sar	fst 1⅛	:474	1:11	1:36	1:491	3↑	Whitney H-G2	3	4	31	2½	2hd	21	Turcotte R	119	b	*.10	94-15	Onion1191Secretariat119½Rule by Reason1192	Weakened	5
30Jun73-8AP	fst 1⅛	:48	1:111	1:35	1:47		Invitational 125k	4	1	13	12½	16	19	Turcotte R	126	b	*.05	99-17	Secretariat1269My Gallant120nkOur Native12017	Easily	4
9Jun73-8Bel	fst 1½	:461	1:094	1:59	2:24		Belmont-G1	1	1	1hd	120	128	131	Turcotte R	126	b	*.10	113-05	Secretariat12631TwiceaPrince126½MyGllnt12613	Ridden out	5
19May73-8Pim	fst 1 3/16	:481	1:112	1:353	1:542		Preakness-G1	3	4	1½	12½	12½	12½	Turcotte R	126	b	*.30	98-13	Secretariat1262½Sham1268Our Native1261	Handily	6
	Daily Racing Form time 1:53 2/5																				
5May73-9CD	fst 1¼	:472	1:114	1:361	1:592		Ky Derby-G1	10	11	69½	2½	1½	12½	Turcotte R	126	b	*1.50e	103-10	Secretariat1262½Sham1268Our Native126½	Handily	13
21Apr73-7Aqu	fst 1⅛	:481	1:121	1:364	1:494		Wood Memorial-G1	6	7	66	55½	45½	34	Turcotte R	126	b	*.30e	83-17	Angle Light126hdSham1264Secretariat126½	Wide,hung	8
7Apr73-7Aqu	fst 1	:231	:451	1:083	1:332		Gotham-G2	3	3	1hd	12	1½	13	Turcotte R	126	b	*.10	100-08	Secretariat1263ChampagneCharl11710Flush1172½	Ridden out	6
17Mar73-7Aqu	sly 7f	:221	:444	1:10	1:231		Bay Shore-G3	4	5	56	53	1hd	14½	Turcotte R	126	b	*.20	85-17	Secretarit1264½ChmpgnChrl1182½Impcunous126no	Mild drive	6
18Nov72-8GS	fst 1 1/16	:241	:472	1:12	1:442		Garden State 298k	6	6	46¼	33	11½	13½	Turcotte R	122	b	*.10e	83-23	Secretariat12231½Angle Light122½Step Nicely122¾	Handily	6
28Oct72-7Lrl	sly 1 1/16	:224	:454	1:112	1:424		Lrl Futurity 133k	5	6	510	53	15	18	Turcotte R	122	b	*.10e	99-14	Secretariat1228Stop the Music1228Angle Light1221	Easily	6
14Oct72-7Bel	fst 1	:224	:451	1:094	1:35		Champagne 146k	4	11	98½	53½	1½	12	Turcotte R	122	b	*.70e	97-12	[D]Secretariat1222StoptheMusic1222StepNicly1221½	Bore in	12
	Disqualified and placed second																				
16Sep72-7Bel	fst 6½f	:223	:453	1:10	1:162		Futurity 144k	4	5	65½	53½	12	11¾	Turcotte R	122	b	*.20	98-09	Secretariat1221¾StoptheMusic1225SwiftCourr1222½	Handily	7
26Aug72-7Sar	fst 6½f	:224	:463	1:094	1:161		Hopeful 86k	8	8	96½	1hd	14	15	Turcotte R	121	b	*.30	97-12	Secretariat1215FlighttoGlory121nkStopthMusc1212	Handily	9
16Aug72-7Sar	fst 6f	:224	:461		1:10		Sanford 27k	2	5	54	41	1½	13	Turcotte R	121	b	1.50	96-14	Secretariat1213Lnd'sChf1216NorthstrDncr1213½	Ridden out	5
31Jly72-4Sar	fst 6f	:231	:462		1:104		Alw 9000	4	7	73¾	3½	1hd	11½	Turcotte R	118	b	*.40	92-13	Secretariat1181½Russ Miron1187Joe Iz1182½	Ridden out	7
15Jly72-4Aqu	fst 6f	:221	:452		1:103		©Md Sp Wt	8	11	66½	43	1½	16	Feliciano P5	113	b	*1.30	90-14	Secretariat1136Master Achiever118¾Be on It1184	Handily	11
4Jly72-2Aqu	fst 5½f	:222	:461	:584	1:05		©Md Sp Wt	2	11	107	108¾	75½	41¼	Feliciano P5	113	b	*3.10	87-11	Herbull118nkMaster Achiever1181Fleet 'n Royal118no		12
	Impeded,rallied																				

Appendix B: Secretariat Racing Record

Acknowledgments

I want to thank *Newsday*, especially editor David Laventhol and sports editor Richard Sandler, whose support and understanding, deadline after deadline, were most deeply appreciated; my friend Mike McGrady, who encouraged me throughout the life of this project, from the day he introduced me to publisher Arthur Fields to the day he read and helped edit the final manuscript; and, finally, Arthur Fields.

I also want to thank Sam Kanchuger, the most helpful and well-organized racing publicist in America, whose copious and instructive files were invaluable; the publisher of *The Thoroughbred Record*, Arnold Kirkpatrick; Bob Van Wert and Jim Bolus of the *Louisville Courier-Journal*, for their help on my research into the 1973 Kentucky Derby; former *Newsday* reporter Mike Quinn, for his research; racing writer Steve Cady and columnists Red Smith and Dave Anderson, all of the *New York Times*, for their support; Amelia Buckley of the Keeneland Library Association; writer Harvey Aronson and designer Corrine McGrady, for their patience; and my parents, for a $600 loan tendered when the ladle was scraping the bottom of the soup bowl.